Knowledge Management in Policing and Law Enforcement

Foundations, Structures, Applications

Knowledge Management in Policing and Law Enforcement

Foundations, Structures, Applications

Geoff Dean

and

Petter Gottschalk

OXFORD
UNIVERSITY PRESS

OXFORD
UNIVERSITY PRESS

Great Clarendon Street, Oxford OX2 6DP

Oxford University Press is a department of the University of Oxford.
It furthers the University's objective of excellence in research, scholarship,
and education by publishing worldwide in

Oxford New York

Auckland Cape Town Dar es Salaam Hong Kong Karachi
Kuala Lumpur Madrid Melbourne Mexico City Nairobi
New Delhi Shanghai Taipei Toronto

With offices in

Argentina Austria Brazil Chile Czech Republic France Greece
Guatemala Hungary Italy Japan Poland Portugal Singapore
South Korea Switzerland Thailand Turkey Ukraine Vietnam

Oxford is a registered trademark of Oxford University Press
in the UK and in certain other countries

Published in the United States
by Oxford University Press Inc., New York

© Geoff Dean and Petter Gottschalk, 2007

British Library Cataloguing in Publication Data

Data available

Library of Congress Cataloging in Publication Data

Data available

Typeset by Laserwords Private Limited, Chennai, India
Printed in Great Britain
on acid-free paper by
Biddles Ltd, King's Lynn, Norfolk

ISBN 978-0-19-921407-5

10 9 8 7 6 5 4 3 2 1

Foreword

Policing has become more complex, more knowledge based, and more professional in the last decade. These changes are felt across the world—a fact recognized by a growing international sharing of practice and personnel between major police forces in different countries. However, there has been a strong tendency to rely on anecdotal exchanges of knowledge rather than systematic, evidence-based approaches. The transformation from a learned craft to a highly knowledge-intensive profession has happened relatively slowly in policing.

This book focuses on knowledge management and its potential application to policing. The authors show how the approach to knowledge management in policing has tended to be overfocused on information technology and insufficiently on the personal, cultural, and organizational context.

The book is timely, as police leaders across the world wrestle with how to deliver security at a personal, community, national, and international level. These layers are connected and knowledge transfer between them and between different organizations in different jurisdictions has become critical.

A professional police force for the 21st century will, increasingly, be one with a segmented and highly specialized workforce, supported by expert systems and highly integrated information technology. For this sort of policing, knowledge management is a key aspect of success and this book is a useful signpost to the future.

Peter Neyroud QPM
Chief Constable and Chief Executive,
National Policing Improvement Agency

Acknowledgements

Words do not do justice to the sacrifices, small and large, my partner Robyn, and children Megan, Amber, Simon, and Jeremy, as well as too many friends to name, have borne graciously from my being stuck 'in my head' for days and weeks at a time over several months while contributing to the writing of this book. To them all, a very heartfelt thanks for being there when my head was elsewhere!

This book would also not have been possible but for the many fine police officers I know, have worked with, and in some cases celebrated too much with, from a host of countries around the world. I hope I have done some measure of justice throughout this work to their experiences, insights, understandings, and tacit knowledge they shared with me. For their generosity of spirit I abundantly thank them.

Geoff Dean

Without encouragement from and discussions with experienced police officers and criminology faculty in many parts of the world, this book would never have achieved the quality we are proud of. I would like to thank several scholars in particular: Dr Stefan Holgersson at the Stockholm Police in Sweden, Mr Rune Glomseth and Mr Ivar Fahsing at the Norwegian Police University College in Oslo, Dr Anne Puonti at the National Bureau of Investigation in Finland.

I am celebrating my silver anniversary with my partner Grethe this year. Twenty-five years of marriage have produced two wonderful daughters, Anne and Mette, who are pursuing their adult life in a way that makes their parents especially proud. A silver anniversary means that myself and Grethe look forward to the next 25 years together. I am grateful to Grethe, who is excited about this new book. She didn't mind my getting up in the middle of the night to finish it, as long as I had morning tea ready for her when she woke up. Small mercies never fail to please.

Petter Gottschalk

Both of us would like particularly to thank the team responsible at OUP for making this book a reality. To Andrea Oliver for her vision in originally commissioning the work, to Katie Allan and all those emails, Michelle Reid, Peter Daniell (who Geoff probably drove crazy with all his complicated diagrams), and the assistance of Lindsey Davis. All of these people in vital ways have provided generous support, encouragement, and wise advice. We are very appreciative to the team.

Geoff and Petter

Contents

Special features

This book is designed as both a practical text and a policy guide for Knowledge Management in policing, law enforcement, and related fields of local and global security. Hence a number of special features are included to assist your reflection on the material contained within this work.

- **Diagrams**—there are over 50 diagrams of several types that illustrate concepts, ideas, systems, processes, and convey information.
- **Discussion Boxes**—these are used as a forum to reflect on the issues and arguments raised about a particular topic.
- **Case Examples**—these are used to illustrate one or two key points on a topic.
- **Case Studies**—there are a series of in-depth studies that provide extended treatment on a case. These are mainly used to demonstrate how a particular application system operates in a policing context.

Abbreviations

ACPO	Association of Chief Police Officers
AFP	Australian Federal Police
AI	artificial intelligence
AIM	Action Information Management
AN	analyst notebook
ATM	automated teller machine
BADMAN	Behavioural Analysis Data Management Autoindexing Networking
BEA	behavioural evidence analysis
C+C EKRS	Cross+Check Experiential Knowledge Reasoning System
CADDIE	Crime and Disorder Data Information Exchange
CATCHEM	Centralized Analytical Team Collating Homicide Expertise and Management
CBAU	Criminal Behavioural Analysis Unit
CDRP	Crime and Disorder Reduction Partnership
CGT	criminal geographic targeting
CMS	content management systems
CNS	Center for Nonproliferation Studies
CPAS	Crime Pattern Analysis System
CRIS	Crime Report Information System
CSPS	Criminal Suspect Prioritization System
CUBICON	Command, Control and Communication system
DAMS	digital management systems
DBMS	database management systems
DIS	digital imaging systems
DMS	document management systems
DSS	decision support system
EKRS	Experiential Knowledge Reasoning System
EKS	expert knowledge systems
ES	expert systems
FLIR	forward-looking-infrared-radar
GIS	geographical information systems
GMAC	Greater Manchester Against Crime
GP	geographic profiling
HITS	Homicide Investigation and Tracking System
HOLMES	Home Office Large Scale Major Enquiry System
IE	inference engine

ILP	intelligence-led policing
IMS	information management systems
IP NNMS	Investigative Pathways Neural Network Mapping System
IS	information systems
ISS	intelligence surveillance systems
IT	information technology
ITC-KMS	'Interlocking Terrorism Contexts' Knowledge Modelling System
JI	Jemaah Islamiyah
KAM	Knowledge Acquisition Module
KBS	knowledge-based systems
KM	Knowledge Management
KMS	Knowledge Management system
KMT	Knowledge Management technology
KOS	knowledge outcome space
LMS	learning management systems; also library management systems
MO	method of operation
NIJ	National Institute of Justice
NIM	national intelligence model
NNPCP	Neural Network for Psychological Criminal Profiling
NNS	neural network systems
PIN	personal identification number
PKMP	police Knowledge Management policy
PKT	Police Knowledge Triangle
PMI	passive millimetre imaging
PSC	private security company
RDBMS	relational database management systems
RMS	record management systems
RNC	Royal Newfoundland Constabulary
S-A	state-action
SECI	socialization, externalization, combination, and internalization
SIO	senior investigative officer
SNA	Social Network Analysis
SOP	Standard Operating Procedure
SPIKE	Surrey Police Information and Knowledge Environment
TAS	Timeline Analysis System
VCM	volume crime management
VICAP/ViCAP	Violent Criminal Apprehension Program
VICLAS	Violent Crime Linkage Analysis System

Introduction

This book is written for operational police on the street and at the management desk. Our view is that for too long Knowledge Management (KM) in policing and law enforcement has remained relatively inaccessible to working police. In keeping with the long established police tradition of being suspicious of anything new or fancy-sounding, KM is either regarded as a fad or a mystery to the average police officer. Irrespective of which view an individual police officer favours they all tend to agree that the pragmatic impact of KM is yet another form to fill out imposed by some techno-head for yet another database or IT system that is supposed to make their working life easier.

Our aim in this book is to debunk the faddish bits of KM and demystify the rest. In so doing we hope the average working police officer and police executive will find practical guidance and innovative ideas they can take hold of and use in their daily practice, whether they are doing street patrols, sitting at a desk, managing an investigation, or overseeing a covert operation.

The layout of the book comprises three main parts that revolve around bringing together in one text a wide and diverse range of knowledge which can be related to policing and law enforcement. In so doing, a specific body of police knowledge and its management can be built up. In keeping with the building metaphor, each of the the main sections, as you will see from the table of contents' is referred to respectively as 'laying foundations', 'building structures', and 'using applications' to do with police Knowledge Management.

The history of science continues to show that many breakthroughs in various disciplines are the result of exposure to a cross-fertilization of ideas from outside of a particular discipline. Policing is no different. Its professionalism depends on openness to new ideas and new ways of doing things from a solid foundation of experience-based practical knowledge.

Police manage their knowledge every day in a variety of ways and situations. There are never days off from knowledge discovery, only lost opportunities. For example, a detective on a day off is doing his grocery shopping in a busy market area in Singapore. He notices a hawker selling canned abalone at half the normal price. The detective becomes curious about why the abalone is so cheap. The hawker tells him the cheap price is because of over-supply. The detective is still curious. He buys a can and examines it closely. He discovers it was canned in Indonesia. He knows, because of his local knowledge, that most of the abalone that comes into Singapore arrives from Malaysia under a local brand name. The detective waits for the hawker to pack up for the day and follows him to his car. He takes down the vehicle registration number.

Back at his office the next day, the detective does a trace on the hawker's vehicle registration and gets his address. He then makes extensive inquiries around the hawker's home area and discovers the hawker is a compulsive gambler who cannot hold down a job. He also discovers the hawker is not related in any way to any seafood dealers.

The detective now suspects that he is dealing with a case of smuggling. He tips off one of his contacts in the Customs and Excise Department. Together, the detective and his Customs contact 'place' an order for a few cartons of abalone as a joint operation and then keep the hawker under surveillance. The hawker orders his 'shipment' of abalone from his friends in Indonesia. The 'shipment' arrives by an Indonesian-registered speedboat off Changi beach in a remote area of the coastline. The illegal hawker and his smuggling ring are arrested at the pick-up point (personal communication, 2001).

In terms of 'Knowledge Management' what this case story tells us is that KM is not, in the first instance, about IT but rather how a person, in this case a detective, chooses to think about the wealth of accumulated 'knowledge' carried around in his head, and furthermore how he chose to create and discover new knowledge to add to his reservoir of experience. The detective could just as easily have 'not noticed' the cheapness of the abalone or, if he, he could just as easily have 'not bothered' to become curious or follow up on investigating the hawker. However, as the case shows, he chose to use his experience-based police knowledge to follow through on his curiosity and in so doing crack an organized crime smuggling ring because he 'bothered' to listen to the knowledge in his head and then successfully manage that knowledge.

However, while technology does not do the thinking that underpins 'Knowledge Management', IT does play a significant role in supporting the storage, retrieval, transfer, and sharing of police knowledge. For example, the Homicide Investigation and Tracking System (HITs), a relational database system used by Washington State in America, keeps track of sexual offenders and regularly updates their whereabouts, vehicles, and other details. The value of this knowledge is paramount in helping to solve serious crimes like rape and murder. For example, an extremely brutal rape and attempted murder took place in Washington State and the investigator requested HITS information about any offenders with a particular physical description and method of operation (MO). HITS provided the investigating detective with a list of known sexual offenders who had been released from prison within the last five years and the areas where they lived. The investigator was also provided with photographs of the suspects. When shown the photographs the victim was able to immediately identify one of the suspects as her attacker (Keppel and Weis 1993).

Our long association with police and policing in and from various countries around the world continues to reaffirm our belief that the real value of 'Knowledge Management' lies in how it strengthens policing as a profession to think in a conceptually holistic and operationally pragmatic way, as the case examples above, and those that will be presented throughout the book, affirm.

Finally, it is our fervent hope that as you dip into the pages of this book you will find the experience both intellectually engaging and intriguingly informative. We trust you will find practical cutting-edge guidance for carrying out the complex and vitally worthwhile job of policing and law enforcement for society by doing what you do to the best of your ability and knowledge.

Geoff Dean and Petter Gottschalk
(Brisbane, Australia and Oslo, Norway)

PART ONE

Knowledge Management in Policing: Laying Foundations

The first part of the book outlines the foundations of Knowledge Management (KM). Given that KM is a very broad church which spans several disciplines, only those aspects of KM that have particular relevance to policing and law enforcement will be the focus of this book.

These police knowledge 'foundations' are presented across three interrelated chapters. The first chapter provides a brief potted version of what knowledge is, how it is defined and classified, and more importantly what all this means for policing. The second chapter discusses the fundamentals of KM and how they impact on policing. The third chapter lays out the guiding framework of KM used in the book. This framework locates policing and law enforcement at both a local and national level within the wider context of a global perspective.

Knowledge Work
in Policing

Introduction

Policing is a profession heavily reliant on knowledge. The form such knowledge takes varies from information to intelligence. What does not vary is the 'value' of knowledge for police work. Initially, the chapter discusses just what this notion of 'knowledge' means in so far as its usefulness and application in policing and law enforcement is concerned.

Furthermore, the chapter details the value of 'Knowledge Management' (KM) as a cross-disciplinary field of study with direct applicability to the practice of policing and law enforcement. Finally the chapter looks at the form and shape of 'police knowledge' and sketches out how it works. Hence, this chapter sets the stage for the rest of the book.

What is knowledge?

Policing has always been information-dependent and information-driven (Chen *et al.* 2002). What makes policing different now from past practices is the explosion in the breadth and depth of informational sources available to police and law enforcement agencies (Hughes and Jackson 2004). However, the price of informational richness and diversity is information overload (Luen and Al-Hawamdeh 2001).

Hence, a major problem facing policing in the globally connected society of today is how to find the 'value' in the phenomenal amount of information generated by the knowledge explosion. Police like most other professional practitioners are playing a game of catch up when it comes to finding information that adds value to their practices and can be leveraged into useful operational knowledge.

The logical solution, of course, is to 'manage' the knowledge. Enter KM on the global stage. There is nothing wrong with the logic. However, the problem with most simple sounding solutions is just that: simple to say, hard to achieve.

The initial euphoria when KM—as we know it today—first hit the headlines[1] in the 1980s (Wiig 1999) has been replaced by a more tempered and prudent awareness that KM is not and possibly cannot fix the knowledge explosion, no matter how smart technology becomes. As Prusak (2001: 1) notes:

> we have seen a tendency—especially among vendors of software—to reductively define knowledge management as moving data and documents around[;] knowledge management grew out of an understanding of the critical value of these other, less digitized factors, and the clear need to devise ways to support and benefit from them.

The 'other less digitized factors' that Prusak is referring to concern the way humans reason as well as the context in which such reasoning takes place. These are matters we will return to repeatedly throughout this work for they are the essence of what it means to manage knowledge.

For the moment, the point we are making is not that KM has had its day in the sun; however, the wild glory days may be over for KM as a guaranteed fix-all solution marketed by various hardware and software vendors in the IT industry. But does this not mean KM is of little or no 'value' to police? However, before we can really address the value question, we need to know what 'knowledge' is.

Defining knowledge

Any definition of knowledge involves making a distinction between the related notions of 'information' and 'data'. A common approach in the KM literature (Wiig 1999; Barclay and Murray 2000) is to define knowledge as 'the most valuable form of content in a continuum starting at data, encompassing information, and ending at knowledge' (Gottschalk 2005: 59). Knowledge therefore is presented as existing at the top end of a hierarchically arranged content continuum from data to information to knowledge. Sometimes wisdom is included on the continuum as the ultimate end goal (Davenport and Prusak 1998; Spiegler 2000).

Figure 1.1 below presents this depiction in the literature of a 'knowledge ladder' type of continuum. Included on the Figure is 'intelligence' in order to relate this knowledge continuum more specifically to a policing and law enforcement context.

---

[1] Prusak (2001) records that the first conference specifically devoted to KM was held in Boston in 1993.

Figure 1.1 Hierarchy of police knowledge expressed as a continuum

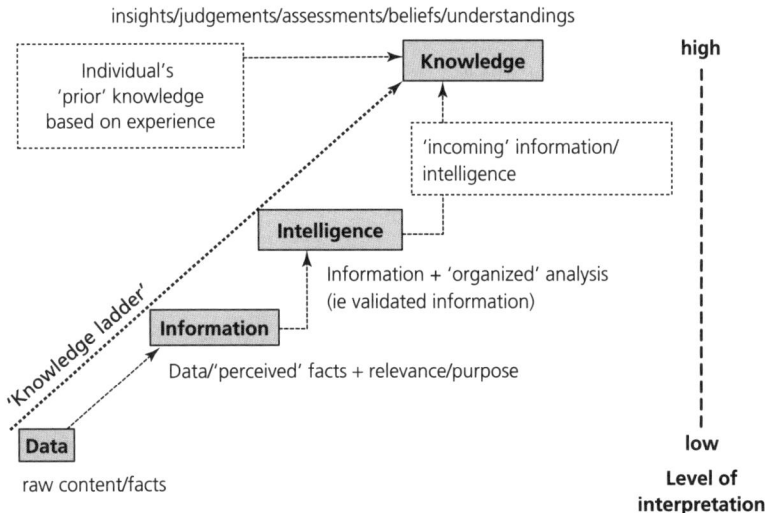

insights/judgements/assessments/beliefs/understandings

'Data' is considered the raw material out of which 'information' develops. As Drucker (1995) notes, information is 'data endowed with relevance and purpose'. The same can be said about 'intelligence' in that it is a form of data to which some relevance has been attached through an attempt to offer an 'organized' analysis of the information received by a crime analyst and/or intelligence officer. Hence, this is why 'intelligence' is placed between information and knowledge on the continuum in Figure 1.1 since ideally intelligence represents, as Brodeur and Dupont (2006: 9) argue, a form of 'validated information'.

A core process of policing and law enforcement is investigation. It is a policing truism that information is the lifeblood of an investigation (Dean 1995). An investigation goes nowhere if information is not forthcoming about an incident. Information is the raw data that supplies the oxygen which breathes life into an investigation. Information is collected by ordinary rank-and-file police officers either working on the street, patrolling and talking to the public, or sitting at a computer doing searches, background checks, or more sophisticated crime mapping and intelligence analysis reports.

'Information' and to a similar extent 'intelligence' then consists of facts and other data which is 'organized' to characterize or profile a particular situation, incident, or crime and the individual or group of individuals presumed to be involved. This 'organizing' of the data to form meaningful information of necessity involves some level of 'interpretation' of the 'facts' as presented. However, the role of interpretation here in 'information' is relatively minor in comparison to its role in terms of 'knowledge' construction. In this regard, the role of interpretation in 'intelligence' is greater and more explicit than in 'information' but not as full-blown as in the making of 'knowledge'.

'Knowledge' as implied operates at a higher level of abstraction and consists of judgements and assessments based on personal beliefs, truths, and expectations about the 'information' received and how it should be analyzed, evaluated, and synthesized—in short 'interpreted'—so that it can be used and implemented in some form of action.

The reasoning behind this 'knowledge continuum' is that if 'data' becomes 'information' when some value is added to it (relevance/purpose) so likewise, up the continuum, 'information' becomes 'knowledge' when some insight, abstraction, or better understanding is added to information to transform it into usable knowledge (Spiegler 2000).

We are not so sure about the smooth, unbroken logic chain argument behind this 'knowledge ladder' conceptualization of a hierarchical continuum containing different content forms. We tend to agree with Wiig (1999) that there is more of a discontinuity between 'information' and 'knowledge' than most people appreciate. The process of creating knowledge by transforming 'incoming information' is more complex than this simple conceptualization allows for in reality. The accuracy and/or the abundance of information does not in itself guarantee success in a police or law enforcement investigation and/or operation. Rather how that information is 'interpreted' and hence turned into knowledge is the key consideration (Sutcliffe and Weber 2003).

The seminal work of Ericson (1981) in his aptly titled book *Making Crime* provides a rich and detailed account of how detectives use their 'police discretion' to take the information they receive from the public, witnesses, victims, and informants and either transform it into a 'crime' or choose to downgrade the information received into 'not a crime'. However, discretionary practices like this are not the sole domain of the 'detective' and their particular brand of 'investigative culture' (Innes 2003). Police discretion is at the very heart and soul of police work. It is enshrined in the office of 'Constable' in the early beginnings of the British system of policing. Street police also have 'discretionary' power to take the same information and upgrade or downgrade its significance.

For example, the eventual police 'outcome' in a physical assault in a domestic violence situation will very much depend on how the responding officers choose to 'perceive' and hence define the 'interpretation' of the incident. This 'interpretation' then becomes part and parcel of their collective 'police knowledge' about 'domestics' as well as part of the 'knowledge-sharing' experience of other officers to whom they tell their 'war stories'.

In the case of a female spouse being the recipient of a domestic violence incident by a male partner this can be 'interpreted' in one of two ways by the responding officers. First, the incident can be upgraded to the status of grievous bodily harm to the female spouse victim if enough 'perceived facts' (eg presence of bruising, blood, cuts, and so forth to the spouse, continuing threats and aggression from the partner, use of a weapon such as a broken beer bottle, knife, etc) in the situation resonate with the responding officers for them to 'interpret' the domestic incident 'as serious' and hence arrest the perpetrator of the violence.

The second way the responding officers can handle this domestic incident is to downgrade it by using their 'police discretion' to 'interpret' the facts as a common assault where a 'domestic argument' (not violence in their perception) got a little out of hand and so a bit of rough handling of the female spouse took place. There may be some bruising and blood present but no weapon and the aggressive partner may appear a little more contrite by the time the police arrive. All of these 'perceived facts' justify in the opinion of the responding officers that no further action should be taken other than to advise the couple to seek counselling.

This 'perceptual reading' of the scene by the officers is filtered through their lens of similar 'domestics' they have attended. It is a common view in police culture that nothing really changes with so-called 'domestics'. The view is based in part on bitter police experience with some domestic violence situations, and in large measure on stereotypical attitudes towards 'domestics' in general. Where the stereotypical police attitude might be that, even if we (the police) intervene with locking up the abuser for a night and going to the trouble of taking out a restraining order on him, in all likelihood the abuser will be back home and forgiven by the spouse before the ink is dry on the order.

If such a culturally transmitted view has taken hold in the 'police experience' of the responding officers to this latest domestic incident then they are already biased in their perception about the futility of doing anything worthwhile in 'domestics'. Therefore, this subtle influence is at work in the back of their minds that given what they 'see' (ie 'see' with eyes but 'perceive' with 'brain') at the scene they are more than likely to take the 'no action' option. Thus, such 'police experience' becomes transformed into 'folklore knowledge' about how to handle 'domestics'.

Clearly, as this hypothetical domestic violence incident shows, the 'discretionary power' of police and other law enforcement officers involves a process of police 'knowledge construction' that operates in a fairly wide 'interpretational space'.

The width of this 'interpretational space' for 'constructing police knowledge' becomes even wider when other elements of the knowledge continuum get added to the mix. In the realm of police intelligence, acting on 'information received' about a particular situation or group of people can get transformed into specific and sometimes idiosyncratic and/or stereotypical ways of characterizing particular situations, incidents, crimes, and the person or people involved. Examples might include racial profiling, or mistaking someone for a terrorist with deadly consequences, or still trying to find years later the weapons of mass destruction that we 'know' through 'our intelligence' Saddam 'definitely' had according to the Bush Administration in its justification for invading Iraq.

Hence, for 'information' to become 'knowledge', a person must evaluate the incoming information against their own prior knowledge or experience of the context out of which the information has arisen. If a person has no direct experience of the informational context then they will have to rely on the prior knowledge of others (eg the shared assumptions and understandings of the police culture) or make a judgement based on ignorance. Either way, the received information cannot be handled 'objectively' in the purist sense of the word.

Some subjective element of prior or imagined experience is 'projected' onto the incoming information. This is the nature of what it means to be human. There is no value judgement implied here that this is a good or bad process, just that it is a process of knowledge construction we as human beings all engage in daily on a moment-by-moment basis. The value judgement comes once the 'outcome' of the action taken on the basis of the interpreted information (knowledge) is itself interpreted as being a 'good' or 'bad' decision by oneself and/or by others.

Therefore, the creation of 'knowledge' is as much a function of prior knowledge as it is of received 'information'. Hence, the reason for the broken dotted lines in Figure 1.1 between 'information/intelligence' and 'knowledge'. These signify that, far from being a smooth, unbroken chain of logical, rational progression in terms of moving up the ladder from information to knowledge, there is a built-in human-related discontinuity inherent in the knowledge creation process which makes such orderly progression an idealist fantasy.

The domestic violence incident discussed above clearly illustrates that a host of unforeseen consequences can result when 'information' gets transformed into 'knowledge'. The transition up the 'knowledge ladder' is more like a game of snakes and ladders in the policing domain than a smooth logical progression as the knowledge continuum suggests.

To sum up, the crucial difference is that if one thinks acquiring new knowledge is just a simple mechanistic input–output type (information 'in'–knowledge 'out') arrangement then the implications for how an organization like policing 'manages' its knowledge are profound. Any organization that believes this simplistic conception about what knowledge is will feel very at home and comfortable with the reductionistic tendency to define KM as just 'moving data and documents around' (Prusak 2001: 1).

Let us be very clear that our view in this book is to remind the reader of the word order in the label 'Knowledge Management'. That is, the most important point to remember is the 'K' comes first in the order of things then follows the 'M'. In other words, valuing 'Knowledge'—its creation, storage, retrieval, transfer, sharing, and application is the name of the KM game. Not the other way round. 'Management' always takes second place to 'Knowledge'.

Classification of knowledge

Ever since the concept of 'knowledge' has been around people have been trying to classify it. Aristotle made an essential distinction between 'know-how' and 'know what' (Prusak 2001). Polanyi (1962, 1966, 1969), building on this distinction, emphasized two distinct types of knowledge—'tacit' and 'explicit' knowledge, where 'tacit' or implicit knowledge is the knowledge people carry around in their heads as mental models and experiential learnings. By contrast, 'explicit' knowledge is knowledge that can be documented and represented as formal models, rules, and procedures.

Many other ways of classifying and categorizing knowledge can be found in the KM literature. For example, lawyers' professional knowledge has been classified into declarative, procedural, and analytical knowledge (Gottschalk 2006). Such classification is based on knowledge in use (Schön 1983). Several researchers (Nordenstam 1983; Göranzon 1990; Gustavsson 2000) have divided professional knowledge into three different types—statement or theoretical knowledge; skill or practical knowledge; familiarity knowledge or practical wisdom.

However, it is very common in the KM literature to stick to the tacit and explicit classification of knowledge. With regard to policing, a number of researchers directly or indirectly conclude that police officers need a wide and substantial variety of 'tacit' (implicit) knowledge (Bayley 1994; Brodeur 1998; Waddington 1999; Finstad 2000).

Finstad (2000) considers the police profession to be a handicraft; not in the sense of mass production, but rather as a form of art handicraft. Waddington (1999) states that the skills and knowledge that a police officer possesses are difficult to describe in theoretical principles, because it is a handicraft. Bayley (1994) believes that police officers require a large 'knowledge bank' to do their job.

Alavari and Leidner (2001) view tacit and explicit knowledge as two sides of the same coin in the sense that they are mutually dependent and reinforcing qualities of knowledge not dichotomous entities or states of knowledge in and of themselves. Hence, they refer to this formulation as a 'knowledge space' (Alavari and Leidner 2001: 112). This concept of a knowledge space will be developed further in later chapters in relation to the mutually dependent processes of knowledge transfer and knowledge sharing.

What is Knowledge Management?

There are about as many definitions of what KM is as there are sun spots on a body baking on a beach. King, Marks, and McCoy (2002: 93) make the comment regarding the nature of KM that there is a 'high level of confusion'. Definitions[2] also keep appearing in the literature just as often as sun spots. Leaving aside such definitional difficulties for the moment, what 'value' KM holds for policing and law enforcement in a global context is the subject matter of concern

---

[2] Readers interested in understanding more about the definitional difficulties of KM are referred to Barclay and Murray (2000); Wiig (2000); Spiegler (2000); and Prusak (2001) for a fuller treatment of the topic.

in this book. Hence, what is of interest here are two aspects of 'Knowledge Management'. These are KM as a 'practice' and KM as a 'philosophy'.

Knowledge Management as practice

To cut to the core of KM as an applied practice it is essentially about a set of distinct yet complementary processes. KM as a practice involves the processes of knowledge creation and capture, storage and retrieval, transfer and sharing, application and integration into the operating philosophy and work practices of an organization. This pragmatic understanding of KM (Gottschalk 2005) is used as a thematic link for the rest of the book. There is a logical progression in this implicit understanding. That is, KM is about 'creating' and then 'capturing' knowledge so that it can be 'stored' and 'retrieved' in order to 'transfer' and 'share' it with others who in turn 'apply' this new knowledge to the problem at hand, and if successful then 'integrate' such new knowledge into the organization at various levels.

Again, it looks like a simple recipe; but not everyone knows how to follow even a simple recipe. It's a bit like the notion of 'common sense'—it's not common to all. With regard to KM in the policing field, one senior police officer made the comment that 'in the ranks of policing, knowledge management is still relatively unexplored' (Colaprete 2004: 82).

However, the relatively easy bits to do in the KM cookbook are the 'storage and retrieval' processes. The IT industry is well geared up to do these bits for a police organization. There are a host of hardware platforms and a multitude of software programs and plugs-ins available to do the mechanical side of information storage and retrieval for police and law enforcement agencies. A quick look through any police magazine in any country will reveal the wonders of having your own Knowledge Management Technology (KMT) goodies sitting on your desk or held in the palm of your hand. On this matter Sheptycki (2002: 84) observes:

> The extensive market in new information technologies—from case management systems, to crime pattern analysis and offender profiling software, and much more—is testified to by the healthy amount of advertising in police trade magazines.

The problem with KMT gadgets is they do everything for you quicker and better bar the thinking. That still has to be supplied by the police officer. Human thinking looks like it will still need to be around in policing for the foreseeable future.

Don't misread the message. KM has enormous potential and value for policing that is unequivocally clear. Knowledge Management and the IT systems and technologies that support the KM processes—capture/creation–storage/retrieval–transfer/sharing and application/integration—can significantly enhance the range of policing/security activities available and hence provide a strategic advantage in the fight against localized forms of crime as well as international and transnational criminal activities and terrorism.

A very simple illustration of the strategic advantage of KM supported by IT systems in the fight against local crime is contained in the following case study.

Case study: 'Intelligence-led' murder investigation

A murder occurred in Singapore, in late 2005, of a 37-year-old Chinese homosexual (personal communication with SIO). Singapore, from a police intelligence perspective, is very well set up to conduct what is known as 'intelligence-led' policing investigations. Within its intelligence gathering capacity there are a considerable number of different relational databases that can be searched by police.

Background checks revealed some known associates of the deceased. One of these became a suspect along with another unknown male. The lead detective on the case conducted a very skilful interview with the suspect during which the suspect revealed unwittingly that he and the other unknown suspect had been hassled and spot-checked in the street recently by some police officers. This slip of the tongue was the breakthrough the detective was hoping for in the case. The detective did an electronic search through the 'Persons Screening Detail Statistics' database of the Command, Control and Communication System (CUBICON), which led to the establishment of the complete identity of the previously unknown suspect. He was traced to Malaysia through the use of a series of other police databases and an ambush was planned which led to his arrest for the murder.

As can be seen in this murder case the level of sophistication that KMT can bring to bear on a crime problem in Singapore is substantial. Various police services around the world are similarly equipped to a greater or lesser extent with KM systems and technologies.

Hence, the IT industry should and will play a major role in the development and adaptation of KM systems for policing needs and ever more so with the rise of fundamentalist terrorism since 9/11. But no matter how sophisticated and 'expert' KM systems get it is still the human head that must supply the technology machine not the other way around.

The silliness of some IT manufacturers' claims in the current global 'politics of fear' climate is where KM gets a black eye by default. For example, a software package much touted statistically, and dubbed 'Matrix' in true Hollywood style by the manufacturing company is currently the favourite relational database used by some American states in the wake of 9/11. Matrix—short for Multistate Anti-Terrorism Information Exchange—combines state records and data culled from a so-called 'Terrorist Handbook'. Matrix purportedly reveals how terrorists 'penetrate and live in our society' using software to arrive at a 'terrorism quotient' which gives a high terrorist factor (HTF) to people who show a statistical likelihood of being terrorists (<http://newspaper.asia1.com.sg/> 2004).

None of the 'home-grown' terrorists that brought London to its knees in 2005 would have been registered on Matrix at the time. Every youth that 'fits' the statistical profile of the suicide bombers will most likely be 'red flagged' on Matrix now. How useful that 'information' is when it fits a large segment of the entire youth population in the UK is a very moot point.

The fact that such KMT 'profiling' systems exist is more a case of 'grabbing at something rather than nothing' as well as a testament to the power of marketing over any independently demonstrated effectiveness in picking out terrorists from the crowd at an airport or in a train or boarding a double-decker bus. Again, the theme of terrorism and the relationship of KM to it will be taken up in later chapters.

Knowledge Management as philosophy

The philosophy, or more accurately the philosophical orientations, underlying the field of KM has its feet firmly rooted in essentially two camps—one mechanistic and the other dynamic in nature. This divergence in perspectives is due in part to the fact that KM by its very nature is a field made up of many disciplines (Barclay and Murray 2000). The width of this cross-disciplinary field is large, very diverse, and made up of some strange bedfellows from IT, information science, and artificial intelligence through business, management, and organizational studies to social, group, educational, cognitive psychology, and some esoteric areas of philosophy. Such a straddling act across this range of philosophical positions and cross-disciplinary boundaries by the KM field makes for some interesting and intriguing combinations.

However, the point is from a philosophical perspective police and other law enforcement organizations suffer from the general misconception that KM equates to IT. That is, KM is all about IT systems. This one-sided equation has, of course, been deliberately fostered and over-emphasized by hardware and software manufacturers to sell more of their wares. We term this a 'Platform and Cable' (P&C) approach to KM. This P&C approach shows no sign of abating, as previously noted by Sheptycki (2002), given the marketing push by the IT industry in police trade magazines.

The other side of the KM equation in so far as its philosophy is concerned is the view that 'knowledge' cannot be 'managed' (Anderson 2003; Chia 2004; Tsoukas and Mylonopoulos 2003; Brown and Duguid 2001; Tsoukas and Vladimirou 2001) in the mechanistic way envisioned by the P&C IT-driven approach. Rather, the only thing that can be 'managed' is the 'context' in which 'knowledge' occurs. This perspective emphasizes a 'learning organization' approach and is conceptually linked to movements like Total Quality Management (Prusak 2001; Spiegler 2000).

This philosophical side of the KM equation will be termed the 'Context and Culture' view in this book as it also emphasizes the cultural dimension of knowledge construction and knowledge transfer (Glisby and Holden 2003; Wensley 2001; Al-Rasheed 1994) and has its roots in complexity theory (Dreyfus 2002; Tsoukas and Hatch 2001).

This Context and Culture conception of KM is another thematic link that will be drawn upon throughout this book to underscore the notion of 'global policing' as a concept of significance for police and law enforcement agencies that engage with each other on the international stage.

What is police work?

Policing is about people and place. At its most general level, police work is the application of a set of legally sanctioned practices designed to maintain public order by imposing the rule of law on people who live in or travel through a given place which is internationally recognized as a geographically defined territory under the control of a particular nation state (Sheptycki 2002).

The set of policing practices cover core issues like law enforcement through crime investigation and crime prevention, security issues involving mainly surveillance and counter-terrorism on a population, and jurisdictional issues in relation to having the legal authority to act in a particular place and under what legal framework and conditions.

The essential point here is that 'police work' no longer exclusively takes place in a local 'territorial' context within a nation state. Traditional conceptions of policing relate to terrain and the population contained within its legally defined boundaries. However, newer conceptions of policing are recognizing that 'policing' and 'the state' have been uncoupling (Walker 2003; Sheptycki 2002) for some time, driven in large measure by the profound consequences of globalization on the nation-state system. Policing like society has gone 'global'.

Hence, at this juncture in the book it is useful to provide some understanding to the reader of our notion of 'global policing'. At a very simple level the term denotes any type of policing and/or security activity that is conducted on the international stage. There are two dimensions to the use of the term in this book.

First, 'global policing' acts as an umbrella concept to bring together under one term the diversity that exists in policing in relation to different sectors[3] (public/private) and different levels (local/national/international) with their different foci of jurisdictional boundaries and primary allegiances.

Secondly, the term 'global policing' also acts as a contextual concept to mark out the emerging form of this new type of policing context in which the world finds itself post-9/11. The distinction between 'policing' and 'security'

---

[3] A fuller treatment of the distinctions between global policing and its relationship to policing sectors and levels will be expanded on in Chapter 3.

has become so blurred with the advent of new fundamentalist forms of terrorism since 9/11 that policing has taken on a national security focus which was once only the domain of the government security services to a large extent. Hence, the term 'policing' itself as used in this book is inclusive of this 'police–security' nexus.

Similar terms like 'international' and 'transnational' policing are not appropriate to use as either umbrella terms or context markers for the emerging of the police–security nexus post-9/11. These older terms are firmly tied to the policing sector as such and not to the more recent emergence 'globally' of the large-scale security sector and how it intermeshes with policing functions and activities.

Post-9/11, policing is based in a new alliance of professional disciplines. Hence, this contextual dimension of 'globalized' policing practices encompasses both public and private forms of the policing–security nexus.

One further theme to be explored in the book, which is related to this focus on the 'global context' of policing, is encapsulated in the phrase 'think globally, act locally'. This phrase was originated by Rene Dubos as an adviser to the United Nations Conference on the Human Environment in 1972 and refers to the argument that global environmental problems can turn into action only by considering ecological, economic, and cultural differences of our local surroundings (Eblen and Eblen 1994).

This 'think globally, act locally' phrase captured the imagination of many environmental activists at the time and was soon hijacked by the business community to support the push for greater globalization of markets. Hence, 'think globally, act locally' is now a common form of sloganeering and is repeated as a mantra-like rallying cry by businesses wanting to expand into the global marketplace.

Police organizations and related agencies have also taken up this catchphrase with enthusiasm. In the UK the Chief Inspector of Constabulary in 2002 used the 'think globally, act locally' phrase to describe his view of 'globalization' being 'about understanding the links between the local and the global' (Povey 2002: 60). Similarly, the Turkish Nation Police in conjunction with the International Police Executive Symposium based in America hosted an international conference in 2006 titled 'Local linkages to Global Security and Crime: Thinking Locally and Acting Globally' (<http://www.ipes.info>).

This business-oriented formulation of 'thinking globally and acting locally' may work well for supplying cheap imports of consumer goods, or finding new markets, but is problematic for policing. Police are not in the business of selling goods or chasing markets. The 'core business' of policing is conducting criminal investigations, maintaining public order, and safeguarding homeland security. And although police are working in a 'globalized' context this business-oriented dictum to 'think globally, act locally' should be reversed when applied to policing.

For police and other law enforcement agencies the imperative should be to 'act locally, think globally'. This reformulation more accurately reflects the fact that any 'global' action taken by police is always firmly rooted to and within a 'localized' context. Police action requires an evidential chain to be produced in a court of law to show how the 'global' connections are linked to 'local' manifestations and vice versa; that is, where evidence exists to show 'local' criminal activity is linked to 'global' criminal networks in some way.

Therefore, we argue in this book from a 'context and culture' perspective on KM that while police continue to 'act locally' they must also learn and train their minds to 'think globally' simultaneously. This is because the daily realities of local policing in a nation-state context have the potential to flow right up to global policing issues. For example, the arrest of a 'local' drug dealer is inevitably connected to a 'global' syndicate of an organized criminal network. However, local police while acting 'locally' are rarely encouraged on many policing issues to think beyond their territorial boundaries like this one to a global level. Hence, the need for operational police officers, in particular, while 'acting locally' to also be 'thinking globally'.

Police knowledge-at-work

Policing in a global world, as the previous section indicated, has been shaped by forces of globalization which have moulded society into a networked world of virtual reality that collapses space and time and transcends the old realities of how work used to be done.

Police work is now firmly rooted in what has become known as 'knowledge work'. This knowledge revolution in policing is not just a simple matter of out with the old and in with the new—a sort of 'business as usual' approach. The only real difference now being a police officer enters a record of interview into an electronic form on a computer rather than writes it up in a notebook.

Technology is not neutral. It has a transformative power far beyond what most of us first imagined when we got a computer. The role of technology in policing and its impact is a theme that will be taken up in later chapters; our intention here is to show how the 'knowledge base' of operational policing or 'knowledge-at-work' is multi-dimensional in nature. The implications of this understanding are substantial for how a police organization goes about 'managing' such operational knowledge.

Figure 1.2 below depicts this multi-faceted structure of police work in relation to three main dimensions of an individual's tacit knowledge—cognitive, technical, and social. Previous research in domains other than policing have found tacit knowledge to be a combination of these cognitive, technical, and social dimensions (Leonard and Insch 2005; Sternberg *et al.* 2000; Sternberg and Horvath 1999; Sternberg *et al.* 1995; Sternberg, Wagner, and Okagaki 1993; Nonaka and Konno 1998; Wagner 1987; Wagner and Sternberg 1986; Nelson and Winter 1982).

Figure 1.2 Multi-dimensional structure of police knowledge

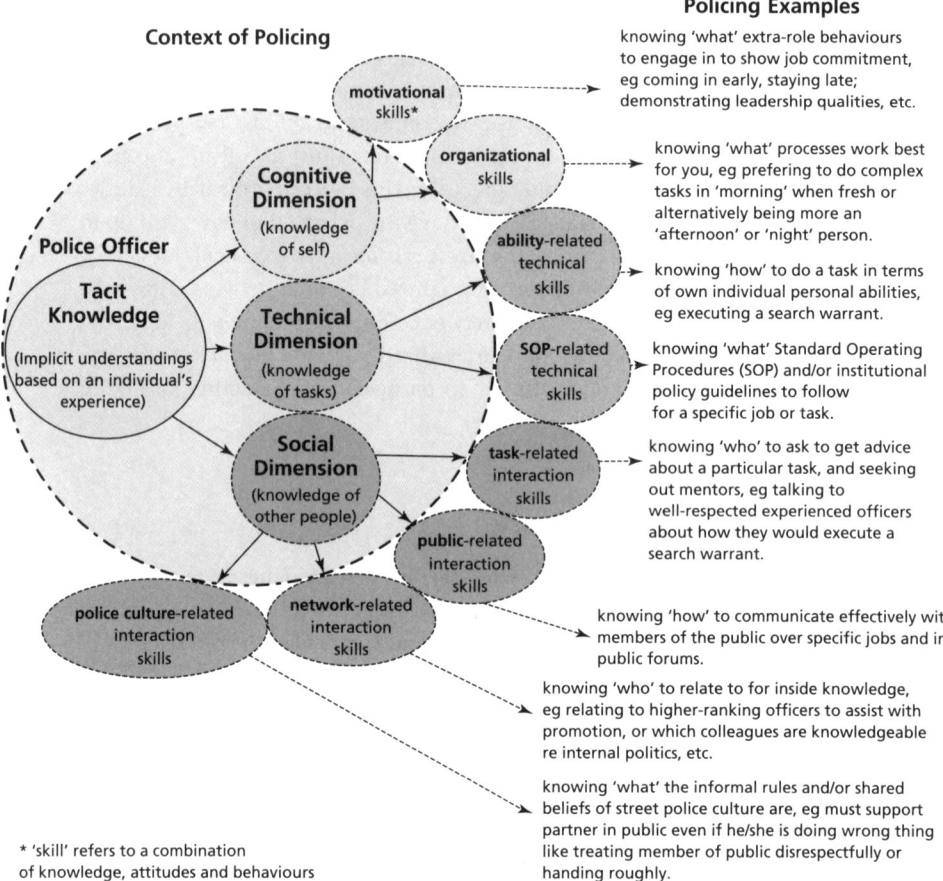

Policing Examples

knowing 'what' extra-role behaviours to engage in to show job commitment, eg coming in early, staying late; demonstrating leadership qualities, etc.

knowing 'what' processes work best for you, eg prefering to do complex tasks in 'morning' when fresh or alternatively being more an 'afternoon' or 'night' person.

knowing 'how' to do a task in terms of own individual personal abilities, eg executing a search warrant.

knowing 'what' Standard Operating Procedures (SOP) and/or institutional policy guidelines to follow for a specific job or task.

knowing 'who' to ask to get advice about a particular task, and seeking out mentors, eg talking to well-respected experienced officers about how they would execute a search warrant.

knowing 'how' to communicate effectively with members of the public over specific jobs and in public forums.

knowing 'who' to relate to for inside knowledge, eg relating to higher-ranking officers to assist with promotion, or which colleagues are knowledgeable re internal politics, etc.

knowing 'what' the informal rules and/or shared beliefs of street police culture are, eg must support partner in public even if he/she is doing wrong thing like treating member of public disrespectfully or handing roughly.

* 'skill' refers to a combination of knowledge, attitudes and behaviours

The diagram clearly illustrates with the examples provided how wide-ranging and deep the 'knowledge base' of police officers needs to be in order to effectively carry out their job and the diversity of duties and functions associated with it.

As can be seen, there are a number of sub-sets of skills for each dimension. In relation to the 'cognitive' dimension this primarily involves police officers, knowledge about themselves, specifically in relation to demonstrating motivational skills about job commitment and dedication, as well as their own organizational skills in how they prefer to work in terms of things like case, resources, and project management amongst other things.

The 'technical' dimension on the other hand consists of two sets of skills divided between personal task ability and specific task-related skills involved in following standard operating procedures (SOPs) of policing various situations officers may be called upon to respond to in the course of their work. As to be expected this 'technical' dimension of tacit knowledge is very much related to what a police officer has received by way of basic training at recruitment and ongoing specialist courses in their career pathway.

The 'social' or more precisely the 'interactional' dimension of policing contains at least four sub-skill sets based on a qualitative longitudinal study of a police officer's work patterns throughout the 21 police districts in Sweden (Holgersson 2005).

The first tacit knowledge social skill set is task-oriented and differs from the 'technical' dimension of task performance in that the focus of these skills is directed towards the interactions of others. Similarly, the public skill set involves the projection of one's self in relation to communication ability with others and the presentation of an appropriate policing 'persona' as discussed earlier. The last two skill sets involve networking in the police organization and the influences of the police culture in so far as how it effects the carrying out of street policing.

It should be borne in mind that the term 'police culture' is a more or less catch-all phrase which subsumes a number of subcultural groupings within its ambit, most notably the 'managerial' and 'operational' police subcultures which are well documented in the literature (Reuss-Ianni 1993; Ekman 1999; Foster 2003; Paoline 2003). Moreover, the 'operational' culture of policing can be further subdivided along the lines other researchers have found: for example, the 'investigative culture' of detectives (Wright 2002; Maguire 2003; Innes 2003) as well as the 'street culture' of general duties police.

The pervasiveness of the social/interactional dimension of policing, especially in relation to its culture and network, can be exceedingly powerful for a police officer's career. That is, the direction an officer's career can take if they fail to 'obey' or give due cognizance to the informal rules of the police culture and their subcultural grouping within it, as well as their network of 'mates', can be changed in an instant.

To conclude, Figure 1.2 is but one example of the depth of the working knowledge of police to which KM can be usefully applied to enhance the human capital and strategic resources of a police organization. Hence, the 'value' of 'police knowledge' and its effective 'management' is the core business of policing and law enforcement.

Summary

Several themes were introduced in this chapter. Such themes concerned the nature of knowledge and what its management means in the context of policing on a global scale, especially since the redrawing of the boundaries between public and private forms of policing and law enforcement and their nexus with the ever expanding security industry.

We argue the creation of 'knowledge' is as much a function of prior knowledge as it is of received 'information'. We note that KM is a multiple cross-disciplinary field of study where the 'K' comes first in the order of things before the 'M'. That tacit and explicit knowledge are two mutually dependent aspects of the same 'knowledge space' in which the processes of knowledge—creation/capture, storage/retrieval, transfer/sharing, application/integration—are played out.

Furthermore, we highlighted the implications for policing and law enforcement of how KM operates both at the level of IT systems support and at the policy level of 'context and culture' in an organization. Moreover, we introduced the theme of 'global policing' as a new term arising out of a post-9/11 police and law enforcement operating environment to signify a new alliance between professional disciplines to encompass public and private forms of the policing–security nexus and their practices. From an international perspective, this notion of 'global policing' is based in the operational imperative of 'act locally, think globally' to underscore the fact that any 'global' action taken by police is always firmly rooted to and within a 'localized' context where the realities of policing take place.

Fundamentals of Knowledge Management for Policing

Introduction

It should be apparent by now that 'Knowledge Management' (KM) is like 'beauty' in that it resides in the eye of the beholder. Hence, the perspective from which one views KM is fundamental to how it is understood. The purpose of this chapter therefore is to sketch out and highlight which 'fundamentals' of KM have relevance for policing. The chapter should instil an appreciation of KM not only in terms of how it can benefit policing but also how it can impose limitations on the effectiveness of policing if the fundamentals of KM as they apply to policing are not well understood. This is a relatively short chapter as anything fundamental should by definition cut to the essential elements involved.

While police organizations function as a 'business', as any large government bureaucracy must, it is a mistake to assume policing is a business like any other. Police and law enforcement organizations are users with specific and special needs for KM. The distinctive mission and particular characteristics of policing therefore make it imperative to appreciate what KM has to offer policing.

Disciplinary diversity of Knowledge Management

One of the first fundamentals to appreciate about KM is that it is a 'system of thought' with no fixed address in any one discipline. KM wanders over many terrains but lives nowhere in particular although plenty of disciplines lay claim to KM. For example, Wiig (1999) provides a list that includes disciplines like business—particularly in the areas of management and organizational studies; cognitive sciences; economics; library and information sciences; information technology (IT) and related knowledge engineering approaches like artificial intelligence (AI)—social sciences (especially cognitive, organizational, social, and group psychology); and a host of diverse areas affiliated with these and other disciplinary approaches like sociology and philosophy (Prusak 2001). Other writers (see King, Marks, and McCoy 2002; Barclay and Murray 2000; Spiegler 2000) provide similar lists.

The point is that KM is so broad that terms like multi-disciplinary and cross-disciplinary do not adequately describe its diversity or its complexity. The proliferation of material written on and about KM is enormous as a quick googling of the term 'Knowledge Management' will attest with the gigantic number of hits such a search reveals. This staggering explosion of information surrounding KM adds more confusion to the definitional nightmare that already exists. One way to make some sort of sense out of such broad and deep disciplinary diversity is to explore the notion of 'perspective' as mentioned previously. That is, the perspective from which one 'views' KM is fundamental to understanding it.

For example as Barclay and Murray (2000: 6) note 'KM in Europe is almost synonymous with groupware (ie computer-supported collaborative work)'. Groupware as the name suggests is an IT-based platform that supports knowledge sharing and collaboration in and between organizations. Hence, the linking of groupware with KM reveals a particular 'perspective' or view of KM as being intrinsically tied to IT infrastructure in particular and information systems (IS) in general. Such a perspective is alive and well in the business management community according to King, Marks, and McCoy (2002: 93): 'executives tend to view KM as a natural extension of the IS function; a number of surveys show that IS is responsible for most KM implementation and management'. From this IS perspective then KM is fundamentally understood as adding new applications to existing IT infrastructure or where incompatibilities exist 'bolting' on a new IT platform to the IT infrastructure.

The focus of the next section is to get a firmer handle on the richness and complexity of the perspectives that underpin KM as a field of endeavour across the wide diversity of disciplines it migrates through.

Differences in orientation to Knowledge Management

KM as a 'system of thought' involves both a 'philosophy' and a 'practice'; or, more precisely, two different philosophical orientations (mechanistic and dynamic) to Knowledge Management as well as a set of distinct yet complementary processes (knowledge creation and capture, storage and retrieval, transfer and sharing, application and integration). The differences in philosophical orientation are the subjects taken up in this section. The next section will round up the discussion about KM processes.

In relation to philosophical orientations, just as the business management community in general has a mechanistic understanding of KM as primarily an IS function, it will come as no surprise as noted in the previous chapter that police and other law enforcement organizations have also come under the influence of the same philosophical perspective or mechanistic orientation that equates KM with IT. This 'platform and cable' approach to KM is good for business but is it good for policing as the only view of KM to hold? The alternative view involves the more dynamic philosophical perspective termed in this book as the 'context and culture' approach to KM.

The argument being advanced here is not that one philosophical orientation or approach to KM is better than another, only that to have 'good sight' one needs both eyes to see with. Furthermore, it is clear that the KM market is dominated by the IS/IT industry to such an extent that police organizations are at risk of seeing out of only one eye and hence perceiving the value of KM as only residing in new and better 'platforms and cables', applications and software.

Falling prey to this one-eyed IS/IT view of KM misses the essential message provided by the other philosophical eye, that it is ignorantly presumptuous to think that 'knowledge' can be 'managed' like a sack of paper potatoes by moving information and data bits around in virtual reality. At best this is an impoverished notion of 'knowledge' and at worst it is grossly arrogant. The only thing that realistically can be 'managed' and not without a great deal of difficulty is the context and culture in which knowledge occurs, if one works at developing the necessary conditions required to stimulate such a broad-based knowledge management strategy.

The notion of 'managing the context' in which knowledge evolves is not some abstract idea that sounds great but has no legs to it. Essentially, it comes down to effectively managing people; because it is people who are the ones that carry a vast storehouse of tacit knowledge around in their heads. People management in the context of KM means that any KM practice has to be people-centred in ways that are meaningful and respectful to them and the knowledge they have. This is the only way to effectively manage people as a valued knowledge resource and it is not easy. People management is the most difficult part of any management job. In general, managing technical difficulties can be overcome if enough money and time is spent. Managing people is not a matter of time or money in most cases. Personalities clash, rigidities set in, and inappropriate assumptions are acted on. HR departments constantly do battle over personal issues.

However, when enlightened management operates in an organization it becomes possible to effectively manage its people assets. Managing people knowledge is the asset of concern here. There are some KM practices that offer some promise for managing the context and culture of knowledge acquisition. Some examples of this people-centred type of KM practice include establishing a lessons-learnt system (King, Marks, and McCoy 2002) to capture and store the wealth of knowledge people have in doing their particular job. This is just one example of using a knowledge repository in a more innovative way than just to store organizational policy and procedure-type documents. Another example of a people-centred KM practice is what is termed in the literature as 'communities of practice'. These 'communities' are made up of members who have a professional interest in some area and who seek out others with similar interests and thus a self-organizing group evolves over time. The links often begin in an informal manner and may become formalized at some point. No matter what form such a 'community of practice' may take the really essential element is the richness and depth of the knowledge sharing that takes place in them. Organizations that explicitly encourage the development of such free-forming self-organizing work-related communities of practice are investing in the future of KM and its as yet unrealized potentialities.

The problem such self-organizing communities of practice presents to a police organization is exactly that—its free-forming self-organizing nature. Police organizations, regardless of how they present themselves to the public, have essentially a paramilitary structure and operate by necessity on a command and control basis. The long-term effect is that police executive management find it hard to let go or free up this ingrained command and control mentality. They like to micro-manage everything. Such an attitude is counterproductive to establishing viable communities of practice in a police organization. This theme of communities of practice in policing will be returned to in later chapters.

Hence, in closing this brief but important section the one fundamental thing to bear in mind is that, when it comes to instigating a KM strategy within a police organization, having 'wisdom' is a far more important consideration. 'Wisdom' in this regard means using two eyes by adopting a 'dual-vision' approach to seeing the way forward for integrating KM throughout a police and/or law enforcement organization.

Key processes in Knowledge Management

Having outlined the strategic choice entailed in adopting a 'dual-vision' approach to KM by not only investing in suitable IT infrastructure but also stimulating people-centred KM practices, this section outlines at a very practical level the KM processes required to enact this strategic choice in relation to police and law enforcement organizations.

As a practice KM relies on and revolves around a set of distinct complementary processes concerned with knowledge creation, capture, storage, retrieval, transfer, sharing, application, and integration. In the original formulation of this systematic framework by Alavi and Leidner (2001) they listed four of these key processes, namely knowledge creation (also referred to as construction), storage and retrieval, transfer, and application. We have expanded on this framework to include the additional processes of knowledge capture, sharing, and integration. While this framework gives a clear indication of what KM involves in practice such a list does not highlight the inter-relationships involved in this intertwined set, either of activities or their significance when attempting to integrate a KM strategy across an organization.

In this regard, one way to usefully conceptualize this set of complementary KM processes is to depict them as involving four inter-related phases rather than in a linear sequence, as shown in Figure 2.1.

The diagrammatic model in Figure 2.1 depicts this systematic framework of KM processes as a set of elliptical circles that interconnect and overlap at certain points with one another. The advantage of this depiction is that it allows the inter-relationships in and between these eight KM processes to become clearer so that implications can be drawn about how these processes interact in practice.

As can be seen, each of the four phases contains a paired set of KM processes that logically relate to each other. For example, Phase 1 involves the paired set of Knowledge Creation and Knowledge Capture processes. This is because the ability to create knowledge is useless unless such knowledge is captured by some process. Otherwise, such knowledge remains locked in someone's head and cannot be used by anyone else. However, once knowledge is captured it can be stored in an electronic form.

Hence, Phase 2 involves both Knowledge Storage and Knowledge Retrieval since once knowledge is stored in electronic form such as a database it can also

Figure 2.1 Phase model of KM processes

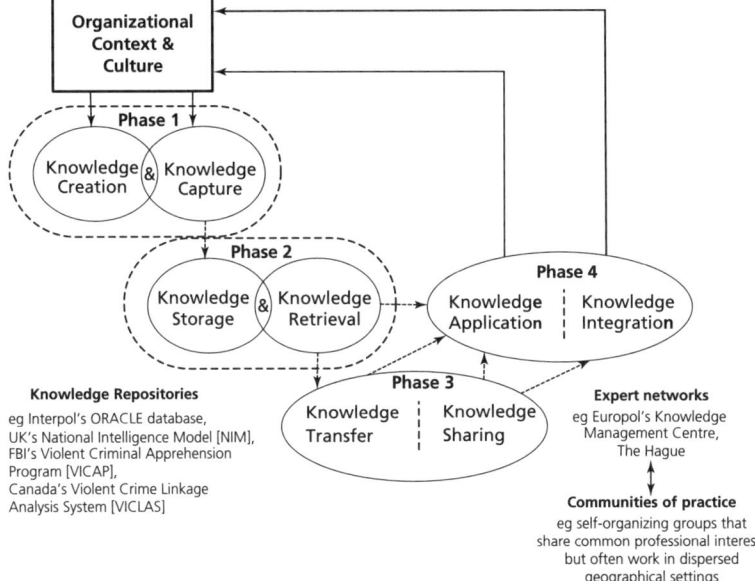

be retrieved from the database by a similar process. Examples of a range of such police-related 'Knowledge Repositories' are also listed in Figure 2.1.

So far so good as indicated by the broken arrow from 'capture' to 'storage', but as can be seen on the diagram Phase 3 appears more problematic and is not so straightforward. Knowledge Transfer and Knowledge Sharing are located in Phase 3 and should in theory go together but in reality a disjunction can occur as indicated by the broken line between 'transfer' and 'sharing'. Also, knowledge transfer is not necessarily the same thing as knowledge sharing although both processes have similar characteristics.

Knowledge can be transferred between individuals and groups and in a very limited sense this can be understood as having 'shared' such knowledge. However, our notion of knowledge sharing has a more active element than just passively moving knowledge around from one person to another. Knowledge sharing involves an active participation in attempting to understand another's knowledge and usually this takes place in a joint exchange of views in dialogue with another rather than simply distributing knowledge between people.

Hence, knowledge transfer is essentially about the distribution of information/knowledge, whereas knowledge sharing is about the participation in understanding information/knowledge. Again, police examples are provided in Figure 2.1 (expert networks and communities of practice) which can relate to both knowledge transfer and sharing at various levels. That is, an expert network can act simply as a distribution point for knowledge expertise (knowledge transfer) but may also include a participative element (knowledge sharing) if the referred expert becomes engaged in an ongoing dialogue with the requesting organization. As indicated in Figure 2.1 this may become a sustained two-way engagement between the people concerned and can over time turn into more of a community of practice about particular policing issues.

Phase 4 is the final phase in which knowledge that has been either directly retrieved and applied, or retrieved and transferred, is then applied and/or shared between people with an eventual applied outcome resulting. The three broken arrows indicate these various pathways to Knowledge Application.

However, while knowledge application and knowledge integration can be logically related, a similar situation arises as with knowledge transfer and knowledge sharing, in that a disjunction can occur between the application of knowledge and its integration back into an organization's context and culture as shown by the broken line.

Applied knowledge can exist in organizational 'silos' and not find its way back into the wider organization as indicated by the arrow from knowledge application to the box that contains the organization's context and culture.

There can be many reasons for such a lack of knowledge integration within a police organization. The range of specialist divisions and departments is such that they may not need to know about some knowledge applications that are not relevant to their specific areas of interest. Also, police deal in very sensitive information and in some cases the strategic nature of the intelligence is such that it can only be available to approved persons on a need-to-know basis. However, there are also situations where knowledge applications should be integrated more widely but where internal police politics sabotage any meaningful attempts to achieve even a minimum level of integration.

Policing is a profession that is well acquainted with the problems of 'integrating' new ways of doing things. Discussion Forum 2.1 below discusses attempts to integrate the philosophy and practice of 'community policing' into police departments and is a case worthy of consideration in regard to seeking to integrate KM as also a philosophy and practice.

Discussion Forum 2.1 Philosophy and Practice of Community Policing

From the 1980s onwards community policing became the dominant strategy of policing for the 1990s. As Cordner (2005: 401) remarks, 'community policing has evolved a few small foot patrol studies to the pre-eminent reform agenda of modern policing'. However, 'community policing' continues to be many things to many people. A common catch cry by proponents is 'community policing is a philosophy, not a program' (ibid.: 402). But there is much confusion over the meaning of the term 'community policing'. For example, in a national survey in the US of 1,606 law enforcement agencies, Wycoff (1994) found that nearly 50 per cent of the responding police chiefs and sheriffs did not have a clear understanding of what community policing means.

In essence, 'community policing' is a crime-fighting strategy that stresses partnership and problem solving. In the US it has been widely practised for about a decade (Sheriff 2002). After the tragic events of 9/11, the idea of involving the community in crime control has taken on new significance. However, in spite of its history and current popularity, the concept of 'community policing' has its detractors.

As Maguire and Katz (2002) note: 'Critics have argued that community policing represents a slogan without action, style without substance, and rhetoric without reality (Bayley 1988; Klockars 1988; Manning 1989; Weatheritt 1988). For some, community policing is an empty reform effort characterized by nothing but "BS and buzzwords" (Hunter & Barker 1993).' Maguire and Katz (2002) further note that 'some influential reformers have expressed concern that community policing has come to mean anything that is new and innovative in American policing (Goldstein 1994; Skolnick & Bayley 1988)'. Cordner (2005: 408) in an up-to-date review of the effectiveness of community policing still concurs with Maguire and Katz's previous findings by noting 'many commentators have taken the view that community policing is little more than a new police marketing strategy that has left the core elements of the police role untouched'.

The diversity of the label 'community policing' is a two-edged sword. 'Community policing' is a very flexible umbrella term for a diverse range of activities and pro-grammes. 'Today, almost every specialised program developed by a police depart-ment is labeled community policing': (Walsh and Vito 2004: 57). The problem this presents for 'community policing' as a philosophy is that in many police depart-ments it is therefore relegated to the level of a sub-unit, not a whole-of-organization approach. 'Although many police departments claim that they are engaged in some form of community policing, the majority of them are still bureau-cratically structured and delivering their services based on the strategies of the rational–legal bureaucratic model.' (ibid.)

While some current research coming out of Canada indicates community polic-ing still has potential to build proactive policing strategies (Clarke 2006; Colvin and Goh 2006) the focal question still remains: is 'community policing' no more than an amorphous concept that is largely meaningless and which can be used by police departments as a 'trendy phrase' to attach to projects to get more police resources, while giving the appearance of legitimacy without making any funda-mental or substantive changes to the way 'policing' has always been done?

Will KM be just another 'trendy phrase' like community policing when it is only given lip service in a police organization rather than well integrated as a philosophy and practice? Hence, is KM doomed to be marginalized in some police organizations so they can get on with doing things the same old way, but now with a set of new high-tech toys to give the appearance that they know all about how to 'manage' knowledge?

Finally, it should be clear that our understanding of 'knowledge integration' is that it is more than just making the knowledge available to staff throughout an organization. Sending information via intranets, emails, posting it on web-sites, and the like is no more than a knowledge transfer process of distribution. That is not integration. Integration is about bringing together aspects of applied knowledge into a unified system of thought that can then be brought to bear on a particular problem when needed in a timely, efficient, and effective manner.

Technological stages in Knowledge Management

Various multistage models have been proposed for organizational evolution over time. These models differ in the number of stages. For example, Nolan (1979) introduced a model with six stages for IT maturity in organizations, which later was expanded to nine stages. Earl (2000) suggested a stage of growth model for evolving the e-business, consisting of the following six stages: external communication, internal communication, e-commerce, e-business, e-enterprise, and transformation. Each of these models identifies certain characteristics that typify firms in different stages of growth. Among these multistage models, models with four stages seem to have been proposed and tested most frequently (King and Teo 1997).

The following diagram in Figure 2.2 illustrates a stage model framework based on work by Gottschalk (2005) and others (Alavi and Leidner 2001) in the business management domain. Although developed for business firms the model is very applicable to police organizations. This framework provides guidance for police executives that are serious about integrating KM in terms of where best to invest in IT resources and also the model provides a benchmark for IT infrastructure.

Figure 2.2 depicts the knowledge management systems (KMS) stage model that conceptualizes on a continuum the stages involved in the growth of KMS and their relationship to the level of IT support required.

The KMS stage model consists of four stages. The first stage is for general IT support for knowledge workers. This includes word processing, spreadsheets, and e-mail. The second stage is information about knowledge sources. An information system stores information about who knows what within the firm and outside the firm. The system does not store what they actually know. A typical example is the company intranet. The third stage is information representing knowledge. The system stores what knowledge workers know in terms of information. A typical example is a database. The fourth and final stage is information processing. An information system uses information to evaluate situations. A typical example here is an expert system.

Figure 2.2 Growth model of Knowledge Management technology

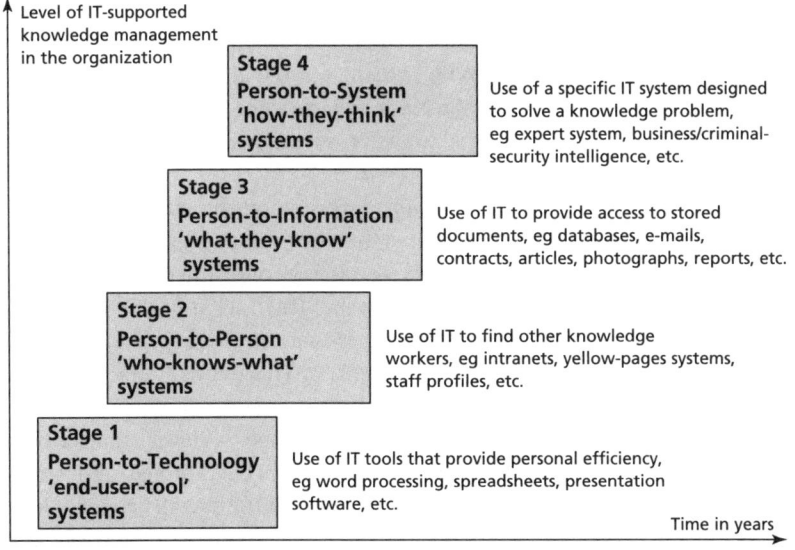

Stages of KMS is a relative concept concerned with IT's ability to process information for knowledge work. IT at later stages is more useful to knowledge work than IT at earlier stages. The relative concept implies that IT is more directly involved in knowledge work at higher stages, and that IT is able to support more advanced knowledge work at higher stages.

The essential point is that the diagram allows a police organization to chart what stage they are at in relation to KM and hence what level of IT support is required at each stage to maximize KM potential in so far as technology can support the practice side of KM. Integrating the philosophy of KM takes longer and is not as easy as plugging in a new 'platform and cable' to run cutting-edge applications. This issue of philosophical integration will be taken up in the next chapter.

Summary

KM is first and foremost a conceptual 'system of thought' that transcends disciplinary boundaries and defies attempts to pigeonhole it.

The analogy of a steam train is a useful way to simplify the complexities surrounding the concept of KM. Envisage KM as the engine of the steam train travelling along a philosophical set of parallel tracks. One track is the 'mechanistic' line that equates KM solely with IS/IT functions that are held together by a 'platform and cable' approach to KM. This line of thinking is systems-centred and is exemplified in the quest to build better IT hardware and more sophisticated software programs. The other track is the 'dynamic' line that recognizes IT systems are fundamentally about managing the conceptual outputs of people in the form of tacit and explicit knowledge products and therefore takes a holistic 'context and culture' approach to KM. This line of thinking is people-centred and finds expression in diverse forms of networked 'communities of practice'.

If KM is the engine in the train the 'steam' to run it along both 'tracks' is provided by the fuel that comes from releasing the practice processes of knowledge creation, capture, storage, retrieval, transfer, sharing, application, and integration throughout an organization.

However, as the envisaged KM train powers along the tracks propelled by these KM processes it is well to be advised that the journey is by no means direct, clear, or smooth. As a practice KM relies on the set of distinct yet complementary and inter-related processes noted above but this 'fuel' is unstable by nature and tends to swirl around in elliptical circles that interconnect and overlap in strange and unpredictable ways (see Figure 2.1). This makes KM a potent and dangerous concoction to pour into the tank of an organization.

KM processes (knowledge creation, capture, storage, retrieval, transfer, sharing, application, integration) as 'fuel' can themselves be 'captured' and 'stored' in organizational 'silos' and therefore not 'shared' for the overall benefit of keeping the organizational train on the tracks and going in the right direction. Even when 'information fuel' is distributed (knowledge transfer) there may be little participation (knowledge sharing) in harnessing its energy potential.

The risks in terms of getting the 'fundamentals' of KM right for police organizations that want to jump on the KM train as this chapter outlines are essentially twofold.

The first risk is conceptual: having 'dual vision' to see the two parallel tracks of KM as illustrated in the train analogy and therefore not losing sight of the fact that both tracks must have resources invested in them. If one track is favoured over the other in terms of investment then it is just a matter of time before the KM train will be derailed. Both tracks have to be kept in working order.

The second risk to KM is one of organizational marginalization: making a new sub-section called 'Knowledge Management' or appointing a 'Chief Knowledge Officer' to oversee the implementation of KM is not a strategy that has proven to work well in police organizations. Integrating KM requires more thought than that if one does not want to end up with an impoverished version of KM.

The next chapter will provide the scaffolding for some useful ideas about how to keep the KM train on the tracks while avoiding the dangers of a narrow conceptualization and a marginalized containment of KM in police and law enforcement organizations.

Framework for Police Knowledge Management

Introduction

Policing in the twenty-first century is a potpourri of sectors, levels, systems, and models that co-exist in a whirlpool of continual interaction. Policing and law enforcement is stretched and fragmented beyond its usual territorial boundaries into a global context that has transformed the way policing business is done and will be done in the future. Local policing is now global policing and the management of police knowledge requires a holistic global framework.

This chapter provides the conceptual underpinnings for such a holistic framework that incorporates the complexities and diversity of policing sectors, levels, and systems as well as its predominant models of practice in carrying out the business of policing in a global context.

Policing sectors

Policing is a social process (Reiner 1994) and as such it spans both public and private sectors (Button 2002). Public policing is the type of policing most people are familiar with through its social control role of conducting patrols, carrying out investigations, and apprehending offenders for breaches of the criminal law and, where sufficient evidence exists, placing them before a court for prosecution. In a democratic society, the social control aspect of public policing is mediated through a respect for human rights and the rule of law which provides the citizens of that society with the constitutional and legal protections to ensure such rights are upheld. Thus, in this book, when the terms police and law enforcement are used they are meant to refer to this 'democratic' form of policing in the public domain and not to some autocratic or totalitarian forms of policing which exist in other parts of the world.

There are a broad range of public and private bodies engaged in the process of policing and several writers have attempted to classify 'policing' in the literature. For example, Johnson (1992), one of the earlier writers, identified the 'public' police along with the private security sector, various types of 'hybrid' policing (bodies engaged in state security, departments of state, municipal bodies, regulatory and investigative bodies) as well as citizenship and self-policing.

Johnson's 'hybrid' classification of policing bodies is a mixture of both public and private sectors and is similar in many respects to the early classification scheme by Miller and Luke in 1997 according to Button (2002). Jones and Newburn (1998: 122) split Johnson's 'hybrid' policing classification into two categories which they termed 'other bodies of constables' and 'other public policing bodies'. Button (2002) builds on the Jones and Newburn distinctions concerning the 'hybrid' classification and introduces a third category to capture those bodies that are engaged in policing-type activities but are not part of the private security industry, as well as recognizing that there is also a small but significant 'voluntary' element to private policing. The Button taxonomy of policing (2002: 16) therefore involves a spectrum of four main policing sectors. They are:

1. Public Police Bodies (Home Office police forces in UK)
2. Hybrid Policing Bodies (three sub-divisions)
   a. Central and Decentralized Public Policing Bodies
   b. Specialized Police Organizations
   c. Private Policing (non-private security)
3. Voluntary Policing
4. Private Security

Button notes that his categories are more fluid and are not to be taken as mutually exclusive or exhaustive. Finally, Loader (2000) presents an innovative attempt at classifying policing by proposing a set of porous and overlapping categories as follows:

- Policing 'by' government
  (public policing bodies, particularly at a national level)
- Policing 'through' government
  (contracting out to other bodies, eg private security industry)
- Policing 'above' government
  (encompasses international developments in policing like Interpol and Europol)
- Policing 'beyond' government
  (growing demand for private policing services)
- Policing 'below' government
  (state organized surveillance [eg Neighourhood Watch] as well as vigilantism)

31

The above classification systems indicate the wide and diverse array of activities and organizations that fall within the ambit of the term 'policing'. It is also clear that the public–private dichotomy so prevalent in the policing literature is not as simple a dichotomy as it is generally regarded to be.

There is a growing body of literature that documents the increasing 'fragmentation' (Johnston 2000) or 'pluralization' (Johnston and Shearing 2002) of policing. Other terms like 'lateralization' (Brodeur and Dupont 2006) and 'multilateralization' (Cherney, O'Reilly, and Grabosky 2006) refer to the same phenomena whereby the form of 'policing' is being stretched every which way —up, down, and sideways or in Loader's terminology 'by', 'through', 'above', 'beyond', and 'below' government. Other terms are appearing in the literature like 'third party policing' (Mazerolle and Ransley 2005) which try to capture the shifts that are occurring in the nature and forms of policing whereby the responsibility for crime control no longer rests solely with state-based public police agencies but is shared with a wide and diverse range of organizations and institutions.

This exponential expansion of the policing–security nexus went on 'steroids' the day after the fateful date of 9/11 became permanently imprinted in history as the defining moment for world security at the beginning of the twenty-first century (Lippert and O'Connor 2006). Witness the burgeoning private security industry and its takeover of many 'low policing' activities of the public police at local and national levels, and the increasing presence of private security companies (PSCs) in the global policing arena. Avant (2005: 7) underscores how expansive this melding together of policing with security functions has become: 'private security companies provide military and security services to states, international organizations, INGOs, global corporations, and wealth[y] individuals. Every multi-lateral peace operation conducted by the UN since 1990 included the presence of PSCs.'

Furthermore, the private security sector substantially outnumbers the public police in most western countries sometimes by as much as two to one as UK research has shown (Button 2002; Jones and Newburn 1998) and this finding is similar in Australia (Sarre and Prenzler 2005).

A worrying trend about this rapid expansion and stretching phenomenon of the policing–security sector is the blurring of governmental, legal, and accountability boundaries to the point where PSCs in particular operate in a context where this is 'governance without government' as the traditional 'state–policing coupling' (Walker 2003: 115) is being radically reappraised.

Thus, to simply view this public–private dichotomy as a static picture is misleading. This simple characterization of policing fails to capture the shifts in alignment that are occurring in this ever expanding universe of policing forms. A more accurate representation of this stretching phenomenon of policing is that it is a very dynamic process. Moreover, it is a layered phenomenon in the sense that there are degrees of 'publicness' and 'privateness'. A position Button

Figure 3.1 Policing sectors expressed as a continuum

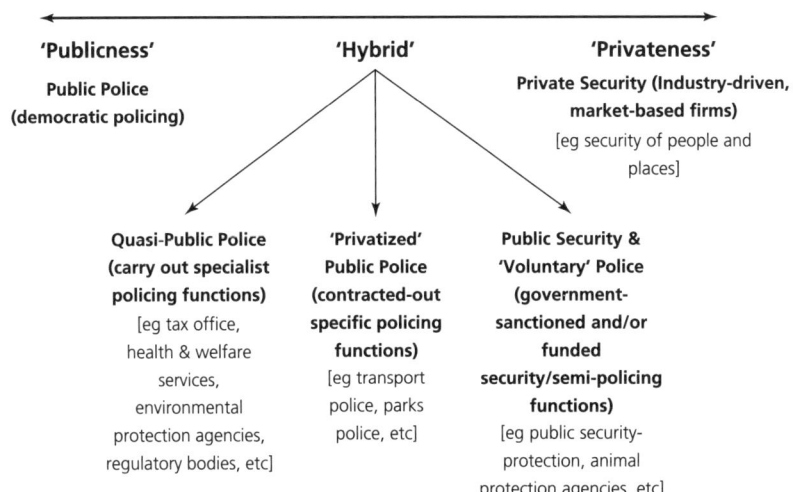

(2002) emphasizes in particular with regard to the various 'hybrid' styles of policing across both public and private sectors.

Therefore, we have developed as part of our overall conceptual framework for KM a graphical representation that locates the array of diverse styles of policing along a sector continuum of 'publicness' and 'privateness'. The purpose of this visualization is to see more clearly the overlapping nature and points of intersection as well as where the grey areas are, which are not so apparent in a simple linear understanding of the public–private dichotomy about the policing–security nexus. This graphical representation is contained in Figure 3.1.

Figure 3.1 depicts the 'publicness–privateness' sectors as a continuum[1] to illustrate the diverse range of 'hybrid' styles that modern policing and its nexus with security can take.

This continuum of policing sectors builds on the work of writers in this area and in particular the work of Button. Although some of the category labels used on the diagram are different to some of Button's terms they essentially reflect a similar categorization. The differences in category classification are for ease of explanation. However, it should be noted that categories 3 and 4 in Button's taxonomy, 'voluntary policing' and 'private security', have been grouped together in our framework as both involve semi-policing functions that are sanctioned or funded by governments in the main which make their similarities more important than their differences.

---

[1] This continuum is also referred to in the literature as a process of 'pluralization' or 'fragmentation' (Johnston and Shearing 2002); or lateralization (Brodeur and Dupont 2006); and/or 'multilateralization' (Cherney, O'Reilly, and Grabosky 2006).

Policing levels

There is a diversity of levels at which policing takes place in a global context. Figure 3.2 illustrates the diversity within the policing and law enforcement domains.

As can be seen from the diagram, policing and law enforcement activity occurs at a number of levels from the local to the transnational. However, the dominant reality of policing is still 'locally' organized. For example, in the UK there is a strong emphasis on local accountability in terms of both local KM and local governance of criminality. In other words, the context of policing is territorial. As mentioned in Chapter 1, policing takes place in a certain location that is internationally recognized as a geographically defined territory under the control of a particular nation state (Deflem 2002; Bunyan 2003; Walker 2003; Jones 2003).

This 'local' territorial element is the public face of policing within a nation state. As such the complexity of policing begins at the inter-related levels of the 'local–national' junction point and becomes increasingly complicated as policing moves into and across 'international', 'transnational' levels. The dotted boxes and adjoining arrows for each of these policing levels in Figure 3.2 are meant to indicate the permeable two-way nature of the multiple points of contact and sets of relationships that develop over time between these global policing levels.

Figure 3.2 Policing levels expressed in a global context

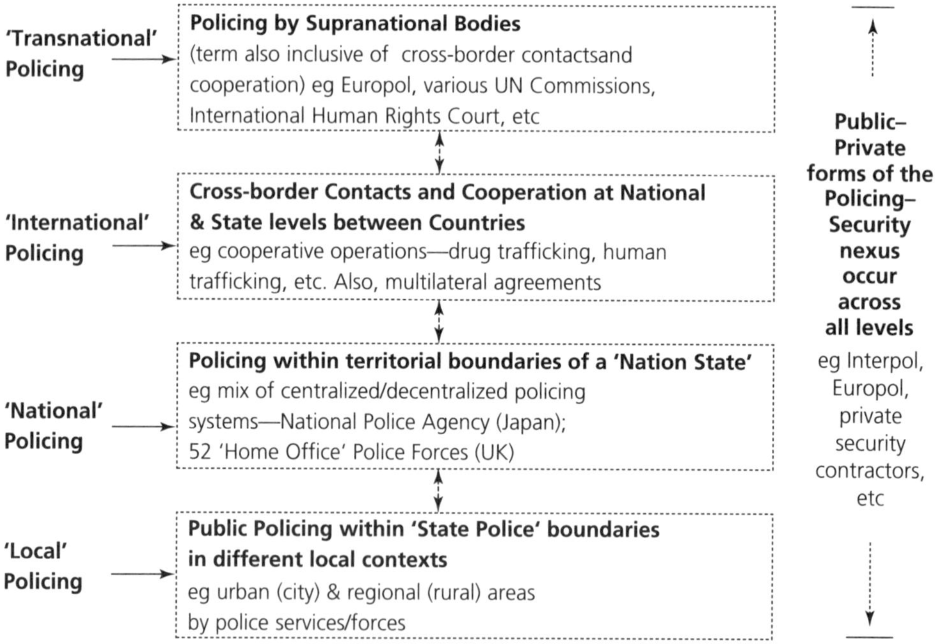

'Transnational' Policing →
Policing by Supranational Bodies
(term also inclusive of cross-border contactsand cooperation) eg Europol, various UN Commissions, International Human Rights Court, etc

'International' Policing →
Cross-border Contacts and Cooperation at National & State levels between Countries
eg cooperative operations—drug trafficking, human trafficking, etc. Also, multilateral agreements

'National' Policing →
Policing within territorial boundaries of a 'Nation State'
eg mix of centralized/decentralized policing systems—National Police Agency (Japan); 52 'Home Office' Police Forces (UK)

'Local' Policing →
Public Policing within 'State Police' boundaries in different local contexts
eg urban (city) & regional (rural) areas by police services/forces

Public–Private forms of the Policing–Security nexus occur across all levels

eg Interpol, Europol, private security contractors, etc

It is important to remind the reader of the discussion in Chapter 1 about the focus of this book being on the 'globalized' context of policing practices and the role and application of KM in such 'global policing'. Hence, there are two key points to be noted in relation to Figure 3.2.

First, 'global policing' is defined for simplicity as encompassing any combination of public–private policing and/or security activity that is conducted on the international stage. Hence, 'global policing' is an umbrella concept that covers the diversity that exists in policing in relation to these different levels (transnational, international, national, local—state, regional, urban) with their different foci of jurisdictional boundaries and primary allegiances.

Second, the term 'global policing' also acts as a context marker for emerging forms of policing and law enforcement in this new post-9/11 policing era in a way that the older terms like 'international' and 'transnational' policing do not adequately capture or convey.

Policing systems

This picture of global policing is further complicated by the enormous variation that exists worldwide in how systems of democratic policing are structured in different countries. Figure 3.3 contains some examples[2] of this variation in terms of two-tiered policing systems as organized in Continental Europe and federal systems as structured in North America in particular.

The examples in Figure 3.3 are self-explanatory. However, it is worth noting the enormity of the situation in the US in relation to the sheer scale and complex structure of its policing system which spans at least six levels of organization (Mawby 2003) as indicated in Figure 3.3. The picture of policing in the US that emerges is one where fragmentation is the name of the game. Such a patchwork pattern of organizational levels of policing makes the comment by the infamous serial killer, Ted Bundy, even more chillingly real: 'jurisdictional boundaries and the inability of law enforcement agencies to communicate with each other allows transient killers to avoid identification and capture' (Killmier 1997: 9).

Also, as indicated in Figure 3.2 at the 'national policing' level, the UK has more of a decentralized policing system with some 43 local forces organized under the Home Office. Mawby (2003: 17) argues that essentially the UK has three types of police force—the London Metropolitan Police, county forces and borough police—rather than 43 different local police forces. These local forces are divided along county and borough lines similar to Canadian and US distinctions between the urban/rural divide. However, like so many aspects of policing,

---

[2] See Mawby (2003) for further discussion of examples in relation to systems of policing in other countries as well.

Figure 3.3 Examples of some policing systems worldwide

Structure of Policing Systems varies greatly both *in* and *between* 'Nation-States'

Two-Tier Systems (most prominent in Continental Europe)
France—*gendarmerie* (ie paramilitary police) under Ministry of Defence.
State police under Ministry of the Interior.
Similarly for **Italy**—*carabinieri* (paramilitary police) and in **Spain**—*guardia civil*.

Federal Systems (North America)
Canada—RCMP (national policing responsibility)
with provinces and municipalities (local policing responsibilities)
USA—six levels* of police organization:
Federal (50 agencies with nationwide responsibilities for public law enforcement)
State (49 state forces)
County (some 3,088 sheriff's departments in counties)
City (around 3,200 city police forces)
Rural (over 13,000 small-town, independent police forces) and
'special district' (separate police forces for such things as parks, university campuses and military bases)

* Note: county, city, rural, and special district are all variants of 'local' policing that often overlap.

---

how such distinctions are interpreted can lead to idiosyncratic ways of classifying police systems in the literature.

The essential point about policing systems that the diagrams graphically illustrate is that complexity and fragmentation abound in policing not only at the local level but also on the global stage. This is one of the major challenges that KM in policing confronts—to find more innovative and creative ways to deal effectively with complexity and fragmentation, rather than adding more weight to already overloaded systems and people.

Policing models

There are three policing models, namely 'community policing', 'problem-oriented', and 'intelligence-led', that are regarded as the current big three in the literature.[3] These dominant models of policing have exerted significant influence in their own ways on the development of policing in the US and the UK over the last 20 years or so up to the present time (Clarke 2006; Brodeur and Dupont 2006; Cordner 2005; Tilley 2003). Figure 3.4 shows each of these dominant models in policing as well as tracing their connections to one another and to other types of policing activity.

As depicted in Figure 3.4 all three such models run 'parallel' (refer to dotted parallel lines) to the 'traditional law enforcement' model characterized by its paramilitary and bureaucratic 'command and control' structure, and focus

---

[3] See Tilley (2003) for an excellent review of these three models in terms of their similarities and differences.

Figure 3.4 Dominant policing models

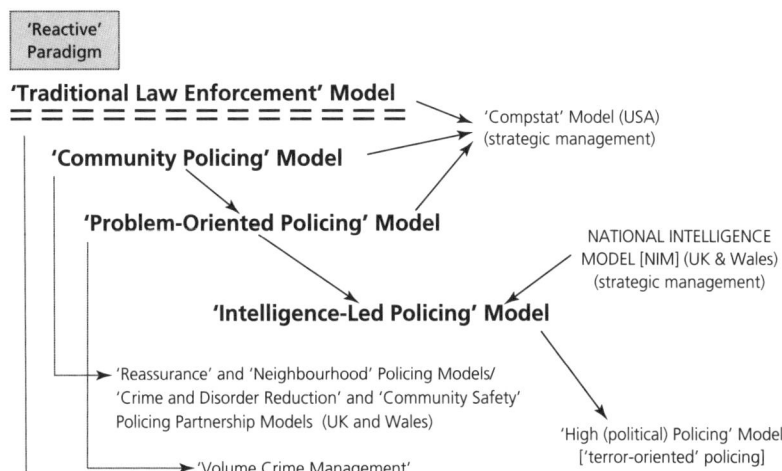

on a reactive, incident-driven response to calls for service. The parallel lines are meant to indicate that these newer policing models have not replaced this type of law enforcement model, as policing will always require a 'reactive paradigm' component, but rather that newer models have broadened the focus and mission of what policing in late modernity is also required to be and do.

In relation to the 'community policing' and 'problem-oriented' models, while they are 'global movements' (Tilley 2003: 311) they have their origins in the US. Whereas, in contrast, the 'intelligence-led' model of policing is a distinct UK development which has been taken up with enthusiastic interest in some other countries (Maguire 2000).

Moreover, as is apparent on the diagram 'community policing' goes by other labels in the UK and Wales. 'Reassurance' policing and 'neighbourhood' policing are models that have some characteristics and features very similar to the various US brands of the 'community policing' model.[4] A comparable situation exists across the Atlantic Ocean in regard to the 'volume crime management' (VCM) model of policing that has been instituted in the UK and Wales as a matter of government policy. This VCM model combines elements of a 'traditional law enforcement' approach as well and has similar features that can be found in US versions of the 'problem-oriented' policing model (Goldstein 1994; Maguire and John 2006) but with a 'Compstat'-type reliance on a defined set of performance indicators used to drive the crime management process.

---

[4] See Maguire and John (2006) for a fuller treatment of these two models ('reassurance' and 'neighbourhood' policing) and their similarities to community policing.

It will also be noticed in the bottom right hand corner of Figure 3.4 that a new 'model' or 'style' may be a better word to describe what is variously called 'high policing' or 'political policing', which has emerged in both the UK and the US. The emergence of this 'terror-oriented' policing model (Simonetti Rosen 2004) is a direct result of the aftermath of 9/11 and the resulting so-called 'war on terror' by various Western governments and their allies through the combined efforts of the policing–security nexus since that time.

Finally, in relation to the policing models, the diagram makes reference to two models of intelligence gathering and analysis (Compstat and NIM) that come under what is termed a 'strategic management' perspective. These two 'intel-based models' are included on the diagram to indicate how they link to various policing models at different levels and in different ways. These strategic management systems are significant processes and therefore are also central for police KM. This theme will be elaborated on in subsequent chapters.

The origin of each 'intelligence' model is also indicated on the diagram. The 'Compstat' model came to prominence in the US, most notably with its application in New York in relation to the 'zero tolerance' policing experiment (Karmen 2004). However, its utility and application has a much wider appreciation than this controversial 'zero tolerance' experiment would indicate. As Walsh and Vito (2004: 57) point out 'Compstat is a goal-oriented, strategic-management process that uses information technology, operational strategy, and managerial accountability to guide police operations'.

In the New York version of Compstat, operational police commanders were expected to focus, manage, and direct in a targeted way their unit's problem-solving processes, or risk losing their commands. While the intention behind such police Darwinism was to empower police managers, in that only the fittest police commanders survived by keeping their post, one of the unintended consequences according to critics of Compstat was that 'most Compstat agencies have in fact opted for a model heavier on control than on empowerment' (Weisburd *et al.* 2003: 63). Hence, Weisburd *et al* argue that Compstat became less of a reform and more of an institutional regression which had the net effect of reaffirming the old and 'discredited management concepts of command and control' (ibid). However, in defence of Compstat, Walsh and Vito (2004) make it clear that like any information management and service delivery system it can also be used to promote innovation. Compstat is just as capable of delivering community policing programmes and problem-oriented solutions as of supporting regression in an organization.

The origin of the other intelligence model on the diagram, the NIM, underpins the workings of 'intelligence-led' policing in the UK and Wales and as such is 'capitalized' on the diagram to indicate its central importance and significance to this model of policing in England. In fact, the British Government's National Policing Plan for the period 2003–06 requires all 43 police forces in England and Wales to implement the NIM by April 2004.

Intelligence-led policing (ILP) is a specific innovation of UK policing that essentially represents a pragmatic model of how to carry out policing better using modern IT (Tilley 2003). ILP involves gathering data to develop up-to-date patterns of crime and criminality in order to plan effective ways to target criminal networks and arrest prolific offenders.

Hence, ILP espouses a similar approach and shares a number of characteristics with Comstat in the US as a goal-directed, IT-based strategic management process (Walsh and Vito 2004). As such both models, ILP and Comstat, adopt a traditional law enforcement focus but with a 'smart' technology edge. However, both models, while underscoring a law enforcement approach, have wider applicability and can be used to support community policing partnership programmes and evidence-based problem-oriented policing initiatives (Tilley 2003; Walsh and Vito 2004).

The core process of any intelligence system like ILP and Comstat is 'strategic intelligence', which conceptually is about prioritizing limited policing resources to best advantage based on in-depth research into particular criminal phenomena. Interestingly, as Dintino and Martens (1983) pointed out a long time ago, 'strategic intelligence' for all its presumed sophisticated-sounding title is nothing more than a new label for old-fashioned social science research.

ILP is the visible face of the NIM in the UK. The rational behind this roll-out of the NIM is the embedding of a 'strategic, future oriented and targeted approach to crime control—broadly represented in the concept of "intelligence-led policing (ILP)"' and thereby providing a 'framework of a rational business process that prioritises and plans the use of resources in the light of objective analysis and assessment of risk' (Maguire and John 2006: 69).

At bedrock, the NIM is a 'straightforward, coherent business management tool' (Christopher 2004). In essence, the NIM is designed to support intelligence-led 'proactive policing' in and across the 43 police services in England and Wales (Flood 2004). The general structure of the NIM is to organize the management of policing at three distinct levels—level 1 deals with the 'local' area issues of police boroughs and counties; level 2 focuses on cross-border issues between forces and regions; while level 3 is concerned with national and international threats. There are four key 'intelligence products' that flow out of the NIM to each level. These 'products' are: strategic assessments, tactical assessments, target profiles, and problem profiles (Home Office 2002a). More detailed information about the actual workings of the NIM can be gained from various Home Office publications as well as the comprehensive review by Maguire and John (2006).

This is a bold move by the government to impose a standardized model of police practice in the form of ILP. Such a move is not without critics, nor without risk. Discussion Forum 3.1 below presents some of the risk factors involved with imposing the NIM.

Discussion Forum 3.1 NIM—comply but not obey?

The nationwide roll-out of the NIM in 2004 (Home Office) was a major shift to a more centralized system of policing in the UK. The NIM as a proactive generic strategic planning and assessment model is 'in theory' the underpinning framework of all policing activities at local, cross-border, national, and international levels for England and Wales (Maguire and John 2006).

The problem with 'theory' is that it rarely translates as intended into 'practice'. The problematic nature of implementing and effectively managing the NIM, and by association ILP, is a mixture of cultural and contextual factors inherent in policing. The police culture as Christopher (2004: 180) points out is 'notoriously immune to reform'. Conservatism and cynicism amongst police make change management difficult (Reiner 2000). Also, enduring rivalries between rank and file and executive police often results in the undermining by street police of strategic change initiatives by top management (Holdaway 1983).

Moreover, sharing information and knowledge is not something police officers are good at doing or even wish to do at the best of times for a host of reasons. 'An enduring characteristic of police culture is the retention and cherishing of information by officers who exhibit an almost perverse unwillingness to share knowledge, thereby suppressing its free-flow upon which intelligence-led policing depends.' (Christopher 2004: 181)

A complicating factor arising from police sharing knowledge is one of 'ownership'. ILP and the NIM by their very labels were always going to have perception problems in terms of who owns them. That is, ILP/NIM were and to some extent still are seen as intelligence tools primarily for intelligence officers who therefore take centre stage in policing. The unintended consequence of this shift to make the NIM the central plank of UK policing is to question how relevant such an intelligence management system is to wider policing concerns like community safety, fear of crime, and so forth, particularly in relation to locally based policing.

A further difficulty is the manner in which the implementation of the NIM was rolled out. In the initial phase of the National Policing Plan (2003–06) it became apparent that there was significant organizational apathy across various police forces in the UK, with quite a number not putting in for funding for the NIM or allocating staff to join the national implementation team. Hence, the Home Office response was to resort to the heavy hand of legislation to get compliance. As Christopher (2004: 185) has observed, 'ultimately, therefore, the government intends to engineer intelligence into policing centrality through legislative coercion'. Such a legislative response may prove in the longer term to be counterproductive. For rather than 'embedding' ILP in the minds and hearts of police it may well turn out that, in a police culture familiar with strategies of resistance, legislation can achieve compliance but not necessarily obedience.

Before moving on to the next section each of these three influential policing models of 'community', 'problem-oriented', and 'intelligence-led' policing will also be drawn upon and referred to in subsequent chapters where appropriate in relation to KM and the processes and technologies that underpin the use of KM in policing.

The next section will now look at the various policing sectors in which these diverse policing forms and models operate.

'Tension spaces' in policing

The nature and face of policing is changing rapidly and evolving dramatically with every new twist and turn in the so-called 'war on terror'. As Sheptycki (2002: 15) asserts 'policing is being re-invented as a key modality of security in the global networked society'. Whilst the new wave of fundamentalist terrorism provides an overriding rationale for tighter global policing and security by governments, the current changes in policing and law enforcement must also be seen against the backdrop of globalization. In this regard, Gill (2006: 30) argues that:

> globalisation—the process that has brought about the current territory for policing and security—manifests itself along three dimensions: a 'deepening' of levels so that there is increased interaction between local and transnational developments; a 'broadening' of sectors that are involved in governance; and, third, spatial 'stretching' so that developments in one part of the globe can have immediate and world-wide impact. (McGrew 1992)

The foundations for a conceptual framework for police KM is contained in the four diagrams (Figures 3.1, 3.2, 3.3, and 3.4) presented and discussed in this chapter. When all four diagrams are combined together as in Figure 3.5 it is possible to 'see' these foundations as a 'cube' of intersecting 'tension spaces' for managing police knowledge globally.

As can be seen in Figure 3.5 the planning 'cube' graphically illustrates the 'deepening', 'broadening', and 'stretching' effects that globalization has on policing and law enforcement.

The goal of this visualized 'cube' is to bring together in a holistic way the four key elements (policing sectors—Figure 3.1; policing levels—Figure 3.2; policing systems—Figure 3.3; and policing models—Figure 3.4) that provide the foundation for this overall conceptual framework depicted in Figure 3.5 for the implementation and development of KM in policing and law enforcement. The 'cube' allows us to plan for police KM using a holistic framework.

What is readily apparent from the diagram is the enormous complexity of what is involved in policing in a global context. The 'planning cube' graphically illustrates the variety of policing sectors that combine at different levels with different models applied in different policing systems that are structured

Figure 3.5 Global framework for planning the management of police knowledge

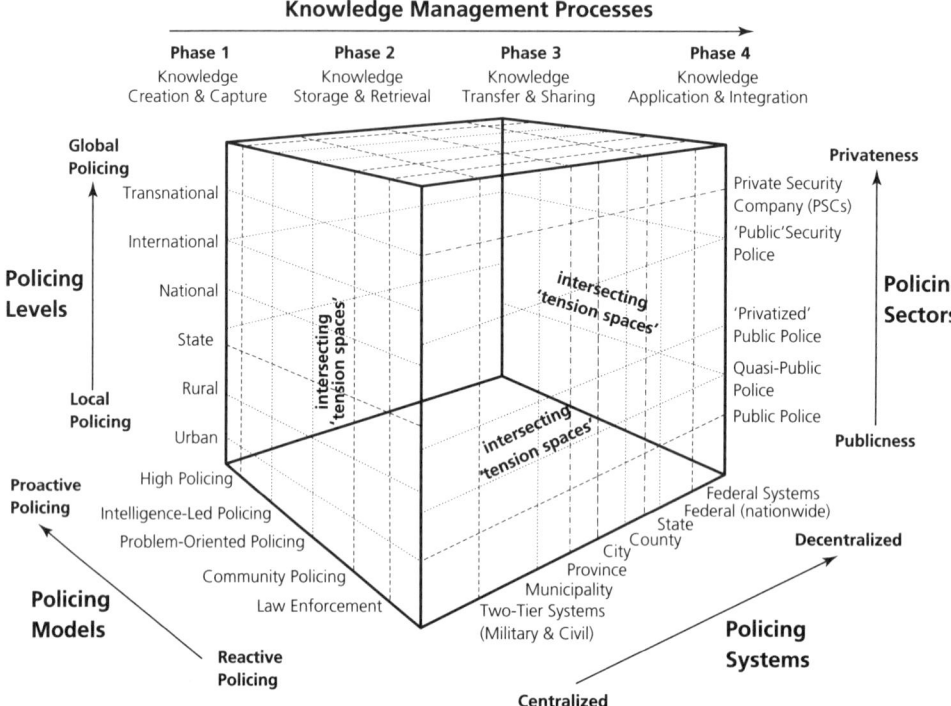

in diverse ways. Each side of the cube is subdivided according to the types of distinction discussed previously for the four key policing elements—sectors, levels, systems, and models.

What is also apparent on the diagram is that the criss-crossing of the subdivision lines creates intersections where a 'space of tension' may be formed from the resulting incompatibilities of the various trajectories of the dividing lines. It can be further noted on the cube that not all the criss-crossing lines are the same thickness nor do they necessarily neatly connect with another line. This depiction is intended to show that reality rarely works in neat harmonious ways —especially where planning is concerned!

The point of this planning cube is not to overwhelm with the sheer complexity of the task but rather to remind oneself that whatever is done in one area has consequences in other areas and in other ways, some intended and some unintended. It is of fundamental importance to view policing and law enforcement from a holistic perspective and be constantly mindful of this fact that intersecting connections exist everywhere. Having a holistic perspective helps prevent out-of-context decisions being made in isolation and independently of what else is happening in the wider policing environment, as well as discouraging 'silo thinking'[5] in various police organizational units.

The job of managing knowledge 'successfully' is to be aware of the 'context and culture' in which knowledge is embedded. Again to re-emphasize the point made earlier in Chapter 1, KM is not just about plugging in a new 'platform and cable' and therefore thinking you have 'done' KM. KM is also fundamentally about better managing the context in which knowledge occurs.

The planning cube is essentially a simple graphical illustration of the global policing context in all its complexity and depth. The aim of the cube is to ensure the interconnectedness of sectors, models, systems, and levels of policing is not lost sight of in planning and implementing better ways to create, capture, store, retrieve, transfer, share, apply, and integrate police knowledge.

With regard to the notion of 'intersecting tension spaces' mentioned earlier, as can be seen on the diagram, such spaces of tension can be formed anywhere by the intersecting connections made in different sectors, models, forms, and systems of policing and at various levels, and to varying degrees of connectedness.

Managing knowledge processes involves first, recognizing potential 'intersecting tension spaces', hence the value of the planning cube with its grid lines. Second, planning 'strategically' how to handle them given that any such tension space will have its own set of specific considerations.

An example of one such 'intersection tension space' in which police knowledge was poorly managed is contained in Discussion Forum 3.2 in relation to the Australian Federal Police's (AFP) involvement in the so-called 'Bali 9' drug trafficking case in Indonesia.

Discussion Forum 3.2 The 'Bali 9' and role of the Australian Federal Police

On 18 April 2005 nine Australians (the Bali 9) were arrested for drug trafficking in a series of police raids on hotels at Kuta and at Denpasar International Airport on the Indonesian island of Bali. Some were caught with bags of heroin taped to their bodies at the airport (*Illawarra Mercury* 2006).

The Bali 9 were only apprehended after a tip-off from the Australian Federal Police (AFP) who had the group of mostly young Australian drug mules under surveillance in Australia for some time prior to their departure to Bali to collect the drugs to bring back to Australia (Johnson 2006).

What makes this case more complicated is the fact that the father of Scott Rush, a 19-year-old who was one of the drug mules caught in Bali at the airport raid had

---

[5] Maguire and John (2006: 84) define 'silo thinking' as 'a concern only with one's own patch, rather than aiming to contribute to a wider system'.

reported his son to the AFP prior to his departure to Bali in order to stop him from getting involved in this drug smuggling ring. An AFP officer allegedly told the father through his barrister that AFP agents had spoken to his son, Scott, at Sydney airport and 'warned the teenager he would be watched' (Michelmore 2005).

The AFP has strongly defended its role in providing the intelligence to the Indonesian Police which resulted in the nine arrests and subsequent death penalty for several of the drug mules, including the 19-year-old Scott Rush.

This case has understandably generated much heated debate in the Australian community over the moral and legal legitimacy of the role of the AFP in knowingly providing information to a country where the death penalty operates for such drug offences (University of Sydney, 'Australians and the death penalty' Seminar 2006).

Irrespective of the level of culpability displayed by the Bali 9, the larger issue highlighted by this case is about the 'tension space' over a citizen's rights. Where citizens of a country that does not have the death sentence, like Australia, get caught up in international and transnational crimes in other countries where the death penalty is a real possibility, the question becomes to what extent should the human and legal rights of those citizens be protected by their country from such capital punishment?

It is apparent from the 'Bali 9' discussion box above that this case falls within the ambit of the 'International Policing' sector in Figure 3.2 and hence the involvement of the AFP. Moreover, the model of ILP was obviously used and KM process of 'Knowledge Sharing' took place by the AFP with their Indonesia Police counterparts. In planning this operation the AFP no doubt took several operational factors into consideration when sharing their intelligence with the Indonesian police. However, it is a very moot point how much consideration was given, if any, to what the likely consequences, both intended and unintended, would be by doing so; especially in the light of the apparent AFP reassurance to the parents of Scott Rush that he would be taken care of and would be intercepted before he left Australia so as not to place his life in danger by being arrested in Indonesia.

This is of course exactly what happened. The latest court appeal by Scott Rush saw his life sentence upgraded to the death sentence by an Indonesia Court (Australian National News Wire, September 2006).

Whatever position one takes on this issue the AFP's action in sharing such intelligence with Indonesian authorities is not the issue being debated here, but rather how, in this international level intersecting 'tension space' between Australian and Indonesian police, the knowledge could have been better managed by taking more consideration of the 'context and culture' dimension of KM processes.

With regard to this cultural context dimension it is somewhat surprising, given the elaborate surveillance carried out by the AFP of the Bali 9, that they did not appear to give enough consideration to what should be a well-known fact in policing, as noted by Mawby (2003: 35), that 'police systems are closely embedded in the wider structure and culture of their societies'. The cultural embeddedness of policing is most certainly the case in Indonesia where the political dimension of policing should never be underestimated. In fact, the term 'futures work' is considered to be of central importance in strategic criminal intelligence (Quarmby 2004) and this is exactly the type of cultural-contextual analysis carried out by 'futures work' in police intelligence. Unfortunately, as Quarmby also points out 'law enforcement has a history of piecemeal, stove-piped or self-directed approaches to futures work' (2004: 129).

There are several other options available which could have been considered in the planning phase of this operation if, as is being suggested, a more holistic perspective via the 'planning cube' in Figure 3.5 had been used to map out and plan contingencies for the likely 'tension spaces' when dealing with the Indonesian policing system. It is not appropriate here to outline such operational considerations other than to point out that a more comprehensive understanding of the complexities involved would have revealed other pathways through the 'tension space' that has clearly tarnished the image of the AFP for some of the Australian community. No one would seriously argue this was a 'good outcome' for the AFP no matter what the perceived 'benefits' such cross-border policing may have achieved.

Policing themes

In this final section of the chapter several themes are brought together to produce a snapshot of some of the present and emerging issues related to laying a comprehensive foundation for police KM. There are five themes in all and each is discussed in turn.

Theme 1: Stretching of policing sectors and levels

Policing and law enforcement is being stretched into a plurality of multi-levelled sectors along the public–private continuum and the local–global dimension. The effects of this multilateralization phenomenon are many and substantial in their impacts. Further fragmentation of crime control efforts is to be expected. An important implication of this stretching phenomenon of policing sectors at multiple levels for KM is the potential risks such fragmentation presents for the various phases to do with KM processes.

With reference to Figure 2.1 (Chapter 2) about the four-phase model of KM processes (phase 1: knowledge creation and capture; phase 2: knowledge storage and retrieval; phase 3: knowledge transfer and sharing; phase 4: knowledge application and integration) a number of scenarios are possible. To take just one example, with more fragmentation into a host of policing/law enforcement/ regulatory/security agencies the practicality, quite apart from the vexing issue of desiring to share information, makes phase 3 of the KM model—knowledge transfer and sharing—much more problematic that it already is in policing. With more organizational boundaries to negotiate at a range of levels—locally, nationally, and internationally—the risk of expanding informational gaps is very likely to increase considerably.

The 9/11 Comission Report (Kean and Hamilton 2004) documents in frightening detail not only the unwillingness of various agencies to share information and intelligence but also the alarming inability because of incompatibility at an IT systems level of even being able to transfer knowledge reliably from one sector to another.

Theme 2: Diversification of policing models

Policing has a tendency to be a profession in search of a practice. This has been most evident since the early 1960s when policing embarked on a period of experimentation with different styles (Flood 2004). The public has witnessed a proliferation of models that ebb and flow in and out of fashion. Once a new project, programme, or style gets a hold police practitioners and academics are apt to label it as a new approach that is usually heralded with claims of success, much like the following list of some of the more memorable models —'Team Policing', 'Unit Beat Policing', 'Policing by Objectives', 'Sector Policing', 'Community Policing', 'Community-Based Policing', 'Problem-Oriented Policing', 'Zero-Tolerance Policing', 'Evidence-Based Policing', and the current fascination with 'Intelligence-Led Policing' and its newer variants like 'Terror-Oriented Policing'.

While the merit or otherwise of labelling anything new or different in policing is debatable, such experimentation is laudable. However, since the 1980s and into the 1990s, as is apparent in Figure 3.4, three policing models (community policing, problem-oriented policing, and intelligence-led policing) have emerged to occupy prominent places in policing and law enforcement. Since 9/11 the role of intelligence has taken centre stage. Hence, it is clear that for the foreseeable future models like ILP and 'high policing' and its variants will dominate the scene in policing and law enforcement.

Theme 3: Integrating 'globally' levels and sectors of policing

Marketing gurus, business executives, and criminal/terrorist networks know the world is a global village and act accordingly. Police organizations talk about making global connections but are still bound to act within territorial and jurisdictional boundaries. Figure 3.5 illustrates this 'local–global' dimension and the permeable boundaries that exist at multiple contact points within the formally and informally established relationship networks between policing levels and sectors. However, there are encouraging signs that the push to move to more integrated ways of doing police business on a global scale is occurring as Brodeur and Dupont (2006: 21) note:

> High policing organisations ... pressured from all sides to end their compart-mentalization, are attempting to harness the power of informal 'knowledge networks' through the creation of integrated structures that act as connecting platforms. In the United States, the National Counterterrorism Center ... and the local Joint Terrorism Task Forces represent the most prominent efforts at integration. Canada has also moved to create Integrated National Security Enforcement Teams that bring together analysts from various law enforce-ment agencies.

Similar initiatives in integrating policing levels and sectors have also been doc-umented in Europe (Sheptycki 2002), particularly in relation to transnational crime. A comment in the 9/11 Commission Report (2004: 401) aptly sums up this theme: 'a "smart" government would integrate all sources of information to see the enemy as a whole'.

Theme 4: Complexity of policing systems

The management of the complexity that abounds in all the various policing sys-tems globally requires proactive leadership to come from police executives as well as politicians. Police leaders must take the front foot and be able to clearly articulate the issues they face in dealing with the complex web of policing agen-cies that of necessity they must join forces with in meaningful ways to combat crime and terrorism on the local–global dimension where it exists.

Without such policing leadership in policy and practice it will be very difficult to find innovative and creative ways to deal effectively with such law enforce-ment systems of complexity. Part of this leadership solution will necessarily involve the effective use of KM processes and IS/IT tools.

Theme 5: Planning 'in' tension spaces

The KM 'planning cube' as illustrated in Figure 3.5 provides a visualized appre-ciation of the complexities faced by policing in a global context that has deepened, broadened, and stretched policing and law enforcement beyond its territorial boundaries. As such the KM cube can assist policing organizations in mapping out the likely intersections where potential 'tension spaces' may arise and thereby give them ability to plan 'in' such tension spaces into their opera-tional contingency planning orders.

Moreover, 'tension spaces' in policing and law enforcement occur not only at the outer boundaries with other policing levels and sectors—a point noted by Ronald Noble (2002: 40), then Secretary-General of Interpol: 'changing the willingness of police forces to share information may, however, be the greatest challenge confronting fighting transnational organised crime'—but also from within policing organizations themselves. This is especially true with regard to police intelligence as Brodeur and Dupont (2006: 20) highlight: 'the creation, conversion, and distribution of knowledge are not isolated acts but are embedded in social and institutional networks, whose function is to both include and exclude'. Formal and informal relationship networks within police organizations thus act as gatekeeping mechanisms for who gets to 'know what' and 'how much' of what.

This point underscores the importance of getting the fundamentals of KM right, as outlined in Chapter 2, particularly with regard to recognizing that 'dynamically' KM is about managing the conceptual outputs of people's tacit knowledge by adopting people-centred approaches like networked 'communities of practice'.

Furthermore, the 'products' of 'futures work' in strategic criminal intelligence like 'background, current, warning and estimate intelligence' (Quarmby 2004: 130) have a significant role to play in sensing where potential 'tension spaces' lie as indicated in the KM cube in Figure 3.5 so they can be planned 'in' and contingencies developed long before any intelligence-led operation gets the green light.

One thing is certain: policing will morph into even more complex forms, types, and styles and this will create opportunities for more intersecting 'tension spaces' arise locally, nationally, and internationally and which police and law enforcement organizations will have to deal with in the future.

Summary

In this third and final chapter of the first part of the book, concerned with 'laying the foundations' for a guiding framework for KM in policing and law enforcement, several themes and issues have emerged. These themes and their associated issues and implications are central to establishing police KM on a firm footing now and in the future.

It is a somewhat ironic twist that 'policing', which has seen many 'internal' reform attempts by a progression of governments in various Western liberal democracies for many years, is now being transformed from the 'outside'. The push for more 'pluralization' and 'multilateralization' has policing and law enforcement being stretched beyond its usual boundaries into a global context that is transforming the way policing business is being done and will be done in the future.

There is a growing realization that if public policing is to do its job effectively one of the requirements is to think differently about the interconnectedness of local policing to global policing. 'Local is global' is not just a cute catchphrase anymore. It is embedded in our daily lives in a myriad of ways from the clothes we buy to the credit cards we use and call centres in another country we are connected to every time we have a problem with our Internet and mobile phones.

The future effectiveness of public policing lies in 'acting locally and simultaneously thinking globally'.

This chapter has identified at least five themes that revolve around this 'local is global' mindset, which police executive management need to be cognizant of when implementing and developing policies and practices for KM in their organizations. The core issue associated with each of these five themes is summarized as follows.

The core issue that theme 1, the 'stretching of policing sectors and levels', presents is how to reduce and counter the worst effects of the increasing risk associated with 'information/knowledge gaps' when policing has to be done in a globally fragmented context.

The core issue that theme 2, the 'diversification of policing models', engages with is to ensure a balance is kept between the current need for 'intelligence' to be the dominant paradigm in policing and the need for further experimentation in developing other policing models and alternative forms of policing.

The core issue that theme 3, 'the global integration of levels and sectors of policing', is concerned with is that until the difficulties of jurisdictional and operational integration is given the highest priority by governments then terrorist activities and organized crime will continue to increase unabated with only minimal disruption to their networks caused by ad hoc police and law enforcement interventions.

The core issue that theme 4, the 'complexities faced by diverse policing systems', centres around, is the need for positive, proactive, policing leadership in developing policies and KM practices to deal effectively with the diversity of policing systems.

The core issue that theme 5, 'planning for tension spaces' in operational orders, revolves around has to do with the comprehensiveness of police KM. Any police operation must be looked at from multiple perspectives and a 'respectful appreciation' in the context of such planning must allow for critical analysis and divergent points of view to be heard. Policing can no longer tolerate a 'groupthink' mentality, where everyone must fall in line with the view from the top or risk being isolated, ridiculed, or having a 'black mark' put against their promotional prospects.

In sum, the future of KM in policing and law enforcement organizations lies in developing and nurturing people-centred practices for sharing and capturing the richness and depth of the conceptual outputs of their staff's wealth of tacit knowledge and lived experience.

PART TWO

Police Knowledge Management: Building Structures

This second main part of the book is concerned with the types of KM 'structure' which can be usefully employed by policing and law enforcement organizations to build a specific body of police knowledge.

The 'structures' considered in this part of the book are arranged on a continuum from the more abstract notion of 'approaches' to KM in terms of the extent of relevance to policing, to 'systems' of KM where various elements are linked into a structure like an expert system, and finally to the 'technologies' that operate within a KMS like a spreadsheet application, or a purpose-built crime records management program.

Each of these structures—approaches, systems, and technologies—are outlined and discussed in respective chapters. Each of the chapters provides examples relevant to policing and draws out their implications for police and law enforcement organizations.

Approaches to Police Knowledge Management

Introduction

This chapter is the first of three chapters concerned with looking at the structures that exist within the domain of Knowledge Management (KM). These structures represent the conceptual 'building blocks' behind KM. Hence, police organizations need to know in a very practical sense what they are getting when they invest in KM.

Such knowledge must include not only the presumed benefits of the 'systems' and 'technologies' they buy but also the 'approaches' that underlie and come with such systems and technologies. Only by having this sort of understanding can police and law enforcement organizations really know for themselves how relevant and necessary are the bewildering array of technologies and systems touted as KM tools to their own policing and law enforcement needs.

Therefore, the focus of this chapter is on the 'approaches' part of KM. The term 'approach' is used in this book to denote the conceptual abstractions associated with a 'school of thought' that reflects a preference for a particular perspective or way of looking at KM and hence the subsequent adoption of a philosophical orientation (approach) that is aligned with this perspective.

Conceptions of knowledge

Perspective is everything. At the most fundamental level of cognition everything a person does flows from how they 'perceive' something. The chilling reality of religion-based terrorism in which a person is willing to end their own life for the 'perceived' greater cause of an extreme interpretation of a religious belief system is testament to the power of one's perspective.

The essential problem with religious fundamentalism is not its logic but its premise. That is, once a person comes to accept the premise of a fundamentalist's perspective and hence its philosophical worldview such a perspective has a logic to it. Such terrorists are not 'mad' or 'insane' in any psychiatric sense. To them it makes perfect sense to be committed enough to follow though on their 'jihad' perspective. In fact, such commitment to a worthy perspective can bring a sense of calm to a person as evidenced by the videotaped interviews of 'martyrs' released by some terrorist organizations after suicide attacks.

The point being made here is that one's perspective, be it at an individual, group, or even organizational level, is very influential in determining the possibilities of what happens next to an individual, a group, or within an organization.

With regard to KM therefore the perspective a police organization adopts towards it will to a large extent dictate what the possibilities are for KM within that organization.

The core component of a perspective is its essential idea or conception. For example, a 'jihad' perspective contains at least three qualitatively different ideas or conceptions about how to interpret the meaning of jihad in Muslim texts. The first conception can be labelled 'Jihad as Moral Warfare'; the second conception is closely related to the first but belongs to a different realm of understanding than just morality, it is termed 'Jihad as Spiritual Warfare'; the third conception may or may not include the other two conceptions but its emphasis is distinctively different and leads to terrorist activities for those who believe 'Jihad as Physical Warfare'. As can be appreciated the outcomes vary dramatically depending on which interpretational perspective one believes in for 'jihad'.

Similarly, there are a range of perspectives on KM that can be classified according to the essential idea (conception) they espouse. Earl (2001) identified seven 'schools of thought' (systems, cartographic, engineering, commercial, organizational, spatial, and strategic) within the literature which can be broadly understood as reflecting a particular perspective on KM.

Earl (2001) presents each school of thought as an abstraction in the form of an 'ideal type'. He makes no claim that any one school is better than the other. Only that they are different in orientation. Also, such schools should not be seen as mutually exclusive. In reality, various schools of thought co-exist in the minds of managers and hence interact with each other in often strange and diverse ways. Not all these schools identified by Earl are directly applicable to policing and law enforcement.

Therefore, in keeping with the practical nature of our book, we will briefly outline and discuss what we have identified as the five essential 'conceptions of knowledge' relevant to police practitioners and managers and what implications they have for policing and law enforcement.

Figure 4.1 Approaches to Knowledge Management

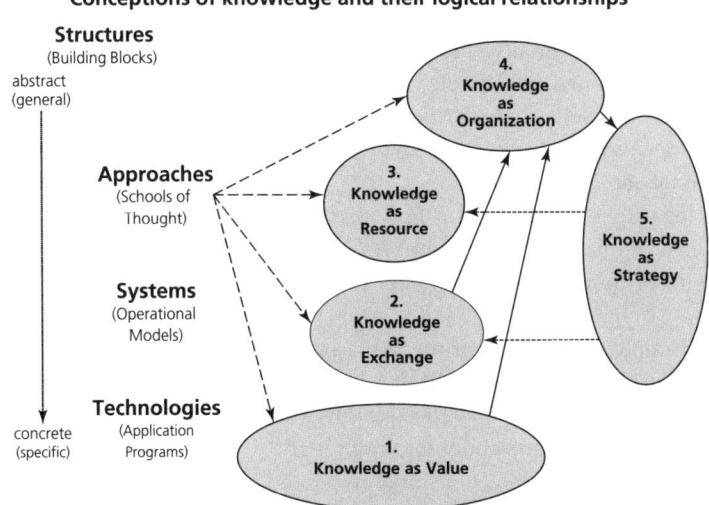

The five conceptions of knowledge are: 'Knowledge as Value'; 'Knowledge as Exchange'; 'Knowledge as Resource'; 'Knowledge as Organization'; and 'Knowledge as Strategy'. Figure 4.1 depicts our understanding of the nature of the relationships between these 'conceptions of knowledge' in relation to policing and law enforcement.

As can be seen in Figure 4.1, the labels for each conception reflect how they essentially conceive of knowledge. Furthermore, they are numbered from 1 to 5 according to the relative importance of their logical relationship to each other.

For example, unless 'knowledge' is seen as having 'value' then there is no point to it. Thus, logically, the first conception of importance must be 'Knowledge as Value'. From this starting point, the next conception of logical significance is 'Knowledge as Exchange'. The reason being that 'knowledge' cannot be known outside the knower unless it is shared or in other words exchanged with another. If an idea is never shared it only remains an 'idea' in the mind of the inventor. No only else knows about it until it is talked about or exchanged in some transactional way with other people. Sharing knowledge gives it its utility.

From here, logic dictates a few routes in terms of the other three conceptions. The numbering therefore from this point on reflects our preference for this relative ordering of the next three conceptions as shown in Figure 4.1.

We would argue that it makes some sense to view 'Knowledge as Resource' as the next logically related conception after 'Knowledge as Exchange'. Our reasoning is that once 'knowledge' has been 'exchanged' with others it does not take long for others to realize that such 'knowledge' is potentially a 'resource' they can use in a variety of ways. When people want something its value increases as a 'resource'. However, to realize that value of knowledge as a resource it has to be further exchanged or explored or exploited in some way. That takes organization. Hence, 'Knowledge as Organization' enters into the picture as the next logical conception. Finally, once knowledge becomes organized by having tacit knowledge turned into explicit knowledge through capture in documents, procedures, and policies then 'Knowledge as Strategy' is able to work its magic. Finding new ways to exchange, explore, and exploit knowledge is what strategizing is all about.

The logically inferred relationships as shown in Figure 4.1 are of course only that—logical inferences that do not necessarily conform to the realities of KM. The point of these conceptions is not to conform to reality but rather to confront it.

For example, it is quite possible that a police organization, or any organization for that matter, may 'in reality' pay lip service only to its collective 'knowledge' or simply not know how to exploit its knowledge. Why is this so? Maybe the culture of the organization does not see the 'value' of the knowledge they have, or only sees the 'value' of certain types of knowledge, or they have failed to realize its 'value' to them because they preferred one form of knowledge over another. Several critical questions like this can be posed to confront this organizational reality based on an understanding of the how the various conceptions of knowledge are being played out in the organization. Such a critical analysis forms the framework for planning solutions to address the deeper issues surrounding the effectiveness or otherwise of KM in an organization, rather than just plugging in a new platform and hoping that will fix the problems. Rarely are KM problems only technical in nature (Hughes and Jackson 2004).

Therefore, Figure 4.1 is another graphical tool for police executives to use in conjunction with the other key tool the 'planning cube' (Figure 3.5) for looking at the KM programme within their organization.

With this understanding of the various conceptions of knowledge firmly in mind we will now turn our attention to discussing each of them in more detail with regard to policing and law enforcement.

'Knowledge value' approach

This conception of knowledge assesses the 'value of knowledge'. This is the baseline from which all the schools of thought identified by Earl (2001) in KM literature play from in terms of appreciating its worth. Where the schools differ is in how they make use of the intrinsic value of knowledge which is reflected in the other conceptions.

This approach to 'knowledge as value' is most evident is the service industry. It has been cogently argued for some time that policing is also a 'service' industry (Avery 1981). Some police forces in Australia, notably the Queensland Police

Service, have gone so far as to change their name from 'force' to 'service' to signify the importance they place on this service orientation to policing as the core principle of their mission in society. Whilst other police organizations in Western democracies may not have gone so far as to officially have a name change a quick look over their vision statement will find an equally strong emphasis on a community service-type orientation.

This 'knowledge value' approach has been operationalized within this service domain of the KM literature in a number of ways. For a long time, Porter's (1985) notion of a 'value chain' was the only value configuration known to managers. Stabell and Fjeldstad (1998) have identified two alternative value configurations, that of a 'value shop' and a 'value network'.

A 'value shop' schedules activities and applies resources in a fashion that is dimensioned and appropriate to solve a specific problem, while a value chain performs a fixed set of activities that enables it to produce a standard product in large numbers. Examples of value shops are professional service firms, as found in medicine, architecture, engineering, and law.

A 'value network' links clients or customers who are or wish to be interdependent. Examples of value networks are telephone companies, retail banks, and insurance companies. In the domain of policing and law enforcement, organized crime networks and terrorist cells can also be perceived as forming value networks along with Interpol, Europol, the FBI, and NIM in the UK among others as law enforcement examples of value networks.

An example of the value configuration of a 'value shop' being applied to policing is presented below in relation to the police investigative process.

'Value shop' of police investigative processes

The police investigation process can be conceptualized as having the value configuration of a 'value shop'. The value shop is an organization that creates value by solving unique problems. Knowledge is the most important value that police and law enforcement organizations have in the fight against crime and terrorism. A value shop is characterized by five primary activities: problem finding and acquisition; problem solving; solution choice; solution execution; and control and evaluation, as illustrated in Figure 4.2.

As can be seen in Figure 4.2 these five activities are interlocking and, while they follow a logical sequence, much like the management of any project (Woods 2002), the difference from a KM perspective is the way in which knowledge is used as a resource to create value in terms of results for the organization. Hence, the logic of the five interlocking value shop activities in this example is of a police organization and how it engages in its core business of conducting reactive and proactive investigations.

Also, noted on Figure 4.2 is how in practice these five sequential activities tend to overlap and link back to earlier activities, especially in relation to activity 5 (control and evaluation) in police organizations when the need for control

Figure 4.2 Police investigation as 'value shop' activities

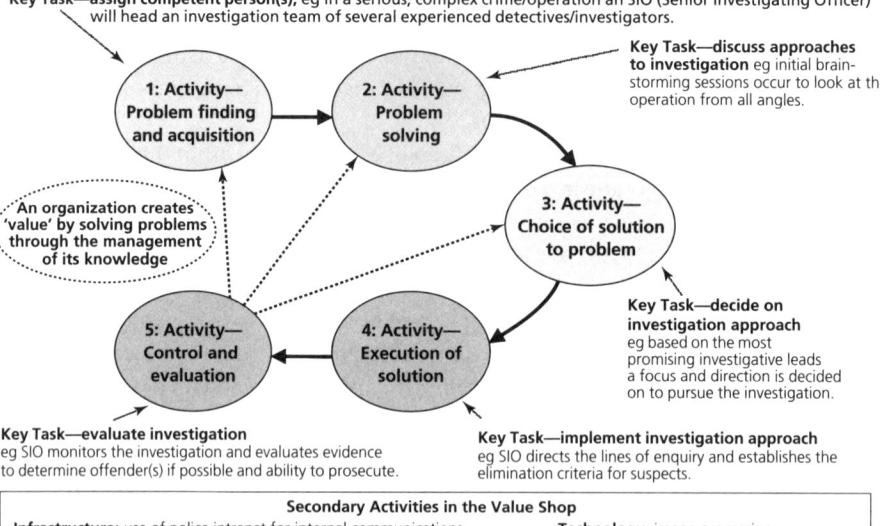

Key Task—**assign competent person(s)**, eg in a serious, complex crime/operation an SIO (Senior Investigating Officer) will head an investigation team of several experienced detectives/investigators.

Key Task—**discuss approaches to investigation** eg initial brain-storming sessions occur to look at the crime/operation from all angles.

1: Activity—Problem finding and acquisition

2: Activity—Problem solving

An organization creates 'value' by solving problems through the management of its knowledge

3: Activity—Choice of solution to problem

5: Activity—Control and evaluation

4: Activity—Execution of solution

Key Task—**decide on investigation approach** eg based on the most promising investigative leads a focus and direction is decided on to pursue the investigation.

Key Task—**evaluate investigation** eg SIO monitors the investigation and evaluates evidence to determine offender(s) if possible and ability to prosecute.

Key Task—**implement investigation approach** eg SIO directs the lines of enquiry and establishes the elimination criteria for suspects.

Secondary Activities in the Value Shop	
Infrastructure: use of police intranet for internal communications	**Technology**: image processing
Human Resources: use of police intranet for competence building	**Procurement**: use of public agreements

and command structures are a daily necessity because of the legal obligations that police authority entails. Hence, the diagram in Figure 4.2 is meant to illustrate the reiterative and cyclical nature of these five primary activities for managing the knowledge collected during and applied to a specific police investigation in a value shop manner.

These five primary activities of the value shop in relation to a police investigation unit can be outlined as follows:

• *Problem definition and information acquisition.* This involves working with parties to determine the exact nature of the crime and hence how it will be defined. For example, a physical assault in a domestic violence situation, depending on how the responding officers perceive it and/or choose to define it, can be either upgraded to the status of grievous bodily harm to the female spouse victim or it may be downgraded to a less serious assault where a bit of rough handling took place towards the spouse. This concept of making crime, a term describing how detectives choose to make incidents into a crime or not, is highly apt here and is why this first activity has been changed from the original problem-finding term used in the business management realm to a problem-definition process here in relation to police work. Moreover, this first investigative activity involves deciding on the overall investigative approach for the case, not only in terms of information acquisition, but also as indicated on Figure 4.2 in undertaking the key task, usually by a senior investigative officer (SIO) in a serious or major incident, of forming an appropriate investigative team to handle the case.

- *Problem solving approaches.* This involves the actual generation of ideas and action plans for the investigation. As such it is a key process for it sets the direction and tone of the investigation and is very much influenced by the composition of the members of the investigative team. For example, the experience level of investigators and their preferred investigative thinking style might be a critical success factor in this second primary activity of the value shop.

- *Solution choice.* This represents the decision to choose between alternatives. While the least important primary activity of the value shop in terms of time and effort, it might be the most important in terms of value: in this case, trying to ensure as far as is possible that what has been decided on is the best option to follow to get an effective investigative result. A successful solution choice is dependent on two requirements. First, alternative investigation steps need to be identified in the problem-solving approaches activity. It is important to think in terms of alternatives, otherwise no choices can be made. Next, criteria for decision-making have to be known and applied to the specific investigation.

- *Solution execution.* As the name implies, this represents communicating, organizing, investigating, and implementing decisions. This is an equally important process or phase in an investigation as it involves sorting out the mass of information coming into the incident room and directing the lines of enquiry as well as establishing the criteria used to eliminate a possible suspect from further scrutiny in the investigation. A miscalculation here can stall or even ruin the whole investigation.

- *Control and evaluation.* This involves monitoring activities and the measurement of how well the solution solved the original problem or met the original need. This is where the command and control chain of authority comes into play for police organizations and where the determination of the quality and quantity of the evidence is made as to whether or not to charge and prosecute an identified offender in a court of law.

We might define police investigation success in terms of the effectiveness of these five primary activities of police work organizations as value shops. Success is achieved if the unit is successful in understanding problems, finding investigation approaches, choosing an optimal investigation approach, implementing the optimal investigation approach, and solving the problem. Rather than a purely sequential procedure to solve a crime, police investigations move back and forth between these five activities.

The value shop approach is very much in line with the investigative process as defined by Smith and Flanagan (2000). The process begins with an initial crime scene assessment where sources of potential evidence are identified. The information derived from the process then has to be evaluated in order to gauge its relevance to the investigation. During the next stage, the information is interpreted to develop inferences and initial hypotheses. This material can then be developed by the SIO into appropriate and feasible lines of enquiry. The SIO will then have to prioritize actions, and to identify any additional information that may be required to test that scenario. As more information is collected, this is then fed back into the process until the objectives of the investigation are achieved. Providing a suspect is identified and charged, the investigation then enters the post-charge stage, where case papers are compiled for the prosecution. Subsequently, the court process will begin.

A 'value shop' configuration requires a knowledge-based strategy that starts by looking at the activities carried out. A total of five primary activities are defined, in addition to secondary activities. The focus of a knowledge-based strategy is what kind of knowledge is applied in the different 'value shop' processes or activities within the overall conduct of a police investigation.

'Knowledge exchange' approach

This conception of knowledge emphasizes the value of 'knowledge as exchange'. It is most closely aligned with the 'commercial' school of thought identified by Earl (2001). Hence, it favours economic and business models of KM where 'knowledge' is perceived within the narrow frame of intellectual assets to gain and keep a competitive advantage in the marketplace. In this sense 'knowledge as exchange' is a market-driven approach.

This 'knowledge market' approach is explicitly concerned with both protecting and exploiting an organization's knowledge or intellectual assets to produce results. With regard to policing and law enforcement, it is concerned with managing knowledge as an asset, where knowledge or intellectual assets include at least three levels of 'knowing':

- Know-what (what kind of crime occurs in this district?): crime pattern analysis
- Know-how (how are criminals doing it?): *modus operandi* of criminals
- Know-why (why do criminals do it?): motivational elements of criminals

The concept of 'knowledge markets' recognizes the interest that individuals have in holding onto the knowledge they possess. Police know only too well that in their marketplace 'knowledge is power'. Hence, police like other security organizations have access to privileged knowledge and as a consequence like to hold onto their 'knowledge power' as a bargaining chip both within and outside the organization.

Therefore, there has to be something in it for a police and law enforcement agency to part with their knowledge power. In other words, they need to receive something in exchange. Policing, like any organization, is a knowledge market in which knowledge is exchanged for other things of value—money, respect, promotions, or other knowledge (Grover and Davenport 2001).

Another aspect of the knowledge market approach is that 'knowledge transfers' occur in knowledge markets. This is a transactional perspective, where knowledge exchanges occur in a marketplace. In defining a knowledge market as a system in which participants exchange a scarce unit for present or future value, one must be clear about two fundamental dimensions—first, who are the 'buyers and sellers', and second, what 'pricing system' exists—to determine what the knowledge consumer pays for a product or service.

Knowledge markets exist within every organization. These markets include not only knowledge that has been codified or synthesized (realized) into an organization's processes, structure, procedures, guidelines, technology, or strategy, but also all dynamic exchanges of knowledge between consumers (buyers) and suppliers (sellers).

According to Grover and Davenport (2001), organizations can be viewed as having two categories of buyers of knowledge—local buyers and global buyers. This is especially relevant to the globalization of policing as discussed in Chapter 1 and commented further on in Chapter 3 in terms of its thematic implications.

The 'local' knowledge buyers are people who are searching for knowledge assets to address an issue that they need to resolve. They require more than information. Expertise, experience, insight, and judgement are needed to bring to bear on the issue. They could pay for knowledge in hard currency via, for example, a consultant from outside the organization, or buy the knowledge from internal suppliers.

The 'global' knowledge buyer is the organization, which has a vested interest in realizing knowledge assets into valuable policing services. The global knowledge buyer, represented by organizational stakeholders whose benefits are tied to organizational level outcomes, has a strong interest in transferring local knowledge to global knowledge. Doing so reduces dependency on knowledge sellers—in case they choose to leave the organization. Knowledge sellers are people who have knowledge (usually tacit) to sell. The quality of this knowledge might be high or low depending on the credibility of the source.

Davenport and Prusak's (1998) concern with knowledge markets also includes the roles of buyers, sellers, and brokers in which they highlight other aspects of these roles other than the 'local' and 'global' elements.

Knowledge buyers or seekers are usually people trying to resolve an issue whose complexity and uncertainty require knowledge. They seek knowledge because it has distinct value to them. With regard to policing this equates to a detective as a knowledge buyer when asking another detective for advice.

Knowledge sellers are usually people in an organization with an internal market reputation for having substantial knowledge about a process or subject. Although almost everyone is a knowledge buyer at one time or another, not everyone is necessarily a seller. Some people are skilled but unable to articulate their tacit knowledge. Others keep themselves out of the market because they believe they benefit more from hoarding their knowledge. Again, in relation to policing, a detective is a knowledge seller when giving requested advice to another detective.

Knowledge brokers make connections between buyers and sellers. Typically, managers are in the knowledge broker role by making connections. Librarians frequently act in this role as information guides us to the task of making people-to-people as well as people-to-text connections as do personnel leaders and resource allocators. In this regard, police managers have an overview of knowledge possessed by different police officers and the skill mix of an investigative team.

We turn now to the second consideration of a 'knowledge market' approach, that of a 'pricing system'. All markets have a price system so that value exchanges can be efficiently rendered and recorded. The price system of a knowledge market includes reciprocity, repute, and altruism (Davenport and Prusak 1998). Each of these terms will be explained before providing some examples for policing and law enforcement.

Reciprocity implies payment in terms of knowledge. A knowledge seller will spend the time and effort needed to transfer knowledge effectively if the person expects the buyer to be a willing seller when he is in the market for knowledge. Reciprocity may be achieved less directly than by getting knowledge back from the same person. In firms structured as partnerships, such as law firms, knowledge sharing that improves profitability will return a benefit to the sharer, now and in the future.

Repute implies being known as a knowledge source. A knowledge seller usually wants others to know him as a knowledgeable person with valuable expertise that he is willing to share with others in the organization. Repute may seem intangible, but it can produce tangible results. Having a reputation for knowledge sharing makes achieving reciprocity more likely: being known as a knowledge seller makes one a more effective knowledge buyer. Having a reputation as a valuable knowledge source can also lead to the tangible benefits of job security, promotion, and all the rewards and trappings of a policing guru. Although a seller does not receive cash directly, he may receive a higher salary or bonus from sharing knowledge with others. In professional service firms such as consulting and law firms, success hinges on repute.

Altruism implies that a knowledge seller may be so passionate about his knowledge that he is happy to share it whenever he gets a chance. This seems to be the case with many university professors, where the joy of having students listening compensates for the often lousy pay. Many knowledge sharers are motivated in part by a love of their subject and to some degree by altruism, whether for the good of the organization or based on a natural impulse to help others. The payment achieved is in terms of attention, admiration, and time spent by others listening to the knowledge seller.

'Pricing system' of knowledge in policing market

A pricing system revolves around the three elements as noted above—reciprocity, repute, and altruism. How these elements interact in a police knowledge market is an area ripe for research. At this stage only some tentative comments can be made. Further empirical research is needed to establish just exactly how such a 'pricing system' works in policing.

'Reciprocity' in police organizations often occurs among close colleagues and colleagues who have known each other for a long time. Whether or not a knowledge seller (police officer) expects to be paid with equally valuable knowledge from the buyer (another police officer) is an open question. A consideration in this regard is that he/she may believe that their being known for sharing knowledge will readily make others in the organization more willing to share with them. However, given that 'knowledge is power' and the notorious reluctance of police to share information (Brodeur and Dupont 2006) this is a moot point.

'Repute' in law enforcement agencies centres around the reputation in terms of management's perception of each officer's knowledge. This management perception will in turn influence the extent to which the officer enters into desired positions. For example, a patrolling police officer who would like to join a criminal investigation unit is likely to be successful if his knowledge reputation is outstanding.

'Altruism' in policing is something that most recruits indicate spurs them to join policing (Criminal Justice Commission 1995). That is, be of service to the community by doing a difficult and sometimes dangerous job. Furthermore, older officers have a tendency to help younger officers. They spend time explaining, informing, and discussing. Hence, altruism can be an effective element in the police knowledge pricing system when experienced officers transfer knowledge to inexperienced colleagues.

'Knowledge resource' approach

The key focus in this conception of knowledge is the value of knowledge as a 'resource'. This conception fits comfortably with the 'systems' school of thought in the taxonomy proposed by Earl (2001). The primary idea in the systems school is to capture specialist knowledge in knowledge repositories for use as a resource throughout the organization. Hence, IT is both necessary and central to a 'knowledge resource' approach in order to capture, store, organize, retrieve, and display knowledge in knowledge-based systems.

A central tenet in a resource-based approach is that unique organizational resources of both a tangible and intangible nature are the real source of competitive advantage. With resource-based theory, organizations are viewed as a collection of resources that are heterogeneously distributed within and across industries. Accordingly, what makes the performance of an organization distinctive is the unique blend of the resources it possesses. An organization's resources include not only its physical assets such as plant and location but also its competencies. The ability to leverage distinctive internal and external competencies relative to environmental situations ultimately affects the performance of the organization.

Knowledge is the important organizational resource in focus in this book. Unlike other inert organizational resources, the application of existing knowledge has the potential to generate new knowledge. Not only can knowledge be replenished in use, it can also be combined and recombined to generate new knowledge. Once created, knowledge can be articulated, shared, stored, and recontextualized to yield options for the future. For all of these reasons, knowledge has the potential to be strategically applied across time and space to yield increasing returns (Bock *et al.* 2005; Garud and Kumaraswamy 2005).

Following the logic of a 'knowledge as resource' approach to police KM, law enforcement agencies should explore and exploit strategic knowledge resources to perform their tasks successfully. The activities and work carried out by police forces are increasingly based on knowledge. Managing the required knowledge at the individual as well as the organizational level as a resource requires attention to knowledge needs.

Hence, identification of knowledge needs in an organization is important. Three common methods used to identify the need for knowledge are illustrated in Figure 4.3.

The problem decision analysis method aims at identifying and specifying problems that knowledge workers have, solutions they can find, decisions they have to make, and what knowledge they need to solve problems and make decisions. For a detective, the problem can be an unsolved robbery case, the decision can be what investigative steps to apply (interrogation, surveillance,

Figure 4.3 Methods to identify knowledge needs

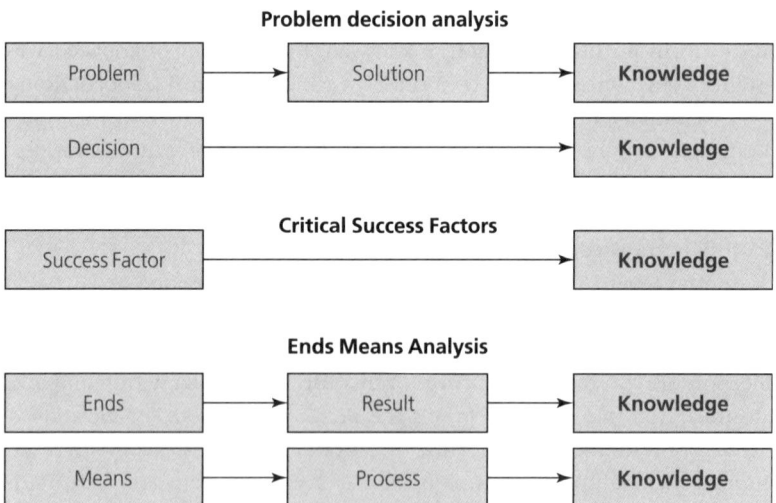

office search, etc), and the knowledge needed can be outcomes of similar cases handled by the police force.

The critical success factors method aims at identifying and specifying what factors cause success. Success can be at team level, individual level, or individual case level. For a detective, critical success factors at the individual case level can be the quality of evidence and access to witnesses. Critical knowledge in this case includes legal knowledge as well as procedural knowledge.

The ends means analysis method aims at identifying and specifying external demands and expectations of services from the police. For a detective, the expectation from society might be that he or she solves the criminal case. The end is winning the case in terms of conviction of the guilty person(s) in court. Knowledge needs associated with winning a case include legal, procedural, and analytical knowledge of successful cases in the past. The means for winning a case might be access to resources of various kinds, such as smart, cooperating people. Knowledge needs associated with means include historical records and analysis of legal client practice.

Strategic value of 'knowledge resource' in policing

Resources are considered strategic resources if they are (i) valuable, (ii) original, (iii) non-imitable, (iv) non-transferable, (v) non-substitutable, (vi) exploitable, and (vii) combinable.

Knowledge as a resource is valuable if there is a need for the knowledge in policing. Knowledge is original if not everyone else has it. For a law enforcement organization, it might be important that neither criminals nor lawyers have the knowledge. Knowledge is non-imitable if it cannot be copied by rivals of the police. Knowledge is non-transferable if it does not leave the force with officers who are leaving. Typical examples of non-transferable knowledge are found in working styles and investigative practices. Knowledge is non-substitutable if it cannot be replaced by other kinds of knowledge. Knowledge applied to money laundering might not substitute for knowledge applied to murder cases. Knowledge is exploitable if it is applicable to policing situations when needed. Finally, knowledge is combinable when different kinds of knowledge merge in an effort to handle a specific policing situation.

A survey was undertaken at a seminar in 2005 with participants from police investigation units in Norwegian law enforcement. Detectives were asked to list strategic knowledge resources in their units as well as rate the relevance of the seven resource characteristics of knowledge. The results are listed in Figure 4.4.

Figure 4.4 illustrates different levels of strategic value from knowledge resources. For example, the computer crime knowledge is valuable, original, non-substitutable, exploitable, and combinable. But this knowledge is at the same time both imitable and transferable. Of more strategic value is Schengen cooperation police knowledge, which is a knowledge category satisfying all seven strategic criteria.

Figure 4.4 Survey results for strategic knowledge resources

Knowledge Resources Characteristics	1 Valuable	2 Original	3 Not imitable	4 Not substitutable	5 Exploitable	6 Not transferable	7 Combinable
Analysing handwriting	Yes	Yes	Maybe	Maybe	Yes	Yes	Yes
Analysing pictures	Yes	Yes	Yes	Yes	Yes	Yes	Yes
Analysing weapons	Yes	Yes	Yes	Maybe	Yes	Yes	Yes
Schengen cooperation	Yes	Yes	Yes	Yes	Yes	Yes	Yes
Analysing documents	Yes	Yes	No	No	Yes	No	Yes
DNA identification	Yes	Yes	No	No	Yes	No	Yes
Police intelligence	Yes	Yes	Yes	Yes	Yes	Yes	Yes
Computer crime	Yes	Yes	No	Yes	Yes	No	Yes

A 'problem-oriented' policing example of the strategic application of knowledge in the Norwegian police force is how knowledge is used to identify crime patterns. Like other police forces around the world, in Norway strategic knowledge resources are applied to identify patterns in crime behaviours along different axes such as time, geography, and demography. Here, the pattern of incidents is more important than each single incident. Police actions are focused more on preventing crimes by removing the root causes, rather than finding the criminals as an effect of the situation.

Likewise, the efficient and effective deployment of resources is becoming central in police work. For example, UK central government has become increasingly focused upon the setting of targets in efforts to improve the efficacy of public services and demonstrate value for money from increased expenditure (Ashby and Longley 2005).

A 'knowledge resource' approach to police knowledge management requires a knowledge-based strategy. Strategic management models traditionally have defined an organization's strategy in terms of its tasks and work priorities. The resource-based approach suggests, however, that organizations should position themselves strategically based on their original, valuable, combinable, exploitable, non-transferable, non-substitutable, and inimitable resources and capabilities rather than the services derived from those capabilities. Resources and capabilities can be thought of as a platform from which the organization derives various services for various tasks. Leveraging resources and capabilities across many policing activities, rather than targeting specific services for specific situations, becomes the strategic driver. While criminal situations may come and go, resources and capabilities are more enduring. Therefore, a knowledge resource-based strategy provides a more long-term view than the traditional approach, and one more robust in uncertain and dynamic environments.

Finally, a central component of such a knowledge resource strategy is higher education for police officers. Acquiring knowledge training through higher education equips officers to handle a variety of situations better given the complexities of societies today (Roberg and Bonn 2004).

'Knowledge organization' approach

This conception of knowledge views the primary value of knowledge as being derived from its location in the 'organization'. Naturally, this conception is directly linked to the 'organizational' school of thought identified by Earl (2001).

This approach to 'knowledge as organization' is all about the use of organizational structures and networks, both formal and informal, to share or pool knowledge. The engine that drives this knowledge organization approach is 'knowledge communities'. This is where a group of people with a common interest, or problem, or experience come together in an organizational context to share and pool their knowledge and expertise. These communities are designed and maintained for a business purpose that develops through exchange and sharing a 'common knowledge'. Dixon (2000) defines common knowledge as the knowledge that employees learn from doing the organization's tasks. Common knowledge is managed through knowledge transfer mechanisms. Such knowledge communities can be intra- or inter-organizational communities.

In this perspective, organizational units in law enforcement 'ideally' represent 'communities of practice' sharing knowledge to fight crime. Unfortunately, an ideal design and the real workings of the design are not always in alignment. This aspect of knowledge transfer and sharing is a theme that will be taken up further in this and later chapters. However, before knowledge can be transferred it first has to be either created or existing knowledge captured. This is what organizations need to excel at from a knowledge perspective.

Organizations create and define problems, develop and apply knowledge to solve the problems, and then further develop new knowledge through the action of problem solving. In many organizations, developing new knowledge is even more important than keeping track of existing knowledge. The organization is not merely an information processing machine, but an entity that creates knowledge through action and interaction. It interacts with its environment, and reshapes the environment and even itself through the process of knowledge creation.

Hence, Nonaka *et al.* (2000) argue that the most important aspect of understanding an organization's capability concerning knowledge is the dynamic capacity to continuously create new knowledge out of existing organization-specific capabilities, rather than the stock of knowledge that a firm possesses at any one point in time. With this view of an organization as an entity that creates knowledge continuously, we need to re-examine our organizational theories, in terms of how organizations are organized and managed, how they interact with the environment, and how organizational members interact with each other.

Fighting economic crime by non-criminal organizations represents an interesting example of desperate knowledge creation needs. While economic crimes by criminal organizations represent a knowledge field where police have some experience, economic crimes (tax fraud, manipulation of share prices) by legal organizations represent a field where many police organizations are lacking basic knowledge of accounting, marketing, business strategy, money transfer, and hierarchical structures.

Knowledge creation is a continuous, self-transcending process through which one crosses the boundary of the old self into a new self by acquiring new context, a new view of the world, and new knowledge. One also transcends the boundary between self and other, as knowledge is created through the interactions among individuals or between individuals and their environment.

To understand how organizations create knowledge dynamically, Nonaka *et al.* (2000) proposed a model of knowledge creation consisting of three elements: (i) the SECI process, the process of knowledge creation through conversion between tacit and explicit knowledge, where SECI stands for socialization, externalization, combination, and internalization; (ii) *ba*,[1] the shared context for knowledge creation and the place to create knowledge; and (iii) knowledge assets, the resources required to enable knowledge creation, such as inputs, outputs, and moderation of the knowledge-creating process.

The three elements of knowledge creation have to interact with each other to form the knowledge spiral that creates knowledge. An organization creates knowledge through interactions between explicit and tacit knowledge. This interaction is called knowledge conversion. Through the conversion process, tacit and explicit knowledge expands in both quality and quantity. There are four steps in knowledge conversion: from tacit to tacit, from tacit to explicit, from explicit to explicit, and from explicit to tacit. As mentioned above, these four steps are called socialization, externalization, combination, and internalization (SECI) (Nonaka *et al.* 2000).

Socialization is the conversion of tacit knowledge to tacit knowledge. New tacit knowledge is converted through shared experiences, and acquired the same way, such as through spending time together or living in the same environ-

---

[1] The Japanese word 'ba' can be translated as 'place'. However, this is not necessarily a physical place, more of a place at a specific time. 'Ba' therefore can be described as the real cultural, social, and historical context which is of importance to each knowledge worker.

ment. Socialization takes place when new skills are acquired by spending time with others who have those skills. Socialization also occurs outside the typical workplace, when mental models and opinions are shared among persons who are present. Socialization is the sharing of tacit knowledge between individuals, usually through joint activities rather than written or verbal instructions. For example, by transferring ideas and images, apprenticeships allow newcomers to see the way others think. Knowledge is produced in a group setting not only through mere acquisition of the individuals' knowledge, but also through the sharing of common understanding. Social processes play an important role in the transition of knowledge across individuals or groups. This phenomenon can easily be observed when new graduates from police academies join their older colleagues in patrolling and investigations. New police officers look, listen, and follow their experienced colleagues, without necessarily understanding why they do it in this way.

Externalization is the conversion of tacit knowledge to explicit knowledge. Tacit knowledge is articulated into explicit knowledge. Explicit knowledge can be expressed in words and numbers and shared in the form of data, scientific formulae, specifications, manuals and the like. This kind of knowledge can be readily transmitted between individuals both formally and systematically. The successful conversion of tacit knowledge into explicit knowledge depends on the common knowledge space as well as the use of means such as metaphors, analogy, and mental models. Externalization involves the expression of tacit knowledge and its conversion into comprehensible forms that are easier to understand. Conventional learning methodologies require the externalization of the professor's knowledge as the initial step in the students' learning process. Conventional investigation procedures require the senior investigative officer to present the case to the team in a meeting. Externalization involves techniques that help to express ideas or images as words, concepts, visuals, or figurative language (eg metaphors, analogies, and narratives), and deductive/inductive reasoning or creative inference.

Combination is the conversion of explicit knowledge to explicit knowledge. Explicit knowledge is converted into more complex and systematic sets of explicit knowledge. Explicit knowledge is collected from inside and outside the organization and then combined, edited, and processed to form new explicit knowledge. The new knowledge is then disseminated among the members of the organization. When the financial controller collects information from all parts of the organization and puts it together to show the financial health of the organization, that report is new knowledge in the sense that it synthesizes explicit knowledge from many different sources in one context. When the senior investigative officer applies the cross-check framework presented in this book, then pieces of explicit knowledge are combined into a coherent set of explicit knowledge. Combination involves the conversion of explicit knowledge into more complex sets of explicit knowledge. Focusing on communication, diffusion, integration, and systematization of knowledge, combination contributes to knowledge at the group level as well as at the organizational level. Innovative organizations seek to develop new concepts that are created, justified, and modelled at the organizational, and sometimes inter-organizational, level. Complex organizational processes require the cooperation of various groups within the organization, and combination supports these processes by aggregating technologies and knowledge.

Internalization is the conversion of explicit knowledge to tacit knowledge. Individuals convert explicit knowledge into tacit knowledge. By reading documents or manuals about their jobs and the organization, new employees can internalize this explicit knowledge in such documents to start doing their jobs. When internalization has occurred, the new knowledge becomes part of existing mental models and know-how. This tacit knowledge accumulated at the individual level can stimulate a new spiral of knowledge creation when it is shared with others through socialization. Internalization requires the individual to identify the knowledge relevant to oneself within the organization's explicit knowledge. In internalization processes, the explicit knowledge may be embodied in action and practice, so that the individual acquiring the knowledge can re-experience what others go through. Alternatively, individuals could acquire tacit knowledge in virtual situations, either vicariously by reading or listening to others' stories, or experientially through simulations or experiments. Learning by doing, on-the-job training, learning by observation, and face-to-face meetings are some of the internalization processes by which individuals acquire knowledge.

Knowledge creation is a continuous process of dynamic interactions between tacit and explicit knowledge. Such interactions are shaped by shifts between different modes of knowledge conversion, not just through one mode of interaction. Knowledge created through each of the four modes of knowledge conversion interacts in the spiral of knowledge creation. Nonaka *et al.* (2000) emphasize that it is important to note that the movement through the four modes of knowledge conversion forms a spiral, not a circle.

One of the important developments in police theory and research is the recognition of the institutional contexts in which law enforcement agencies participate. Institutionalized organizations, such as police organizations, are about meanings and values. Rational decision-making, based on cost-effectiveness calculations often found in business, occurs within the context of broader values (Crank 2003). The institutional context for law enforcement organizations is found in the society and in communities where police officers do their job. Knowledge management in this context is not just a question of effective problem solving. It is also a question of filling the policing role in society.

Police organizations are abandoning the bureaucratic model and are developing into learning organizations and intelligent organizations. The theory behind the intelligent organization draws attention to the discrepancy between societal values and the way in which organizations are structured, citing the lack of choice, freedom, and community in many organizational cultures. McLeod

70

(2003) suggested that police organizations will develop through a transition from bureaucratic, to post-bureaucratic, and finally, to restorative organizational models characterized by learning and intelligence, where KM is a requirement for success.

Organizational mechanisms for 'knowledge transfer' in policing

Knowledge transfer in an organization can be defined as the process by which one unit (eg a group, department, or division) is affected by experiences. Another definition suggests that knowledge transfer at the individual level is how knowledge acquired in one situation applies to another situation. Both these definitions describe knowledge transfer as something that manifests itself through changes in knowledge or performance of the recipient units. Dixon (2000) distinguishes between serial transfer, explicit transfer, tacit transfer, strategic transfer, and expert transfer of knowledge:

- *Serial transfer* takes place when the same group of knowledge workers perform the same work one more time by applying their own knowledge. The nature of the task is frequent and non-routine, and the type of knowledge that is transferred can be both tacit and explicit. When the same team of investigative police officers get a new criminal case to solve, then serial knowledge transfer takes place when individuals in the team share experience from the previous case. Serial transfer is a process that moves the unique knowledge that each individual has constructed into a group or public space so that the knowledge can be integrated and made sense of by the whole team. A team can be defined as a group of people with a shared commitment who strive for synergy among its members.

- *Explicit transfer* takes place when a group of knowledge workers perform the same work as another group has done before by applying knowledge from the other group. The knowledge from the other group is transferred explicitly as words and numbers and shared in the form of data, scientific formulae, specifications, manuals and the like. The nature of the task performed by the team is frequent and routine. When one police district experiences the same kind of crimes as another police district for the first time, then transfer of knowledge between the two districts will represent explicit transfer.

- *Tacit transfer* takes place when a group of knowledge workers performs the same work as another group by applying knowledge from the other group, but in a different context. The knowledge from the other group is transferred through social activity as tacit knowledge. The nature of the task that the group is engaged in is frequent and non-routine. This is also called near transfer—not because of the geography involved but because of the similarity between the source team and the receiving team. In national bureaus of investigation, tacit knowledge transfer occurs when officers investigating narcotics share their knowledge with officers investigating trafficking or money laundering.

- *Strategic transfer* takes place when a team has taken on a task that happens only infrequently—a one-off project—and wants to benefit from the experience of others, within the same organization who have achieved a similar task. Typical of this transfer mechanism is that the senior-level managers are often involved and define what kind of knowledge is needed to solve the task. The type of knowledge that is transferred can be both tacit and explicit. When a police district reorganizes to fight organized crime, then knowledge of organized crime cases has to be transferred and transformed into knowledge of criminal organizations.

- *Expert transfer* takes place when generic and explicit knowledge is transferred from an expert source inside or outside the organization to enable the team to solve new problems using new methods and knowledge. This knowledge transfer is applicable when the team is performing a task that is infrequent and routine, and faces an unusual technical problem beyond the scope of its own knowledge. Typically, the knowledge that is requested is not found in a manual or in standard documentation. When Kosovo-Albanian mafia expand their operations in Norway, then Norwegian police officers that have been on UN missions in Kosovo and Albania have expert knowledge about the origins of such criminals (Arnesen 2005).

Police management has to emphasize all five mechanisms for successful sharing and creation of common knowledge in policing organizations. For serial transfer, management has to stimulate meetings and contacts between group members, while for explicit transfer documentation of work by the previous group needs to be stimulated. For tacit transfer, management has to stimulate contacts between the two groups, while for strategic transfer strategic knowledge and knowledge gaps have to be identified. For expert transfer, management has to create networks where experts can transfer their knowledge.

'Knowledge strategy' approach

This conception of knowledge sees the key value of knowledge in terms of its 'strategic' use. This conception is directly associated with the 'strategic' school of thought identified by Earl (2001).

This approach to 'knowledge as strategy' represents an eclectic mix of systems, networks, knowledge repositories, and IT tools since it is essentially concerned with raising the consciousness within the organization about 'the value creation possibilities available from recognizing knowledge as a resource' (Earl 2001: 217). Hence, there is a close alignment with all the conceptions of knowledge discussed so far but in this approach a strategic twist is given to them. This is certainly the case with the 'knowledge as organization' approach.

For example, a strategic knowledge focus in an organization would begin with making a set of distinctions between organizations that are more expertise-driven, experience-driven, and efficiency-driven. Such distinctions help to clarify the strategic advantages of different types of knowledge and their extent as well as how the best value can be derived from such organizational knowledge.

Each of these distinctions between an expertise-driven organization, an experience-driven organization, and an efficiency-driven organization (Hansen *et al* 1999) are outlined below:

- *Expertise-driven organization* solves large, complex, risky, new, and unusual problems. Law enforcement success is achieved through continuous improvisation and innovation. Knowledge workers apply general high-level knowledge to understand, solve, and learn. Learning from problem solving is important to be able to solve the next new and unknown criminal problem. An expertise-driven organization is characterized by both new problems and new methods for solution. An example might be a policing organization fighting economic crimes, where crime types are unfamiliar (ie money laundering) and procedures are not developed (ie working with banks and law firms when fighting money laundering).
- *Experience-driven organization* solves large and complicated problems. The problems are new, but they can be solved with existing methods in a specific context every time. Law enforcement success is achieved through effective adaptation of existing problem-solving methodologies and techniques. Continuous improvement in effectiveness is important to be able to solve the next criminal problem more efficiently and more effectively than the previous one. An experience-based organization is characterized by new problems and existing methods for solution. An example might be a policing organization investigating homicides, where a well-known set of investigative procedures and thinking styles is applied to a variety of criminal situations.
- *Efficiency-driven organization* solves known problems in known ways. The quality of the solution is found in fast and inexpensive application to meet needs. Law enforcement success is achieved in the ability to make small adjustments and improvements in existing procedures. An efficiency-driven organization is characterized by known problems and known methods for solution. An example might be a policing organization controlling car speeding on roads, where well-known approaches are applied to well-known situations.

Few knowledge-intensive organizations are only active in one of these businesses. Most policing organizations are active at several of these levels. For example, detectives in criminal investigations are mainly in the experience-driven business of solving new problems with known methods. Sometimes, they are in the expertise-driven business of solving new problems with new methods. Similarly, lawyers in a law firm are often in the expertise-driven business, but most of the time in the experience-driven business. In some engineering firms, engineers are often in the efficiency-driven business, but most of the time in the experience-based business.

We introduce these three categories of organization, because knowledge focus will be different in expertise-driven, experience-driven, and efficiency-driven businesses. In the expertise-driven organization, learning is important, while previous knowledge of both cases and methods quickly becomes obsolete. In the experience-driven organization, know-how concerning methods is important, while knowledge of previous cases quickly becomes obsolete. In the efficiency-based business, all knowledge concerning both methods and cases is important in an accumulation of knowledge to improve efficiency. Policing is performed by different police organizations, some of which are mainly efficiency-based, while others are mainly experience-based or expertise-based respectively.

The distinction between efficiency-driven, effectiveness-driven, and expertise-driven law enforcement organizations leads us to the contingent approach to information storage. The difference leads us to make distinctions between the following three knowledge management strategies—stock strategy, flow strategy, and growth strategy (Hansen *et al* 1999):

- *Stock strategy* is focused on collecting and storing all knowledge representations in information bases in the organization. Information is stored in databases and made available to knowledge workers in the organization and in knowledge networks. Knowledge workers use databases to keep updated on relevant problems, relevant methods, news, and opinions. Information on problems and methods accumulates over time in databases. This strategy can also be called officer-to-database strategy. Police officers have access to well-proven methods and previous cases, which enable them to handle the same policing situations in the same way as in the past.

- *Flow strategy* is focused on collecting and storing knowledge representations in information bases in the organization as long as the information is used in knowledge work processes. If certain kinds of knowledge work disappear, then information for those work processes becomes obsolete and can be deleted from files and databases. This is a yellow-pages strategy where information on knowledge areas required in work processes in the organization is registered. The link to knowledge sources in the form of individuals performing tasks is made specific in the databases, so that the person source can be identified. When a knowledge worker starts on a new project, the person will search company databases to find colleagues who already have experience in solving these kinds of problem. This strategy can also be called officer-to-workflow strategy. Police officers have access to well-proven methods that they apply to new policing situations.

- *Growth strategy* is focused on developing new knowledge. New knowledge is developed in innovative work processes taking place when knowledge workers have to solve new problems with new methods. Often, several persons are involved in the innovation, and together they have gone through a learning process. When a knowledge worker starts on a new project, the person will use the intra-organizational as well as the inter-organizational network to find information on work processes and learning environments, which colleagues have used successfully in previous innovation processes. This strategy can also be called officer-to-innovation strategy. Police officers have access to novel methods and novel cases that they apply to new policing situations in a creative manner.

As might have become evident, there is a strong link between these three knowledge management strategies and the three types of organization: expertise-driven, experience-driven, and efficiency-driven. In Figure 4.5, characteristics of the three strategies are presented. Typically, efficiency-driven organizations will apply the stock strategy, while experience-driven organizations will apply the flow strategy, and expertise-driven organizations will apply the growth strategy.

The stock strategy is concerned with storing and retrieving all kinds of information from previous work, since police officers will do the same things in the same way again. The flow strategy is concerned with storing and retrieving only information that is relevant to solving new cases in known ways. The growth strategy is concerned with storing and retrieving only information relevant to thinking differently in terms of new cases to be solved in new ways.

Figure 4.5 Characteristics of Knowledge Management strategies

Characteristics	Stock strategy	Flow strategy	Growth strategy
Knowledge focus	Efficiency-driven organization	Experience-driven organization	Expertise-driven organization
Important persons	Chief knowledge officer Chief information officer Database engineers	Chief knowledge officer Experienced knowledge workers	Management Experts
Knowledge base	Databases and information systems	Information networks	Networks of experts, work processes, and learning environments
Important elements	Access to databases and information systems	Access to knowledge space	Access to networks of experts and learning environments
Management task	Collecting information and making it available	Connecting persons to experienced knowledge workers	Providing access to networks
Learning	Efficiency training applying existing knowledge	Experience accumulation applying existing knowledge	Growth training developing new knowledge

When following the growth strategy, the most important knowledge management task is to prioritize important information for the future. All kinds of information not important for the future should be deleted. This task of deleting is not easy. We know from personal experience that throwing away items at home that we don't need any more is not always easy. Similarly, we tend to store reports and binders on shelves in the office that we know for sure that we will never need. Similarly, we store junk information on personal computers and shared databases. The danger of the latter is retrieval, as computer programmers might spend time organizing and retrieving electronic information that is no longer needed. Therefore, cleaning storage space is very important in the growth strategy and to some extent also in the flow strategy.

Strategic applications of 'knowledge focus' in police organizations

There is considerable variability in police organizations and indeed right across agencies in the justice system in the knowledge focus they adopt both within organizational units as well as the organization as a whole.

Some police organizations apply mainly strategic knowledge, which will typically be expertise-based knowledge. As a case example, the Norwegian police can be mapped in terms of its foci of knowledge types as shown in Figure 4.6.

As can be seen the central police directorate, which manages the whole police force in Norway, can be characterized as mainly drawing on expertise-based knowledge. Employees in the police directorate have to develop new knowledge

Figure 4.6 Distribution of knowledge focus across police agencies in Norway

for new policing challenges based on changes in society and in politics. Most of the knowledge they apply is based on educational qualifications.

On the other hand, the central bureau of criminal investigations is characterized by operational, experience-based knowledge. When investigating homicides, narcotics, or trafficking, detectives use mainly investigative steps that have been successfully applied before.

Figure 4.6 mainly serves the purpose of illustrating the variation that exists in a strategic knowledge focus that is applied within law enforcement in a country. However, from a knowledge management point of view, police leaders have to approach the management of a police directorate very differently from the management of a central bureau of investigation, because the required knowledge (operational *versus* strategic) and the knowledge sources (experience-based *versus* expertise-based) are so different.

Summary

Approaches to KM in policing and law enforcement can be aligned with five conceptions of knowledge, which are: 'knowledge as value'; 'knowledge as exchange'; 'knowledge as resource'; 'knowledge as organization'; and 'knowledge as strategy'.

The first approach, 'knowledge as value', is a baseline conception to which all the schools of thought identified by Earl (2001) in the KM literature connect in various ways in the other conceptions. This 'knowledge value' approach is most evident in the service orientation of policing. A policing example of this approach is presented in a 'value shop' configuration of the investigation process. Such a 'value shop' approach defines police work, especially police investigations, as an iterative process of problem understanding, approach, decision, action, and evaluation. Knowledge supports each of these five primary activities in the value shop.

The second approach, 'knowledge as exchange', is a market-driven approach. It is closely aligned with the 'commercial' school of thought (Earl 2001) and favours economic and business models of knowledge management. Police trade in this 'knowledge market' through the organization's intellectual assets is measured in terms of its economic value to produce results. The 'pricing system' for police knowledge in this market of knowledge buyers, sellers, and brokers revolves around the elements of reciprocity, repute, and altruism.

The third approach, 'knowledge as resource', fits with the 'systems' school's primary goal of capturing specialist knowledge in knowledge-based systems. Managing such knowledge as a resource at the individual as well as the organizational level requires the identification of knowledge needs through the methods of 'problem decision analysis', the study of 'critical success factors', and 'ends means analysis'. The strategic value of police knowledge resources lies in the organization's ability to capitalize on the various characteristics of knowledge being valuable, original, non-imitable, non-transferable, non-substitutable, exploitable, and combinable.

The fourth approach, 'knowledge as organization', is about the use of organizational structures and networks, both formal and informal, to share or pool knowledge. The engine that drives this knowledge organization approach is 'knowledge communities'. Furthermore, an organization is not merely an information-processing machine, but an entity that creates knowledge through action and interaction. It interacts with its environment, and reshapes the environment and even itself through the process of knowledge creation. Four steps have been identified as being involved in knowledge creation. Nonaka *et al.* (2000) have called these steps socialization, externalization, combination and internalization—which together are known as the SECI process. Once knowledge has been created organizations must be able to leverage that knowledge by transferring it to others. Knowledge transfer takes place through five mechanisms (Dixon 2000) termed serial transfer, explicit transfer, tacit transfer, strategic transfer, and expert transfer.

The fifth approach, 'knowledge as strategy', is essentially concerned with raising the consciousness within the organization of the value-creation possibilities of knowledge as a resource. Such a strategic knowledge focus classifies organizations into efficiency-based, experience-based, and expertise-based organizations. While the stock strategy of information storage is appropriate for an efficiency-based organization, the flow strategy and the growth strategy for storing and retrieving information are appropriate for an experience-based and expertise-based organization respectively.

In sum, the five approaches to KM in policing and law enforcement are not mutually exclusive. Approaches interact with one another and are often layered through a police organization in different divisions and sections. What is important from a Knowledge Management point of view is the mix of approaches and ensuring a complementary combination of approaches and their various contributions is achieved to ensure optimal performance.

Systems in Police Knowledge Management

Introduction

The focus of this chapter is on the systems that underpin Knowledge Management (KM) in the policing and law enforcement environment. It is important to be clear about a basic distinction between an 'information system' and a 'knowledge system'. An information system collects, stores, and retrieves information, whereas a knowledge system takes the captured information and creates knowledge. Moreover, depending on the sophistication of the knowledge system, it can then recreate the 'created knowledge' and further recreate the recreated 'created knowledge' in an ever expanding iterative cycle of knowledge creation.

This basic distinction between information/knowledge systems reflects the layered nature of data–information–intelligence–knowledge as noted in Chapter 1 (Figure 1.1) and the technological implications of this basic construct. Modern information systems are technology-dependent systems, but the same is not necessarily true for knowledge systems. That is, a knowledge system is more reliant on 'individual and collective learning than on the power of technology' (Rowe 2005: 782).

This does not mean that knowledge systems can or even should be less technologically driven than clearly they currently are. It would be hard to imagine a knowledge system that is not technology-reliant. The point being made is that 'knowledge creation' is more about nurturing a process of engagement with informational sources and a diversity of ideas from others that can be stored in a computer system, than about relying on a system of technology to create knowledge. Relying on technology to create knowledge is to put the proverbial cart before the horse.

Having clarified this distinction between an information system and a knowledge system we will now turn our attention to, first, the architecture behind a Knowledge Management system (KMS) then, second, a critical look at the various types of computer system available to manage knowledge in a policing and law enforcement context.

Architecture of Knowledge Management Systems

A KMS at its broadest level refers to a diverse array of socio-cultural, organizational, and technological components (Alavi and Leidner 2001) that come together to form a system to manage knowledge for use at the individual, group, and organizational level. Hence, the main objective of a KMS is to support the creation, transfer, and application of knowledge in an organization.

The creation of knowledge as we have already discussed in previous chapters is very much concerned with the capturing the tacit knowledge in the mind of individuals and this is essentially a socio-cultural issue for management to address at an organizational level when designing a KMS. The technological component of a KMS revolves around IT and IS systems. Hence, an information management system (IMS) is regarded as one subset among others in the larger concept of a KMS.

Knowledge management systems facilitate the efficient and effective sharing of an organization's intellectual resources. To ensure effective usage, a KMS has to be designed in such a way that knowledge workers can readily find high-quality content without feeling overwhelmed (Poston and Speier 2005). In other words, not only must the architecture of the systems design do what it is intended to do, it must also do it in a user-friendly way.

The specific needs of policing and law enforcement organizations often require modifications to a system's architectural infrastructure and design in order to make the system relevant to the special demands the policing context places on such systems. Before looking at the particular needs and demands for different types of KMS in policing a basic understanding of the diversity of the architecture behind such police-related KMS is required.

There are a number of ways in the KM and related IS/IT literature that KMS can be classified (Alavi and Leidner 2001). For example, a KMS is often defined in terms of inputs such as data, IT, best practices, and so forth (Malhotra 2004).

Because of the focus in this book on practical policing in a global context we have taken a different approach to classifying KMS according to the essential nature of the architecture of the systems in use in the global policing and law enforcement community. The advantage of this form of classification is that it allows police practitioners and management to appreciate in a non-technical and simple way the core application domain of the information systems they use to manage their police-specific organizational knowledge. There are four types or levels of KMS in our classification system. They are:

- Systems that manage 'documented' explicit information (IMS)
- Systems that manage 'geographical' spatial information' (GIS)
- Systems that manage 'audio-visual' intelligence–surveillance information (ISS)
- Systems that manage 'expert knowledge' tacit information' (EKS)

These four systems of Knowledge Management in our typology are not mutually exclusive. In practice the systems are more inter-related in that one can build upon the information provided by the other in a conceptual sense rather than necessarily in a technical sense. This is because often the platforms are different and therefore getting different KMSs to talk to each other like relational databases do may not be financially or technically feasible depending on the budgetary resources of particular police departments and law enforcement agencies.

With regard to the first level of the typology, IMSs are the most basic form of KMS whereby vast amounts of different types of information are stored in databases. In the context of policing and law enforcement the most useful types of database are relational in nature. In other words they 'talk' to other databases so that information can be exchanged and shared with others. Such relational databases are used in policing by a wide range of users for a variety of purposes from general policing, criminal investigations, crime prevention, to security and intelligence purposes.

The next level of systems architecture within the KMS domain, which has changed the way police work is done, is the use of geographical information systems (GIS). The most well-known example of such a system is the use of crime mapping data to identify 'hot spots' of criminal activity.

The third level of KMS is concerned with what we have termed intelligence–surveillance systems (ISS). We prefer the term 'surveillance' rather than the more general term of security system as 'security' denotes only this area of application rather than the wider use of surveillance in an intelligence capacity, for example in crime analysis. The notion of 'intelligence–surveillance' on the other hand not only draws attention to the distinctive nature of the systems architecture used but also to the distinctive purpose of the system. Surveillance also encompasses a broad definition of any type of audio-visual combination of infrastructure, covering activities like telecommunications interception (wiretapping, intercepting mobile phone calls and emails) to CCTV cameras and imaging technology.

The final level of KMS in our classification is that of expert knowledge systems (EKS). The architecture of such systems differs from the other forms of KMS in that such systems rely on some form of inferential mechanism and/or rule-based production system for knowledge representation. Such knowledge representation is derived from the tacit knowledge storehouse of experts in a particular field or activity to act as the engine that drives the system.

The value to policing and law enforcement organizations of this classification of KMS according to the distinctiveness of their architectural infrastructure lies in how such a typology can be related to various levels of police knowledge. In Chapter 1 we introduced the policing 'content continuum' framework (Figure 1.1) that showed how knowledge goes up in levels from 'data' to 'information' to 'intelligence' to finally 'knowledge'.

By combining this 'content continuum' with the different types of 'systems architecture' within the KMS domain the diagram in Figure 5.1 is derived. Hence, in essence, each type of systems architecture can be regarded as managing a different level of knowledge.

As can be seen in Figure 5.1 the four levels of KMS (IMS, GIS, ISS, EKS) as they go up the 'content continuum' ladder intersect with 'data', 'information', 'intelligence', and arrive at 'knowledge'.

Although the architecture of each of the four distinct systems manage 'knowledge levels' differently there are degrees of overlap between the systems. This is because each system is used by a range of users for different policing purposes. For example, when running a major crime investigation a number of relational databases (IMS) (eg criminal records searches, incident reports, traffic stop searches) will be searched in conjunction with specialized databases for particular crimes (eg HOLMES 2) as well as intelligence crime analysis (eg Analysis Notebook) and/or surveillance (eg CCTV, wiretapping) systems (ISS).

Figure 5.1 Police Knowledge Management Systems related to knowledge continuum

Architecture of Police Knowledge Management Systems

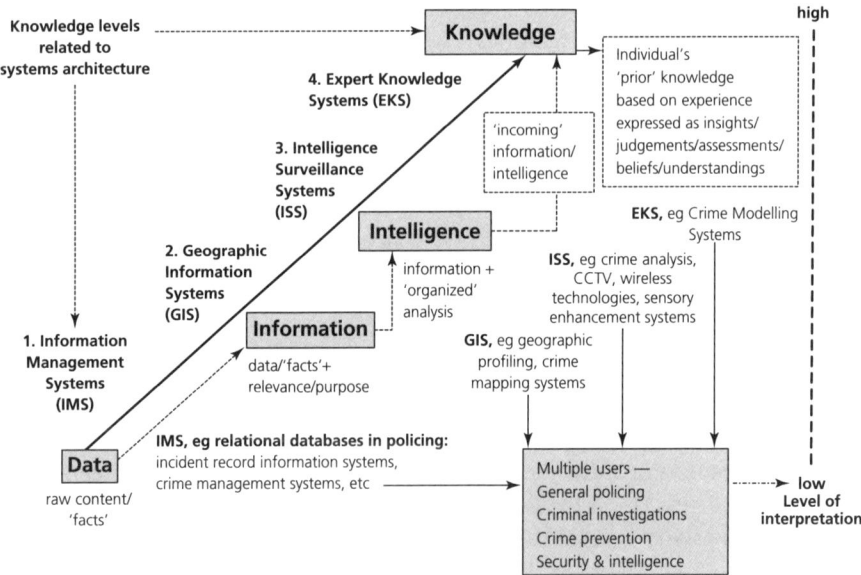

Hence, also depicted in Figure 5.1 are examples of each KMS and various subordinate systems of technological software which can be combined in different ways by different users for their particular purpose.

What should also be apparent from this diagram is the potential for numerous 'tension spaces' to arise. This can occur not only at intra- and inter-organizational levels of knowledge sharing but also at the level of technology in terms of hardware and software compatibilities.

Each of these four levels of KMS and the subordinate systems that are associated with each system's architecture level will now be explored in more detail in the subsequent sections of this chapter.

Information Management Systems

An information system is a computer-based system with the defining characteristic that it provides information to users in one or more organizations. Information systems are thus distinguished from, for example, real-time control systems, message-switching systems, software-engineering environments, or personal computing systems (*Dictionary of Computing* 2004). As such there is no single information management system that is able to cover all Knowledge Management needs in an organization. This is evident from the widespread potential of IT in KM processes.

Despite widespread belief that IT enables KM and KM improves organizational performance, researchers have only recently found empirical evidence of these relationships. For example, Tanriverdi (2005) used data from 250 Fortune 1000 firms to provide empirical support for these relationships.

There are a number of factors that make the design of an IMS difficult. They include the following (*Dictionary of Computing* 2004).

- Their environment is complex, not fully definable, and not easily modelled.
- They have a complex interface with their environment, comprising multiple inputs and outputs.
- The functional relationships between inputs and outputs are structurally, if not algorithmically, complex.
- They usually include large and complex databases (or, in future, knowledge bases).
- Their 'host' organizations are usually highly dependent on their continuing availability over very long periods, often with great urgency attending their initial provision or subsequent modification.

In relation to policing and law enforcement there are further complicating factors. The operating environment is not only complex in scale but global in size. Often multiple databases need to be searched and there is no guarantee that all databases have functional interconnectivity, especially between agencies that may use different platforms. There are also various types of information systems. Some of the more common types available in the marketplace that can be modified for the specifics of police use are as follows (Robertson 2004):

- *Content management systems* (CMS) support the creation, management, distribution, publishing, and discovery of corporate information. Also known as 'web content management' (WCM), these systems typically focus on online content targeted at either a corporate website or intranet.
- *Document management systems* (DMS) are designed to assist organizations to manage the creation and flow of documents through the provision of a centralized repository, and workflow that encapsulates business rules and metadata. The focus of a DMS is primarily on the storage and retrieval of self-contained electronic resources, in their native (original) format.
- *Records management systems* (RMS) are information systems which capture, maintain, and provide access to records over time. This includes managing both physical (paper) records and electronic documents.
- *Digital asset management systems* (DAMS) support the storage, retrieval, and reuse of digital objects within an organization. DAMS differ from document management and content management in their focus on multimedia resources, such as images, video, and audio.
- *Library management systems* (LMS) provide a complete solution for the administration of all of a library's technical functions and services to the public. This ranges from tracking the assets held by the library, managing lending, through to supporting the daily administrative activities of the library.
- *Digital imaging systems* (DIS) automate the creation of electronic versions of paper documents (such as PDF or TIFFs) and are used as an input to RMS. By creating electronic resources, they can be manipulated directly by the records system, eliminating the need for physical filing.
- *Learning management systems* (LMS) automate the administration of training and other learning. This includes registering students, managing training resources, recording results, and general course administration. Learning management systems are designed to meet the entire needs of professional trainers and other educators.

Database systems

The majority of IMS use a database as the heart of the management system. Hence, database management systems (DBMS) consist of a software system which provides comprehensive facilities for the organization and management of a body of information required for some particular application or group of related applications.

Well-known DBMS include the relational database systems ORACLE, INGRES, SYBASE, and INFORMIX, and the earlier systems IMS, IDMS, and ADABAS, still widely used in practice. Some of these products have developed specialist products such as Access and dBASE IV for the PC environment (*Dictionary of Computing* 2004).

In a police and law enforcement context database systems play a very important role in the management of information. Research indicates that database systems allow police officers to easily carry out information searches like background checks, criminal record checks, and so forth (Lingerfelt 1997; Miller 1996; Schellenberg 1997; Hoogeveen and van der Meer 1994; Lewis 1993).

The use of relational database systems (RDBMS) for crime-specific cases like assaults and gang-related incidents, as well as more serious crimes such as homicide and sexual crimes, has proven to be a very effective technology (Pliant 1996; Fazlollahi and Gordon 1993; Keppel and Weis 1993). Relational databases are often used in major criminal cases because they can manage large amounts of information that such crimes like murders and serial rapes generate. Furthermore, the relational nature of such databases means they can 'talk to' and combine relevant information from neighbouring police districts.

Database management in policing

There are a significant number of different IMS and DBMS/RDBMS software brands available to police and law enforcement agencies. Sheptycki (2002) has noted how police magazines are crammed full of advertisements about the latest and best hardware and software products. Marketing police and security-related IMS are a growth industry, hence it is not possible to list all such products available. Moreover, the range of new products and additional features added to existing software systems coming onto the market makes such a listing obsolete and inaccurate within a few years.

As a case in point, the list of crime-recording and investigative systems complied by Adderley and Musgrove (2001) several years ago provides a good overview of some of the types of computer software system still in use in policing and law enforcement, although several of the programs mentioned have been superseded by newer versions. In particular, HOLMES (Home Office Large Scale Major Enquiry System) in the UK has been replaced with HOLMES 2. Also in the US the FBI's original VICAP (Violent Criminal Apprehension Program) has been redesigned as a more user-friendly system with a question form reduced from 189 to 95 items on the new look ViCAP system (Witzig 2003). The Canadian equivalent of the ViCAP system is VICLAS (Violent Crime Linkage Analysis System).

A number of these IMS require designs specific to the needs of particular police forces. This is not surprising given the wide diversity of policing forms, models, sectors, and systems involved in global policing as discussed in Chapter 3. A sampling of some of the different database designs available to policing and law enforcement is presented below.

The first example of an IMS specifically designed for both general policing and specialist use for detectives/crime analysis is COPLINK, described by Chen *et al.* (2002, 2003). COPLINK consists of the two modules 'Connect' and 'Detect'. Connect is an application for information sharing. Detect is targeted for detectives and crime analysts. The system shares the same incident record information system as the Connect module and utilizes the database indexes it generates.

Much of crime analysis is concerned with creating associations or linkages among various aspects of a crime. COPLINK Detect uses a technique called concept space to identify such associations from existing crime data automatically. In general, a concept space is a network of terms and weighted associations within an underlying information space. Statistical techniques such as co-occurrence analysis and clustering functions are used to weight relationships between all possible pairs of concepts (Chen *et al.* 2002, 2003).

In COPLINK Detect, detailed criminal case reports are the underlying information space, and concepts are meaningful terms occurring in each case. These case reports contain both structured (eg database fields for incidents containing the case number, names of people involved, address, and date) and unstructured data (narratives written by officers commenting on an incident, eg witness B said he saw suspect A drive away in a white truck).

Several field user studies have been conducted to evaluate the COPLINK system. For example, a group of 52 law enforcement personnel from the Tucson Police Department in the US representing a number of different job classifications and backgrounds was recruited to participate in a study to evaluate COPLINK Connect. Both interview-data and survey-data analyses support a conclusion that use of the application provided performance superior to using the legacy police records management system. In addition to the statistical data, these findings were supported by qualitative data collected from participant interviews (Chen *et al.* 2003).

Another example of an IMS of a different design is the SPIKE (Surrey Police Information and Knowledge Environment) IMS in the UK. Surrey Police recognized that it needed to transform itself into a virtual organization if it wanted to continue to deliver its unique community-based policing service under the pressure to become more efficient. Only a drastic improvement in productivity and reduced costs would allow their style of policing to survive. The solution was SPIKE, which enables real-time knowledge sharing and has become a catalyst for a quantum change in the organization's structure and the method by which it delivers its services (*Computer Weekly* 2002).

The setting up of SPIKE required a lot of conceptual work to be done by the Surrey Police to develop the information architecture. Staff had to be able to create and access information using a consistent method and interface. Moreover, the criteria for access—ensuring that only those personnel with a right to know can access what it is they are authorized to know, and no more—had to be both pre-set and non-intrusive. All the issues of security levels and clearance were worked out up front.

In the end, the system had to prove itself on the street. Like most people with real jobs to do, police officers tend to regard a heavy burden of administrative paperwork as an unnecessary evil. Since the information utility is only as valuable as the information it contains, convincing officers that taking the time to input that information in the first place can be a challenge. Only when they experience the fruits of that input, by way of receiving the output they need to ease and speed up their real jobs, will it be accepted. Increasingly, information is most useful when it is delivered on the beat (*Computer Weekly* 2002). A key value to be gained from SPIKE or other similar information systems is making it possible for officers to have timely mobile information and access.

Different regional police forces in the UK have other IMS applications like the CATCHEM (Centralized Analytical Team Collating Homicide Expertise and Management) system in the Derbyshire Police and the BADMAN (Behavioural Analysis Data Management Autoindexing Networking) system in the Surrey Police which operates as a specialized IMS alongside the general crime reporting SPIKE system in Surrey as described previously.

A further example of an IMS with a purpose-built relational database system for homicide investigations is the HITS (Homicide Investigation and Tracking System). This program, unlike some others, was developed by detectives for detectives in Washington State in the US (Keppel and Weis 1993). The HITS system performs three functions:

- it evaluates the critical factors necessary to solve murder investigations;
- it identifies the salient characteristics of homicides; and
- it records information unique to a particular offender—such as the offender's method of operation or physical evidence.

Hence, the HITS system allows investigators potentially to link particular suspects or items of evidence to murder cases that have occurred in Washington State.

The HITS program manages information from at least six sources stored in seven different data files—murder, sexual assault, preliminary information, Department of Corrections, gang-related crimes, ViCAP, and timeline. The key feature of the HITS program is its interactive search capability that can search any single query across a potential 250 fields of information for single or multiple field-related information in any order or combination on a person, address, or vehicle.

As can be seen from this short review of IMS, there is a wide diversity of both general and specialized relational databases in use in policing in both the UK and the US in particular. This situation is similar in relation to the next level of KMS, that of GIS.

Geographic Information Systems

A GIS according to Boba (2001: 19) is 'a set of computer-based tools that allow a person to modify, visualize, query, and analyze geographic and tabular data'.

Such GIS software allows a user to create simple point maps up to complex three-dimensional visualizations of spatial and temporal data.

A commonly used term in policing that is associated with GIS technology is 'crime mapping'. However, Boba (2001: 20) prefers to use the term 'crime analysis mapping' because using GIS in the context of law enforcement activity is 'not just the act of placing incidents on a map but also of analysis'.

Crime is not spread evenly across maps. It clumps in some areas and is absent in others. People use this knowledge in their daily activities. According to the National Institute of Justice (NIJ 2005), people avoid some places and seek out others. Their choices of neighbourhoods, schools, stores, streets, and recreation are governed partially by the understanding that their chances of being a victim are greater in some of these places than in others. In some places people lock their cars and secure their belongings. In other places they do not.

Crime mapping is concerned with advancing spatial understanding (Ratcliffe 2004). Areas of concentrated crime are often referred to as hot spots (Bowers *et al.* 2004). NIJ (2005) identified several crime hot spot theories. For example, place theories explain why crime events occur at specific locations. Street theories deal with crimes in slightly larger geographic areas than specific places; that is, over small, stretched areas such as streets or blocks. Neighbourhood theories attempt to explain neighbourhood differences. Other theories attempt to explain differences in crime patterns at much higher levels of aggregation. For example, theories of crime differ among cities and among regions. On the city level, suggested actions may include citywide changes in economic, transportation, education, welfare, and recreation policies.

Researching such theoretical explanations of crime is greatly assisted by GIS. Hence it is little wonder that GIS has become an important tool for crime measures and spatial analysis of criminal activity (Andresen 2006). Classical and spatial statistics have been merged to form more comprehensive approaches in understanding how crime is related to social problems. According to NIJ (2006), these methods allow for the measurement of proximity effects on places by neighbouring areas that lead to a multi-dimensional and less static understanding of factors that contribute to or repel crime across space.

Geographic information systems in law enforcement represent digital repositories for e-government (Amaravadi 2005). Crime mapping is used with Knowledge Management in e-government (Iyer *et al.* 2006; Lytras 2006) and also for change management (Stojanovic *et al.* 2006) in policing (Haugen 2005).

The diffusion of IT in policing is accelerating (Skogan and Hartnett 2005) as technology to support knowledge work in law enforcement is improving (Glomseth and Gottschalk 2005; Gottschalk and Holgersson 2006; Hughes and Jackson 2004). The diffusion of computerized crime mapping in policing is part of this IT revolution in law enforcement (Bowers *et al.* 2004; Ratcliffe 2004; Weisburd and Lum 2005).

Crime mapping systems

The wide and varied diversity of software products in GIS and crime mapping applications can be gauged from the list of categories used to sort the 126 software applications reviewed by the Police Foundation's Crime Mapping Laboratory in the fourth edition of its *Users' Guide of Mapping Software for Police Agencies* which the Foundation produces via COPS funding. The categories covered in this fourth edition (Fall 2002: 8) are: data acquisition/data management; geocoding; crime mapping/crime analysis; internet mapping; redistricting; emergency management; and an 'other' category. This category includes a collection of specialized and more complex software products to do with geospatial imaging, geographic profiling, cartography, routing software, vehicle tracking, drawing/design, and GIS applications development.

As is apparent from such a listing there are many GIS that are applied in law enforcement organizations. Here are some examples of systems in the UK that were reviewed by the Home Office (2006):

- Amethyst: Devon and Cornwall
- CADDIE: Sussex
- COSMOS: Birmingham
- GMAC: Greater Manchester
- JUPITER: East Midlands Government Office region
- LASS: London Government Office region
- NERISS: North East Government Office region
- North West Regional Crime Mapping System: North West Government Office region
- Project DRAGON: Welsh Assembly
- SCaDIS: Surrey

Ashby and Longley (2005) conducted a case study of the Devon and Cornwall Constabulary. They found that geo-demographic analyses of local policing environments, crime profiles, and police performance provided a significantly increased level of community intelligence for police use. This was further enhanced by the use of penetration ranking reports where neighbourhood types were ranked by standardized crime rates, and the cumulative percentage of the crime was compared with the corresponding population at risk.

NIJ (2005) argues that, moving beyond the manual pin-mapping approaches of the past, desktop GIS technologies have introduced crime analysts to new ways of visualizing and mapping crime. Specifically, tools for dynamic visualization and mapping in a GIS environment make it possible inductively to describe and visualize spatial distributions, identify unusual observations or spatial outliers, and discover patterns of spatial association, including clusters and hot spots.

Weisburd and Lum (2005) studied diffusion of computerized crime mapping in policing. The diffusion of computerized crime mapping is based on widely available technologies. Technology is an important factor in explaining the rapid adoption of geographical information systems in mapping crime. However, the availability of a new technology is not enough to explain its widespread adoption. Weisburd and Lum (2005) found three more explanations:

- Diffusion of a new technology generally begins with the wide recognition of a need for change.
- The identification of a need, through some type of crisis or reassessment, is followed by a period of research and development.
- Research and development concluded that law enforcement should be more focused on crime hot spots.

Hence, computerized crime mapping became central to the creation of crime hot spots by identifying clusters of addresses, which evidenced high rates of recorded crime. After the adoption of computerized crime mapping, police organizations develop in terms of crime-mapping maturity. This notion of 'maturity' in terms of GIS technology and in particular crime mapping is the subject of the next section.

GIS maturity framework

The diffusion of an innovation such as crime mapping can be conceptualized as a process in each law enforcement agency. In the next diagram (Figure 5.2) we conceptualize the process in terms of maturity levels as suggested by Gottschalk and Tolloczko (2006). The purpose of this maturity model is to help practitioners and researchers study organizational evolution and determine future direction in a police organization's use of electronic systems when mapping crime.

One of the first maturity models for IT was introduced by Nolan (1979), who suggested a model with six levels of IT maturity in organizations. Later, this model was expanded to nine levels (Gottschalk and Khandelwal 2002). Kazanjian (1988) applied dominant problems to maturity levels. Dominant problems imply that there is a pattern of primary concern that organizations face for each theorized level. In the area of IT maturity, a dominant problem can shift from lack of skills to lack of resources to lack of strategy associated with different maturity levels. More recently, Gottschalk (2006a, 2007) suggested a stage of growth model for KMS in policing, consisting of four stages: officer-to-technology systems, officer-to-officer systems, officer-to-information systems, and officer-to-application systems. Similarly, Gottschalk and Solli-Sæther (2006) suggested a maturity model for IT outsourcing relationships.

Maturity models assume that predictable patterns exist in the growth of an organization. This is conceptualized in terms of levels of maturity. These levels are sequential in nature, occur as a hierarchical progression that is not easily reversed, and involve a broad range of organizational activities and structures. In the case of crime mapping, levels of maturity represent the extent to which geographic information systems are innovating law enforcement.

Figure 5.2 Maturity levels framework for GIS applications

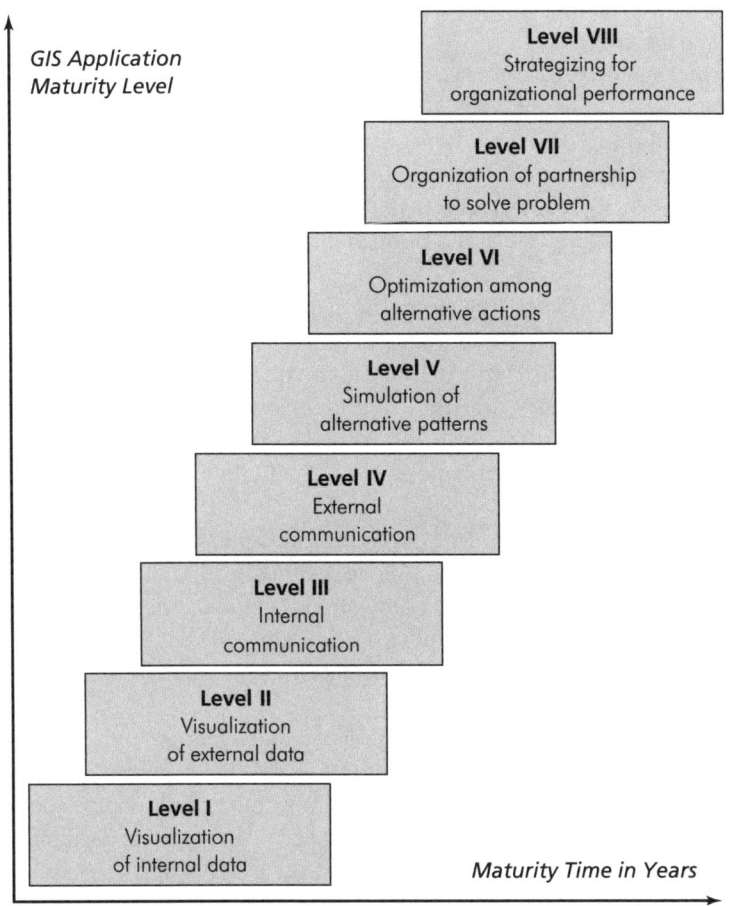

We present a maturity model for GIS applications consisting of eight maturity levels as illustrated in Figure 5.2.

Gottschalk and Tolloczko (2006) define the following maturity levels:

- *Visualization of internal data.* An electronic map is used to visualize geographic areas using police data. A typical example is the mapping of hot spots. Hot spots are areas of concentrated crime (NIJ 2005, 2006). Crime analysts look for concentrations of individual events that might indicate a series of related crimes. Computerized crime mapping is central to the development of a hot spots approach to policing (Weisburd and Lum 2005).
- *Visualization of external data.* An electronic map is used to visualize both police data and external data. For example, the Vancouver Police Department obtained data from the LandScan Global Population Database for spatial analysis of criminal activity (Andresen 2005). The LandScan Global Population

Database has been adopted by many US and international government agencies, as well as the United Nations, for estimating populations at risk from criminal activity.

- *Internal communication.* The electronic map is shared with officers at different locations. For example, COSMOS (Community Safety Mapping On-line System) in Birmingham is an Internet GIS-based community safety tool, designed as a central point of contact for crime and disorder reduction (Chainey and Smith 2006). It provides access to multi-agency data through interactive mapping and data query tools, and through interactive tabular and graphical profiles.

- *External communication.* The electronic map is shared with other public agencies and private organizations that join the problem-solving task. For example, CADDIE (Crime and Disorder Data Information Exchange) in Sussex is an Internet-based solution designed to ensure that all 13 CDRPs (Crime and Disorder Reduction Partnerships) and partners in the county have access to relevant, accurate, and timely information about crime and disorder (Chainey and Smith 2006).

- *Simulation of alternative patterns.* Registered hot spots and other items on the map are statistically correlated with each other, so that different crime patterns will emerge from computer simulations. A typical example is prospective hot spotting, where future locations of crime are predicted. For example, Bowers *et al.* (2004) used a moving window technique to generate prospective risk surfaces.

- *Optimization among alternative actions.* Based on targets and other inputs, the system suggests an optimal solution to the problem. For example, the Devon and Cornwall Constabulary apply geo-demographics for resource allocation in policing. According to Ashby and Longley (2005), geo-demographic profiles of characteristics of individuals and small areas are important in tactical and strategic resource management in many areas of business and are becoming similarly central to efficient and effective deployment of resources by public services.

- *Organization of partnership to solve problem.* The police agency is reorganized to work according to problem-oriented policing. For example, the Project DRAGON provides timely daily exchange of information between probation, the prison service and the police to monitor prison releases and supports partnerships prevention responses to re-offending (Chainey and Smith 2006).

- *Strategizing for organizational performance.* The police agency makes its policing strategy based on GIS results. To be successful, Ratcliffe (2004) argues that there are fundamental training needs for managers to enable a greater understanding of the analyses presented to them, and how to use mapping to further crime prevention and reduction. At this level, executive training of police chiefs is more important than increasing the technical ability of crime analysts. According to Ratcliffe, the challenge for the future of crime reduction practice in law enforcement is to worry less about the training of analysts, and to do more to address the inability of law enforcement management to understand and act on the crime analysis they are given. An emerging example of this maturity level is GMAC (Greater Manchester Against Crime), which operates through a business process model that is changing organizational structures and strategies. GMAC is a structure and process framework for delivering partnership working, utilizing a strategic analytical capability across Manchester (Chainey and Smith 2006).

Finally, in relation to the use of GIS-based crime-mapping applications, an evaluation of geographical profiling software by Rich and Shively (2004) found limitations in all compared software applications. For example, only CrimeStat is able to export results to other mapping software, while only Rigel Analyst has the ability to generate reports. Both Dragnet and Rigel Analyst have the facility to add crime data manually. Based on this evaluation of software applications mature police organizations will have to struggle to find software applications which support levels VII and VIII in the maturity model.

Intelligence–Surveillance Systems

This third level of KMS is concerned with the merging of intelligence and surveillance systems into what is rapidly becoming a dominant systems architecture in policing and law enforcement especially since 9/11 (Nunn 2003; Raco 2003; Lyon 2003).

Lahneman (2004) suggests that intelligence agencies were the world's first knowledge companies. Managing knowledge has always been the primary mission of the intelligence community's leadership. Accordingly, the intelligence community can benefit substantially from Knowledge Management approaches.

Knowledge Management systems that fall within the scope of what we term Intelligence–Surveillance Systems (ISS) involve a very broad range of quite different systems and technologies from crime analysis software to surveillance systems (CCTV) including telecommunications interception technologies to cutting-edge sensory enhancement software based on thermal imaging technologies.

Crime analysis systems

Crime analysis is defined as 'the qualitative and quantitative study of crime and law enforcement information in combination with socio-demographic and spatial factors to apprehend [a] criminal. Prevent crime, reduce disorder, and evaluate organizational procedures' (Boba 2001: 9). Hence, it is little wonder that crime analysis systems have become integral to police models like problem-oriented policing and intelligence-led policing (Tilley 2002; Cope 2003).

One of the key functions of crime analysts is to look for crime patterns by analysing current criminal records then captured and stored in the various police information management systems like the HOLMES 2 system which is used for major investigations in the UK and the CRIS system (Crime Report Information System) for general crime reporting used by the London Metropolitan Police. The FBI's ViCAP system uses pattern analysis to trace travelling criminals who are actively involved in major violent crimes. In Europe, INTERPOL uses ORACLE, which is a relational database system, to provide crime information to its 177 member states.

There is also a wide range of specialist software systems used by different police forces often in the same country. Some of these specialist crime analysis systems are combined with crime-mapping software to enhance the capabilities of the system for local policing. For example, the West Midlands Police in the UK use CPAS (Crime Pattern Analysis System) to provide digital maps on which the density and types of crime can be overlaid to show specific crime called patterns in a defined area. A similar system called the AIM (Action Information Management) system is used by the Suffolk Police to plot crime corridors on a map based on the addresses of all known offenders and their associates (Adderley and Musgrove 2001).

The key difficulty with this task is the sheer volume of data that is generated by the vast array of interconnected databases available to search and which are continually being added to at a faster-than-lighting rate in real-time computing. Such 'information overload' (Eppler and Mengis 2004; Blair and Maron 1985) is well documented.

The task of managing this information overload and then finding potentially relevant information that can be turned into useful operational knowledge for policing is made more manageable if appropriate intelligence analysis software is available to crime analysts. The types of intelligence software will be taken up in the next chapter when dealing with policing technologies.

Surveillance systems

The use of the term surveillance is most closely associated with CCTV as a video surveillance system for providing security for specific locations like public spaces and buildings (Goold 2004) as well as in police stations for suspects held in custody (Newburn and Hayman 2002).

However, a broader use of the term surveillance is used here to include telecommunications surveillance systems like phone interception or wiretapping, electronic surveillance systems like wireless cell phone eavesdropping and tracking, as well as Internet surveillance systems to do with email and chat-room monitoring and so forth.

The domains of policing and security have seen an explosion of growth in the use of video surveillance (CCTV) since the rise of religiously motivated terrorism. In Singapore, it is estimated that on a daily basis the same person will be captured on a security video tape around 60 times on average as they go about their routines of entering shops, stores, banks, and various public places.

In large metropolitan areas like London it is usually double this amount of surveillance, around 150 times a day on average (personal communication).

CCTV is big business in the security-conscious world of anti-terrorism. The second generation of CCTV is called the 'thinking eye' with the main difference between first and second generation being the change from a dumb camera that needs a human eye to evaluate its images to a computer-linked camera system that evaluates its own video images.

This trend towards 'securitization' (Raco 2003) of public space through the use of an extensive CCTV network of cameras has also become a central element in urban regeneration programmes in the UK. One of the most comprehensively planned CCTV systems in any urban space in the UK according to Raco (2003: 1879) can be found in the urban regeneration in Reading in Berkshire where 'there are currently 160 CCTV cameras, operated by a range of public- and private-sector players'. Police forces in the UK are increasingly expected to become engaged with local communities and businesses in policing partnerships (Coleman and Sim 2000) to ensure the securitization of urban renewal spaces like town centres, dockland areas, and old industrial sites as they are turned into what Zukin (1995) has termed 'trophy investments' by private property developers.

However, the securitization of such high-quality property investment developments by CCTV systems is not unproblematic for policing. Often CCTV systems have more of a crime displacement effect than actual crime reduction. For example, the installation of a CCTV network in central Glasgow was found to have significantly displaced crime to other areas across the town rather than reduced it. According to a local crime prevention officer, 'Since we introduced those CCTV cameras in the centre, crime has shifted away to other parts of the town to the east and the west where there is drug dealing and prostitution' (Raco 2003: 1880).

Another area of surveillance that represents a 'tension space' for policing and law enforcement is the rapid development of wireless technology and cellphone surveillance. The traditional statutory framework governing electronic surveillance, wiretapping, and the like does not as yet provide the law enforcement community with clear-cut guidance.

In the US, government eavesdropping over wireless devices was steadily on the increase even before 9/11. From 1998 to 1999, electronic intercepts used to tap into wireless phones, pagers, and email grew by 17 per cent (Carlson 2000). Post-9/11 electronic surveillance of cell phones, emails, websites, etc, has grown exponentially.

With respect to the situation in the US, according to Wesley Clark (2006: 31), 'the only thing certain with respect to the legal requirements for acquisition of cell site information by the government for purposes of identifying the location of a cellular telephone and its user is that nothing is certain at this moment'.

However, this state of affairs is unlikely to remain so for very long as law makers in the US are pushing for legislative provisions to obtain the legal means to compel service providers to provide access to wireless surveillance technologies. Hence, cell-site tracking is headed down the path toward a legislative solution in America. Other Western countries are likely to follow a similar legislative path.

The tension space revolves around ensuring that continuing safeguards against unwarranted privacy intrusions currently present for other telecommunications interception technologies are maintained for wireless technology.

Gips (1999) provides an apt reminder about the tension of balancing competing claims for protection and privacy when he states: 'what security technology giveth toward peace of mind it taketh away in diminished privacy'.

Sensory enhancement systems

There is a range of new emerging KMS that work on enhancing the sensory capabilities of the user. For example, passive millimetre imaging (PMI) devices that literally scan and 'see through' clothes and walls are being used by police and other law enforcement agencies as well as more traditional thermographic tools like forward-looking-infrared-radar (FLIR) for night-vision operations. PMI scanning technology is used primarily for weapon detection and the detection of hidden contraband like drugs (Schiff 1997; Pauper 2001).

PMI technology is based on the principle that 'all objects with temperatures above absolute zero naturally emit a broad spectrum of electromagnetic radiation' (Rosenberg 1998: 4). The human body emits strong electromagnetic waves while objects carried on the body emit weaker electromagnetic waves. The difference in electromagnetic wavelengths allows PMI technology to build scanned image of the human body and everything carried on the body.

Much of this 'sensory enhancement' technology finding its way into the policing and law enforcement domain is a direct result of the 'dual use' funding policy by the Department of Defense for technologies that can have both military and civilian applications (Haggerty and Ericson 2001).

The term 'sensory enhancement', while an appropriate label for such thermographic technologies, is also a little misleading. PMI technologies do more than just 'enhance' the sensory capabilities of the user. For example, they give a police officer the capability to see things that without the technology could not be spotted and hence would for all practical purposes remain 'invisible' to the police officer. As Julie (2000: 14) notes PMI technology is 'capable of revealing any item carried on the person, including those made of metal, liquid, ceramics, plastic, and powder, regardless of the number of layers of clothing being worn, and is even able to take effective readings through wood, plaster, and other materials commonly used in home construction'.

The use of advanced technologies like PMI by the police is not new and can be understood as part of the larger societal trend toward the 'database nation' or the 'surveillance society' (Garfinkel 2000; Lyon 2001) at the beginning of the twenty-first century. What is new is the rapidity, zeal, and excess of these 'technologies of surveillance' (Kiyoshi Abe 2003) trends post-9/11. Nunn (2003: 461) clearly identifies the 'tension spaces' such a trend has created in and for policing and law enforcement in the wider society when he comments:

> Heinous events like 9–11 create massive social and political pressures to use whatever tools are available to identify and locate terrorists and other criminals likely to repeat such acts in the future. In the context of public responses, calls for patriotism, justice, and punishment mute critical analysis of what role these new technologies will play in the future as they become entrenched tools of law enforcement.

The almost 'superhuman' power given to ISS by linking up with thermographic technologies such as PMI scanning devices that allow x-ray examinations of individuals and the ability to see through buildings and walls is a societal issue of substance. PMI technology is intrusive technology. Democratic policing and responsible governments must set appropriate-use policies and procedural guidelines on thermographic technologies to ensure a person's right to privacy is maintained by the rule of law.

Expert Knowledge Systems

Expert systems are knowledge-based systems (KBS) but not all KBS are expert systems. Knowledge-based systems can take a range of other forms and can be found in many areas of artificial intelligence. Furthermore, expert systems can be defined as a system of reasoning used to solve a problem.

In the IS/IT environment the term 'expert system' refers to a computer system that uses a 'knowledge base' to support a reasoning process in order to solve an application problem (*Dictionary of Computing* 2006). The reasoning process in the context of expert systems is based on an 'inference engine' and/or a 'knowledge representation' language structure.

With regard to the inference engine, it is the part of the expert system program that operates on a knowledge base and produces inferences based on a production rule system. A 'production rule system' refers to a programming language in which the programs consist of conditions and action rules of a typical 'if . . . then' nature. Hence, such production systems are often known as rule-based systems in artificial intelligence and form the basis of many expert systems.

'Knowledge representation' is used more in the artificial intelligence community and consists of data-structure techniques and organizing notations like semantic networks, frames, and computer logic. The two most common computer logic systems are propositional calculus and predicate calculus, which have been widely adopted within artificial intelligence as an alternative to the production rules of an inference engine-based expert system. Such computer logic is used for representing the meaning of natural language statements.

However, there are many alternative logics that have been developed in the artificial intelligence community, like 'fuzzy logic', to represent the vagueness and uncertainty of common sense and to represent the tentative nature of common-sense reasoning (*Dictionary of Computing* 2006).

Expert systems that employ rule-based information have been developed to assist in knowledge-intensive activities (Bowen 1994; Brahan *et al*. 1998). These systems attempt to aid in information retrieval by drawing upon human heuristics or rules and procedures to investigate tasks. In a policing context, crime modelling systems like decision support systems for modelling different crime scenarios are examples of the use of expert knowledge systems.

'Knowledge-based' crime scenario modelling

In Chapter 2 we presented a stages-of-growth model for knowledge management technology (see Figure 2.2). Stage 4 of this framework refers to 'how-they-think' systems as encompassing expert systems of the type presented here in the development of a crime-modelling system based on the expert knowledge gained by detectives.

An interesting example suggested by Keppens and Schafer (2006) is the evaluation of evidence performed by detectives. They found that a crucial concern in the evaluation of evidence related to a major crime is the formulation of sufficient alternative plausible scenarios that can explain the available evidence. Therefore, they developed a knowledge-driven methodology for crime scenario construction in terms of a decision support system. The decision support system is devised to find according to Keppens and Schafer (2006: 205):

- The set of all scenarios that explain a given set of available evidence. Scenarios are descriptions of a combination of situations and events.
- The hypotheses supported by scenarios that explain the available evidence. Hypotheses are important features of a presumed crime, such as type of death and characteristics of the perpetrator.
- Additional pieces of evidence that could be found if a certain scenario/hypothesis is true. For example, a further examination by a psychologist into the state of mind of the victim before his death can help confirm a particular scenario.
- Additional investigative actions by means of which evidence can be uncovered, that may help differentiate between two or more hypotheses.

The decision support system has a central inference mechanism that enables a problem solver to make inferences under different hypothetical conditions by maintaining the assumptions that each piece of information and each inference depend on. Knowledge is represented in the system in terms of events, states, and causal relations between events and states.

So far, the theoretical ideas presented by Keppens and Schafer (2006) have only been developed into a prototype decision-support software. Although it is an interesting approach and an exciting example of what might be possible at stage 4 of our Knowledge Management technology stage model, useful practical applications will probably be found several years from now.

The case study below is offered as a further example of what is possible using KMS. The case concerns the organized crime of money laundering.

Case Study: Money Laundering

Money laundering can be defined as the depositing of cash in a legitimate account, most commonly a bank, any movements or transactions which complicate and disguise the origin of funds, and the conversion through the layering process into a form which the perpetrator can control.

Money laundering is concerned with placement, layering, and integration. Money must be placed into the financial system—for example traveller's cheques, postal orders or banker's drafts—retail economy, or smuggled out of the country. Layering is the concealment of the source of the ownership of the funds. Typically, layers are created by moving money in and out of the offshore bank accounts of shell companies through electronic funds transfers. Integration is the stage where the money is integrated into the legitimate economy and financial system (Stedje 2004).

Stedje (2004) evaluated effectiveness in the detection of money laundering in Norway. Her study of effectiveness in prevention and detection of money laundering crime confirmed results in earlier archival studies, that the majority of offenders are known criminals, particularly drug-involved. Except for two cases, all studied criminal cases involved currency. Just about half of the suspects were employed or held business positions. The age was lower than for sophisticated white-collar crime, but higher than for street crime, as the average age was 35. The majority were male with a personal account relationship with the institution.

Stedje (2004) finds it surprising that most of the suspects were of Asian origin, and that all cases, except for two, were of recorded criminals. This suggests that the police do not fight high-class criminals, the man in the suite, but the already known criminal, the man in the street. Additionally, with remarkably bad scores, no persons were convicted of money laundering by the suspicion-based report system in 2001 in the Oslo Police District.

Previous studies of effectiveness in money laundering investigations mostly concur with the findings by Stedje (2004). The studies have in common that the police seem less capable of detecting and the courts less capable of punishing sophisticated money laundering and non-physical currency. The greater universe of criminal financial activity remains largely untouched by the fight against money laundering. None of the studies find that the practice meets the intentions and ambitions of money-laundering legislation, namely to be a substantial method to fight organized crime and terrorist activity.

From a Knowledge Management technology perspective, several applications of information technology might improve the effectiveness in the detection of money laundering. In Figure 5.3 we apply the stages of growth model to illustrate potential applications.

Money laundering involves the creation of layers in order to move money around via electronic funds transfers between offshore bank accounts of shell corporations. Hence, as can be seen in Figure 5.3, such money movements provide several opportunities for law enforcement tracking and interception strategies through the use of KMS at various levels of sophistication.

Summary

This chapter introduced an important distinction that police and law enforcement practitioners need to appreciate: an 'information system' is not the same thing as a 'knowledge system'. That is, it is not simply a case of the trendy term 'knowledge' being exchanged for 'information' and placed in front of 'system' to make it sound better and brighter.

At best an 'information system' can only collect, store, and retrieve information entered into it whereas a 'knowledge system' takes the entered information and creates knowledge out of it in an ever expanding iterative cycle of knowledge creation. Furthermore, the key to knowledge creation rests in the mind of the user of the system not in the technology of the system itself.

Figure 5.3 KMS detection examples in money laundering

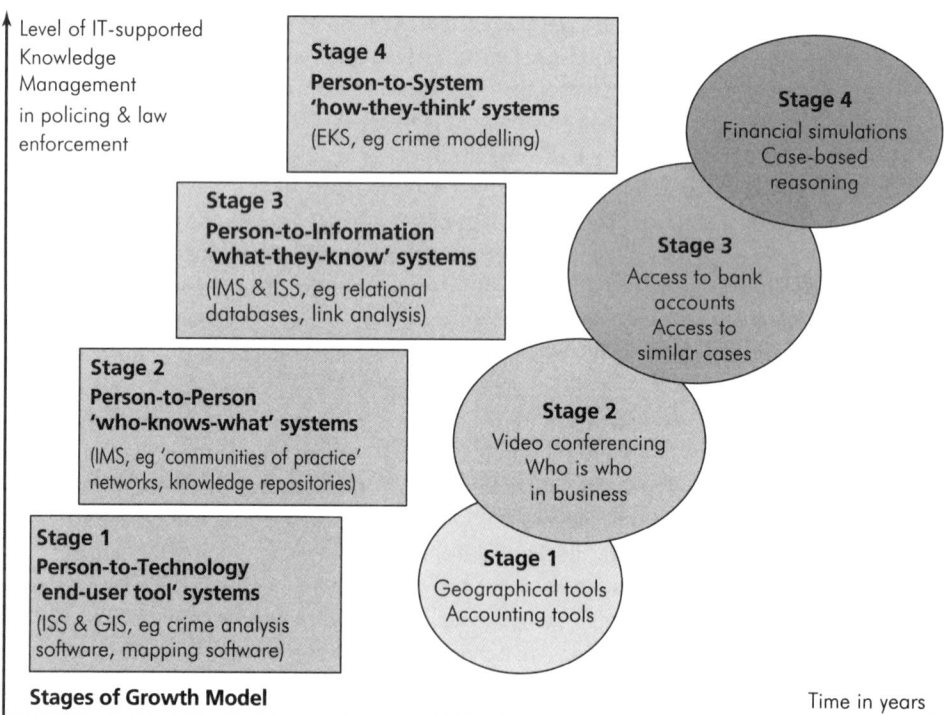

A typology of four systems of knowledge management—IMS, GIS, ISS, and EKS—was also introduced in this chapter based on how each type of systems architecture manages the different levels of knowledge for which the system has been designed.

These four KMS overlap and combine in different ways depending on the particular purposes of the users. Hence, the potential for 'tension spaces' to arise is numerous both organizationally and technologically.

The first level of KMS discussed centred on how police use of IMS is about the management of relational databases in the main. The specific design of an IMS for policing and law enforcement varies considerably and depends on the particular needs of different police forces. Given the wide diversity of policing forms, models, sectors, and systems involved in global policing this is hardly surprising and again adds a level of complexity and even more 'tension spaces' for police and law enforcement organizations to work through in order to ensure optimal efficiencies and maximize the effectiveness of their IMS. Several examples of police database design were sampled in this section.

The second level of KMS concerned the use of GIS technology and in particular crime mapping. GIS-based crime-mapping applications are many and varied in the police and law enforcement environment. Therefore, we presented a model framework of GIS maturity levels to assist police managers and practitioners better to understand and plan the organizational evolution of GIS systems when mapping crime.

The third level of KMS focused on ISS in policing and law enforcement. ISS involves a very broad range of systems and technologies from crime analysis software to surveillance systems (CCTV) including telecommunications interception technologies to electronic wireless and Internet surveillance systems to cutting-edge sensory enhancement software based on thermographic technologies.

The increasing trend towards 'securitization' of public space was discussed along with research evidence that suggests CCTV surveillance can often result in crime displacement rather crime reduction. Furthermore, the 'superhuman' powers conferred on police and other law enforcement officers due to the emergence of sensory enhancing technologies like passive millimeter imaging (PMI) devices that see through clothes and walls was noted. PMI is an intrusive technology which requires appropriate policies and procedural guidelines to ensure the legality of its use in policing operations.

The fourth and final level in our KMS classification scheme was EKS. It was noted that expert systems are knowledge-based systems (KBS) but not all KBS are expert systems. Knowledge-based systems can take a range of other forms and can be found in many areas of artificial intelligence.

Expert systems are defined as a system of reasoning used to solve a problem. They involve the use of an inference engine or knowledge representation structure to solve an application problem. In the context of policing crime modelling systems like decision support systems for modelling different crime scenarios are examples of the use of expert knowledge systems. A case study was offered as an example of what is possible when using a variety of KMS to detect money-laundering operations by organized criminals.

Technologies for Police Knowledge Management

Introduction

The central focus of this chapter is to explore the breadth and depth of technologies in use or that have potential for use in policing and law enforcement. However, this focus is not viewed through the lens of an IT perspective but rather in terms of a Knowledge Management (KM) orientation to police technological resources.

Initially, the foundations for selecting appropriate technologies for police and law enforcement use will be laid with a brief overview of how various technologies have been classified. Next, a new classification scheme or typology using a matrix design is presented along with a range of specific software examples and applications.

Finally, this matrix will be used to map out the type or class of technologies currently available in a police organization as well as relate such technologies to each of the key functions of policing. In this way, police managers are in a position to make informed strategic choices concerning their current and future technological needs.

Policing technologies

There are a number of ways in which policing technologies can be classified. A useful typology proposed by Nogala (1995: 199) consists of several categories as listed below:

- Surveillance and detection technologies
- Identification technologies
- Information-processing technologies
- Communication technologies
- Organization and administration technologies
- Intervention technologies
- Mobility technologies

These categories are not mutually exclusive as there is clearly some overlap with detection and identification technologies. Also, a number of categories can be regarded as falling under Information Management Systems concerning collecting, storing, processing, and communicating information throughout the policing organization.

Manning (2003) on the other hand clustered technologies into five categories based on the salient features of each type of technology in use in policing and law enforcement. They are:

- Mobility technology
- Training technology
- Transformative technology
- Analytic technology
- Communicative technology

As can be seen there are similarities and differences between Nogala and Manning's classification schemes. Both include mobility and communication technologies in their typologies.

With regard to mobility technologies this is not surprising. The public want to see a visible police presence both on the street and in cars as well as a rapid response time to calls for assistance. Hence, mobility technologies like random uniformed patrols undertaken in police vehicles are part and parcel of what the police have to do to satisfy such public demands. Come election time, politicians of all political persuasions regularly beat the 'get tough on crime' drum and promise more resources to the police. This usually translates as more police on the beat and in cars in campaigns designed to trade on citizen fears and win votes using such popularity politics. It is little wonder that mobility technologies continue to take up a large slice of police expenditure.

However, the category of analytic technology in Manning's scheme would by and large subsume a number of Nogala's categories like surveillance, detection, identification, information-processing, and intervention technologies. Since the 'analytic' category covers a wide range of technologies in Manning's classification—like those designed to acquire, store, and aggregate police data to facilitate crime analysis, crime mapping, and aid in crime prevention—other categories like transformative technology have little obvious counterpart in Nogala's classification scheme. However, the way Manning defines the term 'transformative', as consisting of technological devices that extend the human senses and present technical evidence in scientific form, shares some features with surveillance, detection, and identification technologies.

Matrix of policing technologies

It is clear that there is no definitive way to classify policing technologies. Any classification scheme depends on what it is designed to show. Hence, we proposed a classification scheme which builds on the work of Nogala (1995) and Manning (2003) but which takes a different path in terms of how it classifies technologies which are and can be used in policing and law enforcement.

Our classification is based on a combination of the key functions of both 'policing' and the 'technologies' involved. With regard to technologies, there are three categories of technology in which we are interested in relation to managing police knowledge. They are:

- technologies where the primary function is to communicate data, information, intelligence, and knowledge;
- technologies where the primary function is to visualize data, information, intelligence, and knowledge; and
- technologies where the primary function is to reason with data, information, intelligence, and knowledge.

Grouping technologies[1] according to these three specific functions of communicating, visualizing, and reasoning in relation to levels (data–information–intelligence–knowledge) of police knowledge allows police managers to make informed judgements about:

- what class of technology they need to suit a particular purpose;
- what the technology is actually capable of delivering; and
- what combination of these technologies may be required, now and in the future.

For example, the use of databases is widespread in policing but there is nothing dramatically innovative about them in police work (Puonti 2004). This is because essential databases belong to the class or category of technologies concerned with just communicating data (storing, retrieving, and transferring), information, intelligence, and/or knowledge from one place or person to another place or person.

The database revolution is about communicational efficiencies in terms of time saved and global reach, not about a higher order of communicating. It is

---

[1] Clearly, there are purposes for policing technologies other than the ones we have identified as communicating information, visualizing information, and reasoning with information. For example, as Manning (2003) points out, police technologies can be used for a training function or even a transformative purpose. However, the three key functions we have listed are the ones that are of primary concern in relation to the focus of our book.

certainly true that modern relational databases are very sophisticated in how they can communicate and what they can be programmed to do (ie tracking vehicles, people, and events); however this is an argument about the level of communicative sophistication of a database, not about a change in its techno-logical nature.

If a database is combined with a visualization technology that can generate a link or node chart-type analysis based on what is stored in the database then a different order (class/category) of technology is involved which changes the functionality of the database to something different than just communicating. Now the database is capable of visual analysis.

Furthermore, if an 'inference engine', the driver of an expert system, is added to the database then the functional capabilities of the database change to a tech-nology that is capable of reasoning.

An example of linking a communicative technology, such as a police data-base, to a visualization technology, such as a GIS, can be found in the Criminal Suspect Prioritization System (CSPS) developed for the Criminal Behavioural Analysis Unit (CBAU) of the Royal Newfoundland Constabulary (RNC) which is used to correlate crime behaviour and offender characteristics stored in a data-base in order to provide investigators with a prioritized list of suspects (House 1996). The CSPS database is also linked to a MapInfo GIS to visualize the crime patterns. In excess of 7,000 offenders' criminal histories are in the database and it is uploaded with up-to-date overnight arrest information (Adderley and Mus-grove 2001).

With regard to the how the key functions of policing are classified, pre-vious research by Dean (1995) identified three core functions or process-es—investigation, analysis, and prevention—that constitute an integrated set of daily operational policing practices. These policing and law enforcement functions are defined as mutually reinforcing cycles of operational practice as follows:

- investigation is a process centred on analysis which leads to prevention;
- analysis is a process that is used as a tool for investigation; and
- prevention is a process that is the outcome of the investigation.

Investigation, of course, is fundamental to everything the police do. The same is true of analysis. As Peterson and Ridgeway (1990: 13) point out 'analytical ability is what makes a good investigator'. These authors, however, have con-cerns about how analysis is conceptualized in policing for they go on to state that 'law enforcement analytical courses that do exist usually focus on the use of intelligence analysis, not on how to analyze' (op cit).

Prevention is one of those buzzwords in police parlance. Everybody agrees there should be more of it. The difficulty is how to give it operational meaning beyond mere words. Heal (1992: 265) argues that to form a composite strate-gy of crime, prevention needs to be located 'within a broader strategy' and 'set alongside the processes of detection, investigation and court disposal on the one hand, and care of the victim on the other'. Prevention, therefore, is a concept that needs to be more clearly and broadly articulated by police, particularly how it relates to the everyday world of operational practice.

How these three key functional processes integrate at an operational level will be discussed in more detail in subsequent chapters. For our purposes here the significance of these core policing functions lies in how they can be related to the various categories of technology previously mentioned. Using our classification scheme for technologies in use in policing and law enforcement results in a grid or matrix space in which various software programs and technologies can be located under the core policing functions of investigation, analysis, and prevention. This matrix is presented in Figure 6.1.

The purpose of our matrix is not to give police managers a lot of technological jargon and in-depth details about various programs and software packages available but rather to provide a conceptual understanding of policing technologies in terms of what they are designed to do and how they relate to the larger context of Knowledge Management Systems (KMS)—the focus of this book.

It needs to be borne in mind that the matrix diagram is suggestive only of where various technologies and/or software programs can be located. The matrix

Figure 6.1 Matrix of technological and policing functions

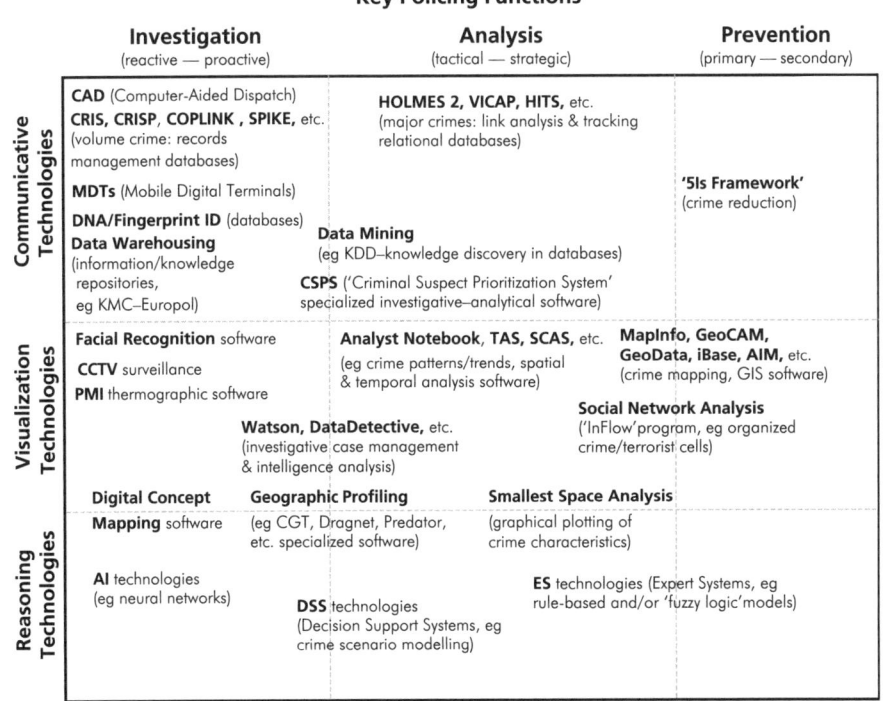

is not meant to be comprehensive or exhaustive. Furthermore, as can be seen on the matrix, there are a range of illustrative examples of policing technologies across functional categories. Also, any 'product names' that appear are used as examples not as an endorsement of any kind.

The first category of Communicative Technologies contains hardware and software programs whose basic functional purpose is to communicate information both externally to the public and within the policing and law enforcement environment.

Web-based services allow police agencies to disseminate selective information to the public about police-related matters and activities like crime-stopper news items, recruitment information, and so forth.

With regard to internal police and law enforcement use, some typical examples of communicative technologies are indicated in Figure 6.1 and include technologies like CAD, MDTs, and a host of application databases for automatic fingerprint identification, facial recognition, DNA, and so forth. The details of such technologies are well covered in several publications[2] in law enforcement and hence will not be repeated here.

The next category, Visualization Technologies, is concerned with those technologies that use visualization as the core process for user functionality for the software. This term 'visualization' may seem jargon at first but it does point to a fundamentally important underlying concept about the use of such technologies. Tergan *et al.* (2006: 168) note that 'according to Ware, the "power of visualization comes from the fact that it is possible to have a far more complex concept structure represented externally in a visual display than can be held in visual and verbal working memories"'.

Police investigations of any serious crime become very complex very quickly. As information flows into an investigation the relationships between victims, suspects, and other persons of interest begin to branch out in multiple directions. This is where visualization technologies come into their own as a class of technologies which harness the power of various visual representations of data, information, and intelligence to create operational police knowledge in an investigation. The examples noted in Figure 6.1 of various visualization technologies will be discussed along with others in more detail in later sections.

The third category of Reasoning Technologies clusters together those technologies that have the ability to mimic human reasoning. The level of reasoning with such technologies can vary considerably from being relatively low in comparison with the higher capabilities of the human brain to quite sophisticated and complex neural operations. Clearly, the fields of influence in this category are cognitive and computer sciences and the field of artificial intelligence (AI), as well as related sub-disciplines such as DSS (Decision Support Systems) and ES (Expert Systems), as noted in Figure 6.1 on the matrix diagram.

---

[2] See Chu (2001) *Law Enforcement Information Technology: A Managerial, Operational and Practitioner Guide.*

Each of the categories of policing technology will be discussed in turn with reference to the three key policing functions.

Communicative technologies

It is clear from the matrix in Figure 6.1 that the investigative function has a high concentration of such communicative technologies. In Nogala's (1995) classification scheme our communicative category would typically subsume his information-processing, organization–administration, and mobility technologies as well as Manning's (2003) mobility and communicative technologies and to some extend his training technologies category.

With regard to Manning's (2003) 'communicative technology' label his category is more restrictive than our use of the term. For example, Manning only considers communicative devices used to diffuse information to the public at large not those used to gather, analyse and then disperse such data/information throughout a police department. Such information diffusion to the public through the external network of police communications has expanded greatly since the advent of the Internet and the profusion of police websites.

In 2000, about 5 to 6 per cent of criminal justice agencies maintained sites registered with search engines. One use of the Internet involves the posting of crime information for citizens. For example, police use their department's website to show maps, diagrams, statistics, and pictures. In June 1997 the FBI placed some 16,000 pages of case files on the Internet and plans to post a total of 1.3 million pages. The rationale for such case file posting is seen as part of a freedom of information service to public requests for such information. Other uses of the Internet in the US in particular include posting the names and offences of sex offenders in several states. Also, websites feature people who are delinquent in their child support payments and provide search engines to find arrestees' home addresses in Philadelphia and San Antonio.

Furthermore, some departments use the Internet, email, and visuals for information and educational purposes. The San Diego and Chicago police have created elaborate videos for distribution to publicize their community policing programmes. The Chicago police have a large media budget for advertising on the radio and television, preparing and distributing their tapes to neighbourhood associations and the media.

Moreover, the Hartford (Connecticut) Police Department has provided computers for community groups to access crime reports and other data. Hence, distribution of low-grade police information that had previously been imparted through newsletters, handouts, adverts, or meetings can now be done via such websites and citizen-accessible terminals (as in Hartford and Chicago). San Diego has the capacity to distribute warnings to local areas (of tornadoes and other disasters) via e-communication, faxes, and telephone and can alert officers via email on their laptops.

It is clear that such 'communicative technologies' have allowed for greater direct contact with the public and hence greater sharing of certain types of police-related information publicly as well as internally within the organization. Such communication technology has also created newer, more efficient forms of communication among officers. However, Manning (2003) notes that emails are generally not favoured within police departments for direct orders or commands, even when available, because of the lagged or temporal feature of the communication. That is, messages might not be read, and another rule must be created and enforced requiring acknowledgement or response to emails. However, email communication, as well as that afforded by cellular or digital phones, does have its advantages. Chan's (2001) study in Australia showed that IT has facilitated information sharing among officers, accountability, and improved communication, resulting in a more cooperative and positive work atmosphere.

Apart from information diffusion to the public communicative technologies can be used for crime investigation, analysis, and prevention.

As is apparent in Figure 6.1 the communicative technologies are used extensively for the investigative function and consist mainly of database-type technologies that are used for a host of different policing purposes. Several examples are listed on the matrix ranging from CAD systems to data-warehousing designs like the 'Knowledge Management Centre' (KMC) based at the Hague as part of EUROPOL (2006). This Centre functions as a knowledge repository and international search facility for policing expertise.

Volume crime by its very nature relies heavily on databases. Systems like CRIS used in the UK and CRISP used in Australia by the Queensland Police Service, and others like COPLINK (the Connect module in particular) in the US, function in a similar manner to record and manage large amounts of data concerning everyday crime.

It will also be apparent from Figure 6.1 that 'Data Mining' (Firestone 2005) as a communicative technology falls somewhere on and over the arbitrarily drawn boundary (see broken-dotted lines) that separates the investigative and analysis functions of policing technologies. This indicates that data mining can be put to an investigative use as well as for crime analysis, and even crime prevention. For example, the Dutch police have used DataDetective since 2001 to match and mine crime databases (DataDetective 2006).

Thus, all the broken-dotted lines on the matrix represent the relative nature of these conceptual distinctions and serve to show the fluid flexibility of where the boundaries can be drawn, in that data mining, along with other technologies like GIS-based 'MapInfo' type systems, straddles and stretches across some and often all three policing functions of investigations, crime analysis, and crime prevention. However, whilst such boundary blurring does occur across operational policing contexts it should not be lost sight of that, as our classification system makes clear, any policing technology has one primary technological function it excels in, be it to communicate information, visualize it, or reason with it. Therefore, the policing technologies listed in Figure 6.1 are located in the 'matrix space' that indicates the nature of their primary contribution to police investigations, analysis, or prevention but are not solely restricted to this use.

For major crimes some sort of 'analysis' function (see Figure 6.1) in relational databases is of primary concern to not only record and manage crime data but also to link and track similar crimes (eg HOLMES 2, ViCAP, VICLAS, HITS, etc). Specialist software such as ARGOS is used in combination with other databases by various police services to keep track globally of crimes like paedophilia.

As noted previously, the CSPS developed by the CBAU of the Royal Newfoundland Constabulary, is one such example. CSPS is essentially an analytical tool that is used to suggest viable lines of inquiry for investigations (House 1997).

Systems like this do not solve crimes; police officers will always have that task. However, relational databases like CSPS, HITS, and so forth help police to focus on an investigation based on the systematic development of information that is already in the possession of the police.

An interesting example of such focusing associated with the CSPS system is reported in Adderley and Musgrove (2001) concerning the originator of the system, who had property stolen from his car. He used CSPS to profile likely suspects. The system produced a list and the 'top' five suspects were investigated. The offender was found to be the suspect ranked third.

In relation to crime prevention technologies there are no particular specialist programs as such but rather the adaptation of existing technologies that are customized for crime prevention purposes. For example, the '5Is framework' (Ekblom 2003) in the UK is a good example of such technological adaptation to crime reduction. The framework is a practical tool for transferring and sharing crime prevention knowledge. The 5Is stand for intelligence, intervention, implementation, involvement, and impact. The 5Is framework is organized as a sequence of stages which emphasizes the merging of evidence and experience—of the crime problem, the context, what works, and how to realize it. This often requires the involvement of a range of different people. The five stages illustrate the type of 'good practice' knowledge which can be captured and shared under each of the '5Is' noted above. Ekblom (2003) provides the following description of each stage.

- *Intelligence*—gathering and analyzing information on crime and disorder problems and their consequences, offenders and *modus operandi* causes of crime, and (with longer-term, developmental prevention) the 'risk and protective factors' in young children's life circumstances associated with later criminality.
- *Intervention*— blocking, disrupting, or weakening those causes. The interventions cover the entire field: acting through both civil prevention and traditional justice/law enforcement, addressing both situational and offender-oriented causes, and tackling causation at different levels—

immediate 'molecular' causes of criminal events, higher-level causes in communities, networks, markets and criminal careers, and remote 'upstream' causes influenced by manipulation of risk and protective factors in children's early lives.

- *Implementation*—converting the intervention principles into practical methods that are customized for the local problem and context targeted on offenders, victims, buildings, places and products, on an individual or collective basis, planned, managed, organized and steered, monitored and quality-assured, with documentation of inputs of human and financial resources, outputs, and intermediate outcomes assessed for ethical issues.
- *Involvement*—mobilizing other agencies, companies, and individuals to play their part in implementing the intervention, or acting in partnership, because crime prevention professionals must often work through or with others, rather than directly intervening in causes of crime. In both cases specifying: who were involved, what broad roles or specific tasks they undertook, how they were alerted, motivated, empowered or directed (eg by publicity campaigns, financial incentives), how a broadly supportive climate was created in the community, and how hostility was reduced.
- *Impact*— nature of evaluation (how the project was assessed, by whom; whether this was a reliable, systematic, and independent evaluation; and what kind of evaluation design was used), impact results (what worked, how), cost-effectiveness, coverage of crime problem, timescale for implementation, and impact process evaluation (what problems/trade-offs were faced in implementation, how they were resolved at each stage), replicability (which contextual conditions and infrastructure are helpful, or necessary, to successfully replicate this project—or particular elements of it—at each of the 5Is stages), learning points—both positive and negative (what to do, what not to do).

Such customization of existing technologies for more proactive crime prevention activities often falls under the banner of problem-oriented policing (Tilly 2002) or community policing projects. For example, since the early 1990s the Swedish police have changed their work practices to be more 'proactive', 'which, in Sweden, is called "problem oriented policing" or "community policing"'. (Borglund 2005: 3).

One of the advantages of communicative technologies is the presumed time saving for other tasks in policing, for functions like crime prevention. For example, freeing up of patrol time in order to provide opportunities for problem-oriented and community-policing crime-prevention activities. However, research has found technology only provided marginal gains in uncommitted blocks of time for patrol officers (Welsh 2002). Moreover, what little time was saved did not translate into more crime prevention-type activities in this study. Welsh (2002: 130) argues that 'these are lost opportunities for preventing crime and strengthening police–community relations, among other (non-crime prevention) aims that problem-oriented and community policing, especially the latter, espouse'.

Finally, as this review of various communicative technologies makes clear, relational databases are the main technological systems that police organizations rely on so heavily, especially for investigative purposes and the subsequent analysis and prevention of crime. Given this heavy reliance Puonti (2004: 148), along with other researchers, makes a very important observation about the use of databases when she notes that 'the problem with databases is that they are easily filled up with everyone's material, they are not selective enough, and they are very difficult to use when they contain so much information (Brown and Duguid 2000: 112)'. Similarly, Bowker (2000) argues that a database is increasingly seen as an end itself rather than as a working archive that is robust and flexible enough to work as a tool for a diverse group of users.

In operational policing practice, this fundamental problem of the non-selective nature of database accumulation is further complicated by the fact that, at some point, someone has to make a choice about what is relevant and important and what is not for the crime situation under scrutiny. Hence, vital information can be left outside the database because someone makes the wrong choices. This potential pitfall is magnified if the person doing the selective culling is inexperienced in the area or lacks proper training and supervision.

Visualization technologies

This second group of technologies where the primary function is to visualize data, information, intelligence, and knowledge is a rapidly developing domain, especially since the development of GIS. GIS technology and its use in policing through various crime-mapping applications, as presented in the previous chapter, is growing exponentially.

At the conceptual level this area of technology is based on similar yet discrete fields of academic study: research and application known as 'information visualization' and 'knowledge visualization'. Both these approaches are grounded in similar theoretical assumptions regarding various features of how humans process information and knowledge (Tergan *et al.* 2006). Whilst both information visualization and knowledge visualization focus on how we as humans use our innate abilities to process visual representations effectively, they differ in the manner in which each domain uses these abilities. For example, in the information visualization field the aim is to explore large amounts of abstract data, text-based in the main, in order to derive and/or develop new insights into how to make the stored data more accessible. In contrast, the field of knowledge visualization is concerned with helping individuals to assess, structure, and manage their knowledge in order to facilitate knowledge transfer and sharing as well as stimulating knowledge creation among other things (Eppler and Burkhard 2005).

Concept mapping

One of the visualization tools that both information visualization and knowledge visualization have in common is what is termed 'concept mapping'. There are a number of complementary terms used like mind maps, conceptual diagrams, and visual metaphors, which are related in similar ways to the idea of a 'concept map' which can also be used for knowledge construction and sharing (Eppler 2006).

The notion of 'concept maps' has a long tradition in educational research and practice as a tool for knowledge visualization (Novak and Canas 2006). The cognitive structure of concept maps is generally hierarchical in nature with more general abstract concepts at higher levels and more specific concrete concepts subsumed at lower levels under higher order concepts. However, this traditional concept map method of representing knowledge has been criticized because of its strict adherence to this hierarchical representational scheme. Hence, such hierarchical techniques are not well suited for visualizing knowledge in less structured ways while at the same time remaining comprehensive in manner (Tergan *et al.* 2006).

This shortcoming of traditional concept mapping has been overcome with the development of advanced computer-based concept-mapping tools. There are a range of visualization software programs which can support the knowledge-based work of police and law enforcement that provide for various forms of visual representations of knowledge other than in a hierarchical scheme.

Furthermore, the types of visualization software programs available allow for multimedia representations of information and knowledge as episodic events, images, animations, simulations, and hyperlinks to video clips, audio clips, and other content stored in digital repositories. The dynamic nature of such visual representations significantly enhances the ability to put together not only concept maps of relevant related data and information to show criminal and/or terrorist network connections but are also foundational to the development of 'knowledge maps'.

The term 'knowledge maps' refers to the use of a concept map to represent the knowledge of a domain expert (Coffey *et al.* 2006). There are many aspects of an expert's domain knowledge that can be represented comprehensively in an integrated format which can be used to develop Expert Knowledge Systems (EKS) (eg the Decision Support System (DSS) devised by Keppens and Schafer (2006) for crime scenario construction that was presented in the previous chapter). This DSS modelled an example of a possible money-laundering scenario using an integrated format to represent knowledge in the system in terms of events, states, and causal relations between events and states.

As the matrix in Figure 6.1 indicates there is a wide variety of visualization software programs available to police and law enforcement practitioners. We have already covered under the area of Intelligence Surveillance Systems (ISS) in the previous chapter a number of these technologies like CCTV and PMI software. As can also be seen in Figure 6.1 visualization technologies extend from the investigative function into the 'analysis' function and to a lesser extent to the 'crime prevention' function. Furthermore, visualization technologies extend into the domain of reasoning technologies across all operational policing functions as well. In fact, visualization technologies can be considered as foundational applications for many reasoning technologies.

With regard to the 'analysis' function this is closely linked to visualization technologies. This is because, as discussed previously, the power of the visualization process allows patterns of criminal activity and trends to be easily accessible and understandable. Hence, it is little wonder that policing models like problem-oriented policing (POP) and intelligence-led policing (ILP) rely so heavily on this visualization form of technology for crime analysis and crime prevention. Therefore, some of the visualization software programs to do with crime investigation and analysis will be elaborated on briefly in the next section.

Visualization software

The 'Analyst Notebook' (AN) is one example, along with other software applications, that offers sophisticated visualization techniques such as link analysis diagrams and network analysis diagrams. The AN software also includes a range of charts, for example, time-line analysis charts to see how related events unfold, and transaction-pattern analysis charts to examine significant activity between subjects under investigation.

A similar example is the Timeline Analysis System (TAS) which helps crime analysts to examine large amounts of information visually by illustrating cause-and-effect relationships. This system graphically depicts relationships found in the data in order to identify trends or patterns (Pliant 1996).

The 'Watson' software is an integrated suite of investigative case-management and intelligence-analysis software and is similar in many respects to the AN. It is also used by several UK and Australian police forces, many US police departments, and various UK and US government departments, according to the sales literature for the software (Adderley and Musgrove 2001).

Where Watson differs from other programs on the market like DataDective is in its particular emphasis as a case-management tool that enables senior investigative officers (SIOs) to maintain a structured and methodological approach to the investigation.

Watson, according to Adderley and Musgrove (2001), was used in the notorious UK murder case of Naomi Smith to harness HOLMES data and produce links between people, vehicles, crime scenes, etc. The output could be displayed visually with a search query like 'is there any relationship between Mr X and Mr Y?'. Using this investigative search process a large number of attributes could be matched at one time. While detectives were utilizing this information, forensic scientists were able to make a breakthrough by identifying

115

the offender's DNA through adopting an investigative strategy of testing all males between 15 and 28 years old. Watson, together with HOLMES, identified a reduced set of males to be tested initially and, during the testing phase, the offender's DNA matched one of the first 15 samples.

With visualization technologies producing such impressive results it is clear that they are here to stay within the realms of policing and law enforcement and are big business for the companies who develop such programs. For example, the 'i 2' company that owns the 'Analyst Notebook' has marketed their AN visualization suite of software successfully to UK, Dutch, Swedish, and New Zealand police forces, as well as some state police services in Australia, and some legal departments in the US, including the FBI (Adderley and Musgrove 2001).

A rapidly expanding development in the area of crime analysis and intelligence is Social Network Analysis (SNA). Since 9/11 in New York and the London bombings by 'home-grown' Islamist extremists on 7 July 2005 the importance of understanding and tracking the social groupings of persons who are of interest to police and security services by conducting a comprehensive network analysis has been highlighted.

SNA is a mathematical method of 'connecting the dots' (Krebs 2006). It allows the user to map and measure complex, and sometimes covert, human groups and organizations such as terrorist cells or organized crime groups. One software application for SNA is 'InFlow' (2006) which, according to its developers, is being used in both business and counter-intelligence circles (<http://orgnet. com/>). The notion of network analysis and related software applications of visualization technologies will be examined further during subsequent chapters in the applications section of our book.

GIS-based software

The use of GIS and spatial data analysis techniques is another rapid area of growth in policing and law enforcement (Althausen and Mieczkowski 2001), particularly in the variety of software applications for mapping crime (Weisburd and Lum 2005). Again, visualization is the key process for managing the knowledge generated though crime-mapping applications. Moreover, GIS is a prominent tool for analysing criminal behaviour and the impacts of the criminal justice system in general on society (Andresen 2006). According to NIJ (2006), classical and spatial statistics have been merged to form more comprehensive approaches in understanding social problems from research and practical standpoints. These methods allow for the measurement of proximity effects on places by neighbouring areas that leads to a multi-dimensional and less static understanding of factors that contribute to or reduce crime across space. As stressed by researchers such as Ashby and Longley (2005) and Clarke (2001), it is important that law enforcement keeps pace with new developments in effective crime prevention and crime investigation.

Another specialized area within policing that uses GIS is concerned with visualization technologies that can be grouped together under the umbrella term 'Geographic Profiling' (GP). Several products are on the market like 'Dragnet' developed by the Centre for Investigative Psychology (IPC) at the University of Liverpool in England; 'Predator' developed by Godwin, a former student at IPC; 'Crime Stat' developed by the National Institute of Justice in the US; and 'Criminal Geographic Targeting' (CGT) developed by Rossmo. These are typical software applications of GP (Ramsland 2001). Originally it was the innovative work of Rossmo (1997) that popularized GP. Rossmo was a police officer with the Vancouver Police Department in Canada who was able to demonstrate the utility of his CGT software. This technology is a form of spatial crime analysis that investigates the likely spatial behaviour of an offender by examining information which can be found at known crime site locations such as encounter/apprehension sites, murder sites, body/property dump sites.

The innovative aspect of the CGT system reverses the approach of environmental criminologists who use sociological information such as the offender's background, peer influences on criminal careers, and so forth to describe, understand, and control criminal events by focusing on the relationship between an offender's home and the crimes he or she commits. The spatial analysis that results from looking at an offender's various crime sites is a three-dimensional plot where the height represents the relative probability that a given point is the residence or workplace of the offender and this information is then overlaid onto a local map.

The system was initially validated on several solved crimes locating the offender's residence in the top 5 per cent of potential locations (Adderley and Musgrove 2001). Since then CGT has had a number of successes. For example, in one sensational case investigative systems at the time suggested that the killer could have lived within a 2,000 square kilometre area. The CGT software developed by Rossmo indicated that the search should be restricted to a 10 square kilometre area. The offender, who lived within that restricted area, was subsequently captured and convicted. CGT was also used in a case where a 16-year-old girl was murdered and another left to die. The software suggested a search area of 1.5 square kilometres from a possible area of 26 square kilometres. The offender who lived within that search area was arrested and charged with the offences.

However, not all uses of CGT or any other GP software meets with such success all the time. The key difficulty with using geographic-based software programs lies in the fact that there must be a series of crime sites to work with and they must be reliably linked to the same offender. These conditions are not always possible and hence the accuracy of the software is dramatically reduced.

Finally, as can be seen in Figure 6.1, GIS technologies such as 'MapInfo' and other GIS-based crime-mapping products are used predominantly for crime analysis and crime prevention. GIS and crime-mapping software has been extensively covered in Chapter 5 so, rather than go over familiar ground again, a case study of the use of crime mapping is presented below in relation to its use in Norway using a problem-oriented policing approach.

Case Study: Crime mapping in Oslo

The Norwegian Police Directorate set out a new strategy for crime prevention and community safety to be implemented by all Norwegian police districts in 2002. The strategy is based on a problem-oriented policing approach and was initiated because of the Parliamentary White Paper no 22—*Police Reform 2000*. The police directorate defines problem-oriented policing as a work philosophy. The intention of this philosophy is to make the police more efficient in crime prevention and crime reduction (CPOP 2005; Goldstein 2003).

Problem-oriented policing has since been taught and implemented on several maturity levels in police agencies. There are 27 police districts in Norway, each headed by a chief of police. The chief of police has full responsibility for policing within his or her district. Oslo police district is the largest with more than 2,300 employees. The Norwegian Police Directorate manages all police districts and reports to the Department of Justice. Since 2002, the directorate has arranged seminars and workshops for top-level police management in the theory and practice of problem-oriented policing.

An example of GIS and the use of crime-mapping software in Oslo, the capital of Norway, is illustrated in Figure 6.2. In the centre of Oslo, pickpockets were becoming very active. Application of GIS revealed a pattern, and one of the hot spots was identified. The hot spot was the restaurant Uncle Donald in University Street. Police officers contacted the owner of the restaurant as well as the doormen. A problem-oriented approach was taken based on 'situational crime prevention' principles (Center for Problem-Oriented Policing 2005) to reduce the opportunities for pickpockets. Hangers for clothes were installed underneath each guest table as well as a wardrobe for guests' clothes. In addition, policing information was shared with people employed in the restaurant. As a consequence, the number of pocket thefts dropped in this restaurant.

As a result of the successful situational crime prevention further GIS-based analysis showed that pocket thefts were also prominent in or near other restaurants in the city as a whole.

With reference to Figure 5.2, our GIS maturity model, it is apparent that a number of levels were involved in this crime-mapping analysis. That is, visualization of both internal (level I) and external (level II) data as well as internal communication (level III) and external communication (level IV) with city authorities resulted in alternative patterns simulations (level V), and identification of optimum actions (level VI), and establishing partnerships (level VII) initiated problem solving. Figure 6.3 presents this GIS-based analysis of the 'hot spots' identification process based on crime-mapping data.

Restaurants became important partners in this crime prevention initiative and similar strategies used by restaurants, as presented in the case study in Figure 6.2 where they

Figure 6.2 Crime mapping applied to pocket theft in Oslo

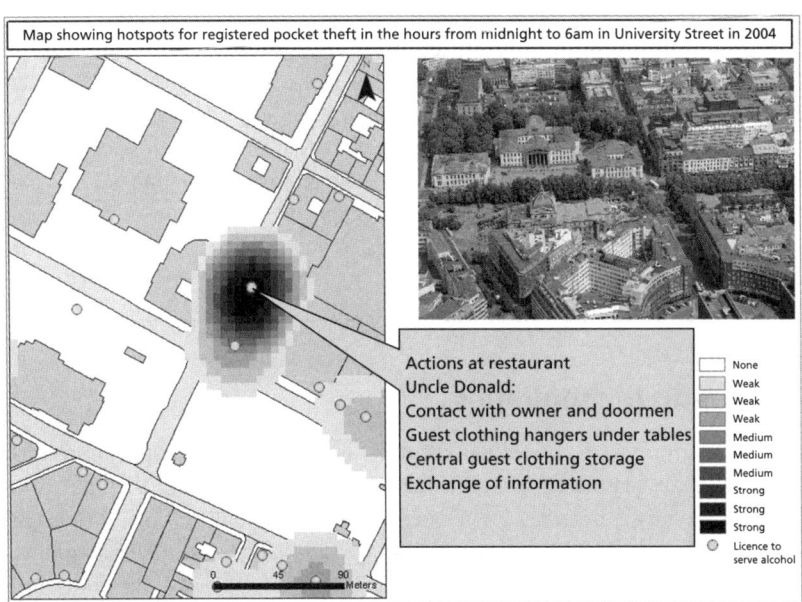

Figure 6.3 'Hot spots' of pocket theft in Oslo

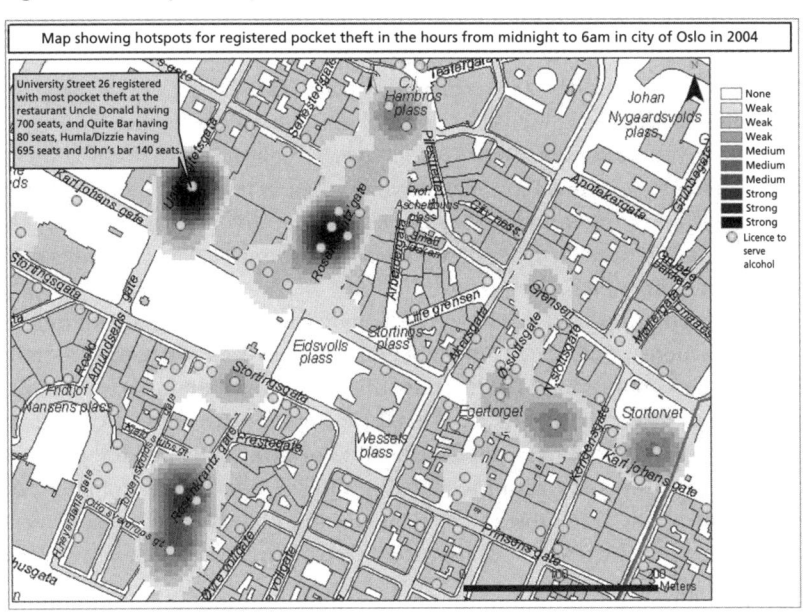

opened wardrobes and installed hangers under guest tables, dramatically reduced the number of pocket thefts city-wide in Oslo.

In terms of the notion of 'GIS maturity' introduced in Chapter 5 it is evident that the Oslo Police District has reached maturity level VII. Other police districts in Norway are found at lower levels. One reason for the variation in maturity is the variation in population density. Oslo, being the capital and the largest city in Norway, with a population of 550,000 inhabitants, will typically have more geographically concentrated crimes than other police districts. In other words, the geography of different police districts in a country will to a large extent determine the value and utility of using a GIS approach like crime mapping.

Reasoning technologies

This third group of technologies revolves around software applications that mimic human reasoning at some level. As can be seen on the matrix in Figure 6.1 there are overlaps at the boundaries with visualization technologies. In fact, visualization technologies can be considered as foundational applications for many reasoning technologies. As discussed previously the notion of 'concept mapping' is central to the way in which humans reason. Technological advances allow very sophisticated digital concept maps to be developed as well as other similar conceptual reasoning applications such as diagrammatic and graphical representations, and self-organizing maps can be generated with appropriate software. Several statistical packages like Smallest Space Analysis (SSA)[3] also allow data to be scaled in a multi-dimensional way to produce sophisticated graphical plots of the crime characteristics of offenders.

In the investigative domain there are several applications that specialize in specific areas like offender/criminal profiling (Cope 2003). Such profiling applications operate more like expert systems, in that they involve making inferences about the likely characteristics of an offender or criminal based on a detailed analysis of their crimes.

Other profiling-related databases use a neural network and data mining to carry out a more sophisticated linking activity than traditional databases (Strano 2005: 2). This application of artificial intelligence and data-mining technology is a research project by the Italian Neural Network for Psychological Criminal Profiling (NNPCP) that has been developed to overcome the limitations other profiling programs have with investigating single crimes. Most profiling software is only really applicable to 'serial' crimes like homicides and rapes where there is a series of crime scenes that are linked to the same offender(s) rather than a single crime scene.

---

[3] See Merry and Harsent (2000) article on the 'interpersonal dimension of burglary' in Canter and Alison (eds) *Profiling Property Crimes*, for an example of the use of SSA.

The outputs of the system comprise 24 investigative areas and 200 specific types of information which are used to draw the offender's psychological, psychopathological, and motivational profile. This data is constantly being loaded into the NNPCP system to make it more precise and statistically efficient in reducing the margin for errors. Furthermore, during a crime scene inspection a police officer can use a laptop to connect to the dedicated website for the neural network and generate a possible profile very quickly.

The domain of reasoning technologies extends into the other operational policing functions of crime analysis and crime prevention. For example, there are a number of systems that serve as intelligence analysis tools for policing and law enforcement. Many of these crime analysis systems use neural networks to solve problems by developing associations between information objects and then comparing known information objects with unknown objects. (DataDetective 2006)

This ability of computers to mimic human reasoning is the basic enterprise of the field of AI and its related sub-disciplines of DSS (Decision Support Systems) and ES (Expert Systems), and is a rapidly expanding area in a range of disciplines, especially medicine and the biological sciences, to identify and treat different diseases.

Often there are spin-offs and crossovers to other areas of professional activity where applications in one area have potential in another. For example, medical biological research has developed sensors to detect the presence of odourless and colourless deadly nerve gases like tabun and sarin, which were used in the Japanese subway terrorist attack. Because one or more gases could be used in a potential attack neural networks have been integrated into the sensors' in order to process the sensors' electrical signals and report on the levels and types of gases present (Marks 2006).

In spite of the large amount of research activity invested in AI, DSS and ES applications in several areas, policing is not in general one of them. Policing and law enforcement is lagging behind in basic foundational research necessary to develop sophisticated AI-related applications in its domain of operational practice. This issue will be looked at in more detail in Part 3, the applications section of this book.

Disruptive technologies

The term 'disruptive technology' was popularized by Harvard Business School Professor Clayton Christiansen to refer to those technologies that bring radical change by introducing a new way of doing things (Wormeli 2005). Disruptive technologies are often the cause of changes in business leadership as new and more flexible companies emerge to take advantage of these newer technologies. Such smaller innovative companies are not tied to past traditions about the way things are done. Occasionally, major companies get beyond the inertia of their own procedure-bound processes and policies and manage to reinvent themselves and use new technologies to develop whole new business models.

When this notion of 'disruptive technologies' is applied to the realm of policing and law enforcement it is not only the disruption caused to an organization by changes in the way things are done which is of interest. Equally important is the impact such technologies have upon society which policing organizations need to consider. As Chan (2003: 656), quoting Postman (1992), reminds us 'every technology is both a burden and a blessing'. Policing technologies are no exception and may in fact have greater potential to magnify both the blessings and the burdens for themselves and for society at large.

It is clear that some recent technological advances used in policing have potential to be 'disruptive' in both a positive and negative sense. For example, 'sensory enhancement' technologies, such as the passive millimeter imaging (PMI) devices discussed in Chapter 5, give to intelligence and surveillance systems (ISS) almost superhuman powers to see through buildings and walls. From a policing point of view this is a very positive outcome. However, a disruptive technology that changes the way police can carry out surveillance and gather intelligence in ways that were once invisible to them is also an 'intrusive' form of technology which can have negative consequences for innocent citizens. The 'tension space' that such technologies like thermographic imaging creates can be disruptive to a person's right to privacy. It remains to be seen from a legal point of view if such intrusions can strike the right balance between security and privacy.

With regard to police forces in general the term 'transformative technologies' used by Manning (2003) is similar in notion to the idea of a newer technology having the potential to be 'disruptive'; although not all technologies that have a transformative quality are by necessity disruptive. However, it is clear that any form of change in policing, technological or operational, faces some strong opposition from an inherently conservative police culture. Stroshine (2005: 182), in a review of IT innovations in policing within the US context, elaborates on this point by stating:

> The police culture is one that is very resistant to change. Even with the capabilities available today, some departments (usually smaller agencies) are reluctant to part with old practices, or simply don't have the budget to do so. The ability of most officers to utilize the available technology is also in question. Although it is becoming more and more common that at least some college education is a necessary condition of employment, many forms of data analysis (eg crime mapping) requires special expertise not readily possessed by most police applicants.... [also] law enforcement agencies at the local level, are ill prepared to deal with the burgeoning problem of cyber crime.

Furthermore, the concept of 'technological frames' was coined by Orlikowski and Gash (1994) to describe certain cognitive schemas about the nature, capabilities, and uses of technology that are shared by members of social groups.

Clearly technological frames about how helpful or constraining a given technology is to them vary between members of work groups. Hence, there is an ever present potential for 'tension spaces' to arise when a clash of technological frames becomes evident in a work context such as policing. In an Australian case study about e-Policing Chan *et al.* (2001) found evident of a clash in technological frames of the users of policing systems and the architects of such technology. The most important lesson learnt from this study was that 'giving police access to computers, increasing the range and quality of information that is stored electronically and automating what were previously manual processes will not necessarily increase organizational effectiveness or change how the business of policing is conducted by the agency' (Chan *et al.* 2001: 116).

In the final analysis, technology can only be as good as the people who use it. As Abt Associates (2000: 154) point out technology alone will not turn police forces into 'thinking' or 'learning' organizations. However, a police force can use technology to approximate a 'thinking' organization if it learns to manage the context of its police knowledge through the proper selection of appropriate technologies and the training of its staff. This is the high road to Knowledge Management.

Selecting technologies

It should be clear from this review of the wide and diverse range of technologies available for police use that choosing what class, capability, and combination of technologies are needed now and in the future to combat crime and terrorism is a challenging task for any police organization.

The matrix in Figure 6.1 is also designed to be used as a mapping tool to assist police organizations in selecting the right mix of technologies to suit their current and future needs. The construction of the matrix incorporates a 'sliding scale' concept which is illustrated in Figure 6.4 in terms of a hypothetical situation.

Imagine a medium-sized police agency that wants to upgrade its technological resources. It does a technology audit throughout the agency. A list is produced for the police executive. However, having a list of technologies in use in the police agency does not tell police managers much about what is the class or capability or combination they need to upgrade their technology resources. Figure 6.4 is helpful in order to obtain a more informed view.

First, the technology audit list is overlaid onto the matrix as originally shown in Figure 6.1 to give a 'big picture' appreciation of where their technological resources are likely to fit on the matrix.

Secondly, those technologies that the agency does have are mapped onto and cross-indexed in Figure 6.4 in the appropriate 'matrix space' that aligns with key policing and technological functions as shown.

Figure 6.4 Mapping tool for police technology audit

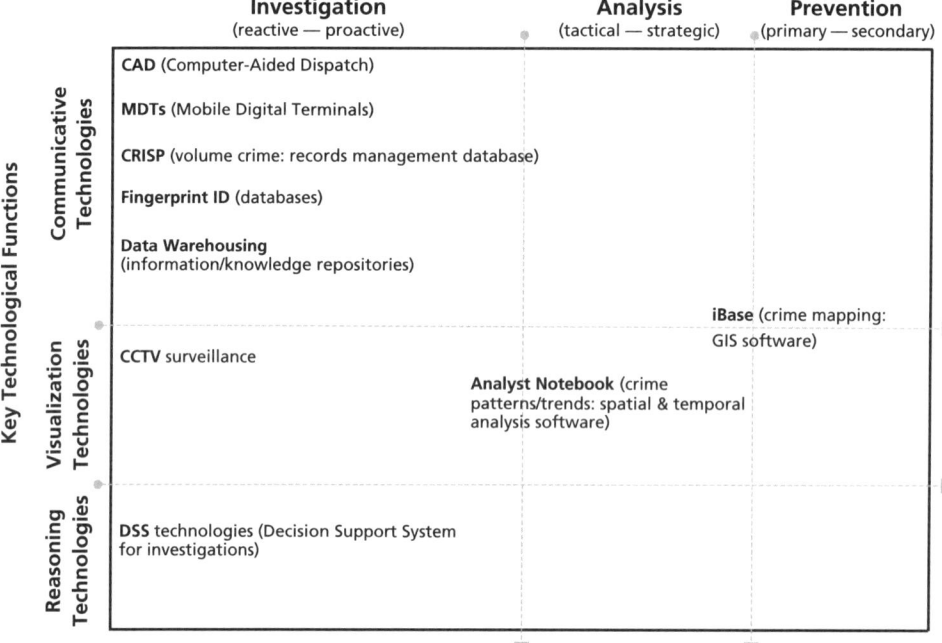

Hypothetical Map of Current Police Technology in a Medium-Sized Police Agency

Key Policing Functions

	Investigation (reactive — proactive)	Analysis (tactical — strategic)	Prevention (primary — secondary)

Communicative Technologies

CAD (Computer-Aided Dispatch)

MDTs (Mobile Digital Terminals)

CRISP (volume crime: records management database)

Fingerprint ID (databases)

Data Warehousing (information/knowledge repositories)

iBase (crime mapping: GIS software)

Visualization Technologies

CCTV surveillance

Analyst Notebook (crime patterns/trends: spatial & temporal analysis software)

Reasoning Technologies

DSS technologies (Decision Support System for investigations)

Key Technological Functions

Thirdly, the boundary markers (broken-dotted lines) between different matrix spaces become 'sliding scales' (see the insertion of a grey knob on each boundary marker). These knobs are used to adjust each boundary marker in order to resize the divisions between matrix spaces to fit the agency's current technologies into the appropriate locations.

As can be seen in Figure 6.4 the bulk of this medium-sized police agency's technologies are of the communicative type and are located in the investigative domain. Apart from the standard CCTV system for surveillance of public places there are only a few other visualization-type technologies for crime analysis and crime mapping which extend into the crime preventive domain. Given the size of the hypothetical police agency there is little need or budget for sophisticated reasoning-based technologies other than a DSS for running and managing serious and/or complex crime investigations.

Now that the agency has a current at-a-glance snapshot of where the strengths and weakness of its technological resources lie, police managers are in an informed position to make strategic choices as to where to invest more in technology. One of the other benefits of such a graphical mapping exercise is that it allows police managers themselves to be knowledgeable enough about the best mix of different types of technologies to plan for their future needs rather than being solely dependent on the 'techno-speak' of IT consultants and advisers. The adjustable Matrix Map puts police managers in charge of the technological support required for informed Knowledge Management.

Summary

This chapter introduced a new classification scheme or typology for police technologies based on a combination of key policing functions (investigation, analysis, prevention) and key technological functions (communicating, visualizing, reasoning).

The typology uses a matrix design to map out the type or class of technologies currently available in a police organization as well as relate such technologies to each of the key functions of policing.

With regard to the grouping of technologies according to their primary function on the matrix, various salient aspects of each of the three technological groups are presented below.

The first group, communicative technologies, represents those technologies whose primary function is to communicate data, information, intelligence, and knowledge both externally to the public, internally throughout a police organization, and globally to other police and law enforcement-related agencies. Such communicative technologies consist mainly of database-type systems that are used for a host of different policing purposes.

In particular, extensive use is made of relational database technologies to carry out the investigative function of policing and law enforcement in both reactive and proactive investigations. However, an important dilemma for police is a database's capacity to absorb vast amounts of information but often in a non-selective manner. This creates significant retrieval problems in terms of locating relevant and vital information.

The second group, visualization technologies, is where the primary function is to visualize data, information, intelligence, and knowledge. This is a rapidly expanding area with diverse applications for policing and law enforcement ranging from specialized analytical software to GIS-based crime-mapping software.

Visualization technology is based on extensive ongoing academic research in fields like information visualization, knowledge visualization, AI, and cognitive sciences. It is to be expected that other emerging technological applications will develop out of such research activity, which may be suitable for adaptation in policing and law enforcement in the future.

The third group, reasoning technologies, involves software applications that mimic human reasoning. Such reasoning technologies are closely related to visualization and make substantial use of digital concept maps to explore the way human beings reason.

As with visualization technologies there is a large amount of research activity focus on reasoning technologies in the discipline of AI and related DSS and ES applications. This is an area of future growth in policing as currently it is lagging behind in necessary basic foundational research needed to develop sophisticated AI-related applications for operational police and law enforcement practice.

In all three technological groupings—communicative, visualization, and reasoning—there is potential for new emerging applications to become 'disruptive technologies' since they can often cause substantial changes by introducing new ways of doing things. However, not all such technologies having a transformative quality are necessarily disruptive. It is clear that any form of change in policing, technological or operational, will have to overcome effectively the inherent conservatism of the 'police culture' as well as clashes in different 'technological frames' to realize its full potential.

One of the distinct advantages of this Matrix Mapping is that it allows police managers themselves to be knowledgeable enough about the best mix of different types of technologies to make informed judgements about their current and future technological needs, rather than being solely dependent on the 'techno-speak' of IT consultants.

However, the central issue for police executives with regard to technological resources is that they must first learn to manage the context of police knowledge and then engage in an informed strategic selection of appropriate technologies based on the class, capability, and combination of such technologies to suit current and future needs.

PART THREE

Police Knowledge Management: Using Applications

The third part of the book looks at the use of three police-specific Knowledge Management applications developed by the first author. Each of these applications addresses several issues in the investigative domain that are of ongoing concern for police and law enforcement institutions and agencies.

These applications are low-tech 'expert' systems which have the potential to be transformed into high-tech application programs. However, the inherent knowledge value lies in the execution of each low-tech application by individual police officers not in the sophistication of the software.

Finally, this third part concludes with a chapter devoted to setting out the practices and policies for the way forward in relation to meaningfully integrating 'Knowledge Management' as a diversified yet distinct field of endeavour that has much to offer the policing and law enforcement community.

'Cross+Check' System: Experiential Knowledge Reasoning Application

Introduction

This is the first of three practical application chapters on specifically designed technological systems for the management of police knowledge. The importance of these applications, presented over the next three chapters, rests on the fundamental distinction made in various ways throughout this book that information lies outside the brain but knowledge is to be found inside it. All three application systems seek to exploit the 'inside' or tacit knowledge in the head of experienced police officers.

This chapter introduces an experiential knowledge reasoning system called 'Cross+Check' which is designed to capture and utilize police expertise in the investigative domain. The rich diversity of the cumulative experience of individual officers contributes directly to the intellectual capital of a police/law enforcement agency.

The chapter begins by laying the groundwork for the Cross+Check (C+C) system by introducing the notion of 'police knowledge triangles' and their 'fuzziness' which form the knowledge base for this human reasoning system.

Next, the chapter looks at how utilizing the intellectual capital of police requires Knowledge Management applications at the top end of 'how-they-think' systems based on expert systems of human reasoning. An 'expert system' is a particular kind of knowledge-based system which is designed to handle real-world human problems that require human expertise to solve them. The underlying notion behind an expert system is that expertise built up over time by a person's (ie police officer's) tacit knowledge in a relatively specific domain (ie investigation) can be structured in such a way as to allow a less experienced person (ie probationary constable and/or new officer) to access this expert knowledge in order to assist them in solving a similar problem (crime).

The remaining sections of the chapter look at, first, the necessary component parts for a police/security investigation system to reason like an 'expert system'. Then, it looks at how the C+C model operates as a experiential knowledge reasoning system by capitalizing on the tacit knowledge of investigating officers as both 'expert' and 'user' of the system. Third, a case study of a murder is used to illustrate the operation of the C+C system as an additional application tool for use in police and law enforcement investigations.

Triangles of police knowledge

In Chapter 1, Figure 1.2 depicted the nature of police knowledge as comprising a multi-faceted structure along three main dimensions concerned with the cognitive, technical, and social aspects of an individual officer's tacit knowledge. Building on this understanding of a police officer's tacit knowledge a further way to conceive of police knowledge is as a triangle that consists of information which, when combined with an individual officer's experience, forms the basis of the understandings, insights, and judgements that constitute police knowledge.

Figure 7.1 illustrates this triangular structure of police knowledge within the context of a policing and law enforcement organization.

Figure 7.1 Components of police knowledge conceptualized as a triangle

Information
• includes data, and
• police intelligence

Experience
combination of elements:
• length of time in job
• diversity of jobs
• breadth and depth of training
• 'learning' personality

Police Knowledge Triangle

Knowledge
• tacit and 'know-how' knowledge
• explicit and 'know-what' knowledge
• resource 'know-where' knowledge

As can be seen each side of this Police Knowledge Triangle represents a different dimension of policing where information[1] and experience combine to complete the police knowledge side of the triangle.

The notion of 'experience' in Figure 7.1 requires further elaboration. Experience itself is a composite notion made up of many aspects. For our purposes within a policing context there are four significant aspects to our view of experience that are of interest. They are: length of time in policing; the diversity of jobs experienced in policing; the breadth and depth of police training; and the adaptability/flexibility of an officer's personality to 'learn' from their experience.

In relation to length of time in the job 'experience' should not necessarily be equated with duration of time served or age of an officer. It is often assumed that the longer a person has been in a job the more experience they have. This can be a very misleading assumption. Clearly, there is an optimum time that a person needs to be in a job to gain a competent level of experience, but beyond that optimum point there may well a diminishing return in terms of further knowledge acquisition through spending more time in that particular job. For example, a police officer with 20 years' experience in the traffic division where issues are more black and white, in terms of whether a driver was either speeding or not speeding, would find such 'experience' less valuable when policing a domestic violence situation where areas of grey abound. Moreover, the longer one spends in a particular job after having gained competence the more the risk of rigidity occurring where one stops learning anything new and just relies on repeating the same old patterns based on experience.

Hence, the second aspect of 'experience' concerned with the diversity of policing jobs acts as a moderating variable on the duration of time served in a job by highlighting the quality of experience gained through engaging in a range of different job experiences. Relying just on how long an officer has been in the job is at best a very crude measure of 'experience'.

In a similar manner the third aspect relating to the breadth and depth of police training is also a qualitative measure of 'experience' as such training helps an officer to think outside their own area of expertise.

Finally, the fourth aspect of 'experience' concerns an officer's ability to foster a 'learning' personality in the sense of being open and mentally flexible enough to learn from and apply their experiences to other policing situations and contexts.

With regard to the 'knowledge' side of the triangle in Figure 7.1, it is a cumulative and multi-faceted concept. For policing purposes the key ingredients of knowledge, apart from its tacit and explicit dimensions, are concerned with

---

[1] The concept of 'information' and its relationship to data and intelligence within a policing context were described in detail in Chapter 1 and illustrated in Figure 1.1. Thus, they will not be elaborated on further other than to note that the term 'information' is used here in relation to this notion of Police Knowledge Triangle in its broadest sense to include crime data and police intelligence.

'know-how','know-what', and the further type of resource knowledge (Tergan, Keller, and Burkhard 2006), 'know-where' to find the knowledge needed to do the job.

Therefore, from an organizational perspective police knowledge is a triangulated mixture of information and the cumulative experience of a diversity of individual officers both past and present who have contributed to the overall intellectual capital of the organization.

How this conceptualization of Police Knowledge Triangles works at the operational level of police practices is illustrated in the next set of four Figures, 7.2, 7.3, 7.4, and 7.5. The basis of operational policing in terms of the key processes of investigation, analysis, and prevention has been written about by Dean (1995) previously and is used as the conceptual framework for the embedding of the Police Knowledge Triangle (PKT), as will been seen in the following set of figures.

The circle in the figures represents the boundary or operational policing circle of a particular investigation that marks its sphere of reach and influence as dictated by the nature of the crime and the laws that apply to it. How this diagram works is as follows.

The 'information side' of a PKT is formed when an 'information line' (solid line on Figure 7.2) is drawn from where the information flows into an

Figure 7.2 Police Knowledge Triangles relating to key processes of policing

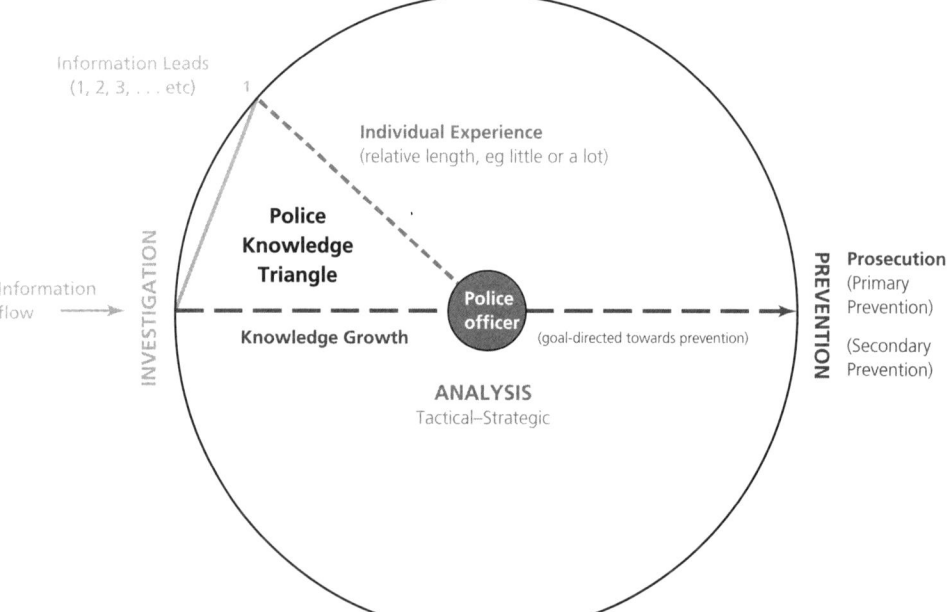

investigation to the particular 'investigative lead' the information suggests. Each such 'investigative lead' is drawn in a numbered sequence on the circumference of the operational circle starting at the nearest point to the information flow. With regard to the 'length' of the information line, it varies according to how far along the circumference it is placed. Hence, as more information in the form of 'investigative leads' is added these extra lines of inquiry 'move' the investigation along towards the prevention goal due to their 'extended' length (see Figures 7.4 and 7.5 below for a graphic depiction of this movement effect).

The 'experience side' (broken line on Figure 7.2) of the PKT extends from the 'central point of the police officer' doing the investigation to connect up with the particular 'investigative lead' being considered (ie analysed) by the officer. In relation to the 'length' of the experience line, it varies but only to a relatively slight degree in comparison to the extended length possible with the information lines as more lines of inquiry are added. For example, the next Figure 7.3 shows this relationship of length of experience in regard to a police officer with 'little' experience in the investigative process.

However, to sum up Figure 7.2, once the information and experience lines join up then an increase in knowledge results (ie understandings, insights, assessments, judgements, inferences, and so forth) and a triangle of such 'police knowledge' for the particular crime/security problem under investigation is formed by the intersecting lines. Hence, the area contained in the triangle represents the current state of the knowledge growth for this specific investigation so far as analysed and articulated by the investigating officer.

Naturally, as more 'information leads' come in and are added to the circumference of the operational policing circle more PKTs are formed and the knowledge growth increases towards solving or at least dealing more effectively with a crime/security problem.

The reason the knowledge growth (dashed) line is fixed along the horizontal plane from the 'Investigation' end to the 'Prevention' end is to underscore the fact that police knowledge is always goal-directed towards some type of prevention. At a primary level the investigation may result in a successful prosecution. Secondary benefits like a focused crime prevention strategy targeting certain crimes may also be an outcome from such knowledge growth.

Figure 7.3 illustrates the 'role' that experience plays in police knowledge. As can be seen, the experience line is shorter than that depicted in the previous Figure 7.2. Hence, it should be clear from comparing these two graphic representations that the previous police officer has substantially more experience than the one shown in Figure 7.3. Therefore, as the 'experience' line moves around the circumference of the investigation in relation to its linking up with extra 'investigative leads' as they are added its 'length' will only increase relatively slightly.

Such an effect is consistent with what happens with actual on-the-job experience, in that experience is gradually accumulated over years. Rarely are there sudden large growth spurts or jumps in experience for most people. There may

Figure 7.3 Police officer with 'little' investigative experience

well be sudden insights but this is not the same thing as experience. To become experience insights take time to be integrated into one's life by much practice and trial and error before they take root as a learned experience.

Therefore, the experience of a police officer doing an investigation is a relatively stable but not a fixed entity and is made up of the accumulated sum of time and diversity in the job, breadth and depth of training, as well as adaptability and flexibility of a learning personality.

Figure 7.4 offers a more developed depiction of the police/security knowledge growth process as several PKT's are formed as a result of further investigative leads coming into play in the operational cycle of a reactive crime.

Figure 7.5 is included to show how even in a reactive investigation there are proactive strategies that can be used. As can be seen in the bottom half of the operational cycle further PKT's can be formed in a variety of ways that can add value not only to the current investigation but also to secondary crime prevention measures. For example, the crime-mapping case study in Chapter 6 about a series of pocket thefts that took place in restaurants throughout Oslo in Norway is illustrative of this secondary prevention aspect. For example, a simple measure like designing the storage of coats and jackets differently in restaurants was all that was necessary to successfully reduce the number of these types of restaurant thefts throughout Oslo.

The essential point that the set of diagrams, from Figures 7.1 to 7.5, shows is how PKTs are the base of the 'expertise' of an officer through the cognitive integration of the constant flow of information and experience as they mesh and accumulate knowledge inside the head of the investigating officer. Thus, PKTs represent the knowledge base of the C+C experiential knowledge reasoning system which is presented in the latter section of this chapter.

Figure 7.4 Police Knowledge Triangles related to reactive operational strategies

Figure 7.5 Police Knowledge Triangles related to proactive operational strategies

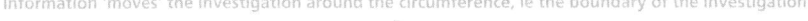
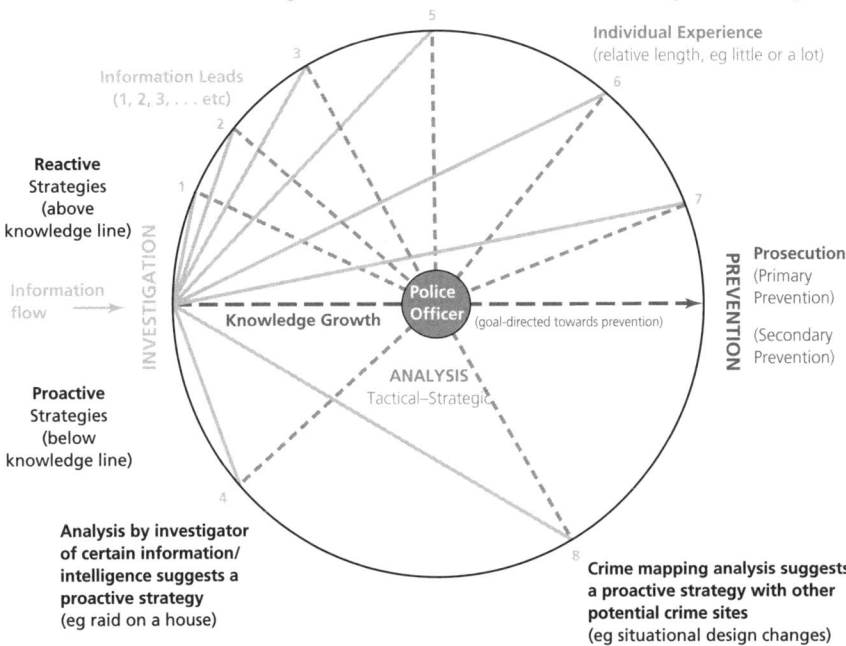

However, PKT like all knowledge bases can contain incorrect or incomplete information as well as personal biases and cultural assumptions. In fact police decision-making takes place in the real world which is a 'world of uncertainty' where as Zadeh (1990: 408) defines 'knowledge...[as] inexact, incomplete, or not totally reliable'. Clearly, police knowledge triangles by their very nature rely on information and intelligence derived from or subject to human reasoning and hence interpretation by individual police officers. We have previously discussed the role of the 'interpretation space' inherent in the discretionary power bestowed on police in relation to incidents of domestic violence.

However, the issue of central concern that needs to be addressed in relation to PKT is how to improve the reasoning ability of police decision-making, given that some of the information and/or intelligence received will be inexact, incomplete, or inaccurate to varying degrees. The next section provides some guidance to address this issue from the most unlikely sounding branch of mathematics 'fuzzy logic'.

'Fuzziness' of reasoning with Police Knowledge Triangles

Fuzzy logic was introduced to the world of mathematics in 1965 by Zadeh (Myers 1986). What is central to fuzzy logic according to Zadeh (1990: 407–408) is that:

> ...unlike classical logical systems, it aims at modelling the imprecise modes of reasoning that play an essential role in the remarkable human ability to make rational decisions in an environment of uncertainty and imprecision. This ability depends, in turn, on our ability to infer an approximate answer to a question based on a store of knowledge that is inexact, incomplete, or not totally reliable...In a nutshell, in fuzzy logic everything, including truth, is a matter of degree.

The formal name in science for fuzzy logic is 'multivalence' (Kosko 1993). The opposite of fuzzy logic is binary logic known formally as 'bivalence' or two-valuedness. Binary logic states that there are two ways to answer a question—true or false, 1 or 0, right or wrong, black or white.

Fuzzy logic is more realistic and recognizes that the world is a much more messy place where the boundaries between black and white, right and wrong are blurred or 'fuzzy' at the edges. In other words, fuzzy logic sees an infinite range of options instead of just two extremes. Fuzziness represents the shades of grey. Hence, as Kosko (1999: 8) succinctly puts it, 'fuzzy logic is reasoning with vague concepts'.

In terms of Knowledge Management fuzzy models provide a means to represent and adapt to inherent vagueness and ambiguities that can occur when applying a more traditional rule-based reasoning system to a specific situation (Klir and Folger 1988). The use of fuzzy logic in expert systems applications is an increasingly important area of research development (Saheb-Tehrani 2005). Compared to traditional expert systems, fuzzy expert systems take less time to develop, reduce maintenance cost, and improve user understanding (Cox 1995; Schneider *et al.* 1996).

One of the distinct advantages of fuzzy logic in the realm of police Knowledge Management is that it allows a person to get involved with science without knowing about mathematics, as you are able to compute with words and shades of grey rather than with algebraic equations. This 'computing with words' is the new 'multivalence' mathematics which lies behind fuzzy logic; however, you do not need to understand this maths in order to use fuzzy logic as the following case example of a murder investigation will make clear.

The important point for police to recognize is that the imprecise nature of police reasoning can be modelled using fuzzy logic to arrive at firmer, more accurate inferences about a crime and/or security investigation. Such fuzzy inferences can provide approximate answers to questions such as what course of action is more likely to advance a 'stuck' investigation; or what degree of risk does a potential terrorist suspect pose to the community?

A case study of the murder of a homeless person will be used to show how 'fuzzy logic' can enhance the reasoning process in such an investigation. A series of diagrams with the concept of a police knowledge triangle embedded within them will illustrate the 'fuzziness' of investigative reasoning in this murder case.

Case Study: 'Band-Aid' Murder

A homeless male was found dead in his room in an inner-city boarding house in a major city in Australia. He had 13 stab wounds inflicted by a large kitchen-type knife all over his body. A number were concentrated around his upper torso and head. Some of the head wounds penetrated his skull about half a centimetre in depth. Such penetration would have required considerable force to be used. The room was in a state of disarray with upturned furniture, drawers pulled out of cupboards, clothes strewn over the floor, and the window in the room was open with broken glass in a few of the panes. Clearly the room had been ransacked.

From interviews with other boarders in the house it was established that several personal items were missing from the victim's belongings, like his wallet, a small portable bedside radio, and so forth. It was further established that the victim had won some money recently 'on the horses' and had last been seen spending lots of money at the pub and getting very drunk, which was his custom. Most of the residents of the boarding house were alcoholics, and lived semi-vagrant lives as derelicts and hobos.

An odd feature of the killing was that the deceased had a Band-Aid applied to one of the 13 stab wounds. The Band-Aid was on one of the head wounds. Forensic tests

Figure 7.6 Murder case information presented in a 'fuzzy'

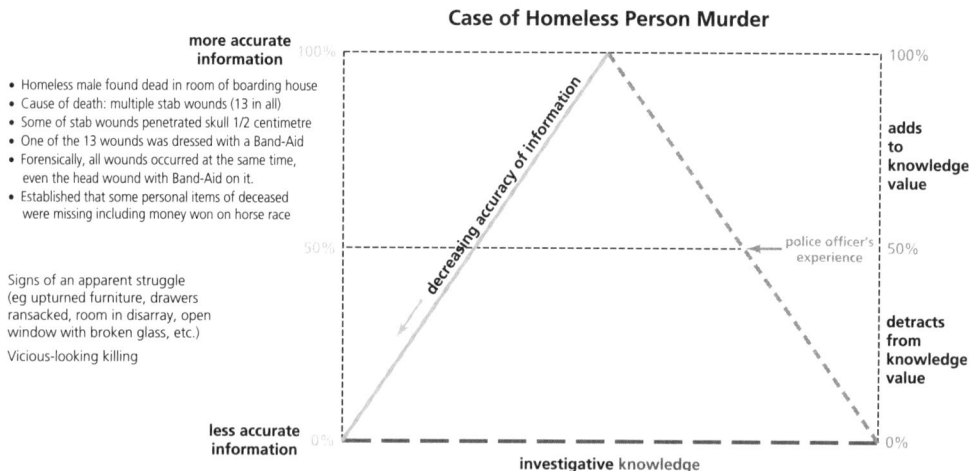

Case of Homeless Person Murder

- Homeless male found dead in room of boarding house
- Cause of death: multiple stab wounds (13 in all)
- Some of stab wounds penetrated skull 1/2 centimetre
- One of the 13 wounds was dressed with a Band-Aid
- Forensically, all wounds occurred at the same time, even the head wound with Band-Aid on it.
- Established that some personal items of deceased were missing including money won on horse race

Signs of an apparent struggle (eg upturned furniture, drawers ransacked, room in disarray, open window with broken glass, etc.)

Vicious-looking killing

more accurate information — 100%

decreasing accuracy of information

less accurate information — 0%

adds to knowledge value

police officer's experience — 50%

detracts from knowledge value

investigative knowledge

confirmed that all 13 wounds had occurred at the same time, including the one with the Band-Aid on it. In other words, it was not an old wound. Hence, the Band-Aid must have been applied by the killer at the time of the murder.

Figure 7.6 illustrates the case details of this murder crime scene in relation to the 'fuzziness' of the case information as represented in a PKT structure.

As can be seen, on the left hand side of the diagram the case information details have been arranged in a series of bullet point items. These information items descend in order of their relative accuracy. That is, items that are regarded as 'more accurate' in terms of factual information are 'clustered' nearer to the top of the percentage range and 'less accurate' or more inaccurate items of information are clustered closer to the bottom of the percentage range.

The 'police experience' an investigating officer brings to a case is a composed of several aspects, as discussed in the previous section with regard to the notion of PKT. Hence, 'police experience' has a sort of 'wild card' status in relation to investigations as it is unique to individual officers and therefore has potential to either 'add to' or 'detract from' the knowledge value for a particular investigation. The same applies to a team of investigators as each bring their own opinions, beliefs, biases, and judgements to any investigation, which is based to some extent on their cumulative years of police experience.

With regard to the homeless person murder case under examination a team of detectives was assigned to the case and a quick arrest was expected. After collecting all the pertinent facts and information a brainstorming session was held to toss around 'case theories' about the murder. Two options A and B emerged from this brainstorming session. Choosing between these two options is where 'fuzzy logic' comes into play.

The 'fuzziness' of each option can be expressed as belonging somewhere on a 'fuzzy' scale in terms of the likely range of correctness of the reasoning process used in support

Figure 7.7 Options—'fuzzy' inferences A or B ?

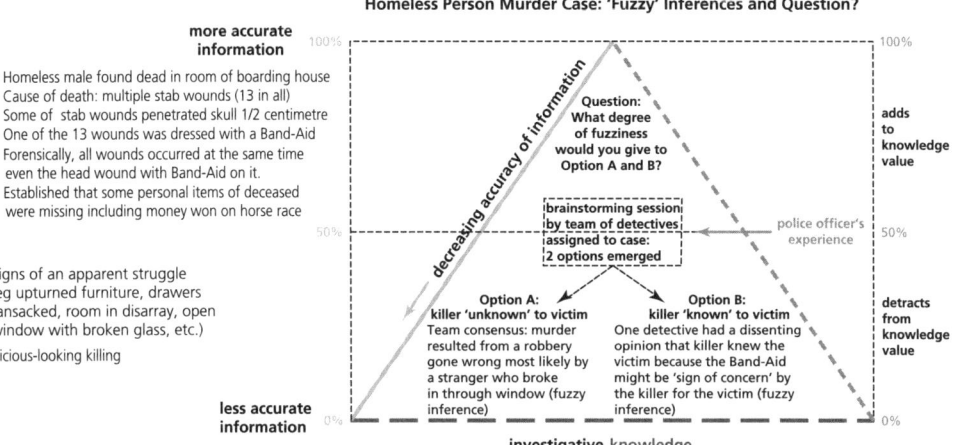

of each 'case theory' option. Figure 7.7 asks the question: how 'fuzzy' is the inferential reasoning process behind each case theory for option A and B?

As can be seen, a consensus emerged from the session (Option A: Unknown Killer) that in all likelihood the murder was the result of a robbery gone wrong by a stranger. This 'case theory' was based on the reasoning that whilst the victim had been drinking his winnings away in a public bar strangers would have seen the state he was in when he finally left for his room in the boarding house. Hence, the stranger could have easily followed the drunken victim to the boarding house and broken into his room via the ground floor window and attempted to rob him of his winnings. From the state of the room it would appear the victim was conscious enough to put up a fight and was killed viciously in the ensuing struggle with the killer.

The 'fuzziness' of Option A (likelihood of killer being unknown to the victim) can be plotted on the PKT for this investigation as shown in Figure 7.8.

Figure 7.8 Option A: 'Unknown Killer' fuzzy inference

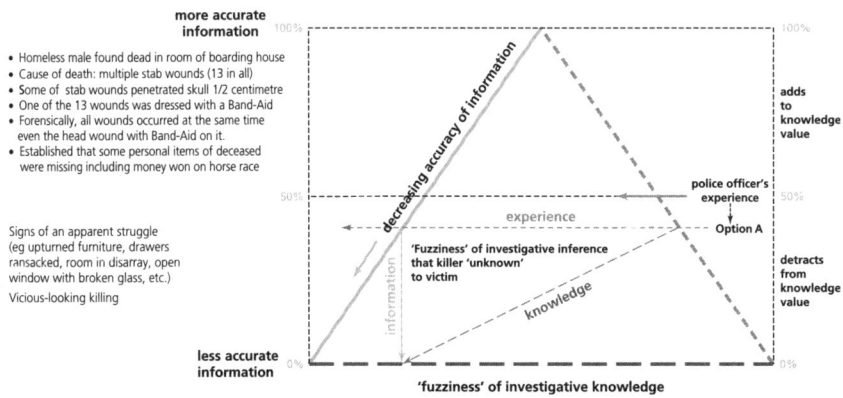

As can be seen the 'fuzzy' factor range based on this reasoning for Option A is plotted on the fuzziness scale of police knowledge (see bottom of triangle) as falling somewhere between a 20 per cent to 80 per cent likelihood of being incorrect. Thus, it should become immediately apparent that with such a wide 'interpretational' range the fuzzy inference that the killer was unknown to the victim presents a rather poor investigative lead to follow.

Option B (likelihood of killer being known to the victim) presents a better fuzzy range as shown in Figure 7.9.

Clearly, Option B's 'fuzzy' factor range of somewhere between a 40 per cent to 60 per cent likelihood of being correct gives better odds to the fuzzy inference that it is more likely that the killer was known by the victim.

As is apparent from the diagram the significance of the Band-Aid having been put on the victim by the killer offers a compelling argument that the killer was trying to 'undo' what may have been an unintentional killing. People put Band-Aids on a wound to stop it bleeding. Psychologically the killer was attempting to undo his action of stabbing the victim in a struggle to rob him. However, once the robber realized the stab wound was fatal and that his actions could not be undone then the issue becomes one of trying to avoid detection.

Hence, the killer attempts to throw the police off the track and misdirect the investigation by staging the crime scene to look like a mad vicious killer with no concern whatsoever for the murdered victim: in other words, the ruthless cold-hearted act of a stranger not that of a drinking buddy or acquaintance. The meaning of the 'Band-Aid' is the key to this investigation as Figure 7.10 illustrates with a comparative analysis of Options A and B.

It is clear from this visual analysis of the relative position and size that Option B is a more accurate and hence reliable inference to follow for this murder case. Option B has

Figure 7.9 Option B: 'Known Killer' fuzzy inference

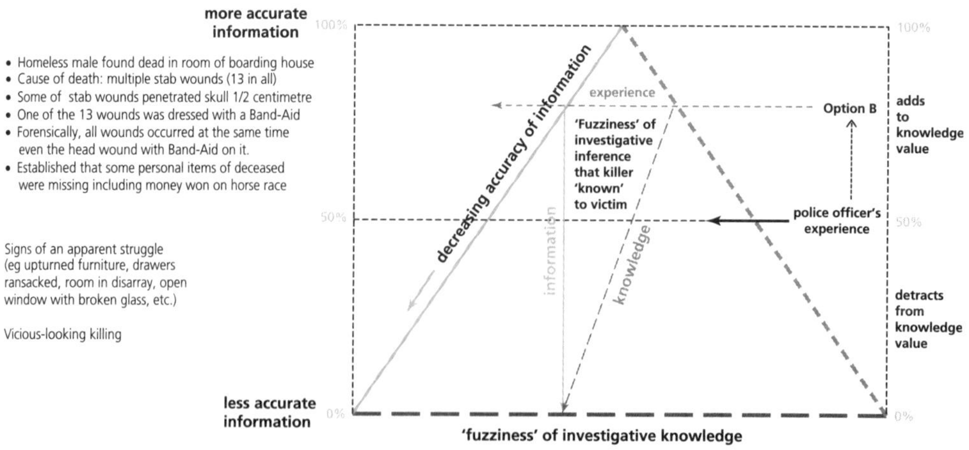

140

Figure 7.10 Comparative analysis of Options A & B 'fuzzy' inferences

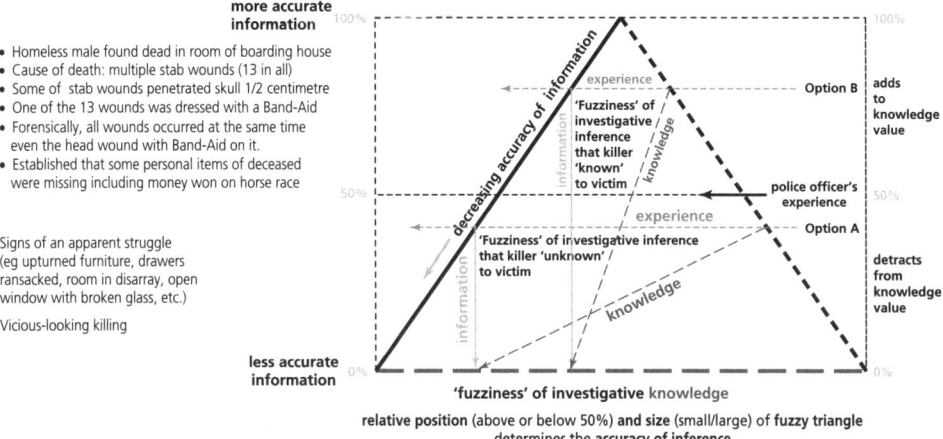

- Homeless male found dead in room of boarding house
- Cause of death: multiple stab wounds (13 in all)
- Some of stab wounds penetrated skull 1/2 centimetre
- One of the 13 wounds was dressed with a Band-Aid
- Forensically, all wounds occurred at the same time even the head wound with Band-Aid on it.
- Established that some personal items of deceased were missing including money won on horse race

Signs of an apparent struggle (eg upturned furniture, drawers ransacked, room in disarray, open window with broken glass, etc.)

Vicious-looking killing

more accurate information

less accurate information

'fuzziness' of investigative knowledge

relative position (above or below 50%) and size (small/large) of fuzzy triangle determines the accuracy of inference

more area above the 50 per cent line where the most accurate crime scene information clusters.

Furthermore, the experience of the investigator who suggested the Band-Aid held some significance for understanding the relationship of the killer to the victim (Option B) is also above the 50 per cent line where the odds are better than chance (ie a 50/50 bet) that the Band-Aid is significant. Hence, this fuzzy inference holds potential to add knowledge value to the murder investigation.

Outcome of 'Band-Aid' murder investigation

The investigator who suggested the Band-Aid might hold some significance for the crime as a 'sign of concern' for the victim was laughed at when he mentioned this in the brainstorming session. Other investigators in the team session made their own suggestions at his expense that maybe he should stop watching so many CSI shows and just concentrate on doing his job properly.

This particular investigator was so annoyed at being ridiculed by his peers that he set off on his own investigation. A few of the homeless boarders left a few days after initially being interviewed by the police to continue their itinerant lifestyle in other locations up and down the coast as well as interstate.

Fuelled by ridicule the lone investigator tracked and interviewed the few drifters who had moved on from the boarding house shortly after the murder. In an extended interview, he eventually managed to break down one of them who then ended up confessing to the murder.

The motive had been to rob the victim of his winnings. But the victim woke up from his drunken stupor when his 'mate' attempted to take his remaining money. A fight broke out and the killer grabbed a knife that was lying on the kitchen table and stabbed

141

the victim. When he realized what he had done he went to the bathroom cabinet, found a Band-Aid and put it over the fatal stab wound to show the victim he didn't mean to hurt him. However, when he realized the victim was really dead he decided to stage the crime scene as mentioned previously.

The case also demonstrates how police use 'case theories' (ie fuzzy inferences) like Options A and B in this investigation to reason with and figure out the possible motive and *modus operandi* of an offender. As Keppens and Schafer (2006: 204) point out the problem is 'not the fact that case theories are used at all, but rather the premature convergence to a single theory without proper consideration of alternatives'.

Such premature convergence on a particular case theory poses one of the greatest risks to the integrity of an investigation. Dixon (1999: 132) reinforces the nature of this risk, by pointing out in relation to police investigative practices that have led to miscarriages of justice, that:

> if any factor in investigative practice had to be nominated as most responsible for leading to miscarriages of justice, it would have to be the tendency for investigators to commit themselves to belief in a suspect's guilt in a way that blinds them to other possibilities.

LeBeuf (2001:15), in a report on criminal investigations and intelligence practices in relation to organized crime and cyber-crime for the Canadian Police College, underscores the point that 'the investigation community seems to be suffering from a quick action syndrome' where case theories are formed at a very early stage in an investigation. Once such hasty case theories are formed, as Greer (1994: 59) asserts, 'the tenacity with which the police have clung to their original view in spite of strong countervailing evidence' is truly astounding.

Therefore, what this murder case example shows is not only how police investigations depend on information which will vary in degrees of accuracy and completeness but also how fuzzy logic can be used to reduce the risk of 'premature convergence' on a particular line of inferential reasoning that police rely upon to develop their 'theories' about a case.

The next section takes up this use of police inferential logic (case theories) in relation to using expert systems as reasoning applications in policing and law enforcement.

Reasoning like an expert system: inferential logic

Our focus in this 'Applications' section of the book is concerned with stage 4 'how-they-think' systems (see Figure 2.2 in Chapter 2). Such 'thinking systems' are at the top end of KMT for reasoning systems developed by disciplines within the domain of computer science, predominantly within the AI community.

Artificial Intelligence (AI) is an area of computer science that studies how to make computers perform like humans. The AI field has two main objectives—first, to create intelligent machines and, second, to find out more about the nature of human intelligence (Charniak and McDermott 1985; Dale 1987).

The AI field is divided into three relatively independent research areas—that of expert systems, natural language, and robotics (Rauch-Hindin 1986). Expert systems are the most significant and practical application of these three branches of AI technology.

Expert systems are, as Sedbrook (1998: 19) points out, an 'attempt to clone human expertise to avoid geographical and time-based limitations of consulting with human experts'.

The terms knowledge-based and expert systems are sometimes used interchangeably in the literature. However, as noted previously in Chapter 6 in the section to do with reasoning technologies, there is a clear distinction between these terms.

Hence, expert systems are a particular type of knowledge-based system that is designed to handle real-world human problems that require human expertise to solve them. That is, expert systems use human-like reasoning processes rather than computational techniques to solve a problem in a particular domain.

The underlying concept of an expert system is that the expertise built up over time by a person's tacit knowledge of a relatively narrow domain is structured so that a less experienced person (novice) can access this expert knowledge in solving similar problems. In other words, the expert's knowledge is recorded so that the system can draw upon this to provide expert advice.

It has been estimated that there are over 12,500 expert systems deployed in manufacturing, medicine, and business alone (Sedbrook 1998) and the number of expert system development tools has been growing at about 16 per cent per year since the mid-1990s (Durkin 1996).

As Blum (1988) states there are two fundamental requirements for a 'system' to qualify as an 'expert system': (a) the knowledge is organized so that inferences can be constructed from it; and (b) there is a mechanism to infer expert guidance for a given situation. Figure 7.11 illustrates the eight key components or elements that make up an 'expert system' (Sagheb-Tehrani 1993) in relation to police use.

These eight elements are largely self-explanatory. What is important to understand from this diagram is how the central mechanism of an expert system lies in the three interdependent components of the Knowledge Base (4), the Database (5), and the Inference Engine (6) as shown enclosed in the larger rectangular box in Figure 7.11.

The knowledge base (KB) contains an expert's knowledge and methods of dealing with problems in the specified domain. The KB interacts with a database or series of related databases in order to derive the intended outcomes. However, it is important to note that the KB is a 'static' component although it gets added to as new knowledge is gained and processed via the Knowledge Acquisition Moudule (KAM) (2).

The database is a collection of data about objects and events on which the KB works. Hence, the database is more 'dynamic' than the KB as the state of the database is constantly changing as new data is updated.

Figure 7.11 Key components of an expert system

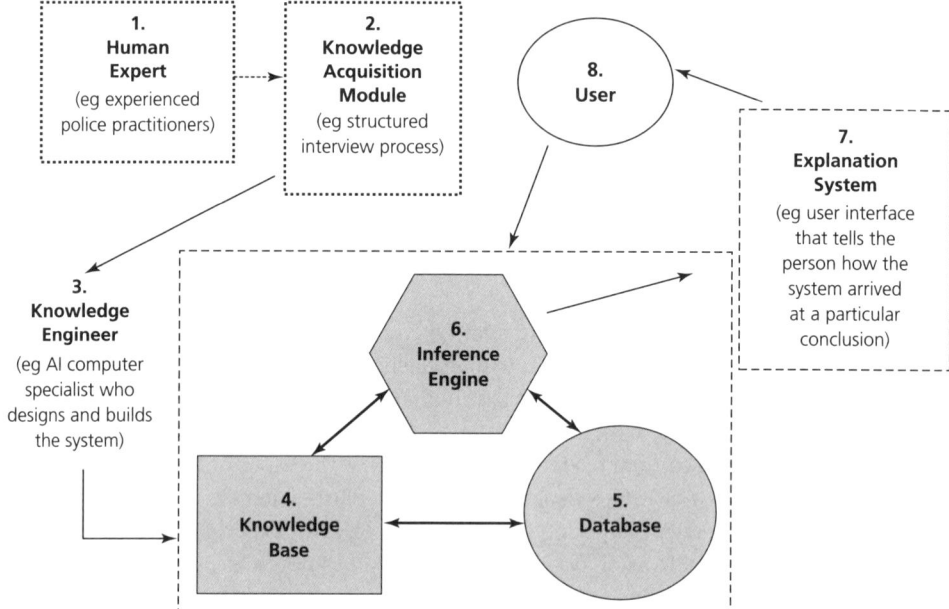

While the inference engine (IE) allows the user to draw inferences from the interactions between the KB and database and/or other interconnected databases, the IE navigates through and searches the KB to develop inferences that are consistent with the state of the database. The IE applies heuristics (ie rules of thumb) to guide its processing. Heuristics are normally defined in 'if this... then that' rules that are used to represent the 'knowledge' that has been extracted from experts.

Another element that is important to be aware of with expert systems is that they should have some sort of 'explanation system' (7) which tells the user how the system arrived at a particular conclusion. This is a useful component because it enables the expert system to explain its reasoning to the user and hence how the IE makes use of knowledge to come to expert conclusions (Hall and Kandel 1992).

Although the principles of an expert system are simple there are substantial difficulties with getting expert systems to work well. One such major difficulty is 'knowledge acquisition'. This is a key problem area or 'bottleneck' for building expert systems (Chen 1988).

The two most popular methods for getting 'knowledge' into an expert system are structured interviews and protocol analysis (Schank 1982; Cooke and McDonald 1986; Hoffman 1987). However, both are interpretative methodologies that depend on subjective interpretations. Therefore these knowledge acquisition methods require an interviewer with a good deal of experience to ensure the knowledge captured is as reliably accurate as possible given the subjective nature of extracting tacit knowledge and 'if this . . . then that' rules from an expert's head.

The main obstacle with an 'if this . . . then that' rule-based approach is not technological but human. That is, humans do not think in terms of rules.

As we have seen already a lot of the reasoning involved with policing is 'fuzzy' because it takes place under conditions of ambiguity, uncertainty, and sometimes danger, as well as being time intensive. In such a constantly changing and unstable environment an 'if this . . . then that' rule-based approach is very problematic.

An alternative approach to a rule-based system is to model the dynamic memory of experts. This approach relies on attempting to capture the mental processes of experts rather than inferring decision-making rules. Such mental models build expert systems incrementally and hence they become self-evolving expert systems with a capacity to learn.

Furthermore, with a self-evolving expert system the nature of the KB component of the system changes. In a conventional expert system the KB simply acts as a static container of the expert's knowledge, usually written in an 'if–then' rule format. However, in a self-evolving expert system the KB is a network constructed from objects and relationships which as Chen (1988) argues forms a Knowledge Space (KS).

Hence, when referring to a self-evolving expert system the term KS will be used to highlight the qualitatively different nature of this type of knowledge acquisition process as well as distinguish it from the more traditional KB of a rule-based expert system. We will take up this point further in the next section concerning the 'Cross+Check' System.

Cross+Check: experiential knowledge reasoning system

It is important to realize that a 'system' can be just about anything. That is anything we choose to regard (a) as a whole, and (b) as comprising a set of related components; and more formally a system, $S = (C, R)$, where C is the set of its components and R is the set of relationships (or interfaces) that combine them into a coherent whole. In computing the word 'system' is freely used to refer to all kinds of combinations of hardware, software, data, and other information, procedures, and human activities. An airline reservation system, for instance, comprises all those things, distributed and connected worldwide. At the other end of the spectrum, an operating system just comprises software components (*Dictionary of Computing* 2004).

As we have seen, the main idea behind an expert system is to transfer expertise from the expert to the computer so users can get specific advice from the computer to assist in solving a problem (Turban and Aronson 1998). In general the expert's role is limited to assisting the knowledge engineer in developing, refining, and testing the KB. Once the KB is up and running the expert is not involved in helping specific users. Nor are users are involved in maintaining the KB.

However, this need not be the case for every type of expert system. In fact, the type of expert system presented in detail here, known as the 'Cross+Check' (C+C) system for use in both criminal and civil investigations in policing and security as well as law enforcement in general, is designed to capitalize on the tacit knowledge of investigator as both 'expert' and 'user' of the system.

Hence, in this section of the book we will use the term 'Experiential Knowledge Reasoning System' (EKRS) rather than the commonly used acronym of ES (expert system) to refer to our computer-based but non-automated system where the knowledge worker (ie the investigating police officer) is both the expert that inputs into the system as well as the user of the knowledge generated by the system.

We use the EKRS acronym not only to identify the C+C system as logically belonging to the field of 'expert systems' as a sub-class in its own right, but more importantly to distinguish the innovative aspect of the C+C system, in that it uses an investigator's experiential knowledge to 'reason like an ES' rather than the C+C system being a machine-based ES for its entire operation.

The C+C system was designed by Dean (2003) as a low-tech, computer-based, human reasoning, KM system for conducting investigations. The purpose of the C+C system is to generate logically derived inferences systematically for analysis and prioritization into investigative leads and strategies to find and develop evidence as well as plan and manage the overall investigation. To achieve this aim the C+C system utilizes different informational sources about a crime/incident case by applying the tacit knowledge expertise of an individual police officer and/or law enforcement/security practitioner in order to infer and reason through investigative leads and strategies to assist in dealing effectively with and/or solving a case. The C+C system as an EKRS is applicable to reactive and proactive investigations and can be used successfully with single as well as serial crimes.

The C+C system utilizes a mental modelling approach to acquiring the tacit knowledge of an investigating officer, rather than inferring decision-making rules, so that incrementally each individual police officer uses the C+C template forms to build their own self-evolving Knowledge Space (KS) component within the C+C EKRS.

As mentioned previously, Police Knowledge Triangles (PKTs) are the basis of a police officer's expertise which is acquired over time and hence represents this pool of tacit knowledge that is drawn upon by individual officers to build their self-evolving KS which is central to the C+C System EKRS.

An investigating officer uses a set of four specifically designed templates or C+C forms that act as the input component (Knowledge Acquisition Module or KAM) of the C+C EKRS. These template forms are designed to be non-prescriptive and hence afford maximum flexibility for the investigating officer to reason with the information contained in them in order to develop well-grounded inferences about the case being investigated.

One innovative aspect of the C+C system is that the investigating officer acts as both 'expert', in the sense of inputting his or her tacit knowledge into the system, and 'user' of the system to reason through an investigation using the set of C+C templates to derive a 'Knowledge Outcome Space' (KOS) that forms the basis for prioritizing a list of investigative leads and strategies to follow up on within the case. Furthermore, using the C+C EKRS teaches an investigating officer to reason systematically using well grounded inferential logic based on the set of differential information sources that the officer uses to input into the system.

Operational framework of 'C+C' model: visual analysis

The core operational innovation of the C+C EKRS is its ability to integrate and visually analyse the inter-relationships between four qualitatively different sources of information, those of:

- *police/security information* which in the C+C model represents the collected police/security knowledge about the incident, operation or case under investigation;
- *descriptive information* which in the C+C model represents police/security knowledge that is gathered from witnesses, informants, members of the public, interviews with suspects, intelligence reports, and the like and captured in various police relational databases used for conducting background checks, crime pattern analysis, and so forth;
- *diagnostic information* which in the C+C model represents socio-cultural and psychological/psychiatric knowledge about those aspects of the incident, operation, or case under investigation that may be of relevance to analyse and examine in more detail like the nature of the offender–victim relationship, psychological patterns/behaviours or motivational themes revealed in the way the crime was carried out, and/or socio-cultural/political elements especially in terrorist incidents; and
- *research information* which in the C+C model represents scholarly knowledge about policing/law enforcement and security that has been published in various journals, books, and so forth on particular crimes and/or aspects of criminal and terrorist behaviour that can be related to the incident, operation or case of current interest in an investigation.

This C+C model operates as an experiential knowledge system by utilizing these four types of qualitatively different information so that the user can develop inferences from such informational sources and then test the veracity of those inferences by cross-checking them through a process of visual analysis against each level of information in the system. This systematic process of reasoning also allows an investigator to place a relative weighting on developed inferences and hence to prioritize investigative leads and strategies.

Figure 7.12 presents a graphic model[2] of the inter-related nature of these four informational sources arranged as levels of analysis in a diamond-shaped pattern that forms the four 'operational quadrants' for the model which together constitute the conceptual scaffolding of this operating framework of the C+C EKRS.

Figure 7.12 Operational framework of C+C Model

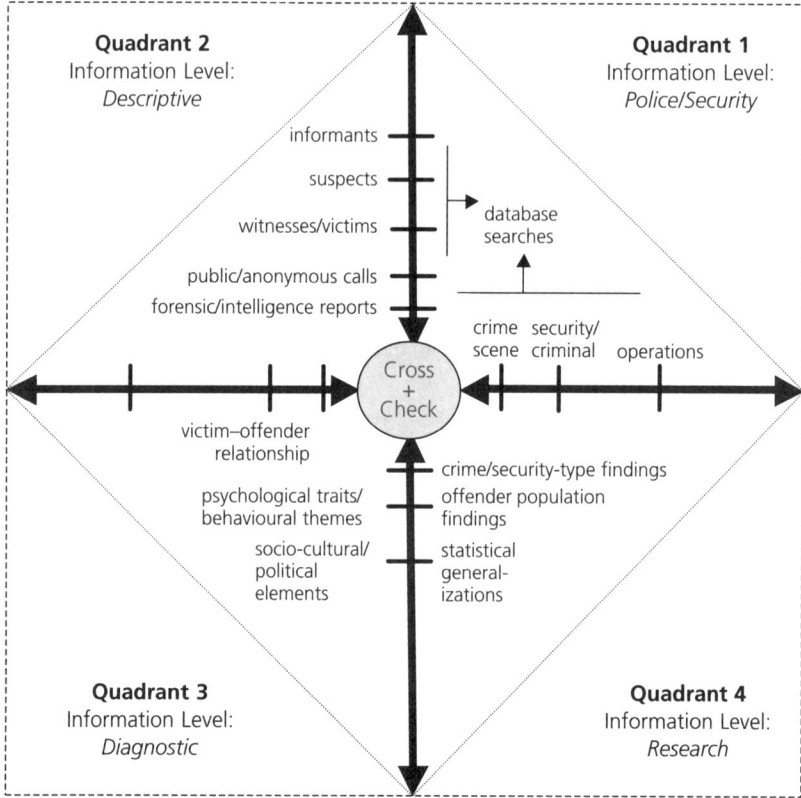

---

[2] The conceptual basis of this graphic model has been written about extensively in another publication and hence will not be expanded here. The interested reader is referred to Dean (2005).

'C+C' model: component elements

The potential information subsumed that is available under the four main quadrants of the C+C model, as illustrated in Figure 7.12, is recorded in a checklist format on a set of six specially designed 'investigative forms' that act as templates. The design of each 'template' uses the same structure to capture information for each of the four quadrants in the C+C model as well as capturing the tacit knowledge of the investigating officer's inferences and analysis of the information on the remaining two forms.

Each of the four quadrant templates is designed as an A4-sized page on which three columns are drawn using the presentation software 'PowerPoint' from the Microsoft Office suite of programs. The 'three column' structure of each of the informational quadrants (Investigative, Database, Diagnostic, and Theoretical) is as follows:

- first column contains a 'checklist' of elements to consider at each level;
- second column is where various 'characteristics' are recorded for each level;
- third column is where the 'tentative inferences' are recorded for each level.

A sample page (PowerPoint slide) of this three-column structure for descriptive information (Database Quadrant) about an incident, operation, or case is shown in Figure 7.13.

The only variation on each of these four quadrant 'template' forms is in the directional flow of the recorded information on the various forms. The information flow changes on some forms from right to left and then left to right. The reason for this change in recording direction is to ensure that when the four information quadrants are laid out side-by-side (see Figure 7.14) and joined up then the four 'tentative inferences' columns will always be aligned together in the middle of the adjoining four forms to form what is termed the 'Knowledge Outcome Space' of the C+C system.

The remaining two investigative forms that make up the template set are the 'Knowledge Outcome Space' (shown in Figure 7.14) and an 'Investigative Priorities' form which records the results of the visual analysis depicted on the 'Knowledge Outcome Space' form. A blank copy of the 'Knowledge Outcome Space' form is illustrated in Figure 7.14 to show how the main four investigative forms are arranged on the page.

As can be seen the fifth investigative form (Figure 7.14) represents the blank 'outcome space' where the tacit knowledge of investigative officers is recorded by them as they draw connecting lines to form a visual 'Cross+Checking' analysis of the incident or case based on the third column of 'tentative inferences' which they cut and paste into each quadrant.

This analysis is carried out by 'aligning' all of the four quadrant forms together on one sheet of paper. The process involves photocopying each of the previous four forms and taping them together in the order shown in Figure 7.14.

Figure 7.13 Example of 'descriptive' information form

'Cross+Check' System Copyright: Dr. Geoff Dean	**2nd Quadrant : 'Descriptive' Information Form** any attachments secure behind form	Case Reference No: Investigating Officer:
2. 'Descriptive' Information Checklist **WITNESS(S) STATEMENTS** Record address, sex, age, ethnicity, marital status, occupation, activity at the time of the crime, witness under influence of drink or drugs, any other specific pieces of information from or about witness(s). **MEMBER(S) OF PUBLIC** Any specific pieces of information about offender, crime, security issue regardless of whether or not it is considered relevant at the time. **INFORMANT(S)/ANONYMOUS CALL** Any specific knowledge/information eg tip-offs, etc, about offender, crime, security. **VICTIM(S) STATEMENTS** Record address, sex, age, ethnicity, marital status, occupation, activity at the time of the crime/security issue, victim under influence of drink or drugs, any other specific pieces of information from or about victim. **FORENSIC/PATHOLOGY REPORTS** Any specific information/evidence eg fingerprints, DNA tests, toxicology, dental records, blood spatter patterns, time of death (if applicable) etc. **INTERVIEWS:** **VICTIM'S FAMILY, FRIENDS** Any specific pieces of information about victim as described by family members, friends, work colleagues, acquaintances, and others regardless of whether or not it is considered relevant at the time. **SURVEILLANCE/INTELLIGENCE REPORTS** Any specific pieces of information about suspects, the crime, victim, security issue gathered from surveillance/intelligence operations eg phone taps, tracking mobile calls, database searches, etc. **OFFENDER(S) CHARACTERISTICS** Sex, age, ethnicity, height, accent, build, hair length, hair colour, facial hair, tattoos, distinctive smell, any other distinctive physical features, use of a disguise, offender under the influence of drink or drugs. Any other specific pieces of information the victim and/or witness(s) described about the offender regardless of whether or not it is considered relevant at the time. **ANY OTHER ELEMENTS**	→ **'Reported' Characteristics** →	**Tentative Inferences**

Figure 7.14 Example of 'Knowledge Outcome Space' information form

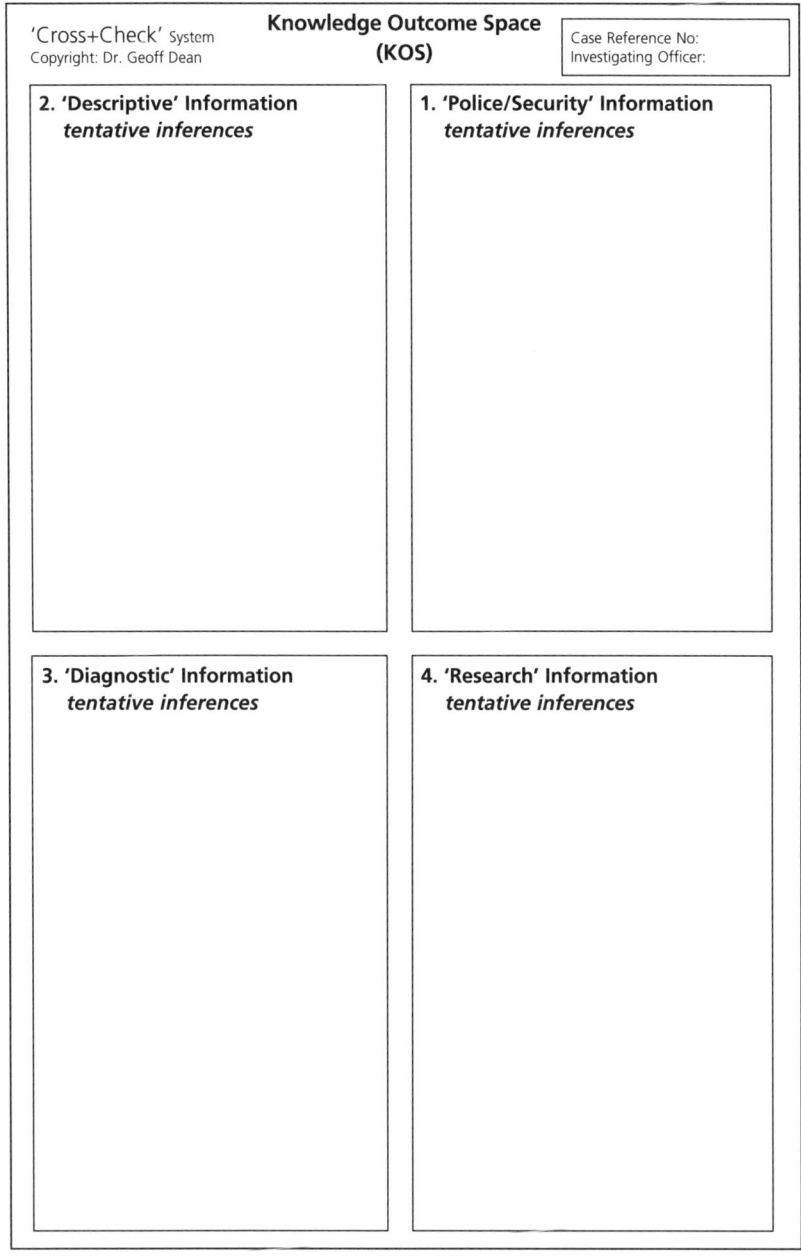

| 'Cross+Check' System
Copyright: Dr. Geoff Dean | **Knowledge Outcome Space**
(KOS) | Case Reference No:
Investigating Officer: |

2. 'Descriptive' Information
tentative inferences

1. 'Police/Security' Information
tentative inferences

3. 'Diagnostic' Information
tentative inferences

4. 'Research' Information
tentative inferences

Hence, what you end up with is an A3-sized piece of paper which is a hard copy version of the 'Knowledge Outcome Space' (KOS).

The reason for using photocopies of the previous four investigative forms is that the process of using a pencil or felt-tip marker to compare and connect up various items of information on this A3-sized KOS can become very messy. Hence, there may be several iterations of this analytical process before the investigating officer arrives at what they consider to be their final knowledge captured on the 'outcome space' product.

The sixth and final form in the C+C system is the 'Investigative Priorities' form which, as noted previously, records the results of the visual analysis depicted on the 'Knowledge Outcome Space' form. These investigative priorities, in terms of leads to follow and/or potential strategies to use, have logically and systematically been derived by the investigating officer from a sustained and reflective analysis of the connections as visually diagrammed on the previous KOS form (Figure 7.14).

'C+C' model: special class of expert system

The C+C system shares the same structural characteristics as a traditional expert system (see Figure 7.15) but where it differs is in some of its uniquely innovative design features. For example, the 'human expert' functions as both the 'knowledge engineer' of what is inputted into the system as well as the 'user' of

Figure 7.15 Component elements of 'C+C' EKRS

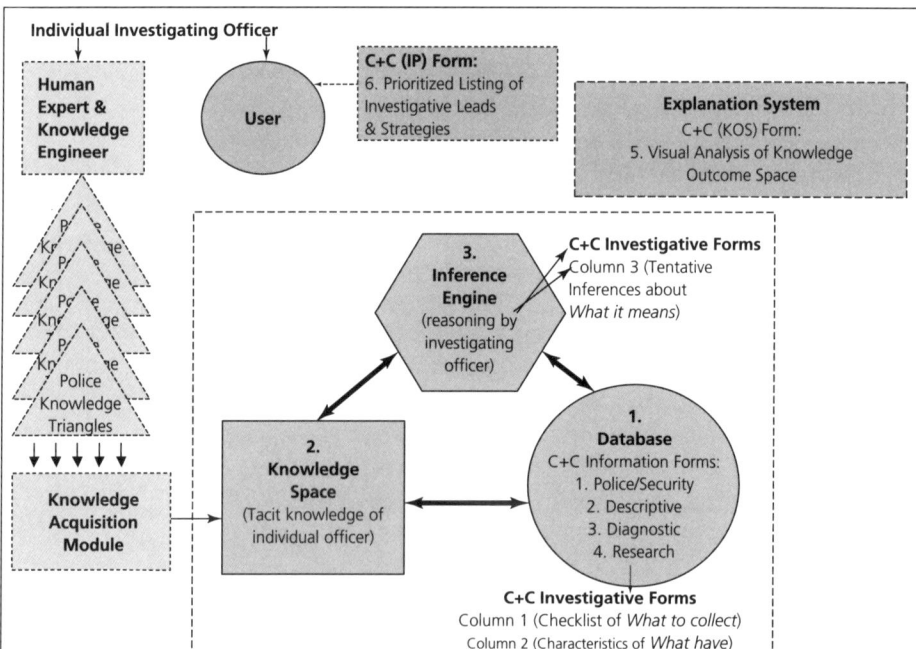

the system's knowledge output. Furthermore, the set of six investigative information forms that comprise the core elements of the C+C model represent and interact in various ways as the 'database', 'inference engine', and 'explanation system' for this type of EKRS.

How the 'three-column' structure of each of the four investigative information forms as well as the other two forms (the 'KOS' form and the 'Investigative Priorities' form) represent and interact as the component parts of the 'expert system' shell of the C+C model is shown in Figure 7.15.

As can be seen the three main components of an expert system, as illustrated in the earlier Figure 7.11, Database, Knowledge Space (Base), and Inference Engine, still stand in the same relationship to each other in this C+C EKRS. The essential difference between the two Figures 7.11 and 7.15 is that the 'Human Expert' is both the 'Knowledge Engineer' in the sense of building their own self-evolving 'Knowledge Space' for the system as well as the 'User'. As is also evident in Figure 7.15 the human expert is responsible for inputting their 'Knowledge Acquisition' based on the cumulative wisdom of years of developing and refining their understanding of PKTs.

Once the information contained on the four C+C template forms is entered into the appropriate first two columns on the templates then this 'Database' can be further utilized by the investigating officer for reasoning purposes by applying their tacit knowledge understandings (Knowledge Space) to develop tentative inferences (Inference Engine) about what they have collected so far in the investigation in relation to police/security, descriptive, diagnostic, and research information on the incident, operation or case and in terms of its relevance, significance, and meaning to the investigation.

Finally, the 'Explanation System' component of the C+C EKRS brings all the tentative inferences together in the KOS form for further visual analysis. The end result of this visual analysis is the production of a prioritized list of investigative leads and strategies. The value of the 'Explanation System' is that it allows the investigating officer to be able to track and show the logical steps they took from the original information they collected about some aspect of the investigation right through to the inference they may have drawn about its significance and how they have weighted such significance in terms of the overall investigative priorities to follow up on leads and develop strategies for the investigation. Having such an explanatory system ensures not only that inconsistencies and differences in informational sources are cross-checked but also that no stone is left unturned.

How this C+C EKRS works in practice will become self-evident in the case study presented in the remaining sections of this chapter.

Case Study: Murder in hotel room

The C+C system is applied retrospectively to an investigation of a solved murder case involving a 57-year-old Chinese male found in a hotel room in Singapore in 1998.

This case is used as a training example of how the C+C system operates as an 'expert knowledge' system.

Brief description of crime scene

A bloodstained Chinese male victim was lying prostrate on the concrete floor of the toilet in the hotel room. The victim was dressed in long brown trousers and white short-sleeved shirt. His hands and legs were bound behind with strips of torn bed sheets. The knots looked tight and secure. His face was covered with adhesive tape and mouth stuffed with a piece of cloth. His face was black from the lack of oxygen. In the hotel room the bed was messy, there was a rolled-up Chinese newspaper on the bed, along with some shoe prints on the top left corner of the bed sheet. There were several bus tickets scattered on the bedroom floor. On the bedside table there was a Nokia mobile phone hands-free earpiece.

In the initial investigation at the crime scene, all the hotel staff were interviewed and hotel records perused. The victim had been a regular at the hotel for the last four months. None of the hotel staff were able to provide any information on the case. However, an elderly chambermaid told detectives that she had bumped into a couple in the corridor who seemed to be walking towards the victim's room. But she was short-sighted and could not give a detailed description of the couple except that they spoke Chinese with a foreign accent. Security cameras were not installed at the hotel nor were any security guards employed by the hotel. Subsequent interviews with the victim's friends and workers at his coffee shop did not yield any information relevant to the case except that the victim liked to mingle with females from China.

Initial input into investigative forms

The investigating officer initially inputs into the set of four different investigative forms (police/security, descriptive, diagnostic, research). This inputting is done by the officer working through the three columns on each form from the first 'checklist' column, which acts as a guide for the sort of information to capture on each form (this will vary depending on the type and nature of the crime or incident being investigated); to the second 'characteristics' column which records the specific details for the crime/incident and relates to a checklist element; and finally to the third 'inferences' column where the investigating officers use their experience and expertise to record their initial tentative thoughts about the likely links and meaning of particular characteristics of the crime/incident.

An innovative aspect of the C+C EKRS forms is that, for most investigations, the type of information recorded in a police information management system is contained on only two of the four investigative forms used in the C+C system: those of 'police/security' and 'descriptive' information.

The 'diagnostic' form is often regarded as the domain of police psychologists and is usually only sought for particular types of crime that give some indication of psychological disturbance in the offender by what he/she says and does at the crime scene. However, by not including some 'diagnostic' information in the investigative collection cycle a valuable source of knowledge is left out of an investigation even into relatively simple and uncomplicated crimes/incidents which can help to focus the investigation. The other investigative form that is generally not included as a distinct source of information in most investigations is the 'Research' form. Again, this is seen as the domain of academics and other specialized experts like crime analysts or intelligence officers who may have a research interest. Some of the research-based knowledge about specific crimes and criminal behaviours is generalizable to other situations when due caution is exercised, and should be again considered as a valuable source of information to 'cross check' against the other three investigative forms.

For the murder case under review each of this set of four different investigative forms is presented in turn below (see pages 156–160).

Visual analysis of Investigative Forms

The next two investigative forms 5 and 6 are at the heart of the C+C reasoning system. Form 5 is where the visual analysis of the four tentative inferences columns comes together to form a KOS (Figure 7.20). Form 6 represents the end result of this visual analysis with the production of a prioritized list of investigative leads and strategies (Figure 7.21).

As can be seen in Figure 7.20, the investigating officer, after substantial reflection and consideration of all this 'inferential knowledge' gathered about the murder, starts to draw connecting lines to form a visual C+C analysis.

Such a graphic analysis, as mentioned previously, is best carried out by 'aligning' all of the four A4-sized investigative forms into one combined A3-sized sheet of paper which is then taped together and photocopied several times to make a number of 'draft' copies in order to arrive at a refined final copy of the visual analysis.

In so far as the actual visual inspection and analysis of this combined A3-sized KOS form is concerned a few guidelines are necessary.

First, the investigating officer takes a 'draft' KOS form and begins to link up inferences by drawing lines (tip—use different coloured marker pens for similar inferences) that connect those inferences that appear to be related in some way to one or more of the inferences contained in the four centrally aligned columns that face each other in the middle of the A3-sized KOS form.

For example, in Figure 7.20, if we look at the first investigative form (police/security information) the investigating officer has drawn arrowed lines from item 1 regarding the location of the murder (cheap hotel room with no sign of forced entry) which directly links specific aspects in total or part with at least seven other inferences from two of the other investigative forms. That is, item 1 on Form 1 connects with specific aspects of items 1, 2, 3, and 5 on Form 2 (descriptive information) and items 3, 4, and 5 on Form 3 (diagnostic information).

A typical example of the 'visual reasoning process' used by the investigator to arrive at these seven links is elaborated on below.

The arrow from item 1 on Form 1 to item 4 on Form 3 is based on the investigator's tacit 'on-the-job' knowledge about this type of 'cheap hotel' in the cultural context of this particular country. This is so also for the arrow from item 1 on Form 1 to item 3 on Form 3 about the likelihood of the prostitute the victim was using being a woman of

Figure 7.16 Investigative Form 1

1st Quadrant : Police/Security Information Form

'Cross+Check' System
Copyright: Dr. Geoff Dean

any attachments secure behind form

Case Reference No:
Investigating Officer:

Tentative Inferences	'Crime/Security' Characteristics	1. 'Police/Security' Information Checklist
Possibly 'planned' crime — murder/robbery. Reasons: **1** Location in hotel room with no sign of forced entry— came with some person(s)? **2** 'Professional' job at tying knots, had experience at this before maybe? **3** Brought 'adhesive tape' so some pre-planning involved **4** Only personal items of value missing—indicative of 'professional' selective robbery; did not just grab everything like an amateur	Murder with personal items of property missing. 30 Jun 1998 at about 6.10 am (no real significance) Budget hotel room—died in toilet area. His hands and legs were bound behind his back with strips of torn bed sheets. Knots looked tight and secure. His mouth was stuffed with a piece of cloth while his face was almost black from the lack of oxygen. His face was covered with adhesive tape.	**TYPE OF CRIME/SECURITY:** Personal/Property/Corporate/Organised crime/security threat **CRIME/SECURITY ELEMENTS:** **Time/Day/Date** (any significance) **Crime/Security location** (indoor/vehicle/outdoor/underwater) **Crime/Security Site** (point of contact/primary scene/ secondary scene/Intermediate scene/ dump-site or disposal site) **M.O. ELEMENTS (Personal Crime):** **Method of Approach** (surprise/con) **Method of Attack** (blitz/surprise/con) **Method of Control** (verbal threats/presence of weapon/ physical force—for compliance and/or restraint/use of weapon) **Method of Escape** (on foot/bike/car) **Precautionary Actions** (disguises–bulky clothing/alteration of voice/blindfold/use of gloves/use of condom if sexual assault/use of fire/ disposal of victim's clothing/looking at or taking victim identification)
	Fully clothed male victim was found lying face down on the toilet floor in a hotel room. Victim's family confirmed that victim's wallet, S$23,000 Rolex Watch and S$1800 gold jade ring with diamonds were missing.	**If a Body** (left at primary crime site or other site/condition/position) **Item Removal** (evidential items/financially valuable items/personal items—as trophy and/or as souvenir) **VICTIM ELEMENTS:** **Victim Selection** (availability/location/vulnerability) (any evidence of relational or opportunistic victim) (any evidence of symbolic criteria/fantasy criteria) **Victim Resistance** (victim compliance/passive resistance/ verbal resistance/physical resistance)
5 Possible sign of a struggle by the victim	The bed was messy. Contained a rolled-up Chinese newspaper. A blue coloured blanket and a pillow case were found on the floor. No damage to the hotel room.	**M.O. ELEMENTS (Property Crime):** **Method of Entry** (no damage/forced entry) **Method of Search** (random/systematic) **Property Damage** (no damage/malicious damage) **Property Removal** (valuables/personal) **Method of Escape** (on foot/bike/car)
6 Bus tickets at the murder scene? The tickets may be linked to the murder otherwise how to explain their presence at the scene as victim owned a car. Unless victim took bus there? **7** Sign of 'forensically careless' offender(s)	(refer to personal items above) but left Nokia mobile phone hands-free earpiece. Seven bus tickets found on the floor. Some shoe prints on the top left corner of the bed sheet.	**M.O. ELEMENTS (Corporate Crime):** **M.O. ELEMENTS (OrganizedCrime):** **M.O. ELEMENTS (Security threat):** **ANY OTHER ELEMENTS**

Figure 7.17 Investigative Form 2

'Cross+Check' System Copyright: Dr. Geoff Dean	**2nd Quadrant: 'Descriptive'** **Information Form** any attachments secure behind form	Case Reference No: Investigating Officer:

2. 'Descriptive' Information Checklist	'Reported' Characteristics	Tentative Inferences

2. 'Descriptive' Information Checklist

WITNESS(S) STATEMENTS
Record address, sex, age, ethnicity, marital status, occupation, activity at the time of the crime, witness under influence of drink or drugs, any other specific pieces of information from or about witness(s).

MEMBER(S) OF PUBLIC
Any specific pieces of information about offender, crime, security issue regardless of whether or not it is considered relevant at the time.

INFORMANT(S)/ANONYMOUS CALL
Any specific knowledge/information, eg tip-offs, etc, about offender, crime, security.

VICTIM(S) STATEMENTS
Record address, sex, age, ethnicity, marital status, occupation, activity at the time of the crime/security issue, victim under influence of drink or drugs, any other specific pieces of information from or about victim.

FORENSIC/PATHOLOGY REPORTS
Any specific information/evidence, eg fingerprints, DNA tests, toxicology, dental records, blood spatter patterns, time of death (if applicable), etc.

INTERVIEWS:
VICTIM'S FAMILY, FRIENDS
Any specific pieces of information about victim as described by family members, friends, work colleagues, acquaintances, and others regardless of whether or not it is considered relevant at the time.

SURVEILLANCE/INTELLIGENCE REPORTS
Any specific pieces of information about suspects, the crime, victim, security issue gathered from surveillance/intelligence operations, eg phone taps, tracking mobile calls, database searches, etc.

OFFENDER(S) CHARACTERISTICS
Sex, age, ethnicity, height, accent, build, hair length, hair colour, facial hair, tattoos, distinctive smell, any other distinctive physical features, use of a disguise, offender under the influence of drink or drugs.

Any other specific pieces of information the victim and/or witness(s) described about the offender regardless of whether or not it is considered relevant at the time.

ANY OTHER ELEMENTS

'Reported' Characteristics

Victim was a regular at the hotel for the last four months. Victim booked the room at 1.00 pm for two hours. He checked in alone on the day in question and also in his previous booking.

Elderly chambermaid told the police that she had bumped into a couple at the corridor who seemed to be walking towards victim's room. They spoke Chinese in foreign accent.

Another chambermaid heard 'thumping noises' in victim's room.

Check with victim's friends—they revealed that victim liked to talk big about his winnings and business ventures. They also said that the victim liked to hang out with a lot of women from China.

Enquiries on the bus tickets revealed that four tickets belonged to Service 65 and three tickets belong to Service 190. All of them were bought with a specific Transit Link Farecard. The ticket holders boarded the bus services at a bus stop along Pipit Road in Macpherson housing estate.

Tentative Inferences

1
Likely that victim checked into the hotel for sexual pleasure.

2
Likely the woman is a Chinese national.

3
Likely victim made himself a target for such a robbery/ murder by possibly dealing with Chinese prostitutes. Hence, very likely the offender(s) may be known to the victim.

4
Given that there are several bus tickets likely that more than one offender may be involved in crime.
Also, offender(s) may be less well off and used public transport to get to the hotel from their place of residence in Macpherson housing estate.

Figure 7.18 Investigative Form 3

3rd Quadrant: 'Diagnostic' Information Form
any attachments secure behind form

'Cross+Check' System
Copyright: Dr. Geoff Dean

Case Reference No:
Investigating Officer:

3. 'Diagnostic' Information Checklist	Motivational Characteristics	Tentative Inferences
BEHAVIOURAL ELEMENTS: **'Staging' Behaviour** 'staging' is a conscious action by an offender to thwart an investigation by attempting to conceal, redirect, or manipulate evidence in such a way as to provide a different motive for the crime. **'Scripting' Behaviour** 'scripting' is *what* the offender said to the victim and *how* the offender said it; as well as what they *command* the victim to do and/or say. The 'script' the offender uses to direct the victim verbally and behaviourally reveals their ideal fantasy about the nature of the crime. **'Signature' Behaviour** 'signature' is behaviours committed by an offender which are not necessary to commit the crime, as they serve to satisfy particular emotional and psychological needs of the offender.		
PSYCHOLOGICAL ELEMENTS: **Behaviour indicative of developmental dysfunction** **Control**—often expressed as an obsessional trait arising from developmentally unresolved problems of jealousy and envy: 1. directed at *victim's actions* 2. directed at the *experience* of being in control of another person.	Victim's mouth was stuffed with a piece of cloth while his face almost black from the lack of oxygen.	**1** Planned to kill victim after robbing him to avoid identification? Since no attempt to remove cloth to allow him to breathe when offender(s) left room.
Power—expressed as threatened or enacted physical or sexual violence. 1. *instrumental violence*—practical function 2. *expressive violence*—personal needs function **Fantasy**—expressed as eroticized power and aggression. Two types of paraphilia: 1. Remote non-intimate contact with a target (fetishism, voyeurism, frottism) 2. Forceful intimate intrusion to the target (sadomasochism, picquerism, ritualized-sexual killings, necrophilia, cannibalism)	Fully clothed male victim was found lying face down on the toilet floor in a hotel room	**2** Was no fantasy involved so appears more likely to be a purely instrumental killing to serve practical function of avoiding any future identification.
Behaviour indicative of cognitive dysfunction **Psychotic Thinking**—expressed in delusions, hallucinations and distorted thinking. **Personality Disorder**—expressed as impulsivity & dissociation, dependency, under- & over-controlled hostility, paranoid projection and displacement. **Chemical Addictions**—pathological intoxication, alcohol or drugs-induced psychotic-type processes. **SOCIO-CULTURAL/POLITICAL ELEMENTS**	Hung around with lots of women from China	**3** Likely victim used hotel for sexual pleasure with Chinese nationals working as prostitutes in Singapore. **4** Cheap hotels often used for sexual encounters with prostitutes.
	Budget hotel room	
SPECIFIC CRIME/SECURITY ELEMENTS	His hands and legs were bound behind his back with strips of torn bed sheets. Knots looked tight and secure.	**5** Likely such binding-up requires more than one person to subdue and tie victim.

Figure 7.19 Investigative Form 4

'Cross+Check' System Copyright: Dr. Geoff Dean	4th Quadrant: 'Research' **Information Form** any attachments secure behind form	Case Reference No: Investigating Officer:

Tentative Inferences ◄	'Generalizable' Characteristics ◄	4. 'Research' Information Checklist (general crime findings)

Tentative Inferences

1
Search of Police Intelligence and AntiVice databases for prostitution records involving Chinese nationals.

2
Likely to live in or work near Macpherson housing estate.

3
Step up surveillance and spot checks by police patrols in the housing estate.

4
Search of Housing & Development Board databases for Chinese national renting rooms at Macpherson housing estate.

5
Check with Ministry of Manpower of the Chinese workers employed or staying at Macpherson estate.

6
Criminality to be likely theme along with the instrumental aggression to avoid identification.

7
Establish a neighbourhood canvass of area within the Macpherson estate with particular focus on Chinese national and Transit Link Farecard.

'Generalizable' Characteristics

Check criminal records for vice activities at the hotel and its vicinity.

Offender(s) may be staying at Macpherson housing estate as ticket holders boarded the bus services at a bus stop along Pipit Road in Macpherson housing estate and bought by a specific Transit Link card.

Offender(s) may be adult Chinese national and a blue-collar worker.

Murder with personal items of property missing. Eg victim's wallet, S$23,000 Rolex watch and S$1800 gold jade ring with diamonds.

Enquiries on the bus tickets revealed that four tickets belonged to Service 65 and three tickets belong to Service 190. All of them were bought with a specific Transit Link Farecard. The ticket holders boarded the bus services at a bus stop along Pipit Road in Macpherson housing estate.

4. 'Research' Information Checklist (general crime findings)

CRIMINAL HISTORY
Most serious offenders have a previous criminal history.

RESIDENTIAL LOCATION
Most criminals will commit their crimes within a relatively short and predictable distance from their base or residence. This is usually the case with the first few crimes in a series.

CRIME LOCATION
The location of a crime is not random. Criminals operate out of a mental or cognitive map of their chosen crime environment. Hence, they develop a working knowledge of where suitable 'target' victims may be found and the safest and quickest route home so as to avoid apprehension.

OFFENDER POPULATION
1. Most crimes are committed by a minority of offenders. Hence, an individual offender will often be responsible for a series of previous offences that may or may not be directly related to the current crime.

2. Most offenders tend to be relatively young adult and adolescent males.

3. Most offenders upon release will probably re-offend, often within a year.

MOTIVATIONAL THEMES
'Scripting' & signature' behaviours reveal the emotional and psychological themes that motivate the offender, eg revenge, rage, etc depending on the type and nature of the crime.

NARRATIVE THEMES
Most serious offenders reveal one or more prominent theme in how they will generally live their daily life by the manner in which they carry out the crime. Four key themes are: criminality/aggression/sadism/intimacy.

SPECIFIC CRIME FINDINGS:

Bus tickets.

Figure 7.20 Investigative Form 5

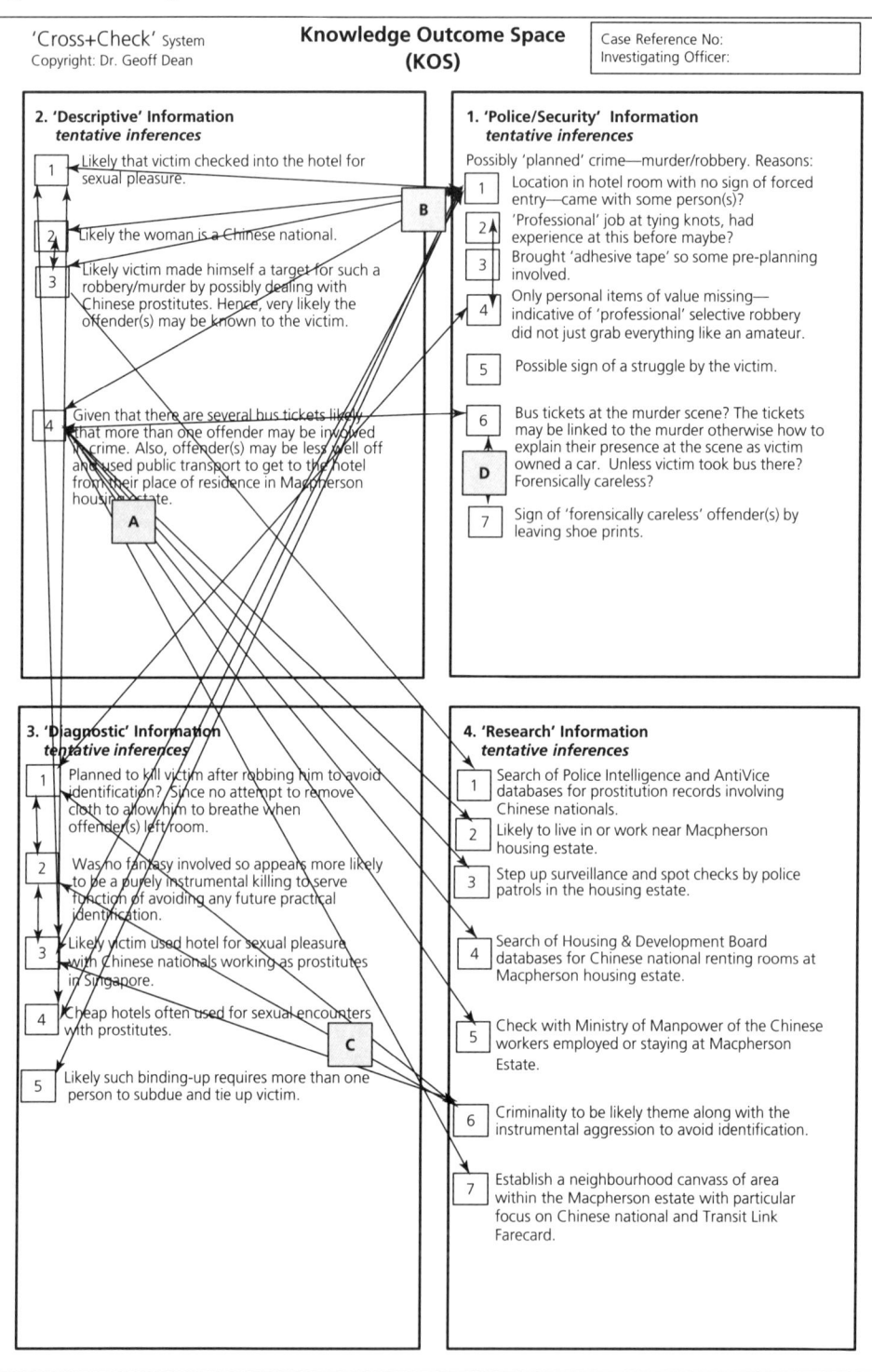

'Cross+Check' System
Copyright: Dr. Geoff Dean

Knowledge Outcome Space (KOS)

Case Reference No:
Investigating Officer:

2. 'Descriptive' Information
tentative inferences

1. Likely that victim checked into the hotel for sexual pleasure.

2. Likely the woman is a Chinese national.

3. Likely victim made himself a target for such a robbery/murder by possibly dealing with Chinese prostitutes. Hence, very likely the offender(s) may be known to the victim.

4. Given that there are several bus tickets likely that more than one offender may be involved in crime. Also, offender(s) may be less well off and used public transport to get to the hotel from their place of residence in Macpherson housing estate.

1. 'Police/Security' Information
tentative inferences

Possibly 'planned' crime—murder/robbery. Reasons:

1. Location in hotel room with no sign of forced entry—came with some person(s)?

2. 'Professional' job at tying knots, had experience at this before maybe?

3. Brought 'adhesive tape' so some pre-planning involved.

4. Only personal items of value missing— indicative of 'professional' selective robbery did not just grab everything like an amateur.

5. Possible sign of a struggle by the victim.

6. Bus tickets at the murder scene? The tickets may be linked to the murder otherwise how to explain their presence at the scene as victim owned a car. Unless victim took bus there? Forensically careless?

7. Sign of 'forensically careless' offender(s) by leaving shoe prints.

3. 'Diagnostic' Information
tentative inferences

1. Planned to kill victim after robbing him to avoid identification? Since no attempt to remove cloth to allow him to breathe when offender(s) left room.

2. Was no fantasy involved so appears more likely to be a purely instrumental killing to serve function of avoiding any future practical identification.

3. Likely victim used hotel for sexual pleasure with Chinese nationals working as prostitutes in Singapore.

4. Cheap hotels often used for sexual encounters with prostitutes.

5. Likely such binding-up requires more than one person to subdue and tie up victim.

4. 'Research' Information
tentative inferences

1. Search of Police Intelligence and AntiVice databases for prostitution records involving Chinese nationals.

2. Likely to live in or work near Macpherson housing estate.

3. Step up surveillance and spot checks by police patrols in the housing estate.

4. Search of Housing & Development Board databases for Chinese national renting rooms at Macpherson housing estate.

5. Check with Ministry of Manpower of the Chinese workers employed or staying at Macpherson Estate.

6. Criminality to be likely theme along with the instrumental aggression to avoid identification.

7. Establish a neighbourhood canvass of area within the Macpherson estate with particular focus on Chinese national and Transit Link Farecard.

Chinese origin from the People's Republic of China. The tacit knowledge of these two links to item 1 on Form 1 can be cross-checked with items 1, 2, and 3 on Form 2. Such cross-connecting of links strengthens the inferential reasoning of the investigator and validates the process.

The next arrow from item 1 on Form 1 is to item 5 on Form 3. This link suggests that more than one offender could be involved in this murder. Hence, 'more-than-one' inference can be subsequently cross-checked to item 4 on Form 2 about the bus tickets and linked back to item 1 on Form 1 as shown. Thus by this process of visual reasoning the seven links to the crime location and what it infers have been literally 'drawn out' and established by this C+C system of analysis.

Second, it is important to bear in mind that this type of visual analysis is more than just a statistically based content analysis where the most number of connections made automatically dictates the first priority lead to investigate further in a case.

As is apparent in Figure 7.20, item 1 on Form 1 has the most number of connections (seven links in all) but is labelled as cluster B on Figure 7.21, which is the second investigative priority on the list. This is because the 'quality' of the knowledge gained by the connections represented in cluster A (item 6 (bus tickets) on Form 1 linked to five other inferences to follow) offers a better investigative strategy to follow than cluster B.

Third, the same reasoning process of visually analysing and connecting up inferences and cross-checking them against all the other inferences is repeated a number of times as shown on Figure 7.20. This iterative reasoning takes place using several draft A3-sized analysis sheets until the investigator is satisfied all possible and potential links have been established and then a final KOS form is produced.

Fourth, this final KOS form functions as part of the 'explanation system' component of the C+C EKRS from which the investigative leads shown in Figure 7.21 are derived and arranged in order of priority. The list of priority leads for this murder case is self-explanatory.

Fifth, each individual investigating officer may draw and make slightly different inferential connections as is to be expected since it is their own fuzziness of experiential knowledge that is being used to 'power' the system. Hence, there is only a uniformity of recording and reasoning involved in the C+C system rather than an imposed conformity of thinking. In fact, such diversity of investigative thinking should be encouraged (this is the subject of the next chapter). For our purposes here, the only requirement is that whatever visual analysis a particular investigating officer may come up with the connections must make logical sense and be able to be defended by such logic.

In sum, what the graphic nature of the C+C system demonstrates quite clearly in this murder case is how the initial tacit, on-the-job, experiential knowledge of the crime location can be captured and used to reason with in a systematic manner, and logically connected to other knowledge inferences to focus an investigation.

Figure 7.21 Investigative Form 6

'Cross+Check' System Copyright: Dr. Geoff Dean	INVESTIGATIVE PRIORITIES FORM	Case Reference No: Investigating Officer:

Prioritized listing of potential investigative leads & strategies
(based on most significant inferences)

> **Results of 'Cross+Checked' Visual Analysis based on Police Expert Knowledge Inferences:**
>
> The visual analysis on the Knowledge Outcome Space (KOS) revealed three substantial inferential patterns identified as clusters A, B, and C and a fourth minor pattern D to follow up for further investigation.

A This inference pattern clusters around the likely residential location (Macpherson housing estate) of the offenders involved. The discovery of the bus tickets (*police/security information item 6*) was linked to this housing estate (*descriptive information Item 4*).

Therefore, the first investigative strategy should be increased surveillance measures in and around the estate with Chinese nationals as target group as well as conducting relevant database searches *(research information items 2, 3, 4, 5, and 7)* to confirm or refute the veracity of this lead and if possible establish further leads.

B This inference pattern centres on the victim's habit of regularly booking a cheap hotel room (*police/security information item 1*) to engage in sex with Chinese prostitutes (*descriptive information items 1, 2, 3, 4*) which brought his displayed personal wealth to the notice of a gang of criminals associated with Chinese prostitution (*diagnostic information items 3, 4, 5*).

Therefore, the second investigative strategy should be concurrently to search police intelligence and anti-vice databases for prostitution records involving Chinese national and known organized crime gangs engaged in prostitution rackets *(research information item 1)*.

C This inference pattern revolves around the motive for killing the victim given that robbery appears to be the main reason for the crime *(diagnostic information item 1, 2, 3)* which suggests a criminal lifestyle (*police/security information items 2, 3, 4*) where strong instrumental violence is prepared to be used to avoid possible future identification *(research information item 6)*.

Therefore, the third investigative strategy should be concurrently to search criminal records for similar cases of robbery with violence.

D This inference pattern involves signs of 'forensic carelessness' on the part of the offenders by leaving bus tickets and shoe prints on bed (*police/security information items 6, 7*). Although this pattern is minor in terms of the number of linked inferences it does indicate that these offenders are not criminally sophisticated.

Therefore, the fourth investigative strategy should be to follow up on all potential suspects with sustained interviews as these offenders are more than likely to unknowingly reveal incriminating evidence on themselves or others if involved in this crime.

Any other comments:

Summary

This chapter presented a knowledge-based application system designed to handle investigative problems in the real world of policing and law enforcement by utilizing the tacit knowledge expertise of police officers. The application known as the C+C system is an experiential knowledge reasoning system that captures and utilizes police expertise in the investigative domain. The C+C system is conceptually located at the interface of the larger expert systems field and the domain of fuzzy logic or multivalence mathematics in which the user can compute with 'words' rather than 'numbers'.

The chapter introduces the concept of 'police knowledge triangles' as the knowledge base necessary for the C+C system to reason like an 'expert system'. One of the main difficulties faced by expert systems is how to deal with the problem of Knowledge Acquisition (KA). The usual methods of conducting structured interviews or doing task analysis surveys of a person's expertise is very labour- and time-intensive. Even if these collection methods were a realistic option, for a police organization to try to get busy working investigators to fill out a detailed survey or make time for an in-depth structured interview presents a major challenge.

One innovative aspect of the C+C system is how it deals with this KA difficulty in a very unique way by capturing the tacit knowledge of investigating officers in the 'real-time' recording of crime information by them as both 'expert' and 'user' of the system. The basic investigative forms used by the C+C system can be easily integrated into any Crime Information Management Database System.

This 'once-only entry' feature of the C+C system allows each individual officer then to systematically generate logically derived inferences for later visual analysis and prioritization into investigative leads and strategies. Hence, the C+C system not only assists an investigating officer in finding and developing evidence in an investigation but also helps in developing an overall investigative and management plan for the entire investigation.

The C+C application utilizes a mental modelling approach to acquiring the tacit knowledge of an investigating officer rather than inferring decision-making rules, so that incrementally it becomes a self-evolving system of the experiential knowledge of each individual police officer.

Thus, the C+C model operates as an experiential knowledge system that integrates four qualitatively different information sources (police/security, descriptive, diagnostic, research) in such a way as to allow the user to develop inferences and cross-check them through a process of visual analysis against each level of information in the system. This systematic process of reasoning also allows an investigator to place a relative weighting on developed inferences and hence to prioritize investigative leads and strategies.

A case study of a murder was used to show how the tacit, on-the-job, experiential knowledge of police can be captured, graphically modelled, and visually analysed in this C+C application system to further enhance police and law enforcement investigations.

163

'Investigative Pathways' System: Neural Network Mapping Application

Introduction

The application system discussed in this chapter builds on the same conceptual foundation as the fuzzy experiential knowledge reasoning system in the previous chapter; in that this 'Investigative Pathways' application also utilizes the notion of police knowledge triangles (PKTs) as the conceptual basis of police work, as well as being related to the 'Expert System' (ES) branch of the artificial intelligence (AI) field.

However, what is different about the application in this chapter is that it works more like a neural network rather than a pure fuzzy system, although fuzzy systems are a sister technology to neural networks (Kosko 1999). In essence, neural networks are 'brain-like' learning systems. Neural systems are pattern computers. They are able to learn, store, and recall the fuzzy patterns in facial recognition software, personal identification, fraudulent insurance claims, and so forth.

Neural Network Systems (NNS) learn from experience just like the cognitive part of our brain learns to recognize recurring patterns out of the flux of our experiences. Hence, a NNS reasons with patterns, which is how police investigators reason when attempting to solve crimes. Empirical research by Dean (2000) has demonstrated the patterned way in which experienced detectives/investigators think when investigating serious and complex crimes.

This chapter will briefly summarize these research findings on investigative thinking before turning to a detailed presentation of the 'Investigative Pathways' (IP) NNS that developed out of this research. Finally, the chapter presents a series of case studies on the use of this IP application.

Patterned structure to investigative thinking

The experience of being a police investigator is the same the world over. There are certainly cultural and contextual differences between police services throughout the world, but the nature of the job is essentially the same. Since all investigators, by and large, have essentially the same sort of experience, then why are some investigators able to solve difficult and complex cases where other investigators cannot?

This variation between detectives who have similar investigative experience is not simply about different 'personalities' doing the job better, or some possessing more inherent 'ability' than others. Like most such 'simple answers' there is often more complexity to the simplicity than people realize.

'Personality' alone does not adequately account for differences in investigative performance. Nor does natural 'ability' sufficiently account for investigative differences in performance. Clearly, 'personality' and 'ability' have a part to play but it is a mistake to assume that all investigative success can be explained in such a simple manner.

A more realistic answer lies in how the investigator 'prefers to think' about solving the crime. A very successful detective who participated in the original research on investigative thinking (Dean 2000) stated that 'the most difficult thing about an investigation is learning to think how to think about the investigation'. The key, therefore, to being a successful investigator, no matter what type of 'personality' you have or how naturally gifted your 'abilities' are, lies in what style of investigative thinking you bring to the case.

A 'style' is a preferred way of thinking. A 'style' is not an 'ability'. That is, an 'ability' refers to how well someone can do something, while, a 'style' refers to how someone likes to do something (Sternberg 1997: 8).

The relevance of 'thinking styles' in relation to the investigative process is that, for example, a particular investigator may be gifted in terms of having certain abilities. But, the central issue for investigation is how such gifted investigators 'prefer' to use the abilities they have. For this 'preference' (thinking style) of the gifted investigator will largely determine the success or otherwise of their contribution to an investigation.

Ongoing qualitative and quantitative research (Dean, Fahsing, and Gottschalk 2006; 2007) has confirmed the existence in other policing contexts of four styles of thinking 'investigatively' originally identified by Dean (2000). The four investigative thinking styles are labelled as Method, Challenge, Skill, and Risk. Each of these four cognitive styles of investigative thinking are patterned thought processes that investigators repeatedly use and rely upon to think through a case. Moreover, each of these four styles or ways of investigative thinking was found to exist in a hierarchy of increasingly conceptual complexity starting with the lest complex Method way of thinking and progressing through Challenge then Skill to the most complex style of Risk thinking.

Furthermore, the thought patterns of each style of investigative thinking vary according to the elements that comprise it. For example, the structure of the Method pattern of thinking begins for detectives when they are given a crime to solve. When handed a case detectives apply the basics of the procedural method they were trained in. There are a variety of procedural steps within the criminal investigation training literature for various types of crime but in essence all such steps follow a logical sequence that can be subsumed under a set of basic steps, referred to as the '5 Cs' of the police procedural method of investigation. The 5 Cs are the procedural steps of collecting, checking, considering, connecting, and constructing information into evidence.

Conceptually, this 'procedural method' presents a problem for detectives in that, since their formal investigative training only equips them with this one way of 'thinking' investigatively, the question becomes how do they learn to think in any other way when investigating?

Certainly 'on-the-job' experience has a large role to play in shaping the next style of investigative thinking because of the challenge the very nature of the job presents to police. As detectives conduct a serious and/or complex investigation, they become driven by the intensity of the challenge, which motivates them to do the best job they can for the victim(s) by catching the criminal(s) and solving the crime through the application of the 'basic 5Cs' of the investigative method style of thinking they were trained in. This challenge style of thinking is all about what motivates detectives. At this level detectives think about the job, the victim, the crime, and the criminal. These four elements (job–victim–crime–criminal) are the key sources of intensity that drive detectives to do the best they can in a particular investigation (Home Office 2005).

In meeting this investigative challenge, detectives require skill to relate and communicate effectively with a variety of people to obtain information so as to establish a workable investigative focus (Kiely and Peek 2002). Such skill also requires detectives to be flexible in the way they approach people and the case, while maintaining an appropriate level of emotional involvement towards victims, witnesses, informants, and suspects. With this skill style of investigative thinking, detectives are concerned with how they relate to people. Detectives must think about how they are going to relate to the victim, witnesses, possible suspects, the local community, and the wider general public in order to get the information they need to make the case.

When exercising their investigative skill detectives seek to maximize the possibilities of a good result by taking legally sanctioned and logically justifiable risks across a wide latitude of influence. Such justifiable risk-taking requires detectives to be proactive in applying creativity to how they seek to discover new information and, if necessary, how they develop such information into evidence. This risk style revolves around how detectives think through being proactively creative enough to discover new information and if necessary develop it into evidence that will stand up to the test in a court of law (Archbold 2005).

Although it is possible for any investigator to use all four styles of thinking (method–challenge–skill–risk) in a particular investigation it is rare that any one detective will give equal weight to all four styles of investigative thinking in a particular case, because detectives, like everyone else, have a preference for maybe one or two particular styles or ways of thinking.

The important point to note therefore is that experienced detectives and investigators 'intuitively' use these four levels of thinking in an investigation without any significant conscious understanding of the incredible complexity of their thought processes as they investigate the case. They, to a large extent, remain unaware of the patterned way they think. Hence, the following sections illustrate in detail how each of these four patterned ways of thinking operates in the minds of investigators.

'Method' thinking pattern

In Figure 8.1 a graphic depiction of this police procedural way of Method thinking shows a detailed representation of the range of elements that can potentially be involved when investigators base their cognitive processing on this pattern of thinking.

Figure 8.1 'Method' pattern of investigative thinking

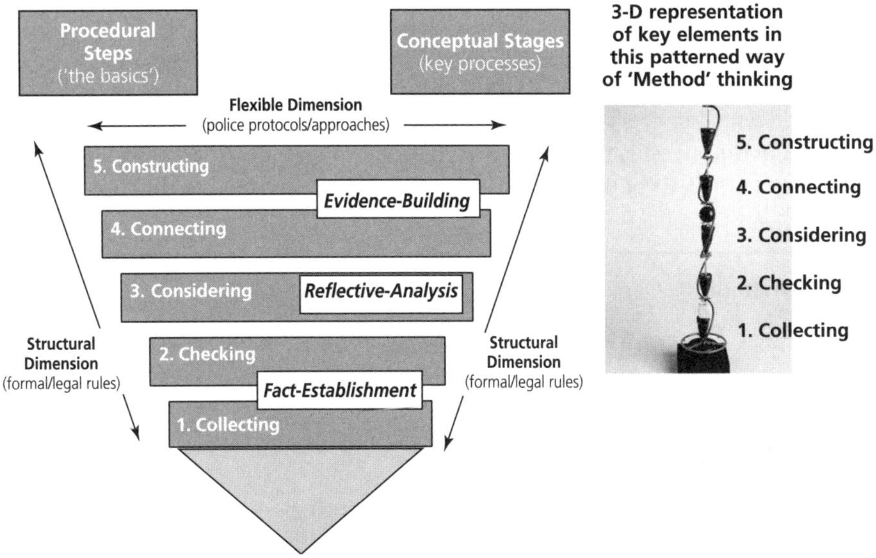

As can be seen an investigation starts 'at the point' of the application of the police procedural 'method' where everything collected may potentially end up as part of the evidence brief. For example, in a reactive-type investigation this 'method' is centred on the initial complaint or crime scene. While, in a proactive-type investigation the 'method' is centred on a piece of information or a preliminary intelligence report that has sparked off a covert operation. The key elements (procedural steps, conceptual stages, and structural/flexible dimensions) of this Method style of investigative thinking are depicted on the large cone-shaped graphic.

The nature of this procedurally driven police 'method' is to uncover facts by 'drilling' or 'spiralling' up in a 'step-by-step' manner (collecting–checking–considering–connecting–constructing) into the information that is gathered about the crime. Such a centring, drilling, or spiralling process is visually conveyed by the point of a 'cone' and its triangular shape conveys how following the method 'narrows down' an investigation and leads to the building up of a brief of evidence to present to a court of law.

It is also evident that this Method understanding of an investigation very much reflects the way detectives are trained. The 'cone' graphic clearly conveys the dimensions of this procedurally driven method of conducting an investigation. The structural dimension of the 'method' is the formal/legal rules that must be followed. The flexible dimension of the 'method' is the discretion that detectives have to stretch the boundaries via various police protocols/approaches while staying within the boundaries set by the formal/legal rules or structural aspect.

The depiction on the right of Figure 8.1 is a 3-D representation of the 5Cs: the key elements in this Method pattern of investigative thinking. As can be seen in this representation there are five 'cones' attached to the central rod of the Method. Each stands for one of the 5 Cs as indicated in an ascending order. The significance of this depiction will be discussed later in the chapter.

For now, some case examples of how this patterned way of Method thinking are presented in order to assist with a more practical understanding of the workings of this investigative thinking style. The two cases below are described in relation to the 5 Cs of the Method style of patterned investigative thinking.

Case 1: ATM theft

This case involved the theft from an Automated Teller Machine (ATM). The victim discovered multiple unauthorized withdrawals of cash from her savings account amounting to $45,000.

1 Collecting and 2 Checking (fact establishment)

The victim was interviewed and the investigator established the following facts: how she discovered the shortage of funds from her bank account; the last time she saw and used her ATM card; whether she revealed her Personal Identification Number (PIN) to anyone; and if she had any suspects in mind.

The victim revealed she had written her PIN on a piece of paper which she kept with her ATM card inside her wallet. More pertinently, she indicated that she co-rented a room with a female colleague, who had recently divulged her financial woes to the victim.

The victim, however, had no particular suspects in mind. A background check was done of the victim's colleague that revealed she had some theft antecedents.

3 Considering (reflective analysis)

Considering her access to the victim's belongings, the prospect of the victim's room-mate being a potential suspect was enormous. The investigator then requested from the bank CCTV footage from the ATM locations where the unauthorized withdrawals took place and managed to secure a photo printout of the suspect, who turned out to be the female colleague.

4 Connecting and 5 Constructing (evidence building)

Meanwhile, the investigator showed the suspect from the CCTV photo to the victim, who confirmed that the suspect was in fact her room-mate. With this positive identification, the investigator was able to connect the crime to the room-mate and construct the whole case. Upon arrest, the room-mate confessed to using the victim's ATM card to make those withdrawals without the victim's consent.

Case 2: Sleeping drunk

Two patrol officers were dispatched to a hotel where a drunken man was reported to be sleeping in the hotel compound.

1 Collecting and 2 Checking (fact establishment)

Upon arrival, both officers tried in vain to wake the drunk who smelled strongly of alcohol. As the officers needed to verify his particulars, they searched his jeans pocket and found his identity card, which gave his name and address.

At this point the officers could have decided that the best option would be to get the hotel staff to order a taxi for the man and send him home rather than waste more police time and resources on what appeared to be a drunk sleeping off a big night out.

3 Considering (reflective analysis)

However, both officers scrutinized the sleeping man. His head was resting on a bag. Upon closer inspection, the officers were surprised to find the bag bore the name of an Indonesian woman. This raised the suspicions of the officers as they reflected on what a man would be doing with an Indonesian woman's bag.

4 Connecting and 5 Constructing (evidence building)

One of the officers tried to rouse the man while the other searched his pockets and found three concealed weapons tucked in his waistband. Sensing something amiss, they decided to check the bag. Upon opening it, they found an assortment of jewellery and a large amount of cash, in local and Indonesian currencies. They realized that this was no ordinary drunk the police would usually encounter in the streets.

Subsequent investigations revealed that the man was responsible for a robbery several days before, where he held up two women at knifepoint, in a hotel some 5 km away, and robbed them of their bag containing jewellery and money. Unfortunately for him, the crime was captured on the hotel's closed circuit camera. Further investigations revealed that he was involved in two other robberies.

'Challenge' thinking pattern

A 20-year veteran of police work captures in his own words the essence of this pattern of investigative thinking:

> I have always felt a high motivation to do very well since the day I graduated from the Police Academy. I see police work as something noble and important such that personal sacrifices are inevitable, for the sake of the community and the country. I was always intensely challenged by the job in every posting. I like investigation because I like to get to the truth of things. I made numerous arrests from the time I was performing street patrols and through my stint in the Investigation Branch. I passionately believe that every police officer has an important role to play in maintaining law and order and ensuring that criminals are effectively dealt with. I enjoy going about my investigations and will not be discouraged by the difficulties I face daily. Each and every arrest and investigation successfully completed gives me great pleasure and fulfilment. I was always so engrossed to perform the job well that I often neglected my breaks, my meals and my family. For many years, I have sacrificed a big portion of my off-duty hours and even leave days for work. I rarely tendered medical leave over my two decades in the service and often would be at work even when I was on medical leave. This obsession with work has caused me to even ignore the symptoms that my family was falling apart. (personal communication 2005)

Figure 8.2 provides a graphic depiction of this Challenge way of thinking and its associated elements and characteristic features.

As is evident the key elements—job, victim, criminal, crime—of this 'challenge' style of investigative thinking for detectives 'surround' and are 'part of' an investigation in much the same way as the four sides of a cube 'surround' and are 'part of' the cube. This Challenge way of thinking for detectives can be thought of as the overall experiential framework in which an investigation is carried out.

Figure 8.2 'Challenge' pattern of investigative thinking

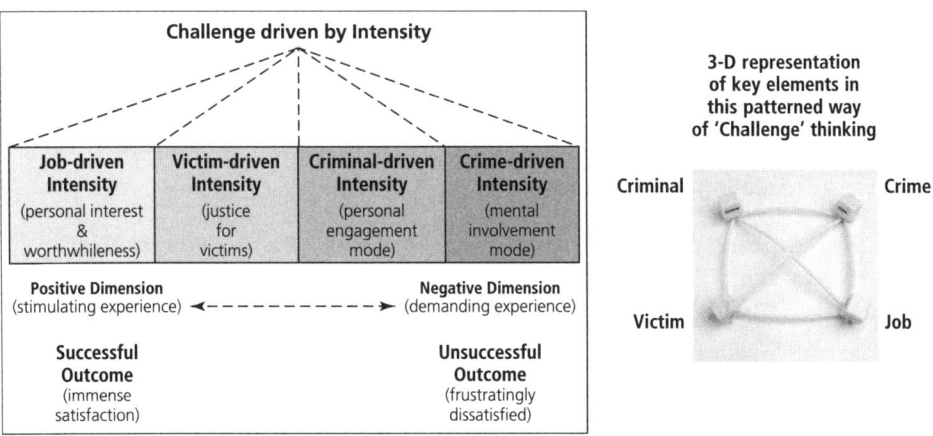

The 'cube' shape conveys this notion that this challenge style of thinking is like a 'container' for a detective's experiential knowledge of the entire investigative process. This experiential knowledge comes with years of investigating a range of wide and varied crimes.

Moreover, the four sides of this challenge-type cube represent the four 'interlocking sources' of 'intensity' (job–victim–criminal–crime) that combine in both positive and negative ways to form this 'experiential container' for a detective. The broken dotted lines in the top half of the figure are meant to signify that the inner cube of intensity has had its sides flattened out to provide this 'four-sided' horizontal view of the cube.

On the positive side, these four 'intensity sources' provide the impetus, energy, and sustenance to meet the many and varied 'challenges' that a serious and complex investigation presents to investigators, especially in protracted investigations. As indicated on the figure, detectives overwhelmingly describe this positive dimension as a very stimulating experience.

On the negative side, any one or any combination of these four 'intensity cubes' can become so powerful in the mind of a detective that it becomes an extremely 'demanding experience' to the point where, in some situations, it can entirely overwhelm a detective. In such circumstances, professional therapeutic help is often needed. This can be the case especially in an investigation of an horrific nature: these 'intensity cubes' not only 'drive' the emotional involvement of investigators but they also 'grow' in intensity as an investigation proceeds.

Again, as in Figure 8.1, a 3-D representation of the four key elements arranged in a 'cube' shape is on the right of Figure 8.2. Likewise the significance of this depiction will be discussed later in the chapter.

Two cases are presented below that reflect some of the key sources of intensity that drive this Challenge style of investigative thinking. Furthermore, what these cases show is how the various elements of Challenge thinking are patterned in different ways depending on which sources of intensity drive a particular police officer in a particular case and how such intensity sources are interwoven with each other throughout an investigation.

Case 3: Stealing from vehicles

Community-based police officers are constantly being briefed about incidents of stolen vehicles that occur on their local turf or patch. In one such case of property stealing the criminal had been breaking the window panels of heavy-duty vehicles and stealing audio components or any valuable that he or she could get access to during the commission of the offence.

Job-driven intensity

One officer took a personal interest in the nature of these offences and established through reading and analysing the mode of operation among reported cases. He deduced that it was highly likely that the same person had committed these offences as they all occurred in close proximity to each other in essentially the same area.

Criminal-driven intensity

The officer became determined to apprehend the offender. What fuelled his anger was a complete lack of respect for authority as the location of these offences was just a stone's throw away from the officer's own police station.

Hence, the criminal had found a way to break into vehicles without drawing any attention to him or herself. The manner by which the criminal escaped undetected and cut through the glass all indicated to the officer that he was dealing with a very confident and experienced criminal. He was determined to pit his wits against the criminal who was taunting police to catch him/her as the crime was being done right under the noses of the police.

Crime-driven intensity

Efforts to mount covert surveillance at the scene of the crime proved fruitless night after night. After a period of time, the police division called for the exhaustive surveillance operation to be stood down. Immediately after the stand-down the offender struck again. The officer who was most 'challenged' by the case was appalled by such luck and did not believe that it was pure coincidence. He became absolutely certain that there was a pattern to the offending.

His intuition indicated that the offender seemed to understand and was aware of the police surveillance operations. The officer decided to test out two possibilities. One possibility was that the offender had one of the local police officers at the station as an accomplice. The second possibility was that the offender had mounted some sort of counter-surveillance on police operations.

The officer confided his thinking to only one trusted team member. He put his theory to the test by seeking help from another friend who was a fellow police officer from another unit. Together they planned a two-pronged operation. His officer partner set up a surveillance 'ambush' in the target location, while he observed the unusual movements or behaviours of shift officers in his station and anyone nearby.

The partner apprehended the suspect red-handed at the scene of an attempted vehicle break-in within a few days of the surveillance operation. They decided to keep quiet about the arrest and not immediately bring the offender back into the local station for processing. The officers were now more determined than ever to arrest any accomplices.

Criminal-driven intensity

The suspect refused to give any information and the officers seized his mobile phone and traced every recent call. One such call resulted in an on-shift police officer's mobile phone ringing. The officers arrested the implicated officer on suspicion. The arrested officer eventually admitted his involvement after further investigations were carried out.

This case also clearly highlights how the crime-driven intensity element of Challenge thinking strongly motivates police officers to engage cognitively in a very deep and personal way with trying to mentally analyse and figure out the jigsaw puzzle of the crime.

Case 4: Suicide or not?

A young woman was found dead at the bottom of her apartment building and preliminary investigations indicated that she had committed suicide. Upon being assigned the case, the investigator understood why it was so easy to dismiss the case initially as a suicide as there were no factors that indicated anything suspicious. Also, a hastily written suicide note was found typed on her computer. The investigator could have written up the case as a suicide and closed it.

Job-driven and victim-driven intensity

However, driven by the intensity to seek the truth and to help the victim's family find closure in the tragedy, the investigator began a search for more information.

He started an intense search of the telephone records of the dead woman. This was a tedious and draining process of verification, cross-checking, and elimination. After almost a week of processing the telephone records and meeting with the subscribers to inquire about their relationship with the victim, the investigator came across a male suspect who had called the victim several times before her death. He appeared out of place, as none of her friends or family seemed to know him.

The male suspect was subsequently discovered to have met the dead woman at a pub and had begun to stalk her after she rejected him. He later admitted to pushing the woman out of the apartment building after they had an argument over his obsessive stalking.

It was indeed fortunate for the family of the dead woman in this case that the Challenge of what the job means was taken so seriously by the investigator that he was able to crack the case of what appeared to be a straightforward suicide.

'Skill' thinking pattern

Figure 8.3 contains a graphic depiction of investigative Skill thinking. The key elements of this Skill style of thinking revolve around the centrality of being able to 'relate' to a diversity of people as investigator. The core characteristic of this 'relatability' is 'effective communication'. Relatability is the fixed point around which the key elements (flexibility, focus, involvement) of this 'investigative skill' thinking revolve at various levels concerning the immediate investigation, the legal system, and the general public.

It is apparent in Figure 8.3 that the key elements within this 'thinking style' are: to have a flexible approach to the investigation; to focus the investigation; and to maintain an appropriate level of emotional involvement, especially with victims and suspects.

This preferred 'style' of thinking by a detective in a sense 'belongs to' the detective in a much more personal way than the other 'styles' since any 'skill' a person has forms part of who that person is. That is, this 'thinking style' emphasizes the personal qualities that detectives bring to any investigation.

As in previous figures, on the right of Figure 8.3 there is a 3-D representation of the three key elements arranged in a 'circle' which revolves around the central skill of relatability. Two cases are outlined below that clearly demonstrate

Figure 8.3 'Skill' pattern of investigative thinking

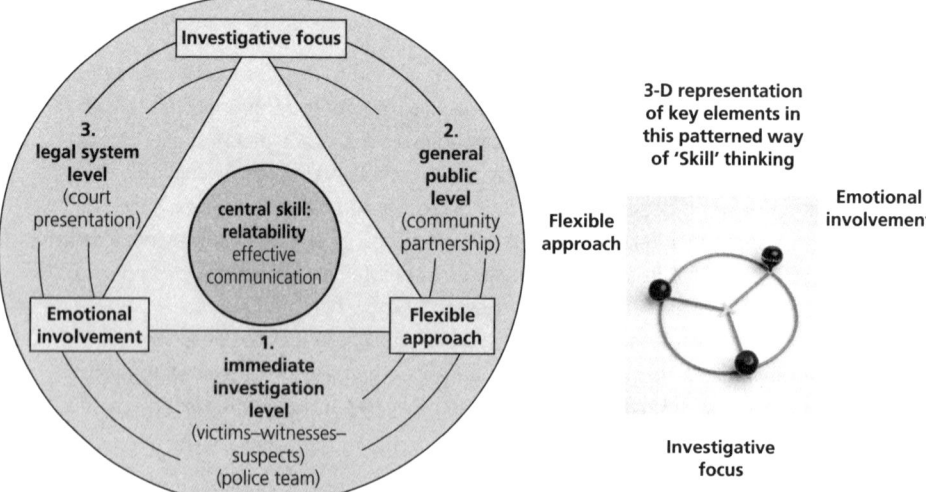

the key elements of 'skilful' thinking by police investigators and their ability to relate and communicate effectively to a diversity of people.

Case 5: Armed robbery

In an armed robbery case the offender had befriended a hostess at a pub and on the pretext of taking her home in his blue van had robbed her of cash and jewellery. The investigation turned cold after all available leads had been exhausted.

During the next month several other robberies (unrelated to the earlier one) were reported. An investigator with a sharp eye noticed that in one such report of a motor vehicle theft a member of the public had witnessed the vehicle being stolen and provided a good description of the thief.

He was a male Indian in his forties, 1.7 metres tall, plump, normal length curly hair, and wearing long dark trousers and a flowery short-sleeved shirt. The stolen van was found abandoned some time later several kilometres away.

Investigative focus

The same sharp-eyed investigator had worked on the earlier armed robbery case and recalled that the offender in that case was described by the pub hostess in a very similar way, even down to the distinctive flowery short-sleeved shirt.

Flexible approach

Further investigations into motor-vehicle theft cases revealed a pattern involving old pick-up trucks and vans. From the location of the thefts and their recovery it appeared that the stolen vehicles were being used for transportation.

As the previous armed robbery case had shown that the offender liked to frequent pubs, an investigative team was set up to conduct enquiries at pubs around the locations of the vehicle thefts and recovery sites.

The perpetrator of the previous armed robbery and the motor-vehicle thefts was subsequently arrested during an ambush at one of the pubs around these locations.

Case 6: Domestic violence

A detective was assigned to investigate a case of severe and prolonged physical abuse, in which the female victim had suffered at the hands of her live-in partner, with whom she had had two children.

She sustained multiple bodily injuries including loss of sight due to assaults over a protracted period of time. However, when the case was brought to court the female victim withdrew her allegations. She refused to testify against her partner despite the serious physical and psychological injuries the assailant had inflicted on her. She insisted that her injuries were caused by a fall. She refused to implicate her partner, and this complicated the investigation process.

- using one's understanding of the importance of the Skill style of thinking to effectively relate to people involved with the particular investigation and get the necessary information to build the case is, generally, all that is usually required of a detective in simple, non-complicated investigations to get a reasonable result.

However, in more serious and complex investigations, this is where the need for the fourth investigative thinking style of Risk comes into prominence. This Risk style of investigative thinking has at its core a preference for engaging in proactive efforts of justifiable risk-taking behaviour to increase the chances of getting a good result in an investigation. The key elements in this Risk style are depicted in Figure 8.4.

As can be seen with regard to undertaking an investigative 'risk' there are three justificatory 'lines' that are concerned: the lawfulness of the proposed risk, how logical the risk is, and the degree of latitude afforded to the risk both economically and conceptually. Each of these three criteria need to be justifiable in order for the 'risk' to be worth it. There is little point in proceeding with an investigative risk if it seems 'logical' and is 'latitudinally' affordable but is not 'lawful' and vice versa.

The three key processes involved in this Risk style of investigative thinking are discovery–creativity–development. Creativity is located in between the processes of discovery and development in this investigative thinking style to indicate its pivotal nature in both of the other processes.

Figure 8.4 'Risk' pattern of investigative thinking

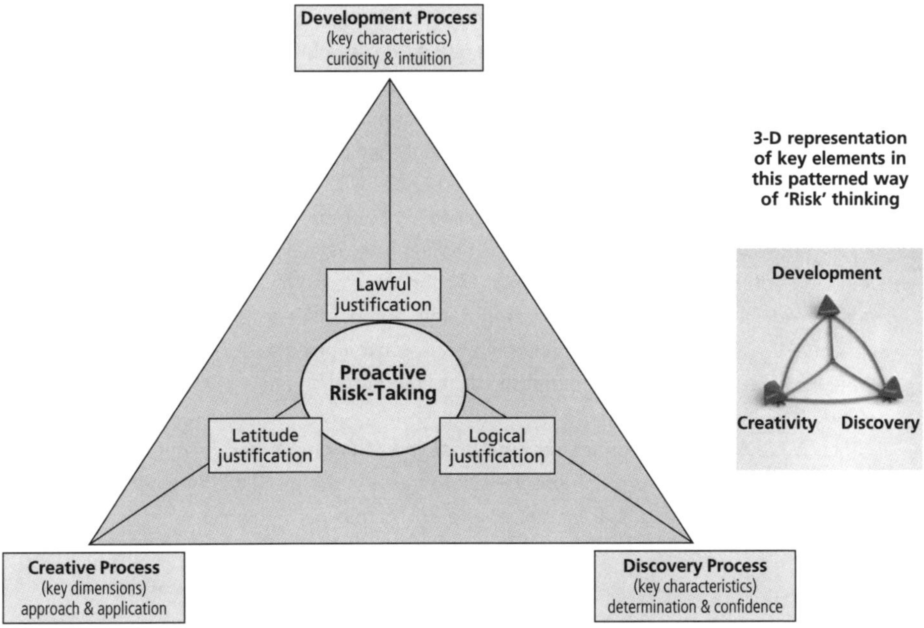

Also, the right-hand side of Figure 8.4 contains a 3-D representation of the three key elements arranged in a 'triangle' shape with proactive risk-taking at the centre point. The two cases below are representative of the Risk style of patterned investigative thinking.

Case 7: Pick-pocketing syndicate

There were several reported cases of pickpocketing from persons in a central shopping district of a large metropolitan city. Most of the victims were tourists and the police management was concerned about such cases affecting the tourism industry.

The investigating team set up to deal with the pickpocketing outbreak was able to ascertain that a well-organized syndicate was involved. The team managed to detain one of the syndicate members, a woman, who was seen loitering suspiciously in the target area. She was brought to the police lock-up. Two detectives were assigned to interrogate her but the result was futile as she refused to cooperate.

Discovery

A senior detective was assigned to the task of producing a positive statement from the accused so that she could be charged in court the next day. The first thing the detective did was to collate intelligence reports on the woman. He discovered the woman had a 15-month-old daughter named Lolita back in the Philippines.

Creativity

The detective then brought two bottles of mineral water—one was a 50 millilitre bottle and the other a 1.25 litre bottle. He brought the bottles to the interrogation room where the woman was held. The detective asked her several questions to assess her level of cooperativeness. She was not willing to answer any of them.

The detective took the two bottles and placed the bigger one on the woman's lap. He asked her to cradle the bottle. He then placed the smaller bottle near to her in a way that a mother would as she prepares to feed her child. The woman was taken aback and wondered what the interrogator was doing.

The detective then instructed the woman to 'imagine the big bottle is your daughter and now you are going to give her milk'. At the same time he said: 'Lolita—mama going to give you milk'. The detective in a very authoritative tone told the woman to 'nurse the "baby" [big bottle] and tell Lolita—mama going to give you milk'. The woman was so thrown off guard that she did as requested for a few minutes and then started to sob involuntarily.

She was so unable to control her emotions whilst thinking of her daughter—who she would miss if she was put in prison—that she started to plead with the detective, saying she would cooperate if the police were willing to expedite her case.

Development

She named the rest of the syndicate members she knew. They were rounded up, arrested, and charged in court.

Case 8: Bomb hoax

A parcel was found in a busy underground train station along with some words suggesting the presence of an explosive. Train services were disrupted to ensure the safe handling of the parcel. It was subsequently found that the parcel contained nothing but some empty food cans and food wrappings. CCTV recordings were obtained from all train stations and viewed. However, no tangible leads to the offender were found. The items found in the parcel were subjected to forensic tests but again, no leads were forthcoming.

Creativity

One investigator suggested the possibility of tracing the offender through the price tags on the empty food cans and food wrappings. The idea was seen as an absurd and a futile waste of time by most of the other investigators.

Discovery

The investigator who came up with the 'absurd' idea managed to convince his supervisor that it was worth following this lead. Subsequently, it was found that the price tag on one of the wrappings was 'unique' to a certain franchise outlet.

Development

A background check at the outlet allowed the investigator to link a possible suspect through his purchase records. The suspect was picked up despite the weak evidence and interviewed. He admitted readily that he was involved in two other similar offences as well as this one. His rationale for engaging in 'bomb hoaxes' was to test the 'readiness' of enforcement agencies in dealing with terrorism. The offender was subsequently convicted in court for carrying out such hoaxes in spite of his 'professed good intentions'.

Reasoning like a neural network: modelling patterns

The detailed examination of each of the four styles of investigative thinking presented in the previous sections, while illustrating the complexity of an investigator's cognitive processes, also reveals that these thinking styles are patterned in specific ways. Such patterned thought processes therefore make it possible to 'model' investigative thinking as a 'neural network', which is also known in the literature as neuro nets, artificial neural networks, and/or neurocomputing (Tafti 1990).

Neural networks have their conceptual roots in neuroscience, which is the study of the human brain. The neural network model of the human brain relies on 'neurons' (ie fundamental brain cells) to interconnect through a complex web of input and output paths so that the brain can function as a decision-making and high-level reasoning system.

The critical point about 'neural networks' is that when neurons are stimulated they produce electrical pulses that strengthen the connections between them (Wilson 1988). Every time the originating stimulus occurs the connections become stronger. Learning, therefore, takes place as a result of increasing the strength and number of connections between neurons. Even a small or partial stimulus may cause a chain reaction of the same type (Weatherall 1990).

Hence, the significance of 'neural network modelling' for training police officers is to add other styles of investigative thinking to the ones they already know and use so they become proficient in all fair ways of thinking 'investigatively'. Hence, the learning process becomes more predictable, in the sense that if a stimulus is strong enough to kick off a chain reaction of neural 'firings' then that particular neural pathway 'learns' to become activated under similar stimuli or in a similar situation. The strength of a stimulus is very much a matter of the degree of mental concentration that an individual gives to a cognitive experience be it a thought, a picture, a particular insight, or understanding.

Recent research in neuroscience has clearly shown how the human brain changes as a function of where an individual focuses their attention. That is, the mental act of focusing attention tends to stabilize the brain circuits associated with this focused concentration on something (Schwartz, Stapp, and Beauregard 2005).

In other words, it is possible to retrain the brain's neural circuitry to learn new pathways of thinking simply by paying enough concentrated attention to what it is one wants to learn. Hence, the value of practising a new way of learning so that over time such focused mental concentration to a specific way of thinking will help to keep the relevant electro-chemical links in the brain circuitry open long enough to become stable physical changes and hence new pathways in the brain's structure.

Such neurological research has significant implications for how to train police and other law enforcement personnel in relation to the importance of 'modelling' specific thought patterns rather than, as so often happens in police academies, concentrating solely on inculcating obedience to required behaviours. Current neuroscience research suggests that behaviour-change training regimes that act in isolation from the cognitive processes that underpin such behaviours may well be ineffectual in the longer term as they fail to lay down the neurological pathways necessary to stabilize such behaviours.

Moreover, such neuro-research helps to explain why human beings become so rigidly locked into certain thinking patterns about particular subjects and beliefs. That is, the repetitious attention of learning as one grows up in effect strengthens to the point of rigidity some specific neural pathways but not others. This 'narrows' the range of thinking options available to a person. In terms of police investigators such a narrowing of thinking options also explains why preferences develop for rigidly sticking to one or two 'tried and true' ways or styles of investigative thinking.

Another implication of this neuroscience research is that individuals, like professionals in business, law, finance, design, and police investigators, who practice their specialty on a daily basis literally 'learn to think differently'. That is, daily practice of a specialized or very specific way of thinking trains the brain to give priority or preference to making and strengthening only those sets of neural connections and not others to the same degree of focused attention.

Hence, it is little wonder that some of these individuals, literally, do not see 'eye to eye' what others mean. Such individuals have 'trained their brains' to think only along certain pathways specific to their profession, or culture, or religion, or creed, and hence have trouble communicating with others who 'think differently'.

Given this understanding of how the human brain functions neurologically, the 'modelling' that a computer-based neural network does is to operate on the principle that a highly interconnected system of simple processing elements (neurons) can pick up complex inter-relationships between a range of variables which in turn can create new structural pathways of thinking.

Therefore, a simple computer model of a 'neural network' can be defined as a 'parallel distributed processing system' consisting of an input layer, an output layer, and a hidden layer of connected neurons or processing elements (Wang and Elhag 2007).

A graphic example is shown in Figure 8.5 of a neural network as it relates to investigative thinking. As can be seen there are four 'tri-layered' (input–hidden–output) processing systems connected in parallel. Each processing system in the hidden layer represents one of the four investigative thinking styles (Method, Challenge, Skill, Risk) as indicated by the letters M, C, S, R of the neural network.

The 'hidden' layer by definition represents an individual police officer's 'internal thought processes' which cannot be seen and can only be inferred from the outputs that result from such cognitive functioning. Hence, the next Figure 8.6 is an attempt to portray graphically the inter-related 'internal workings' of an investigative mind in relation to the four styles (Method–Challenge–Skill–Risk) of the patterned thinking processes police engage in when carrying out an investigation. As indicated on Figure 8.5 this 'modelling' of these four investigative thought patterns is what is depicted in the 3-D representation in Figure 8.6.

As can be seen, the structure of this 3-D model is symbolic of the brain's neural network with its interconnected web of cognitive pathways. The model incorporates and integrates the relational significance of the key elements associated with each of the four 'investigative thinking styles' that constitute the totality of the model.

Figure 8.5 Neural network diagram of investigative pathways

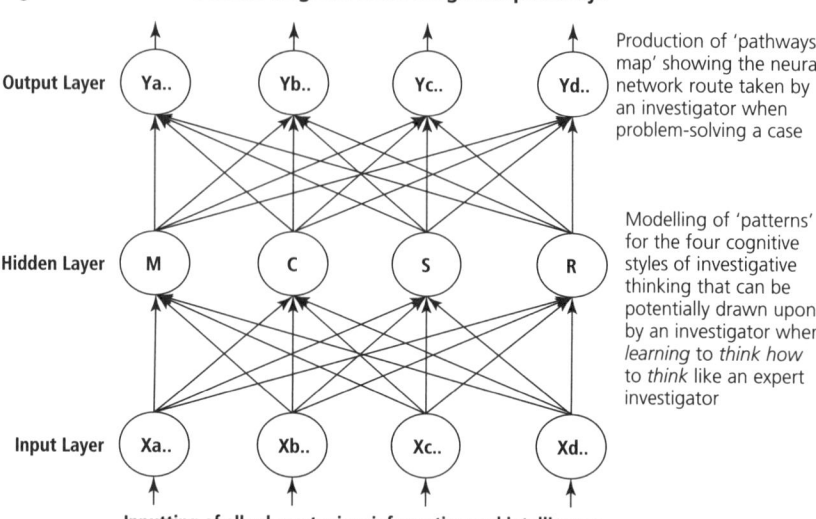

Output Layer: Ya.. Yb.. Yc.. Yd..

Production of 'pathways map' showing the neural network route taken by an investigator when problem-solving a case

Hidden Layer: M C S R

Modelling of 'patterns' for the four cognitive styles of investigative thinking that can be potentially drawn upon by an investigator when *learning* to *think how* to *think* like an expert investigator

Input Layer: Xa.. Xb.. Xc.. Xd..

Inputting of all relevant crime information and intelligence knowledge on case/incident or operation
(eg plug in 'Cross+Check' Experiential Knowledge Reasoning System)

Figure 8.6 3-D 'Neural network-like' model of investigative thinking

more complex pattern of investigative thinking

4. 'Risk' Style of investigative thinking
key elements: proactive processes of:
Discovery
Creativity
Development

3. 'Skill' Style of investigative thinking
key elements: relatability skills of:
Emotional involvement
Flexible approach
Investigative focus

2. 'Challenge' Style of investigative thinking
key elements: intensity sources of:
Crime
Criminal
Victim
Job

less complex pattern of investigative thinking

1. 'Method' Style of investigative thinking
key elements: procedural steps of:
5. Constructing
4. Connecting
3. Considering
2. Checking
1. Collecting

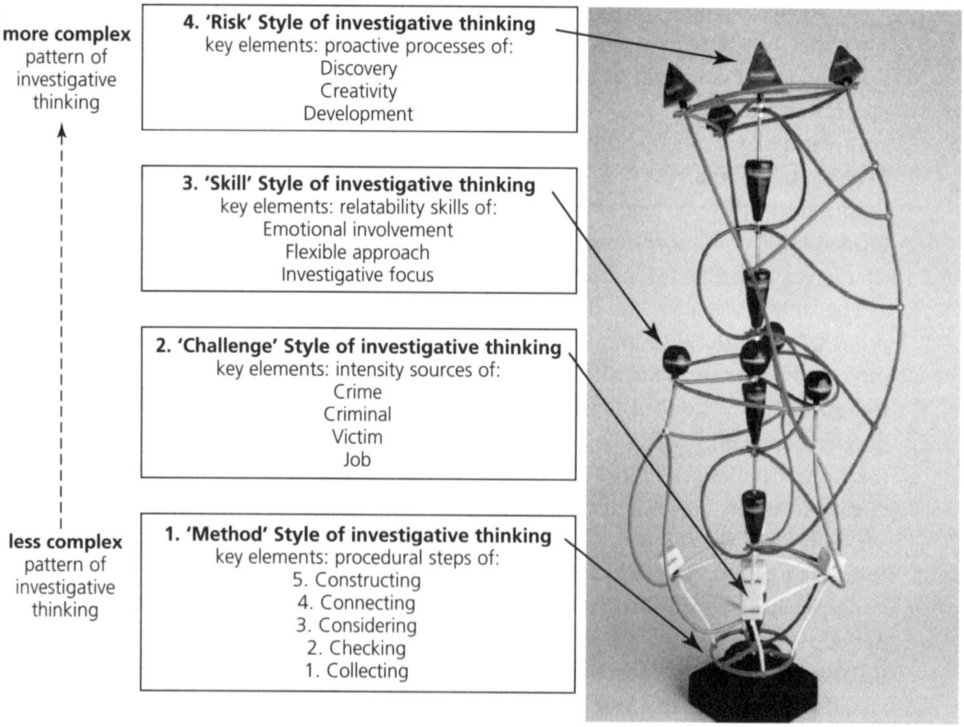

Component Parts (styles & key elements) of Neural Network Reasoning

What is not so obvious from this static representation is the dynamic nature of the model. However, if you visualize the model slowly turning then the 3-D features emerge about the 'shape' for each style of investigative thinking. The inter-related dynamics of each patterned way of investigative thinking captured in this 3-D model is explained as follows.

The central rod of the Method pattern of investigative thinking links (the tubing) the 'cone' shapes of each procedural step of Collecting, Checking, Considering, Connecting, and Constructing information into evidence to various elements of all the other styles.

In relation to the Challenge style, it encompasses the surface area of an investigation's outer boundary (the circle at the base of the model) by sitting above and being connected to the investigative circle through its four key elements—the intensity sources of the Job, Victim, Criminal, and Crime.

In contrast the Skill thinking pattern effects an investigation by ballooning out in the direction of a detective's thinking under the key influential elements of investigative focus, personal flexibility, and level of emotional involvement.

Finally, the Risk pattern of investigative thinking caps off an investigation by enhancing the investigating detective or team's way of thinking that adds multiple connections through the application of creativity, discovery, and development of information into evidence and hence provides skeletal pathways to all the other styles of investigative thinking—Skill, Challenge, Method.

The depicted 'hierarchical structure' of the 3-D model should not be read as implying that investigators always follow a 'temporal sequence' with regard to when, and where, which thinking style or patterned way of thinking is used in an investigation. In some investigations, several of these patterns can occur simultaneously; or can occur in a different order, as well as loop back to other previous patterns. Clearly, the conceptual explanation of the dynamics of this 3-D modelling process will of necessity be simpler and different, in some respects, from the complexity of the actual process of operation by investigators in 'how they prefer to think about' an investigation.

The important point to be clear about in understanding this 3-D model is that investigators may take different pathways when linking up their 'preferred' patterned ways of thinking 'investigatively' about a case.

The particular 3-D representation in Figure 8.6 is just one of a number of possible 'cognitive pathways' an investigator could potentially use to solve a particular crime. The significance of the 3-D model is that it depicts the structural arrangement of the hierarchical layers of thought involved in this one cognitive pathway. Hence, the individual variation in investigative thinking lies in the patterning of the pathways (ie the type and number of cognitive styles and which of their elements are used by a particular investigator) not in the relationship of the parts to one another, as they will always have the same hierarchical arrangement in terms of these four layers of thought patterns. In other words, the architecture of the model will not vary. The four patterned investigative thinking styles and their key elements are stable and constant. Individual variation is in the pathways taken not the parts used. This point will become clear in the case that is presented in the next section.

'Investigative pathways': neural network mapping system

To operationalize the 3-D neural network model depicted in the previous section two investigative forms, shown in Figure 8.7 and 8.8 respectively, are used to map out the investigative pathway taken in dealing with a particular case.

Initially, a form labelled a 'State-Action' case investigation chart (Figure 8.7) is used to capture the key investigative steps taken in this case.

Having charted the sequence of the investigation, these linear procedural steps are then mapped onto a second form which becomes the actual outcome product of the Neural Network Mapping System (Figure 8.8). This form is used to capture the 'investigative pathways' taken by the investigating officer responsible for the case.

It is evident in Figure 8.8 that this form is a diagrammatic layout of the four investigative thinking styles and their associated key elements presented in the same hierarchical order as depicted in the 3-D model in Figure 8.6. As such the diagram depicts a complex visual system of inter-related links and associations that constitutes the web-like structure of the investigative thinking pathway used in a case.

By using these two investigative forms as 'practice sheets' from various solved cases police officers learn how to think like an expert investigator by developing expertise in training their mind to think within the four investigative layers of Method–Challenge–Skill–Risk in different combinations and in different patterns.

The following case is presented to illustrate the use of this neural network investigative pathways mapping system using the two investigative mapping forms that constitute the system.

Case Study: Cyber crime

The neural network mapping system is applied to the investigation of a 'cyber crime' case that occurred in July 2005. The case involved the illegal use of the Internet to post a 'bomb threat' on a public website forum. Given the nature of the case as a potential terrorist attack on a city the police and law enforcement community treated the case with the utmost urgency to avoid a large-scale public panic occurring. The investigation of the case will be presented in line with the tri-structured operational framework of a neural network.

Figure 8.7 'State-Action' chart investigation form

'Investigative Pathways' Neural Network Mapping System [Form 1 of 2]		
Case Investigation Chart: 'State-Action' Sequence of Investigative Steps taken in Investigation		
Type of Case/Incident/Operation:		
State	**Action Tag**	**Descriptive Details**
A		
B		
C		
D		
E		
F		
G		
H		
Etc.		

Figure 8.8 'Neural network' investigative mapping form

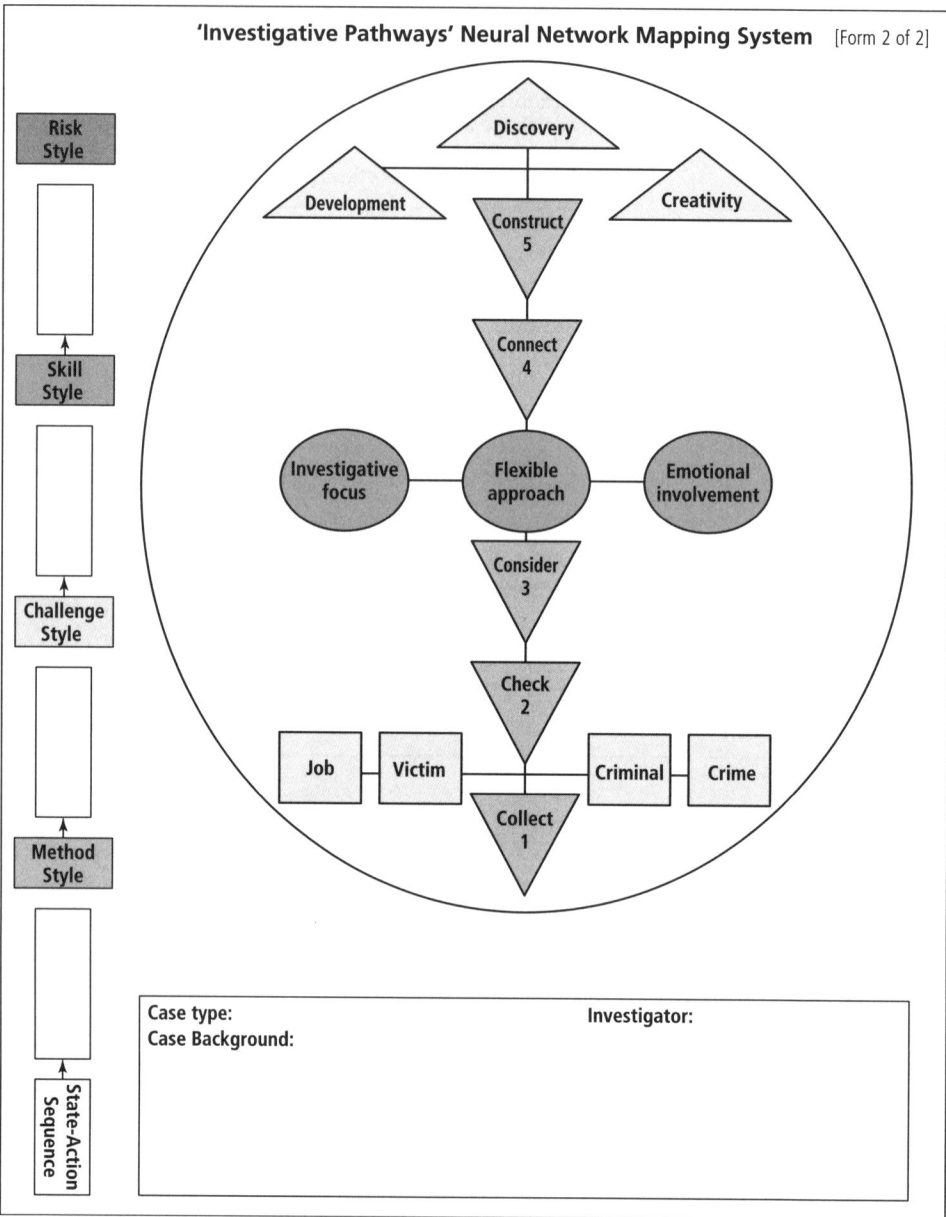

Input layer: 'State-Action' investigative sequence

A 'State-Action' (S-A) chart of the investigative sequence into how this computer-related crime progressed is presented in Figure 8.9. As noted previously, such an S-A chart is used to record the key investigative steps taken in a case.

The chart in Figure 8.9 is self-explanatory. The status of the investigation as it progresses can be gauged by following the chronological order of the various investigative stages to the final outcome for this reviewed case of cyber crime.

This chart can be filled out by the investigating officer or team either as part of the ongoing investigation or at any stage throughout the investigation if so desired. For example, if the investigation stalls at some point it is useful for an investigative team to reflect on the key investigative steps taken so far as a way of stimulating new ideas or potential approaches.

All the necessary information to chart any investigation using a similar S-A structure would be available to an investigation team by searching the relevant crime information management systems and relational databases kept by police and law enforcement organizations.

All the relevant information and intelligence inputted to the S-A chart is then connected up in 'parallel' to the next 'hidden layer' in the neural network system and 'distributed' in this case to the team of investigating officers to stimulate the investigative thinking pathways each investigating officer 'prefers' to use (ie Method–Challenge–Skill–Risk). Hopefully, such parallel 'firing' of information will also stimulate investigators to think outside their usual preferred patterns in order to make new neural connections that lead to alternate pathways of thinking.

Hidden layer: reflective analysis and modelling of thinking patterns

This layer of thinking is by definition 'hidden' from view as it involves the internal thought processes and tacit investigative knowledge of investigators. The only way anyone can know what someone thinks is by the end product such thoughts produce.

Because neural networks reason with patterns the type of analysis required by this 'IP' NNMS is reflective in nature. Hence, practice drafts using the investigative mapping form shown earlier (Figure 8.8) are used to 'model' the investigative thinking contained on the S-A chart at each of the key investigative stages. Often several practice models are required before the investigative officer or investigative team, as users of the system, are satisfied that their final outcome represents their comprehensive reflection of the investigative pathways taken so far with a particular case.

Figure 8.9 'State-Action' investigative sequence for a 'cyber crime' case

	'Investigative Pathways' Neural Network Mapping System	[Form 1 of 2]
	Case Investigation Chart: 'State-Action' Sequence of Investigative Steps taken in Investigation	
	Type of Case/Incident/Operation: Computer Crime—several postings of 'bomb threat' on a public website forum	

State	Action Tag	Descriptive Details
A	'Bomb threat' posting on public website	Members of the public reported an Internet posting on a public web forum that contained a 'bomb attack' threat to blow up a busy bus interchange. The offender of 'bomb threat' posting had the alias of 'Krisurf'. Complaint taken very seriously as the potential for public panic was of great concern to the police.
B	Trace of 'bomb threat' posting	IP address traced to an ISP subscriber who used a wireless router in her home without any password protection.
C	First interview—ISP Subscriber	Interview with ISP subscriber established she was unaware of her router being used by an unidentified offender who had illegally logged onto her network. The only lead was that offender must have been within close proximity to her home at the time of bomb threat posting to have logged on wirelessly.
D	Analysis of previous postings by 'Krisurf'	All previous postings made by 'Krisurf' were collated and IP addresses identified. Analysis of IP data revealed the use of bogus names to register as member of forum as well as using several different IP addresses each time offender logged onto the Internet.
E	Further IP traces (no leads)	Police tracking of IP's found at least six pages of different IP addresses used for postings during a one-week period that were spread city-wide. Also, use of free wireless Internet services in various cafes and other outlets further complicated attempts to identify user as no records kept by such outlets. No useful leads from this tracing exercise.
F	Likely offender 'profile'	Given the IT sophistication of 'Krisurf' in foiling police attempts to uncover his/her identity through bogus membership details and tracing IP addresses, is it a reasonable inference to suggest that the offender is likely to be a young adult of average or above intelligence, employed, owns a laptop that he/she carries most of the time, is highly mobile, sends Internet postings from very different geographical locations across the city.
G	Detailed analysis of IP addresses	Further detailed analysis of IP data carried out by grouping addresses into various neighbourhoods and then into sub-sets of residential zones in close proximity to each categorized neighbourhood.
H	Pattern of repeated use of some IP addresses	This analysis revealed two such categorized neighbourhoods with the most 'hits' (grouped IP addresses). Investigation focused on the 'residential zone' nearest to the neighbourhood with the most hits.
I	Interview IP address owners	Only investigators with significant 'computer knowledge' were assigned to interview IP address owners in order to ensure no potential leads were overlooked due to insufficient investigative knowledge for this specialized type of crime.
J	'Bogus' Internet survey (lead)	Since the offender (Krisurf) might be one of the IP address owners, an 'undercover' exercise was devised. This involved the rouse of investigators posing as 'market researchers' doing a survey of people's Internet experience by conducting in-depth interviews with them. A potential lead was discovered by this 'bogus' strategy.
K	'Bogus' postings by police (no leads)	Investigators attempted to contact and 'befriend' offender by making their own postings on web forum in the hope 'Krisurf' might inadvertently reveal information about him/herself. No useful leads were forthcoming by this strategy.
L	'Favoured' geographic sites for wireless routing	'Bogus' Internet survey identified one residential location in particular that had numerous owners of cafes/shops with wireless routers where their IP addresses had been repeatedly used by 'Krisurf'. The inference was drawn that this location contained a few geographic sites 'favoured' by 'Krisurf'. He/she may even reside near one of them.
M	Surveillance of favourite haunts	Constant observation at several identified Internet cafes/shops eventually led to the discovery of one suspect in particular that matched the 'profile' of the likely offender that was inferred in the action tag 'F' above.
N	Background checks on likely suspects—offender identified	Further investigative effort by way of background checks on the likely suspects eventually led to the identification of the offender. He was formally interviewed and subsequently charged with committing cyber crime.

If the 'IP' NNMS system is being used on a 'live' case then such a mapping product requires ongoing reflection and analysis to update it as new information and/or evidence surfaces for the case in question.

However, where 'IP' NNMS is used retrospectively on a 'solved' case for teaching and learning purposes the issue then becomes, not that a final mapping product is necessarily the 'right' mapping for the case, but rather is such a mapping logical and do the investigative strategies make sense? There are many paths to Rome and learning neural network patterns involves coming up with different ways to reach the same destination.

Hence, the final mapping becomes the 'output layer' product of the investigative thought. For the cyber crime case presented here as an example of how the 'IP' NNMS system works, this involves transposing the data on the S-A chart contained in Figure 8.9 onto a 'mapping' template. This mapping template is shown in the following section.

Output layer: neural network map of investigative pathways

This 'output layer' represents the complexity of the inter-related links and associations that constitute the web-like structure of the investigative thinking pathways neural network model. A visual map as shown previously in Figure 8.8 is reproduced here as Figure 8.10 with the investigative pathways for the cyber crime case mapped on the diagram.

The visualization captures the interconnected complexity of the investigative team's patterned ways of thinking in this case.

The letters A to N refer to the sequential 'state' of the investigation as it progresses and have been transposed from Figure 8.9 (ie the 'State-Action' Investigative Chart). Also, as can be seen alongside each letter the 'action tag' for each of these investigative 'states' is also reproduced from Figure 8.9 to assist with navigating through the map of investigative pathways used by the team in this case.

The easiest way to navigate this neural network map is to follow each letter in sequence starting from A while at the same time reading the 'descriptive details' column in Figure 8.9 that refers to each letter. In this manner, you will notice how you progress up and down and sideways through the mapping at various stages of the investigation as it takes place over time.

Such a zigzagging route perfectly captures how the human brain 'thinks' in an interconnected web of multiple links and reinforcing feedback loops that are in a continuous state of flux until a decision is made and the whole cognitive process starts up again as the next thought, idea, insight, or understanding is mentally processed.

Figure 8.10 Neural network map of investigative pathways in 'cyber crime' case

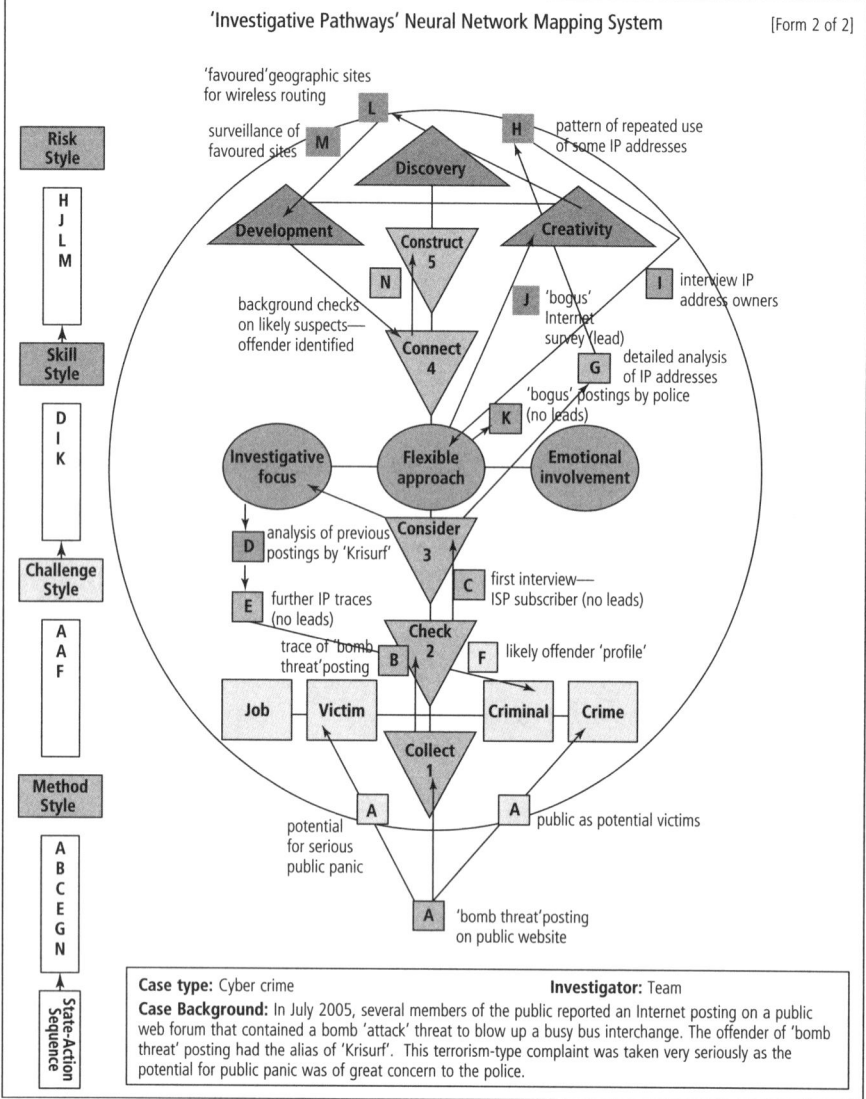

As can be seen, on the left-hand side of the mapping system is a 'sidebar' that contains the four investigative styles as patterned ways of thinking (ie Method–Challenge–Skill–Risk) which have been arranged in the same hierarchical order as on the actual diagrammatic neural network map. This sidebar is included so that an investigator can get an 'at-a-glance' view of which of these four patterned ways of thinking have been in the investigation so far and to what degree. The sidebar is a reference tool to know how many, and how much, and in what sequence, and in what combination the various investigative thinking styles are used. This sidebar is very helpful in establishing when and where another thinking style might need to be considered, particularly in a stalled investigation that has run out of leads or a stuck investigation that has lost focus and direction.

With reference to the cyber crime case that has been mapped in Figure 8.10, it is clear that all four investigative thinking styles were used over the duration of the investigation. As is evident, the investigative Method style, as the backbone of an investigation, not only starts the investigation (A) it must also end it (N) if the case is to be successful. It is also clear from the diagram that the Method in this case did not involve a straightforward application of this style of investigative thinking. There was significant backward and sideways movement in Method thinking happening as the investigation progressed.

As for the Challenge thinking style it manifested itself initially in two prongs or offshoots of the Method style at the start of the investigation at stage (A). The terrorism-related nature of the crime in terms of public panic as well as innocent members of the public becoming possible victims is what links these two elements of the Challenge that the police faced in dealing effectively with this investigation. The other significant Challenge presented to the investigative team as it proceeded occurred when further traces of all the previous postings by the offender known by the alias 'Krisurf' at stage (E) failed to produce any worthwhile leads. At that point, the investigative team realized more fully that they were dealing with a smart offender at least in terms of IT knowledge. This focus on the criminal became a challenge for some members of the investigative team to outwit the offender by trying to figure out who he/she might be and what he/she might be like. This Challenge led to the development of a likely offender profile—the descriptive details of which are recorded at stage (F) of the S-A chart in Figure 8.9.

The patterned way of thinking at the Skill level of investigation is concerned with three key elements or facets of thinking skilfully as can be seen in Figure 8.10. Initially, the conceptual skill of focusing an investigation took the form of deciding to conduct an analysis of all previous postings by 'Krisurf' at stage (D) which led to further traces of IP addresses (E), but this investigative focus led to no real leads or results. It was only after further consideration at the 'reflective-analysis' stage of Method thinking that further detailed analysis of IP addresses (G) led to the 'discovery' of a previously unseen usage pattern hidden within the IP data (H). This discovery led in turn to a series of in-depth interviews (I) with a number IP address owners at a specific geographical location or residential zone that contained wireless Internet access sites (cafes/shops). An important consideration here in regard to (I) is that only investigators with significant IT and computer knowledge were allowed to be used for the interviews. This was to ensure not only that investigators could relate effectively (Skill style) by 'speaking the same language' as IP users, but also to make sure the information gathered was properly understood in order to not lose any relevant information due to a lack of knowledge.

However, at this point in the investigation knowing that the offender might be a sophisticated IT user, the investigative team went back to thinking flexibly (Skill style) and decided to employ two different approaches or strategies in an attempt to identify 'Krisurf'.

The first strategy (J) involved some creative thinking (Risk style) by team members to avoid tipping off the offender if he/she happened to be one of the IP address owners the investigators were going to interview (I). Hence, a 'bogus' in-depth survey about a person's Internet experience was designed and investigators would 'pose' as market researchers for an Internet company as the pretext for the interview.

The second strategy (K) was run at the same time as the 'bogus' survey interviews were conducted. This strategy involved investigators again 'posing' as individuals like-minded to 'Krisurf' by posting their own 'bogus' notices on the website forum used by him/her. In this way the investigators hoped to establish contact with the offender and eventually befriend him so that he/she might unwittingly reveal vital information about his/her identity. However, this strategy did not produce any leads or result.

Fortuitously, the first strategy (J) was more successful in discovering a lead about some likely geographic sites (L) that used wireless routers (Internet cafes/shops) which the offender favoured on a regular basis as places to illegally send electronic postings. This lead was developed into the breakthrough needed in the investigation as constant surveillance by the investigators of these favoured sites (M) eventually led to the identification and arrest of the offender.

As can be seen in Figure 8.10 surveillance led to a number of likely suspects that fitted the offender profile being identified as frequent users at the targeted Internet cafes/shops. Background checks (N) ruled out several of these suspects. Eventually, one of the suspects became the most promising prospect as the offender. A court order to seize his laptop was served and it contained the evidence to convict him of the crime.

As mentioned previously, and as seen in this stage of the investigation in Figure 8.10, for an investigation to be successful the style of investigative thinking must move back to the Method in order to connect offender(s) by evidence to a crime and to construct a case against the offender(s) that is supported by the final brief of evidence.

In summary, it should be noted that the employment of the Risk style of investigative thinking gave this investigation its creative edge. First, by discovering a hidden pattern of usage in the IP data. Secondly, this led to a breakthrough lead when investigators used creativity in posing as market researchers conducting in-depth interviews using a bogus survey instrument. Thirdly, in developing the information gained from the creative lead into evidence that finally identified and convicted the offender.

Summary

This chapter presented an 'Investigative Pathways' (IP) mapping application system based on neural network modelling. The IP application is grounded in extensive empirical research that identified four investigative thinking styles labelled respectively as Method, Challenge, Skill, and Risk. Each of these four cognitive styles of investigative thinking are patterned thought processes that investigators repeatedly use and rely upon to think through a case.

Furthermore, it was found that to a large extent police detectives/investigators remain unaware of the patterned way they think in terms of these four investigative styles. The patterned structure of investigative thinking exists in a hierarchy of increasing conceptual complexity as an individual begins 'to think' further up the hierarchy.

Moreover, although it is possible for an investigator to use all four styles of thinking in a particular investigation, it is rare that any one detective will give equal weight to all four styles of investigative thinking in a particular case. Investigators like everyone else have a preference for maybe one or two particular styles or patterned ways of thinking.

The Method way of thinking is the base level of thought required to carry out an investigation as it encapsulates the procedurally driven nature of basic police training. From there the next layer of thought is the Challenge style which in essence provides the motivational drive to do a good investigation. After the Challenge level of thinking the issue becomes, cognitively, the quality of thinking. That is, the thinking an investigator does at this point needs to rise substantially to the next level of Skill as this style of thinking guides and focuses the investigation. The final layer of conceptual thought is the Risk style of investigative thinking. This top layer is where investigative creativity resides in the mind and requires a proactive outlook to realize its full potential. At this level the Risk style, as the label implies, tends to multiply the potential for either benefits and/or burdens in the investigation. In other words, Risk style thinking can make or break an investigation.

Case examples of the inner workings of each of these styles of investigative thinking (Method–Challenge–Skill–Risk) were presented to illustrate the conceptual sophistication inherent in thinking like an investigator.

The patterned thought processes of investigators made it possible to 'model' investigative thinking as a neural network-like structure. A 'neural network', in computer terms, is a parallel distributed processing system consisting of an input layer, an output layer, and a hidden layer of connected neurons that act as the processing elements of the system.

With regard to 'neural networks' as pattern computers capable of learning, an important finding from recent neuroscience research is that the daily practice of a specialized way of thinking 'trains the brain' to give priority or preference to making and strengthening those sets of neural connections that receive such attention through focused thinking.

A graphic depiction of a 'neural network' system of investigative thinking was presented in detail along with a 3-D model of the 'investigative brain' of the police. This 3-D modelling is symbolic of the brain's neural network with its interconnected web of cognitive pathways.

The significance of the 3-D model is that it shows how individual police officers can take different cognitive pathways based on their 'preferred' patterned ways of thinking when investigating a case.

Therefore, the individual variation in investigative thinking lies in the patterning of the pathways (ie the type and number of cognitive styles and which, of what elements, and when these styles are used by a particular investigating officer) not in the relationship of the styles to one another.

The investigative thinking styles will always have the same hierarchical arrangement in terms of four layers of thought patterns. In other words, the architecture of the neural network model will not vary. The four patterned investigative thinking styles and their key elements (component parts) are stable and constant. Individual variation is in the pathways taken through the styles and their associated parts, not in the styles themselves.

An 'Investigative Pathways' Neural Network Mapping System ('IP' NNMS) is introduced that uses two specifically designed investigative forms as 'templates' for police officers to use in order for them to learn how to operate this application. The two forms are, firstly, a 'State-Action' (S-A) chart used to sequentially record the key investigative steps taken in a case; and, secondly, a neural network mapping form with the key investigative steps transposed from the S-A chart to illustrate graphically the investigative pathways taken in an investigation.

By using these two investigative forms as 'practice sheets' from various solved cases police officers learn how to think like an expert investigator by developing expertise in training their mind to think with the four investigative layers of Method–Challenge–Skill–Risk in different combinations and in different patterns.

The chapter concludes with a detailed case study of a cyber crime to illustrate the use of the 'IP' NNMS application using the two investigative mapping forms that constitute the system. The case study clearly demonstrated the 'zigzagging' nature of investigative thinking and how this neural network-like model captures the interconnected web of multiple links and feedback loops associated with thinking as an expert investigator.

'Interlocking Terrorism Contexts' System: Knowledge Modelling Application

Introduction

The focus of this chapter is on modelling knowledge of the contexts in which terrorism evolves, develops, and operates. From this knowledge foundation an application system is presented for use in the policing and law enforcement community.

The chapter starts with outlining various problematic aspects of defining terrorism and applying a profiling methodology to 'profile' terrorists. This is followed by the argument supported by extensive empirical research that more emphasis should be given to the pragmatically useful approach of profiling the 'process' of terrorism itself rather than the 'person' of the terrorist.

A specifically designed application based on an 'Interlocking Terrorism Contexts' Knowledge Modelling System (ITC-KMS) is then presented along with a case study of the Jemaah Islamiyah terrorist network in the South East Asian region to demonstrate the utility of such a 'knowledge modelling' approach to profiling the process of terrorism.

Problem of 'defining' terrorism

The terrorism field itself is plagued with definitional difficulties as to what constitutes 'terrorism'. As Matassa and Newburn (2003) note, defining terrorism is problematic to say the least. They cite Laqueur who, writing about political terrorism in 1987, argued 'any definition of political terrorism venturing beyond noting the systematic use of murder, injury, and destruction or the threats of such acts towards achieving political ends [is] bound to lead to endless controversies' (Matassa and Newburn 2003: 468). Schmidt and Jongman (1988) cited 109 different definitions of 'terrorism' in the scholarly literature when they undertook a survey of leading academics in the terrorism field. This was in 1988 and the search for an uncontentious definition still has not abated. Much of the definitional debate revolves around trying to split hairs over when so-called 'freedom fighters' become 'terrorists'.

As Townshend (2002: 3) points out the problem of defining 'terrorism' is one of 'labelling, because "terrorist" is a description that has almost never been voluntarily adopted by any individual or group'. It is a pejorative label applied by governments and states to persons who use violent threats and/or force to attack such governments and states. Hence, government and state definitions of terrorism automatically treat any threat and/or use of violence as an illegal act. The problem here, of course, is that this makes the state the sole arbitrator on who has the right to use violence.

The US State Department's definition is a typical example of this self-serving perspective when it defines terrorism as 'premeditated, politically motivated violence perpetrated against non-combatant targets by subnational groups or clandestine agents, usually intended to influence an audience'. (Council on Foreign Relations 2004).

Naturally, having a monopoly of the legitimate use of violence against your opponents is politically and operationally very advantageous for totalitarian states. Even in democratically elected states it is to their political advantage to silence critics by using such self-serving definitions of terrorism as it allows them to side-step the issue of 'state-sponsored terrorism'. This form or type of terrorism is defined as 'a method of warfare whereby a state uses agents or surrogates to create political and economic instability in another country' (Griffiths and O'Callaghan 2002: 307). The use of the CIA by various US government administrations to destabilize a number of countries, especially in Latin America over many years, is a classic case of definitional hypocrisy.

Hence, the clichéd statement used by almost all guerrilla warfare and militant insurrectionary groups that 'one person's terrorist is another person's freedom fighter' underscores the relativity at the very core of the definitional difficulty of terrorism. It depends on who is doing the labelling as to which side you are perceived to be belong to—a fighter for freedom or a terrorist agitator.

It is beyond the scope of this chapter to explore this definitional dilemma any further other than to point out the inherent difficulties that any definition entails. Even the more promising definition offered by Ganor (1998: 6) that 'terrorism is the intentional use of, or threat to use violence against civilians or against civilian targets, in order to attain political aims', and supported by Barker (2003: 23) as a 'definition that works' since it can be applied to governments and their agencies or proxies as well as 'subnational groups', still has labelling problems.

Problem of 'profiling' terrorists

It is apparent, as the previous section makes abundantly clear, that terrorism is a concept that is notoriously difficult to 'define' and 'dangerous' to use. Governments who invoke 'terrorism' rhetoric unwisely often end up having power concentrated in the hands of a few gung-ho individuals at the expense of calmer voices.

The Bush administration's 'axis of evil' talk and lust for war in Iraq after 9/11 against the advice of the majority of the international community on the so-called 'intelligence' of the now non-existent weapons of mass destruction of Saddam has ended up, some four years later, with the ensuing debacle and descent into civil war. Such a tragic state of affairs in Iraq is testament to the dangerous 'solutions' terrorism can breed.

Therefore, once an individual or group has been labelled 'terrorist' it allows a government and its state institutions to wield extraordinary powers of coercion and force. Under other circumstances such power would be seen as unwarranted and unjustifiable and an attempt to subvert traditional notions of law and justice. It seems to evoke the label that 'terrorism' provides 'carte blanche' to a state in the name of 'protection' from terrorist attacks.

However, not only is defining 'terrorism' a difficult task and dangerous undertaking it is also further complicated by the fact that it is an exceedingly thorny issue to establish 'who' exactly qualifies as a 'terrorist'. Hence, the zeal to 'profile' terrorists by the police/law enforcement community and the security apparatus of various Western governments post-9/11 remains unabated.

Such zeal is often misdirected. This is in large measure due to an inadequate understanding of just what 'profiling' can deliver. The limitations of offender/criminal and behavioural profiling as a practice nested in the criminological and psychological literature are not well understood. Thus, attempts to transfer the methodology of criminal and behavioural profiling to terrorism profiling will eventually deliver mixed outcomes—some good, some bad, and others just plain silly to say the least.

What follows is a detailed look at the literature on the 'profiling' methodology. This will establish the necessary background knowledge base for understanding the terrorism model proposed later in this chapter as a useful police knowledge management application for combating terrorism.

Defining 'profiling'

The criminal investigation field is littered with terms that are currently used or have been used to try and capture the meaning behind the concept of 'profiling'. For example, the history of profiling reveals terms like psychological profiling, criminal profiling, criminal personality profiling, criminal investigative analysis, and behavioural evidence analysis have all been used, and some are still used almost interchangeably to describe a similar process of coming up with a 'profile' of a likely perpetrator of a crime.

Given this proliferation of labels, as well as the media's fascination with the notion that has spurned several 'law and order'-type television shows which have their resident 'profiler', it is clear the term 'profiling' needs some careful clarification.

Where the confusion lies is that each of these various profiling terms has its own idiosyncratic additions and omissions. Ainsworth (2001) provides a clear example of just how idiosyncratic the profiling arena has become when he states:

> profilers on either side of the Atlantic often disagree as to the most suitable methods to be used in their work. Furthermore, even profilers in the same country may have fundamental disagreements about the best way in which knowledge might be advanced. Nowhere is this more evident than in the exchanges between Britain's two best known 'profilers', Paul Britton and David Canter. (Ainsworth 2001: 7)

Clearly, the 'profiling' label acts like a covering blanket over very real differences and disparate approaches to profiling. Hence, its meaning has become blurred at best and badly misunderstood at worst.

Moreover, a quick glance over the profiling literature reveals that in England and Europe the literature favours the term offender profiling while in the US the term criminal profiling is more often used. Also, the FBI used to use the term psychological profiling but now label what they do in the 'profiling' arena as criminal investigative analysis.

As well as these terminological differences, there are also definitional differences in regard to what exactly the term 'profiling' means. Several writers (Geberth 1981; Douglas *et al.* 1986; Copson 1995; Jackson and Bekerian 1997; McCann 1992) have their own slightly different twist on what is involved in 'profiling'.

As Ainsworth (2001: 17) observes 'there is no commonly accepted definition of profiling and that the area subsumed under the umbrella is diverse and complex'. Moreover, Harrower (1998: 56) defers to Copson (1996) on this issue stating that whilst 'there is no universally accepted definition of the term' it is used more 'as a "term of convenience" . . . to cover techniques whereby the behaviour shown in a crime is used to draw inferences about the likely offender'.

A very general level of the definition offered by Canter and Alison (1999: 5) best captures the essence of profiling when they state that profiling is 'commonly associated with inferring characteristics of an offender from the actions at a crime scene'.

Aims of profiling

McCann states that 'the ultimate goal of profiling is to assist in the successful apprehension and conviction of the perpetrator' (McCann 1992: 475). While this is certainly a desired outcome for all forms of and approaches to profiling, it is far too general a statement to be of much use as it begs the question—how? That is, just exactly how does profiling 'assist' in apprehending and convicting a perpetrator?

Several researchers (Hazelwood *et al.* 1987; Jackson and Bekerian 1997; Wilson, Lincoln, and Kocsis 1997; Holmes and Holmes 1998; Harrower 1998; Egger 1999) mention in the literature two specific aims associated with 'profiling', regardless of how it is defined, that provides part of the answer to the question of how profiling is useful to an investigation. These two key aims are:

- Profiling can narrow the scope of an investigation.
- Profiling can provide useful strategies for interviewing suspects.

To these two commonly held aims, some writers (Holmes and Holmes 1998, cited in Egger 1999: 13) add other goals like providing:

- 'social and psychological assessments' of the type of offender investigators should be looking for amongst suspects. Also, profiles can provide:
- 'psychological evaluation of belongings' that a suspect may have in his or her possession.

Whilst such goals can be regarded as additional elements they can also just as easily be subsumed under the two key aims noted previously. However, a few comments need to be made about the two key aims of profiling.

With respect to the first aim of 'narrowing the scope of an investigation', this is clearly a very beneficial goal. In serious and complex cases an investigation can yield very large numbers of suspects. Having a process like 'profiling' that reduces the size of a suspect list to manageable proportions is a very useful investigative tool for police departments.

However, like any tool there is a potential downside to it as well. Not only does its 'usefulness' as an investigative tool depend on how it is used and by whom, but also the extent to which it is used in conjunction with other investigative leads and tools.

There is an old saying that 'if the only tool you have is a hammer then you see every problem as a nail'. The risk in the usefulness of profiling, as regards this key benefit of narrowing down a suspect list, lies in the perception that 'profiling' is the right and only tool to use. This 'blind faith' in its inherent value neglects the fact that a 'profile' is, at best, a 'tentative inference' which has yet to be verified and checked against the known facts of a case.

In other words, a 'profile' can just as easily lead an investigation astray as it can 'hit the nail on the head'. It all depends on the type of 'profile' used, how the 'profile' was constructed, who constructed the 'profile', and what other resources and tools can be used to check the 'profile' against. These factors either diminish or multiply the risk of 'profiling'. For example, Egger (1999: 248) in his review of profiling makes the observation:

> Dr. John Liebert, a Washington psychiatrist and a consultant to Seattle's Green River Task Force is distrustful of psychological profiles put together by police agencies and the FBI. He states, 'I think the state of the art [profiling] leaves a lot to be desired' (McCarthy 1984, p.1). Liebert urges police agencies involved in a serial murder investigation to utilize the services of a psychiatrist. He warns that 'superficial behavioural scientific profiling that rigidly reduces serial murder to a few observable parameters can lead an investigation astray' (Liebert 1985, p. 199. Cited in Egger)

Another more chilling example of profiling going astray can be found in the 'Washington Sniper' investigation where 13 people were killed when filling up their cars at gas stations in and around the Washington area in the US during a three-week killing spree that ended in October 2002 with the arrest of two males who did not fit the FBI-produced profile. The offenders were John Allen Mohammed, a 41-year-old Gulf War veteran and his 17-year-old companion John Lee Malvo (*Courier-Mail* 2002: 31).

The failure of the FBI to identify key characteristics of the killers correctly is due in part to the methodological flaws inherent in this 'type' of profiling. The FBI's profiling approach, now known as 'criminal investigative analysis', is still largely based on data they collected in the early 1970s on convicted sexual serial killers. From this very specific and limited sample the FBI generalize the whole population of killers and assume that the same general characteristics will be present in all killings. Blind faith in such 'profiling' can have fatal consequences.

Furthermore, Wilson, Lincoln, and Kocsis (1997) point out that 'profiling' is reductive rather than productive. By this they mean 'profiles' can narrow the list of suspects but they are not capable of specifically identifying the one suspect who is the offender. Evidence is what convicts an offender and 'profiling' at best only produces circumstantial evidence.

In the final analysis, the comment by Egger (1999) in his review of psychological profiling is worth noting. He states:

> Although not all investigators need to be trained profilers, a better understanding of how profiling is accomplished and how it may aid an investigation is recommended. Criminal investigators need to understand that, in some cases, a profile may reduce the universe of suspects to a much more manageable number. Profiles do not have to solve crimes; however, if they are successful, they can make the investigator's job easier. (Egger 1999: 261)

In relation to the second aim of providing useful strategies and suggestions for interviewing suspects, this is a less contentious outcome than the first goal.

Again, the 'utility' of profiling with regard to interviewing suspects will depend on similar factors to do with the 'type' of profiling done and by whom.

For example, a 'profile' that is statistically derived from a certain group of offenders would be less useful in an interview context than a 'profile' which is more clinically based in its construction. Clinical insights and intuitions about how to talk to a certain type of offender are likely to be more beneficial in extracting information than having a list of assumed key characteristics about this group of offenders in general.

Assumptions of profiling

Just as the aims of profiling have the potential to be problematic so also do the assumptions which underpin its use. According to Egger (1999: 5) Holmes and Holmes (1998) identify four assumptions that are made about the profiling process. They are:

1. The crime scene reflects the personality of the offender.
2. The method of operation (MO) remains similar.
3. The signature will remain the same.
4. The offender's personality will not change.

Not all profiling approaches share these assumptions and certainly not to the extent to which some researchers present them more as apparent 'statements of fact'.

Such assumptions should more properly be regarded as at best a form of experiential 'truisms' that might be substantiated in some cases but clearly should not be elevated to proven facts. Assumptions are statements waiting for confirmation.

For example, the assumption that the 'MO remains similar' is based on the first assumption that the 'crime scene reflects personality' which in turn is based on a hidden or implicit unstated assumption that the offender is a 'personality with pathology' (Egger 1999: 5).

Furthermore, this implicit assumption is again in turn based on the sample of offenders from which this list of assumptions is drawn. Since, according to Harrower (1998: 57) '90% of profiling involves murder and rape' it is not surprising that a crime scene displays a 'personality with pathology'.

At this juncture, it is mindful to remember that profiling has traditionally been used with 'criminal' offenders that have some element of 'psychological dysfunction' exhibited through their behaviour, especially in crimes of a serial sexual nature like rapes and murders (Geberth 1996; Holmes and Holmes 1998). For example, Geberth clearly states that profiling is:

> productive in crimes in which an unknown subject has demonstrated some form of psychopathology in his crime . . . sadistic torture in sexual assault, evisceration, postmortem slashing and cutting, motiveless fire-setting, lust and mutilation murders, ritualistic crimes, and rapes. (1996: 711)

The list of crimes that Holmes and Holmes outline is similar, with a few additional crimes suitable for profiling: 'sadistic torture in sexual assaults, evisceration, postmortem slashing and cutting, motiveless fire setting, lust and mutilation murder, rape, arson, bank robbery, sadistic and ritualistic crime, pedophilia.' (1998: 181–182).

Therefore, the key point is that some form of psychological dysfunction is usually evident in most of the crimes to which offender profiling has been applied.

In relation to this aspect, a sub-point that should be borne in mind is that with experience and criminal cunning it may well become the case that a 'pathological personality' can learn to modify and change its MO to evade detection. In such cases, the third assumption that the 'signature remains the same' may be a better yardstick to evaluate if the same offender could be responsible for a series of similar crimes rather than the MO, which with time potentially could change quite considerably.

Moreover, given that profiling has largely been developed on 'low volume' but 'major' crimes like murder, sexual assaults, and rapes with offenders that exhibit personality defects, do the same profiling assumptions apply to 'high volume' or 'minor' crimes like property offences, street robbery, and other more common everyday-type crimes? Or do they break down when 'no pathology' is evident?

This question is of particular relevance to terrorism and will be taken up again in the next section.

Approaches to profiling

The profiling field contains about as many approaches to profiling as there are definitions. However, the task of sorting out approaches becomes a little easier if viewed from the perspective of the nature of the framework or orientation that underpins a particular approach.

Jackson and Bekerian (1997) make a cogent argument that when you look at how each profiling approach analyses offending behaviour it reflects the operation of two quite different methodological frameworks that may be used to support a particular approach. Jackson and Bekerian outline the first of their two main methodological frameworks as follows:

> One framework incorporates concepts and techniques of experimental psychology, such as hypothesis testing or statistical analysis of findings, and it is generally referred to as the scientific approach. Examples of this framework would include research on rape (Davies & Dale 1995, 1996), evaluation of statistical modelling (Aitken, Connolly, Gammerman, Zhan, & Oldfield 1995), diction of offender files from victim and witness descriptions (Farrington & Lambert, as cited in Jackson & Bekerian 1997), and discussion of life narratives (Canter 1994). (Cited in Egger 1999: 8)

The second framework is described by Egger, citing Jackson and Bekerian's work, as follows:

> The second methodological framework relies on the concepts of clinical psychology and forensic psychiatry. In this framework, the profiler is making inferences about the unconscious psychological processes of the offender. Here, 'Conclusions about the relationship of personality and behaviour are drawn from multiple observations of single cases, rather than from population statistics that generalize across multiple cases' (Jackson & Bekerian 1997). The primary example of this framework, aside from private psychological or psychiatric consultants, would be the FBI profiling approach described earlier. (Cited in Egger 1999: 9)

A more appropriate term for the first type of methodological framework identified by Jackson and Bekerian is to define it as a 'statistically based' orientation rather than as a 'scientific approach', as if the second framework which is more of a 'clinically based' orientation is not 'scientific'.

Therefore, in broad terms, the profiling field can be divided into two quite distinct orientations based on whether or not a particular approach is based on a more 'clinical' or 'statistical' methodological framework. A brief review of the types of approach that fit under each of these frameworks or orientations is presented below.

'Clinical' orientation to profiling

This methodological framework includes profiling approaches that are based on a 'clinical' perspective in the construction of a profile. However, this does not mean that each approach has to be practised by 'clinicians' in the sense of a medical practitioner or similarly allied professional, like a therapist or mental health worker. Rather, the emphasis is that the approach is 'clinically based' in terms of the perspective drawn upon involving a psychological and/or psychiatric knowledge base.

For example, the diagnostic evaluations category of Wilson *et al.* fits comfortable into the general orientation of a 'clinically-based profiling' framework as outlined in Egger (1999) following Jackson and Bekerian's analysis of the profiling field. Egger's remarks about this category clearly emphasizes its affinity with this 'clinical' approach to profiling:

> *Diagnostic evaluations* are generally referred to today as *criminal personality profiling* and are done by psychiatrists or psychologists. These are professionals who have very little experience or knowledge of law enforcement or investigation. Their evaluations are generally based on their clinical practice, and drawn from their knowledge of personality theories and various psychological disorders as defined in the *Diagnostic Statistical Manual*. Profiles are constructed by diagnosing the probable psychopathology or personality type likely to have committed the crimes in question. The earliest recorded profiles of

this type would include the Langer and Brussel profiles. (Egger 1999: 6, italics added)

Interestingly, such 'clinically based' profiles have proven to be both extremely accurate on some occasions and less than accurate and even misleading on other occasions. It seems to be a bit of a 'hit and miss' game.

A reasonable inference to draw from this is that to a large extent the 'accuracy' of a clinically constructed profile appears to depend on the experience and ability of the profiler. Hence, one of the main criticisms of this approach is the 'individualistic' nature of the process.

Furthermore, with regard to 'clinically based' profiling a substantial case can be made that the FBI's profiling approach also fits very neatly into this type of framework. For example, the early successes in 'profiling' by the FBI during the 1980s are due in part to the methodology they employed to construct profiles, which was based on their 'organized/disorganized' typology. The development of this classification scheme came out of 36 qualitative, in-depth interviews of convicted sexual killers. Moreover, some of their other typologies, notably the motivational styles of rapists, are directly related to insights developed by forensic psychiatry, in particular, Dr Groth's work on men who rape (Groth 1979).

Therefore, a useful way to think about the profiling approach of the FBI may not be in terms of a distinctly different type of profiling at all but rather as a particular subset of the larger framework of 'clinically based' profiling. The distinguishing feature being that the 'diagnostic evaluations' of the offender are being done by a 'police investigator' at the crime scene rather than a trained clinician like a criminal psychologist or forensic psychiatrist. These trained specialists may well be called in for their expertise when needed by the police investigating team. In summary, approaches that rely on a clinical orientation can be subdivided into two distinct groups of profilers. Those that are more 'investigatively driven' and those that are 'therapy driven' as indicated below:

'Investigatively driven' approaches

This subgroup of profilers can be grouped as having a general clinical orientation, being experientially focused, and tending to rely on their investigative intuition and experience to reconstruct an offender profile from a detailed analysis of the crime scene(s). Typically, such profilers are detectives and police investigators like FBI special agents (eg Hazlewood *et al.*). More recently, the method developed by Turvey (1999) called 'Behavioural Evidence Analysis' (BEA) fits comfortably within this orientation. BEA does not so much present a new approach but rather is a more sophisticated process of much of the FBI's work without being tied to and therefore hamstrung by the original and simplistic 'organized/disorganized' crime scene typology in the earlier work of the FBI.

'Therapy-driven' approaches

This subgroup, because of their professional training, take a more therapeutic insight-oriented approach to profiling. Such profilers are typically forensic psychologists and psychiatrists (eg Paul Britton in the UK and Ronald Holmes in the US).

'Statistical' orientation to profiling

This type of methodological framework is 'statistically based' and hence includes profiling approaches that are deemed to be based on this type of perspective in the construction of a profile. Again, this does not mean that each approach has to be practised by 'statisticians' or only practitioners who are well versed in the rigours of statistical analysis like psychologists or forensic scientists.

The framework emphasizes that an approach is 'statistically based' if it uses various statistical techniques to test hypotheses, model theories, and/or develop databases based on offender populations to augment its knowledge base.

For example, the investigative psychology approach of Canter and colleagues clearly fits within this 'statistically based' framework. Canter's approach uses police records and other data sources to build an empirical database from which to develop theories and test hypotheses. Hence, Canter's approach has been labelled by others as an example of statistical profiling.

Whilst it is clear that Canter's work relied heavily on statistical analysis to profile underlying narrative themes of an offender type, especially in his more recent work where a specific statistical procedure called 'smallest space analysis' (SSA) is almost exclusively utilized to plot a two-dimensional configuration to highlight narrative themes in a sample of similar crime types, it would be misleading to refer to Canter's approach as purely 'statistical'.

That is to say, Canter's approach is more 'theory driven' with statistics playing a supportive role rather than a main role. Hence, it is important not to confuse a 'method of analysis' with the 'conceptual framework' that guides the analysis.

However, one of the difficulties faced by the investigative psychology approach is that, as Egger (1999: 8) notes, 'investigative psychology relies more heavily upon victim information' in order to develop narrative themes about particular crime types. Hence, the accuracy of such victim and witness information is a significant issue, given how notoriously unreliable such information has been shown to be by a number of studies done of memory, victim recall, and the effects of trauma on memory (Ainsworth 2001: 124).

Other examples of statistically-derived profiling approaches are represented in the work of Farrington and colleagues. For example, Farrington and Lambert (1997) use descriptive statistics taken from police records, interviews, victim and witness statements, etc to develop crime-specific databases of likely offender characteristics.

Also, the work of Rossmo (1997) on 'Geographic Profiling' can be related to this framework since, like databases, it is an information-management strategy that relies on collecting geographical data on a crime series and then statistically manipulating such data to assist in targeting an offender's likely home base.

In summary, approaches that rely on a statistical orientation can be subdivided into two distinct groups of profilers. Those that are more 'database driven' and those that are 'theory driven' as indicated below:

'Database-driven' approaches

One group of researchers uses descriptive statistics from police records, interviews, victim and witness statements, etc to develop crime-specific databases of likely offender characteristics (eg Farrington and Lambert). As stated above, Rossmo's work on 'Geographic Profiling' can be related to this group.

'Theory-driven' approaches

The other group of researchers are more guided by theories and hence make specific use of inferential statistics to analyse a crime(s) (eg Canter and his use of facet theory and 'narrative themes' in a crime).

This review of the profiling field presents three main stumbling blocks for transferring this methodology to terrorism in order to 'profile' terrorists. These stumbling blocks revolve around, first, definitional difficulties of profiling itself; second, conceptual confusion over different profiling approaches; and, third, the issue of the extent of psychological disturbance present in a terrorist.

In relation to the first stumbling block, terminological/definitional difficulties regarding profiling, it is clear from the first section of this chapter that the terrorism field is also riddled with terminological/definitional confusion. Hence, the remaining two stumbling blocks of the 'profiling' methodology—conceptual confusion, and psychological disturbance—are discussed in the next section to establish the case that it is the 'process' of terrorism and not the 'person' of the terrorist that should be profiled.

Profiling the 'process' of terrorism

According to Rapoport (2003) the wave of 'religiously inspired' terrorism the world is currently experiencing began in 1979 with the Iranian Revolution. This current manifestation of terrorism needs to be understood within the context of the three previous 'waves' of modern terrorist behaviour.

The 'anarchist' wave began in the 1880s and lasted some 40 years until the beginning of the 1920s. This was closely followed by a second wave of 'anti-colonialism' that started in the 1920s and lasted some 35 years until the mid 1960s. A 'new left' wave took up the mantle of terrorism in the 1960s and again lasted some 30 years, but by the 1990s had largely dissipated (Rapoport 2003).

The fourth wave of 'religious' terrorism, while having its interception in the late 1970s, went largely unnoticed on the world stage as it was mainly confined to the Middle East until the devastatingly effective al-Qaeda terrorist attack of 9/11 when the Twin Towers of the World Trade Center in New York came tumbling down in 2001.

In all four 'waves' of terrorism the dominant aim was revolution. Terrorist organizations often based their 'revolution' on the principle of national self-determination which was to be achieved either by seceding from, overturning, or completely destroying the 'perceived' unjust state or ruling party. Hence, organizations that use terrorist tactics often described themselves as 'freedom fighters' not terrorists. This term 'freedom fighter' has been hijacked and used for so many causes, both legitimate and illegitimate, that it has been corrupted by overuse and abuse and has hence lost much of its credibility.

In relation to the current wave of 'religious' terrorism, it is clear that 'religion' has often played a part in the three earlier waves of 'anarchist', 'anti-colonial', and 'new left' terrorist movements. Religious identity is a potent and powerful component in any movement as it relates directly to a person's sense of purpose and meaning in life and death. Sometimes religion can overlap and becomes intrinsically interwoven in ethnic rivalries as evidenced in the Armenian, Macedonian, Irish, Cypriot, Israeli, and Palestinian conflicts.

However, the crucial point to appreciate about the present al-Qaeda inspired use of 'religion' to support terrorist behaviour is that it is significantly different from the way religion was used in earlier waves of terrorism. Today's religiously inspired terrorist organizations develop from the perspective that their extreme fundamentalist interpretation of religion, and not secular politics, must be on top in society as the governing body and that the rule of 'religious law' not man-made laws must be the standard that operates in this religiously reformed society.

Therefore, the outworking of this 'religious' legitimizing principle supplies the justification for the use of violent terror against the perceived 'godless' ones and the 'infidels' by the 'true believers' who are acting on behalf of God. Such certitude in their own beliefs about the legitimacy of using terror tactics approved by God sets this current wave of religious terrorism distinctively apart from other previous mixes of religion and terrorism.

Islam is the religion that is currently at the forefront of this wave of terrorism as it is being played out in today's contemporary climate. However, such religiously justified terrorist's acts are not the sole or exclusive province of Islam. Other religions, like the Christian Identity Movement in the US, an ultra-right wing extremist group, have engaged in violent terrorist acts with the same certainty about the righteousness of their godly convictions.

Islamic terrorism uses its 'religion' not only to justify the use of deadly violence against anyone it deems an enemy but also to fulfil its larger goal or vision of bringing about a 'pure', non-secular Muslim state governed by Sharia, Islamic law.

Such a vision fuses the 'spiritual' and the 'political' together for the devout Muslim in a way that makes 'terrorism' an acceptable sacrifice for Allah (Gunaratna 2003). The potency of this message was felt on the world stage with the al-Qaeda attack of 9/11 in 2001. The suicide mission was not carried out by a bunch of crazy, insane, lunatics, but as the testimonies of those involved shows they were generally well educated and seriously 'devout' Muslims.

The use of religion as the draw card for terrorism opens up the gates to a very wide pool of relatively 'normal' and religiously 'devout' people as potential applicants for entry into a terrorist organization if the socio-cultural and geopolitical conditions of a community or society are such that terrorism becomes a legitimate option for dealing with 'perceived' injustices in the world. Juergensmeyer (2000) makes the salient point that no religion is immune from having advocates in their midst who push extreme fundamentalist interpretations of God to fix what they perceive as 'problems' in the world. Therefore, the 'process' of terrorism should be the focus of profiling attempts, not the 'terrorist's personality'. This is the theme that will be pursued in the subsequent sections of this chapter.

Terrorist 'profiling systems'

In relation to the 'profiling' field it was shown that there is conceptual confusion over the diverse range of approaches and models available to 'profile' individuals which has led to fragmentation as well as arguments over which approach/model is 'best'. The terrorism field is also in the grip of this fragmentation and argument over the various technological systems being used or that are in development to 'profile' terrorists.

It is worth noting at this point that even if the 'profiling' methodology could be shown to be effective with regard to picking out terrorists in a crowd, there is little conceptual clarity that exists in the profiling domain to guide wouldbe 'terrorist' experts in selecting which 'profiling' approach to use, where and when, and on what type of terrorist. It comes down to personal preferences and idiosyncratic choices rather than any systematic way of assessing the usefulness of any profiling approach.

Of necessity, most 'profiling' attempts rely on 'statistically based' approaches rather than 'psychologically or behaviourally based' approaches, a point discussed previously. These 'statistically based' approaches generally get packaged as software like the much-touted 'Matrix' statistical package favoured by some US states in the wake of 9/11.

'Matrix' is short for 'Multistate Anti-Terrorism Information Exchange' which is a software package that combines personal records of citizens from various US states with data about the personal characteristics of terrorists derived from a 'Terrorist Handbook' in order to produce a score (terrorism quotient or 'high terrorist factor') indicating the statistical likelihood of a person undergoing security screening being a terrrorist. The data culled from the so-called 'Terrorist Handbook', which supposedly reveals how terrorists 'penetrate and live in our society', is also put out by the company that produced the Matrix software. Interestingly, the Matrix program was shut down in June 2005 after US federal funding was stopped due to public concerns over privacy and state surveillance.[1]

Another technological system that claims to be 'a relatively fast and reliable method to determine who is a terrorist and who is not' (Kirsch 2001) is on the market. This technology is based on brain fingerprinting and is referred to as 'computerized knowledge assessment' (CKA). The claim is made that, unlike a conventional lie detector test which can be fooled, brain responses cannot be faked. Hence, it is stated that brain fingerprint evidence has been ruled admissible in US courts where it has been used both to exonerate and convict. CKA works by determining whether or not a stimulus (such as a picture) has been previously seen by a subject. Therefore, it can be used to determine whether someone is familiar with the inside of a specific terrorist training camp or the contents of a particular terrorist code book. Such claims have yet to be independently verified.

What is not in dispute is the fact that such 'profiling' systems exist and may well be more of a testament to the power of marketing than any independently demonstrated effectiveness in picking out terrorists.

Finally, the Center for Nonproliferation Studies (CNS) produced a report on the existing literature on modelling terrorist behaviour. They found their investigation 'revealed a number of promising areas for modelling terrorist behaviour, including multi-agent models, genetic algorithms, cognitive explorations of artificial intelligence, social network analysis and so forth' (2002: 371). Future technological developments will determine how much these promising areas can deliver in preventing terrorist attacks.

'Psychologically disturbed' argument

This third stumbling block with using the profiling methodology to profile terrorists rests on the argument about how 'psychologically disturbed' terrorists are. There is some research that suggests a religious terrorist may suffer from 'one or more mental disorders, including but not limited to, oppositional defiant, impulse-control, antisocial, or other personality disorders' (Schbley 2006). The focus of this research work is on trying to find a common psychosocial profile of Christian and Muslim terrorists who engage in self-immolation usually

---

[1] See <http://en.wikipedia.org/wiki/Multistate_Anti-Terrorism_Information_Exchange>

by carrying out suicide bombings. However, this line of research is narrowly defined and as such does not square up with countless other studies. Furthermore, Horgan (2003: 23) notes the type of research which points to the existence of a 'terrorist personality' is such that 'its propositions are built on unsteady empirical, theoretical and conceptual foundations'.

In fact, Townshend (2002: 16) states categorically that terrorists 'far from being "criminals, crusaders, and crazies" emerge in most good empirical studies as "disturbingly normal" people'. This theme of the apparent 'normality' of terrorists at least in psychological terms is well documented in the terrorism literature.

Rubenstein (2003: 139) asserts that 'thankfully, the search for the "terrorist mind" is now all but abandoned'. He goes on to explain that 'as Walter Laqueur pointed out twenty-five years ago, the task is quixotic, seeing that among those engaging in political violence there exist so many varieties of terrorist organizations and behaviour, sociocultural and political contexts for conflict, and diverse personality types'.

Other writers on terrorism agree with this assessment that a 'typical profile' for a terrorist does not exist. 'No comparative work on terrorist psychology has ever succeeded in revealing a particular psychological type or uniform terrorist mindset' according to Williams (2002: 160) citing the work of David Long, a former assistant director of the US State Department's Office of Counter Terrorism.

Williams (2002: 159) also cites Mohamed Atta, the suicide pilot who flew American Airlines Flight 11 into the north tower of the World Trade Center in New York on 11 September 2001, as a case in point.

> Mohamed Atta came from a privileged Cairo family, and when he was 24, went to Hamburg to study urban planning. Friends who knew him in Cairo and during his first few years at Hamburg's Technical University thought of him as a good guy and basically unremarkable.

In fact, Crenshaw (2003: 99) reinforces just how apparently 'normal' terrorists can be: 'what limited data we have on individual terrorists suggest that the outstanding characteristic is normality'.

Hence the consensus amongst scholars in this area is that in general terrorists do not exhibit the familiar telltale signs or 'signature' characteristics of psychological dysfunction that are found in criminals and serial offenders.

In relation to the specific manifestation of terrorism in the personality of a suicide bomber, the same conclusion that there is no such thing as a 'typical profile' anymore especially in the Middle East, holds true as Reuter's research attests:

> The original assumption—that suicide bombers were exclusively isolated, young, poor, ultra-religious people with no prospects—might have applied in some degree to the first attackers. But nowadays 'none of this is right anymore,' admits Ephrahim Kam, a retired major of the Israeli military

secret service who heads the Jaffe Center for Strategic Studies in Tel Aviv. (Reuter 2004: 109)

A 'profile' of sorts existed in history when the original 'assassins' of the eleventh century refined their art of targeted murder and then suicidally stayed behind to be killed by the target's bodyguards to show their strength of faith by their willingness to die. Hassan-i Sabbah, a preacher and founder of the Assassin sect saw Assassins as the 'true believers' in the struggle against the Sunni rulers of the time who they portrayed as the oppressors and betrayers of true Islam.

The modern day re-emergence of suicide bombing in the 1980s as the terror tactic of choice by Hezbollah (Party of God), a group of Lebanese Shi'ite militants, has long since been successfully exported to a diversity of guerrilla fighters around the world.

Hezbollah cultivated their strategy of suicide bombing to perfection as 'martyr operations' in 1982 and 1983 according to Reuter (2004). They borrowed the 'martyrdom' theme from Iran after thousands of Iranian youths charged to their certain death as 'human wave attacks' on the battlefields of the Iran–Iraq War of the 1980s. Each youth was given a little key to Paradise to wear around their necks as the 'human wave' of these suicidal battalions tried to overrun Iraqi machine gun positions in the name of God and his self-appointed prophet of death and destruction the grand Ayatollah Khomeini and his clerical dictatorship.

Hence, trying to 'pick' this 'suicide bomber' form of terrorism today from the crowd is a naive and futile task. Reuter (2004: 109) quotes from several authoritative sources to underscore this point:

> Psychologist Ariel Merari of Tel Aviv University has painstakingly amassed dozens of biographies of suicide bombers... since the 1970s, no longer sees any way to draw a narrow profile of today's would-be attacker. The more he looks into the biographies, the more the clichés crumble. External factors such as poverty or loneliness seem barely to play any role: the attackers come both from the poorest areas of Gaza and from Ramallah, the West Bank's wealthiest and most cosmopolitan town... You find men from the *lumpenproletariat* along with University graduates, poor people, and also sons of millionaires. They are still primarily—though not only—people of the faith... It is also wrong to assume, he said, that the attackers are picked by some organization without knowledge, then programmed and sent off on their missions like booby-trapped automatons. 'No group can just get someone to do that. At most, they can strengthen existing dispositions, but at the end of the day, it comes from the individual himself, from his experiences, from his beliefs'.

Therefore, it is clear profiling a terrorist, especially suicide bombers, makes little logical sense (Wise 2005) but it is still possible to profile the 'process' used to shape an individual into a potential terrorist. That is, it is important to make a clear conceptual distinction between profiling the person as a terrorist and profiling the process of terrorism.

211

It is also equally clear that the phenomenon of terrorism as we are currently experiencing it around the globe cannot be explained in individual psychological terms using simplistic, single factor notions like they are 'brainwashed', or 'crazy', or 'fanatics', or 'the poor and uneducated' who do these terrible things. As Reuter (2004: 9) points out:

> Individual psychological models of interpretation, important though they are, can't function as the complete explanation. For while they do tell us something about motivations, they are completely incapable of explaining why these attacks begin at a particular time, and in a particular place; why they spread throughout the world in very specific patterns; and why some militant organizations have employed them while others haven't. Using a single model for all deeds of this kind obscures the fact that the paths that lead up to them, and the indoctrination of the attackers, are quite different in each case.

To understand the process of terrorism the focus has to be wider than individual psychology and must include the context is which the shaping of an individual's beliefs and values takes place (Dean 2004). This is particularly so given the contemporary socio-culturo-political Islamic climate that uses religion to legitimize and justify terrorism in the name of God. As Silke (2003: 107) reminds us, 'in the end, suicidal attacks, however dramatic and appalling, are first and foremost a symptom of wider problems'.

The same narrowness of focus approach can also be applied to the use by police and security services of Social Network Analysis (SNA). The utility of SNA as a method for modelling the organizational aspects of terrorism is noteworthy (Krebs 2006; Inflow 2006). However, as the CNS report makes clear it needs to be located within a larger context to fully derive its benefits. The CNS report found that 'current work in this area [SNA] often makes assumptions or obtains results that involve terrorist behaviour. This conceptual and functional intersection between these two areas [organizational and behavioural] means that several of the tools and results of social network analysis could (and probably should) be incorporated into any larger model of terrorist behaviour' (2002: 371).

Therefore, it would appear that to deal effectively with this present-day fourth wave of terrorism it should be recognized that this is essentially a Knowledge Management challenge that the policing/law enforcement/security community is facing. That is, unless police and security officials understand the contexts that are driving this fourth wave of religiously inspired terrorism they will be at a significant disadvantage in knowing how best to respond to such terrorism both conceptually and technologically.

Hence, the next section presents a way of reasoning about the contexts in which the process of terrorism evolves and operates that can be used as a model application for police Knowledge Management in this difficult and complex business of shaping policies and practices to combat terrorism.

'Interlocking terrorism contexts': Knowledge Modelling System

The literature on post-9/11 religiously inspired terrorism reveals three contexts which are of particular significance in relation to developing a Knowledge Modelling application for police and law enforcement use in order to deal more proficiently with the terrorism process that inspires such terrorist behaviour in relatively 'normal' people.

We have termed these three contexts as 'causal', 'commitment', and 'capability' contexts respectively. The 'causal' context refers to the societal or macro level of global socio-culturo-geopolitical systems out of which terrorist grievances emerge when various factors within these systems are mishandled or misaligned by governments, states, or nations.

The 'commitment' context refers to the micro or individual level where disenfranchised and/or disaffected individuals seek 'to align' themselves with the types of 'causes' and/or avenging acts of terrorism that have been incubating in the various 'causal' contexts.

The 'capacity' context refers to the group or organization level where an individual wanting to fight for a cause they have come to believe in passionately can acquire the necessary skills, knowledge, and training, in short, the capacity, to effect a significant impact by engaging in terrorist-type actions.

Furthermore, there are eight aspects or 'factors'[2] in this model spread across these three contexts. Figure 9.1 graphically depicts these three interlocking terrorism contexts and their associated factors as a Knowledge Modelling System.

As can be seen in Figure 9.1 the three terrorism contexts are visualized as a 'process' model which dynamically interlock and interact at multiple levels across a range of factors that combine to stimulate, evolve, and develop religious terrorism into a potent global force.

It is evident in Figure 9.1 that the initial stimulus within the macro 'causal' context for breeding this process of terrorism is multi-factorial. There can be many factors that combine at this societal level which provide the impetus for later terrorist actions. Four such factors gleaned from the literature on terrorism are considered as especially significant in this process model of terrorism as

---

[2] These aspects are considered as 'factors' rather than stages or phases. Stage/phase models of terrorism are too mechanistic to capture the dynamic interplay of these eight aspects of the terrorism process. Hence, the term 'factors' is preferred as it allows for a more flexible understanding of how an individual enters into the process of becoming a terrorist. For example, it means that on this model it would be misleading to suggest that all eight 'factors' must be present for someone to become a terrorist. Whereas, a stage/phase approach suggests an invariant sequence, that if a 'stage/phase' is missed then the process invariably breaks down. While this is a possibility in a 'factor' approach it is not absolutely the case. A person could still go on to become a terrorist without some of the 'group' or 'societal' factors that support the terrorism process. In that case, the type of terrorism will be limited in scope as the potential to inflict damage is restricted only to this one individual rather than a group or network of terrorists.

Figure 9.1 Visualization process model of interlocking terrorism contexts

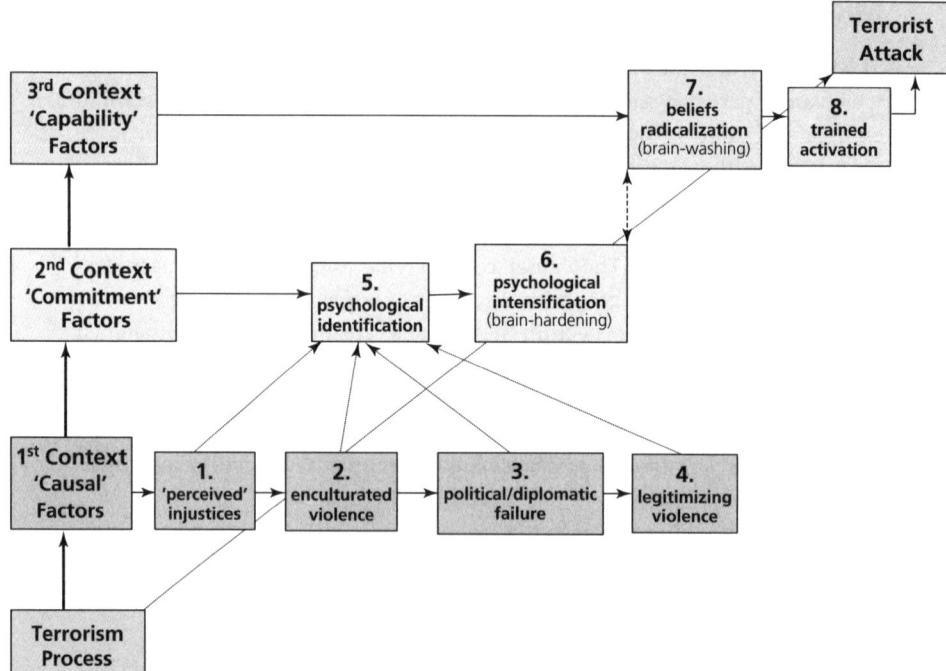

illustrated. They are: 'perceived' injustice; enculturated violence; political/diplomatic failure, and legitimizing violence.

'Perceived' injustices (factor 1) in general are caused by extreme inequalities and the bifurcation that results in a community/society from ethnic tensions, nationalism, tribal rivalries, separatism, poverty, religion, and so forth. When such perceived injustices are left unchecked a process of enculturated violence (factor 2) can take hold. This breeding of a culture of violence in a community/society can lead to the use of force becoming increasingly seen as the 'solution' to these perceived injustices.

If governments, states, or nations and their institutions and/or supranational agencies like the United Nations are not able to broker or bring about a fair and equitable solution to 'perceived' injustices then this inability will be seen as a political/diplomatic failure (factor 3) within a community. This failure to address and resolve perceived injustices will give cause to some to see terrorism as a potential solution or just simply an avenging act.

An enculturated sense of violence can for some be enough of a stimulus to accept terrorism but others require such violence to be legitimized at a community/societal level before they are psychologically comfortable with using such violence. When there is such large-scale legitimizing violence (factor 4) by community/society 'acceptance' of the use of violent force as the only way left to them to 'right' perceived 'wrongs' and 'injustices' then the ranks of terrorist organizations swell, as is attested by the number of volunteers to Hamas for suicide missions in the Middle East.

It is a mistake to assume that 'perceived' injustices (factor 1) are just the whining of the masses, in effect have no legitimacy, and hence can be safely ignored and not taken seriously by politicians. In actuality some 'perceived' injustices are very real. South Africa under the apartheid system is a case in point. As Silke (2003: 51) notes 'many terrorists report that it was violence committed by police officers or soldiers that acted as the final push for them to approach and join a terrorist group'. Moreover, Silke goes on to point out that 'a combination of belonging to an aggrieved group and the experience of violent injustice are such common factors in the backgrounds of terrorists' (ibid).

However, it is not just injustices born of violence that can lead to sympathetic sentiments towards terrorism. Batley (2003), in a case study of the influence of Jemaah Islamiyah in South East Asia, notes that the poor economic conditions for the majority of Muslims in this region continue to ensure the existence of anti-government and anti-establishment sentiments.

A more recent example is the process of enculturated violence (factor 2) that has evolved in the Middle East in relation to the Palestinian situation. Humiliation and hopelessness has been the daily experience of the masses in Palestine. Moreover, the Israeli experience is one of continuing frustration and fear. This is not to condemn or condone either side but rather reflects the way this geopolitical context has evolved. Such a context breeds a 'culture' of violence within Palestinians that is capable of generating in individuals a 'self-sacrificing' desire to kill oneself for the 'cause', 'greater good', 'higher call', or to enter 'Paradise' early. In the Palestinian community approval to go on a 'martyr operation' is well entrenched as research by Reuter (2004: 110) confirms:

> In fact, it's precisely the well-educated, rather than the indigent, who take the lead in advocating violence, as Khalik Shikaki's (head of Ramallah-based Center for Policy and Survey Research) opinion polls reveal . . . 'It goes against the trends in the rest of the world, but here (Middle East) the level of approval for violence rises in line with the level of education.' It's not the mob, nor the illiterate, who are goaded into violence, but precisely the well-educated, well-informed people who conclude that armed struggle is the only way out of the current situation.

At the micro or individual level of the 'commitment' context as shown in the model in Figure 9.1 there are two salient psychological factors in operation. They are personal 'identification' and 'intensification' with a terrorist cause. Psychological identification (factor 5) refers to the belief by a person in the 'rightness' of the 'cause' and the need to use violence to achieve 'justice' for such a cause. Conversely, psychological intensification (factor 6) occurs when the mind of the individual that has 'identified' with terrorism becomes 'hardened' to any worldview other than the radicalized one. In other words a 'brain-hardening process' is involved in such personal intensification with a terrorist worldview. It should be noted here that the 'brain-hardening' process of intensification (factor 6) is distinctly different[3] from what is commonly referred to in the terrorist literature as a 'brain-washing' process.

The psychology behind why a person identifies with terrorism (factor 5) is not unique. As Silke (2003: 51) concludes:

> terrorist psychology is just like that of everyone else [consisting in] the real-
> isation that in the wrong circumstances most people could either come to
> support a terrorist group or possibly even consider joining one. If you, your
> loved ones and your community were discriminated against, persecuted by
> the authorities, intimidated, injured or killed, then terrorism may seem as
> appropriate and justified response.

Where religion is mixed with terrorism then it is not hard to see how a devout person in the wrong circumstances might 'identify' with the use of terror tactics as they perceive this to be the only viable way left to advance their cause. Hence, this fifth factor of psychological identification is a critical element in the terrorism process, regardless of how this identification was achieved, through either the early formative years of indoctrination at religious schools, or in later life from a new-found faith in religion as the supreme guiding principle for one's life.

The third 'capacity' context depicted in Figure 9.1 comes into play in the terrorism process when like-minded individuals join up with each other in order to maximize their capacity for large-scale potential damage. Hence, a terrorist's 'capacity' is contextually a group phenomenon. The grouping can be as small as three or four individuals acting in concert like the London underground bombers of 7 July 2005 or as large as the organizational network of al-Qaeda responsible for 11 September 2001.

There are a number of factors in this 'capacity' context which can be focused on, like skills, knowledge, and training. Most such factors have been well covered in the terrorism and counter-terrorism literature (Beiner 2006; Koepf 2004; Horgan 2003; Seger 2003).

For our purposes here in regard to police Knowledge Management there are two factors of critical importance in this 'capacity' context. They are beliefs radicalization at this group level and then trained activation by the group.

Beliefs radicalization (factor 7) refers to the process of 'systematic indoctrination' or 'brain-washing' by secular extremists of both left/right ideology, and/or

---

[3] This is a crucial distinction between 'brain-hardening' and 'brain-washing' as it draws attention to the subtle process whereby an individual's thinking becomes 'hardened' in a certain direction *willingly through their own efforts*, rather than imposed from the outside by others. Conversely, 'brain-washing' involves a conditioning process of 'systematic indoctrination that changes or undermines one's convictions' (*Macquarie Dictionary* 1982) usually by some charismatic cult leader against an individual's will into believing in a cause. Hence, a 'brain-washing' process is often present in psychological models of terrorism like Stahelski's (2004) social psychological 'conditioning' model. Such a conditioning model may account for some individuals becoming terrorists but by itself, as with most psychological-type models, it is one-dimensional and ignores geopolitical and cultural factors.

religious fundamentalism of any faith be it Islamic, Christian, Hindu, and so forth. Trained activation (factor 8) refers to the decision to join and undergo training for a terrorist mission.

The 'radicalization' of an individual's existing psychological leanings and beliefs involve a systematic, brain-washing indoctrination process. Such indoctrination is often a quite sophisticated cognitive process which such groups and organizations employ on persons they have identified as potential new recruits. That is, such 'brain-washing' can even occur for individuals who have not yet 'psychologically identified' (factor 5) with a particular cause or set of grievances they perceive as unjust.

In an Islamic context, this situation usually arises when young children are sent to fundamentalist religious schools where the uncritical repetition of verse after verse of the Islamic texts takes place. Such a context could be described as akin to a brain-washing process. Strozier and Laughlin (2003: 8) provide some graphic examples of how such indoctrination of children can begin at a very early age in some Middle Eastern communities. These authors cite Murphy (2002) who claims that an official ninth grade curriculum published by the Arabian Ministry of Education proposes as one discussion topic: 'what would be the best weapon to kill a Jew?'.

However, in the case of adults who have already 'psychologically identified' with a cause then this seventh factor of 'beliefs radicalization' has more to do with reinforcing existing beliefs than with changing them. It is precisely because their convictions are 'pre-aligned' with a potential terrorist cause that a terrorist group/organization has little if any 'indoctrination' to do at this point.

These existing beliefs are further reinforced by self-appointed leaders of secular or religious ideologies who relentlessly churn out extreme views that radicalize beliefs (secular and/or religious) in the direction of fundamentalist interpretations where everything involves dichotomized thinking in terms of right/wrong, black/white, good/bad, true/false, holy/evil.

Hence, the end of the terrorism process is reached when individuals fully commit themselves by taking the step from thinking and talking about extremist views to acting on them by undergoing specific terrorist training and mission activation (factor 8).

Finally, an essential point that is not immediately obvious in the depiction of this Knowledge Modelling System in Figure 9.1 is that the key to stopping terrorism is one of alignment. To use an analogy, the process of terrorism can be likened to a combination lock: a combination lock can only be opened when all the wheels (tumblers) on the inside of the cylinder are rotated by a dial or knob to a correct combination in which all the wheels are in the right alignment in relation to each other.

By implication, for terrorism 'to operate', all three contexts—causal, commitment, and capability—are 'wheels within wheels' that need to be 'in alignment' to maximize the effectiveness of terrorist attacks. In other words, terrorism is the result of the alignment of all three contexts. Therefore, if one or more of these contexts is out of alignment then, like a combination lock, it can't be activated. Hence, to stop the current wave of religious terrorism from developing, governments and their police and security institutions need to study each of these three contexts and the factors subsumed under them in order to find points of intervention to prevent their alignment.

Case Study: Jemaah Islamiyah terrorist network

In this section the visualization process model depicted in Figure 9.1 is the backbone of the application known as the 'Interlocking Terrorism Contexts' Knowledge Modelling System (ITC-KMS) which will be applied to a case study of the Jemaah Islamiyah terrorist network in the Asia Pacific region to illuminate the utility of this 'knowledge modelling' approach.

The essential knowledge value of this visualization process model application for the police and law enforcement community is how it looks at the terrorism process at a global 'macro' level in order to deduce points of intervention and prevention at the local 'micro' level of individuals, groups, and organizations within communities that fall under their jurisdiction.

Background on Jemaah Islamiyah

Jemaah Islamiyah (JI) is the most significant terrorist network currently operating in the Asia Pacific region (White Paper 2003). The Council on Foreign Relations (2004) regards Jemaah Islamiyah as a militant Islamic group with strong links to al-Qaeda which seeks to establish a pan-Islamic state across much of South East Asia.

The historical background of JI is that it was formed by a group of radical militants formally known as the 'Darul Islam' or House of Islam who have been trying to establish an Islamic state in Indonesia through armed and violent struggles since Indonesia gained its independence in 1949. During the Suharto regime, the 'Darul Islam' was suppressed by the Indonesian government and members were forced to flee to avoid arrest. They settled in Malaysia and later regrouped and formed the JI in 1985.

The JI membership expanded during this period through recruitments in Malaysia and Singapore. After the fall of the Suharto regime in 1988, some of the JI leaders returned to Indonesia and continue to pursue their vision of establishing a 'Daulah Islamiyah' or Islamic state in the region through the use of violence.

This 'Daulah Islamiyah' vision is to include under its Islamic umbrella the countries of Indonesia, Malaysia, south Philippines and, inevitably, Singapore, and Brunei. This vision was revealed in a JI manual known as 'Pedoman Umum Perjuangan Jemaah Islamiyah' or *General Guidelines of the Struggle of Jemaah Islamiyah* (White Paper 2003).

Whilst there are several recent examples of terrorism and sectarian violence in South East Asia (Abuza 2005), most notably in South Thailand (BBC News 2006; Hatyai bombings 2006, Singapore is used as a case example of an attempted JI operation to illustrate how the knowledge modelling system depicted in Figure 9.1 is used.

Case Target: Singapore (2001–2002)

In 2001 the JI terrorist network planned its most ambitious undertaking so far in the region to explode a series of bombs in Singapore. It can be speculated that the stunning success of the al-Qaeda attack on the Twin Towers in New York in September of 2001 may well have inspired the JI network to up the stakes of the struggle in the Asia Pacific region. Singapore as a nation is strongly aligned with other Western democracies, particularly the US. Hence, it is of little surprise that Singapore should be targeted for a terrorism attack by such a radical terrorist organization as JI.

The JI plans for several attacks to take place in Singapore did not eventuate. Intelligence sources found out about the JI plans just in time to avert the attack. A total of 36 members of the JI network were arrested for terrorism-related activities in Singapore in two separate operations between December 2001 and August 2002 by the Internal Security Department (ISD) of the Singapore Police Force (SPF).[4]

In the first operation 15 JI members were arrested by the ISD. All of these were served with a Detention Order which remains in place for two years under section 8.1(a) of the Internal Security Act of the Singapore government. These members were Muslims and residents of Singapore. In the second operation by SPF against the JI network several months later in August 2002 a further 21 JI members were arrested.

In the main, the 'profile' that emerged of the 36 arrested JI members is as follows:

- male;
- early middle-aged;
- married;
- middle class;
- homeowners;
- employed;
- technical qualifications;
- devout desire for meaning through religion;
- regular attendance at religious school;
- willingness to undergo terrorist training.

Such a profile is entirely consistent with the bulk of the research literature on terrorism that, by and large, 'terrorists' are very 'normal' people, especially in relation to those who identify with the 'religious' or fourth wave of terrorism. From a profiling and behavioural analysis perspective such 'terrorists' could not appear more 'normal'. They 'appear' to be just like the average person on the street.

The only difference that sets them apart from the crowd is that they take their Islamic religion very seriously. They have the 'mindset' of a devout follower not a fanatic. Although it could be argued that some 'devout' followers may become 'fanatical' in seeking to apply their beliefs, this type of 'fanaticism' would be more appropriately termed an obsessive-compulsive drive infused with religious significance rather than a

---

[4] Data presented on JI members is collated from open source information. Also, see Dean (2007) for more details on the individual profiles of these 36 arrested JI members.

Figure 9.2 Visualisation process model of planned JI terrorist attack in Singapore

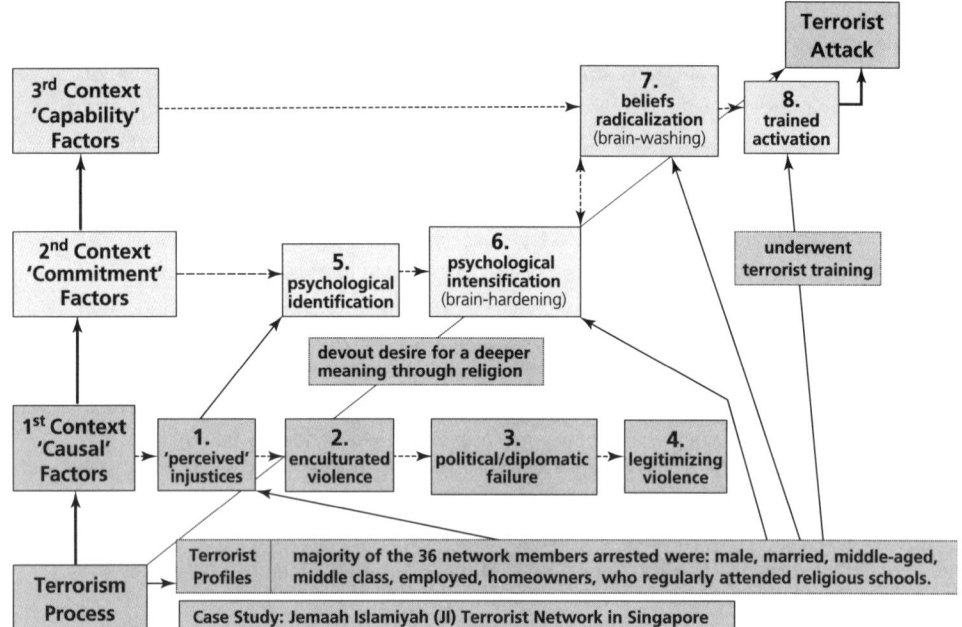

classic psychiatric 'personality disorder'. Needless to say, profiling of any type is not aimed at reading people's minds.

Figure 9.2 presents this JI membership profile on a 'visualization pad' that is used to model this knowledge in relation to the three interlocking contexts out of which terrorism evolves, develops, and operates.

As can been seen in Figure 9.2 the solid arrows link up and track the factors that can be logically related as the terrorism process moves to lock into place the three contexts and their identified factors one after another until the final outcome of a terrorist attack either occurs or is disrupted.

In the Singapore case example it would appear that the most significant causal factor was the 'perceived' injustices (factor 1) faced by Islam from the West insofar as these JI members were concerned. Singapore does not have a 'culture of violence' like in the Palestinian community that is 'legitimized' by many Palestinians. Nor does Singapore play any role in the politics of the Middle East. Hence, the most plausible factor is a globalized sense of 'perceived' injustice to Muslims in general and Islam in particular. These JI members were either led to 'believe' or came to this understanding presumably from the daily dose of media reporting depicting graphic scenes of killing and maiming of innocent civilians caught up in the madness of the Middle East conflict that continually engulfs many Islamic countries.

It is only a small psychological step from this 'perception' to 'identifying' (factor 5) with such conflicts many Muslim people face. From there the key intervening element for individuals who are devout in their beliefs and seek to have deeper meaning through their religion is the type of 'religious education' they are exposed to. The links to factors 6, 7, and 8 visually tell the story of what happened to these 36 JI members.

An implicit conceptual consideration in this terrorism process model is that each specific 'context' determines the individual's 'response parameters'. That is to say, any context, be it a small group context or a larger cultural or societal context, not only constrains but also shapes the individuals at both conscious and unconscious levels of awareness. Hence, in this sense, it is the context that determines what is the tolerable range or parameter of responses an individual should make in such a context to remain a socially or culturally 'acceptable' member of that context.

Hence, the 'JI terrorist members profile' is a product of context-constraining and context-shaping factors that over time individuals have incorporated as sense-making and meaning-creating responses to their life experience. In this light, such a context-constrained and context-shaped individual has only a limited range of acceptable parameters or choices to make in each of these multi-levelled contexts. Thus, from this perspective the relevance of profiling the 'process' of terrorism rather than just focusing on the person of the terrorist makes for better logic on the basis of the existing research literature available on terrorism.

The logic of this constraining-shaping contextual consideration is shown in Figure 9.1 in that under the right socio-cultural and/or socio-political/geopolitical circumstances (with any combination of factors, 1, 2, 3, and 4—causal context) an individual's choices will increasingly become shaped by such factors. At this point not every individual constrained by these contextual factors will psychologically identify with a cause to fight for. Some others will just become overwhelmed, depressed, or give up. Those individuals that have a need to create some sort of meaning out of these constraining factors may seek answers in religion or for that matter any ideological system that appeals to their mind. Religions and other ideological belief systems are potent sources of meaning-making for people. Extremist interpretations of religious and/or ideolog-thought, doctrines, and dogmas supply ready-made answers to the questions of life and thereby provide a sense of meaning and purpose to an individual's existence. Hence, such individuals now enter a different context (factors 5 and 6) where 'commitment' to one's beliefs becomes mandatory for their existence to have any such meaning. Such a commitment context further constrains and shapes the individual to become more psychologically intense towards their religious and/or ideology-inspired worldview. Such mental intensity demands release of some kind. The third context providing a relational outlet for it is here in the context of a group of like-minded individuals who realize their joint capability (factors 7 and 8) to put their commitment into action. At this point in their terrorism journey individuals are totally constrained by this capability context so that there is only one choice left—when to act.

The utility of this 'knowledge modelling' system as depicted in the visualization process model on Figure 9.2 is that, as information and intelligence comes in and is shared with various police, law enforcement, and security organizations, such a visualization of where the terrorism process is for a particular terrorist group or network can be built up over time.

Having a big-picture visualization such as this knowledge modelling of key factors makes it possible to predict likely scenarios and plan accordingly various points of intervention to disrupt the terrorism process. For example, on the basis of this visualization model it was highly predictable that it would be only a matter of time before a terrorist attack by 'home-grown' terrorists (Chance 2005) and not 'outsiders' would be responsible for something like the 7/7 bombings in London in 2005 in which 56 people died. However, hindsight always has 20/20 vision and just knowing there was high potential for a terrorist attack in Britain would not necessarily have prevented the 7/7 bombings. The point being made is such modelling would have dispelled the naive belief that only 'outsiders' could do such a thing not 'home-grown' youths. The same sort of simplistic idea by governments and security services, that terrorism is predominantly about securing borders, by turning a nation into a fortress is not only misguided but a dangerous illusion to foster.

Summary

This chapter presented a 'knowledge modelling' application about the interlocking nature of the contexts in which terrorism evolves, develops, and operates. The application system is based on a visualization model of three particular terrorism contexts: Causal, Commitment, and Capability factors.

There are eight specific factors contained within three Cs of the terrorism process which were identified and explained with supporting research. These factors are: 'perceived' injustices; enculturated violence; political/diplomatic failure; legitimizing violence; psychological identification; psychological intensification; beliefs radicalization; and finally, trained activation.

Various problematic aspects of 'defining' terrorism and applying a profiling methodology to 'profile' terrorists were examined in detail in the chapter. Of particular importance in regard to profiling is the fact that it works best when there is some sign of 'psychological disturbance' within offenders/criminals. In other words, for profiling to be successful some psychological pathology to profile is an essential requirement.

This profiling requirement presents a significant stumbling block to profiling terrorists, as the substantial well-documented research literature on terrorism makes it very clear that terrorists by and large are apparently 'normal', at least in psychological terms. Therefore, such research suggests that a more pragmatically useful approach to emphasize is to profile the 'process' of terrorism itself rather than the 'person' of the terrorist.

In the light of the inherent limitations of profiling terrorists a number of technological 'profiling systems' were noted. Future technological developments will determine how much these promising areas can deliver in preventing terrorist attacks.

Hence, a wider focus than just individual psychological models of terrorists' personality traits and behaviours is required to understand fully and 'model' the process of how terrorism evolves, develops, and operates in and through a number of interlocking contexts.

Hence, a visualization process model of terrorism was presented that depicts the dynamic nature of three such interlocking contexts to do with 'causal' factors, 'commitment' factors and 'capability' factors. The analogy of a combination lock was used as a way to understand how terrorism results from the alignment of all three contexts. This visualization process model is the backbone of the application known as an 'Interlocking Terrorism Contexts' Knowledge Modelling System (ITC-KMS).

Finally, the chapter presented a case study of the Jemaah Islamiyah (JI) terrorist network in the Asia Pacific region and its unsuccessful plans to set off a series of bombs in Singapore. The case study illustrates the utility of this 'knowledge modelling' application.

A composite 'profile' of the 36 arrested JI members revealed that in the main these 'terrorists' were: male, middle-aged, married, middle-class, church-going (Islamic religious schools), homeowners, who were employed, held technical qualifications, and had such a devout desire for meaning through religion that at some point they decided to undergo terrorist training.

Needless to say, such a profile is entirely consistent with the bulk of the research literature on terrorism that, by and large, 'terrorists' are very 'normal' people. However, the essential point that the ITC-KMS application illustrates is how such a 'normal' JI terrorist profile is a product of context-constraining and context-shaping factors that over time individuals have incorporated into a sense-making and meaning-creating religious worldview in which 'terrorism' is seen as a legitimate response to 'perceived' injustices.

The utility of this 'knowledge modelling' system lies in its holistic visualization of key factors that allow terrorism to take root in a community, evolve, and develop. Such visual modelling makes it possible to predict likely scenarios and plan intervention points to disrupt the terrorism process.

Finally, this ITC-KMS is an application that holds substantial benefit for the policing and security community in shaping policies and practices to combat terrorism.

Policy and Practices: Police Knowledge Management

Introduction

This chapter represents the summation of the book. As such it brings together the three main sections of this work that dealt with, first, the conceptual 'foundations' of Knowledge Management, second, the 'structures' required to build a specific body of police knowledge, and, third, specific 'applications' for managing police knowledge.

The focus of this chapter, therefore, is to review the inter-related nature of these Knowledge Management foundations, structures, and applications pertinent to police knowledge. This review will enable policing and the wider law enforcement community to craft a comprehensive policy on Knowledge Management that is applicable to their specific contexts.

The chapter does not provide a prescriptive policy or set of practices on Knowledge Management for policing and law enforcement as various police services/forces/agencies around the world have their own particular context and specific enabling and constraining factors which are unique to them.

However, what is offered in this final chapter is a set of key considerations in relation to developing and implementing a viable and flexibly robust Knowledge Management policy which is timely and relevant to global policing now and in the foreseeable future.

Foundations for police Knowledge Management

The first 'foundations' section of this book covered the nature of 'knowledge work' in policing (Chapter 1), the 'fundamentals' of Knowledge Management (KM) (Chapter 2), and a suggested 'framework' for the new realities of 'globalized' policing (Chapter 3).

Chapter 1 highlighted how 'knowledge work' in policing has an essentially different character to other forms of knowledge like business knowledge or knowledge in medicine, engineering, or IT, although it is also the case that much of KM draws on such disciplines to inform the practice of police knowledge. However, the distinctiveness of police knowledge lies not only in the uniqueness of an individual police officer's storehouse of tacit knowledge based on experience but also how such knowledge is endowed with legal authority and power beyond that which any other individual in society has bestowed on them.

The 'discretionary power' inherent in policing in the office of constable means 'knowledge construction' operates within a wide 'interpretational space' that even allows for the legitimate use of force under certain prescribed conditions and situations. Hence, as Sutcliffe and Weber (2003) have pointed out, how information is 'interpreted' and hence turned into knowledge is the key consideration in the success or failure of a police or law enforcement investigation and/or operation.

Furthermore, tacit (individual, personal, in-the-head knowledge) and explicit (written, documented, assessable knowledge) are mutually dependent sides of this 'interpretational space' in which the processes of knowledge—creation/capture, storage/retrieval , transfer/sharing, application/integration—are interwoven in order to arrive at a policing result.

Moreover, although police knowledge operates within a 'localized' context where the daily realities of policing take place the thinking behind everyday police practices must be 'global' in orientation.

Chapter 2 made it clear that, while much has been written about the 'fundamentals' of Knowledge Management generally, little is written about how these fundamentals apply in the policing and law enforcement domain. It is often assumed that KM business models and their associated IT infrastructure can be easily transplanted into any organizational environment including policing and law enforcement without too much difficulty. In other words, the 'fundamentals' of KM remain much the same regardless of context. This view has some validity in so far as simple Knowledge Management Systems (KMS) and their associated technological infrastructure for using information management systems, databases, knowledge repositories, and so forth are necessary basic requirements to do 'business' for any modern organization.

However, it must be remembered that the notion of KMS is a relative concept that is closely related to IT's ability to process information for knowledge work. The key point is that IT at later stages is more useful to knowledge work than IT at earlier stages. For higher-end IT-supported police knowledge work a key issue to address is one of resources. This resourcing issue is in terms of both specialized staff and significant costs to acquire sophisticated IT infrastructure to run higher-level KMS. This is a major concern for police organizations dependent on the public purse for funding such systems.

Moreover, beyond the basic fundamentals of IT support for KMS significant modifications to existing technologies as well as different types of IT infrastructure will be required to get KM to work effectively for policing purposes. The complexities of policing and law enforcement in the twenty-first century will make it increasingly essential for police and law enforcement organizations to utilize all four stages of KMS comprehensively with specific emphasis on higher-level 'how-they-think' systems, as well as tailoring existing technologies to their specific operational needs and priorities.

Another key emphasis concerned the need for policing organizations to avoid the twin dangers of a narrow conceptualization of KM and its marginalized containment within an organizational department or dedicated section where 'knowledge' resides in the person of a 'Chief Knowledge Officer' (CKO) or similar pretentious title.

With regard to the first risk of promoting a narrow conception of KM, if the IS/IT community's systems-centred 'Platform and Cable' KM approach is favoured over a people-centred 'Context and Culture' KM approach or vice versa then the balance is lost and organizationally KM will fail (Malhotra 2004). KM is all about getting and maintaining the right balance between these two disparate approaches, both philosophically and practically.

In terms of the second risk, if KM is marginalized and contained within an organizational 'silo' then harnessing its potential for knowledge creation and knowledge sharing will remain just a dream (Bundred 2006).

Chapter 3 focused on the development of a planning 'framework' for police Knowledge Management that is capable of addressing the concerns and risks identified in Chapters 1 and 2. To this end, Chapter 3 identified five global themes facing policing and law enforcement organizations in relation to developing a relevant policy and practices for police Knowledge Management.

From a policy and practice perspective, the core issue associated with 'stretching of policing sectors and levels' (first theme) revolved around ways to reduce 'information/knowledge gaps' in a globally fragmented policing/law enforcement and security environment.

This is by no means an easy task as the complexities of the inter-relationships between sectors, forms, models, and systems of policing are formidable as depicted in the global framework for planning the management of police knowledge depicted in Figure 3.5.

It is clear that 'local' policing and law enforcement is continually being pushed and pulled, stretched and shaped by global factors quite beyond their control and in this process 'intersecting tension spaces' emerge and/or erupt in the policing domain.

One clear implication of this constant reshaping process is that policing organizations must be able to adapt to changed circumstances quickly and can no longer remain or afford to be 'silo' organizations where knowledge is compartmentalized and not shared.

The comments by LeBeuf (2001: ix) in relation to the nature of criminal investigations into organized crime and cyber crime in Canada underscore the point about the lack of knowledge sharing in police investigations. He states:

> There definitely is an investigation culture. In this culture, individuals are kept in separate boxes, sometimes referred to as silos, which is an impediment to mutual co-operation, to information sharing, and ultimately to a successful investigation.

How to overcome such a 'silo mentality' and begin to break down a police culture that is reluctant to share information and knowledge is one of the most critical challenges facing KM generally in most organizations but perhaps even more so in policing and law enforcement.

Research by Huysman and Wulf (2006: 40) found resistance to the use of knowledge-sharing tools in the IT field was also alive and well. Their research suggests that 'in order to improve knowledge sharing supported by information technology (IT), tools need to be embedded in the social networks of which it is part'.

Furthermore, policing organizations need to focus on responsive adaptation to changes in the criminal justice and security environments if they are to keep up the fight against crime and terrorism. This point also touches on the second theme identified concerning the 'diversification of policing models'. The core issue here is to ensure a balance is kept between the 'intelligence' model being the current dominant paradigm in policing post 9/11 (New York, 2001), 10/12 (Bali, 2002), 3/11 (Madrid, 2004), and 7/7 (London, 2005) and the need for further experimentation to extend or develop other policing models and alternative forms of policing. Innovation in the way police manage their knowledge should be the cornerstone of any KM policy for policing and law enforcement.

The central issue concerning the third theme about 'the global integration of levels and sectors of policing' is a very thorny one because of the difficulties associated with jurisdictional and operational integration across policing sectors. However, the risks of not creating a globally integrated policing network are significant given the rise of religiously inspired terrorism and the ever-present shadow of transnational organized crime. Supranational bodies like Interpol and to a lesser extent Europol are the sort of networked policing structures that may well require an expanded agenda in order to play a more critical role in globally managing police knowledge in the future.

Given the 'complexities faced by diverse policing systems' this fourth theme can only be dealt with effectively if KM moves beyond just informally networked communities of practice onto a firmer global footing by lead agencies in various policing sectors showing positive, proactive, policing leadership on KM.

The final issue to flow from this framework chapter is about 'planning for tension spaces' (fifth theme). It should be evident from the 'planning cube' graphic in Figure 3.5 that intersecting 'tension spaces' are inevitable and hence unavoidable. Therefore, police and law enforcement organizations that ignore the need for 'planning in' tension spaces as part and parcel of a KM strategy do so at their peril.

Structures for police Knowledge Management

The second 'structures' section of this book considered the range of 'approaches' (Chapter 4), 'systems' (Chapter 5), and 'technologies' (Chapter 6) in the KM field potentially available to police and law enforcement organizations to build the types of KM structure that are relevant to their purposes, functions, and operational demands.

Chapter 4 presented five key 'approaches' to KM in terms of the primary conceptions of knowledge embedded in each approach. By understanding the fundamental ideas behind an approach it is easier to compare and contrast what each of these approaches has to offer to the police and law enforcement organizations. These five approaches are labelled: 'Knowledge as Value'; 'Knowledge as Exchange'; 'Knowledge as Resource'; 'Knowledge as Organization'; and 'Knowledge as Strategy'.

The first 'knowledge as value' approach is fundamental to all other approaches. For unless 'knowledge' is first and foremost seen as having 'value' then why would any organization bother to try to capture and manage it? This 'knowledge value' approach is most evident in the service orientation of policing but also in its crime-fighting function as exemplified in the understanding that the investigation process can be likened to a 'value shop' configuration.

The second 'knowledge as exchange' approach is market-driven and commercial in orientation and therefore favours economic and business models of KM. Its relevance to the 'public policing' model, as opposed to more commercially oriented forms of 'privatized' policing and security models, lies in the fact that policing is a 'knowledge market' in the sense of a police organization's intellectual assets. These can be measured in terms of their economic value to produce results and can be traded like other commodities. However, the 'pricing system' for such police knowledge in the public domain would involve a different set of criteria to do with elements like reciprocity, repute, and altruism.

The third 'knowledge as resource' approach is really about capturing specialist knowledge in knowledge-based systems. The strategic value of police knowledge resources lies in the organization's ability to capitalize on the various characteristics of knowledge being valuable, original, non-imitable, non-transferable, non-substitutable, exploitable, and combinable.

The fourth 'knowledge as organization' approach revolves around the use of organizational structures and networks, both formal and informal, to share or pool knowledge, primarily through 'knowledge communities'. Organizations create knowledge by action and interaction with their environment through what has been termed a 'SECI' process (Nonaka *et al.* 2000). That is, knowledge is created through organized human activity that involves Socialization, Externalization, Combination, and Internalization. However, organizations must be able to leverage that knowledge by transferring it to others in order to maximize the benefits of such a knowledge creation process. This leveraging of knowledge through transfer and sharing is particularly problematic for police organizations not only because of the sensitive nature of the information and intelligence they possess but also because of the well-researched reluctance of police to share even the most basic information even with their own.

The fifth 'knowledge as strategy' approach is perhaps the most difficult to realize as, of necessity, it involves raising the consciousness within the organization of the value creation possibilities of knowledge as a resource. Organizations from a strategic knowledge perspective can be classified as efficiency-based, experience-based, and expertise-based. Such organizational types are often mixed in reality rather than purely one or another of the three types. However, each organizational type tends to adopt a particular strategy with regard to how it tries to create value for its knowledge resources. For example, a 'stock strategy' of information collection and storage in databases and distribution through knowledge networks, internally and externally, is most common for 'efficiency-based' organizations.

A 'flow strategy' also involves storing and retrieving information, but the primary focus is on knowledge-in-use in work processes and hence is more suitable for an 'experience-based' organization. In other words, the 'workflow' processes are the focus, not just holding an unused stock of knowledge in databases. Hence, it is a 'yellow-pages' strategy where information on how a particular current work process is carried out is stored along with links to who the people are that have the knowledge of the process. Thus, when a new project is started, a search of an organization's databases will reveal if similar projects have been carried out and who the people to contact are with the 'know-how' to assist with the project.

A 'growth strategy', on the other hand, also relies on the storage and retrieval of information but only insofar as it is useful in developing new knowledge and innovative work processes and therefore is more suitable for an 'expertise-based' organization. In other words, finding people and innovations internal and external to the organization that have the expertise to develop new knowledge is the focal point of a growth strategy.

The five approaches to KM are not mutually exclusive. Such approaches interact with one another and are often layered through a police organization in different divisions and sections. What is important from a KM point of view is the mix of approaches and ensuring a complementary range of approaches and their various contributions is achieved to ensure optimal performance for police and law enforcement organizations.

Chapter 5 looked at the types of KMS that are relevant to policing and law enforcement in much more detail. The important distinction here is that an 'information system' can only collect, store, and retrieve information entered into it, whereas a 'knowledge system' takes the entered information and creates knowledge out of it. The key factor to knowledge creation is the 'individual mind' of the user of the system, not in the technology of the system itself.

A typology was proposed (Figure 5.1) of four systems of KM for policing and law enforcement based on how each type of systems architecture manages the different levels of knowledge for which the system has been designed. These four KM systems are: Information Management Systems (IMS); Geographic Information Systems (GIS); Intelligence Surveillance Systems (ISS); and Expert Knowledge Systems (EKS).

The importance of these four KMS for policing and law enforcement lies in how they can be combined in different ways to maximize operational effectiveness. However, such combinations can create overlaps which have the potential to create 'tension spaces', organizationally and technologically, which will need to be managed carefully.

Chapter 6 dealt with the variety of 'technologies' available for use by police and other law enforcement and security agencies. Again, as in Chapter 5, a new typology based on a combination of key policing functions (investigation, analysis, prevention) and key technological functions (communicating, visualizing, reasoning) was proposed for classifying police technologies in an easier and more relevant manner for operational purposes. This typology was presented in the form of a matrix (Figure 6.1) which contained the three core technological groupings—communicative, visualization, and reasoning—that police rely upon to investigate, analyse, and prevent crime and terrorism.

A distinct advantage for police executives in relation to technological applications to support KM is the use of this matrix typology to map out and strategically select the types of application based on the class, capability, and combination of such technologies to suit current and future policing needs.

The significant point to note is that new emerging applications coming out of these technological groupings will cause substantial changes both technologically and operationally. Such changes will have to be managed wisely in order to overcome the inherent conservatism of the 'police culture' effectively and avoid what Collier (2006: 114) found in a study of four police forces in Britain: that 'technology' was 'clearly a major impediment to progress in the intelligent application of knowledge in policing'.

Applications for police Knowledge Management

The third 'applications' section of this book took up the key points raised in the previous sections and presented three distinctly different and new applications for managing police knowledge. The key innovative aspect of all three applications systems is how they capture and utilize the tacit knowledge of operational police officers systematically throughout the actual application processes of 'experiential knowledge reasoning' (Chapter 7), 'neural network mapping' (Chapter 8) and 'knowledge modelling' (Chapter 9).

Chapter 7 presented the 'Cross+Check' (C+C) System, which is a knowledge-based application system designed to handle investigative problems by grafting into the system the tacit knowledge expertise of police officers. The tacit knowledge of police is imbued with fuzzy inferences that reflect the 'shades of grey' meanings inherent in police work. Such fuzziness is captured in the notion of 'police knowledge triangles' (Figure 7.1), introduced in this chapter to show how police knowledge grows through a mix of information and experience over time.

The C+C system operates as an experiential knowledge reasoning system that integrates four qualitatively different information sources (police/security; descriptive; diagnostic; and research) in such a way as to allow the user to develop inferences and cross-check them through a process of visual analysis against each level of information in the system. This systematic process of reasoning also allows an investigator to place a relative weighting on developed inferences and hence to prioritize investigative leads and strategies.

Chapter 8 presented an 'Investigative Pathways' (IP) mapping application system based on the neural network modelling of four investigative thinking styles termed Method, Challenge, Skill, and Risk. Each of these four cognitive styles of investigative thinking are 'patterned thought processes' that investigators repeatedly use in varying combinations depending on individual preferences to think through the investigation of a case. These four patterned thought processes exist in a hierarchy of increasing conceptual complexity as an individual begins 'to think' further up the hierarchy. Such patterned thought processes of investigators made it possible to 'model' investigative thinking as a neural network-like structure.

Such a neural network mapping application of investigative thinking pathways holds significant potential for training police to 'learn the patterns' of how to think as expert investigators.

Chapter 9 presented a 'knowledge modelling' application about the interlocking nature of the contexts in which terrorism evolves, develops, and operates. The application system is based on a visualization process model (Figure 9.1) of three particular terrorism contexts to do with Causal, Commitment, and Capability factors. Each of these interlocking contexts and their associated factors are used to profile the 'process' of terrorism itself rather than the 'person' of the terrorist. The knowledge value of such a visual modelling application rests in its potential to predict likely scenarios and plan intervention points to disrupt the terrorism process.

This review of salient aspects and key points related to the three main sections of this book—'foundations', 'structures', and 'applications'—provides the essential background against which to discuss and reflect on the necessary core considerations required for crafting relevant and effective policies and prac-tices to integrate KM successfully in police and law enforcement organizations.

Policy considerations for police Knowledge Management

Organizations run on policy. Practices flow from policy. Therefore, it is impera-tive for organizations to have in place the right sorts of policy to get the types of practice they see as essential to carry out the work of the organization. It is no different for police and law enforcement organizations and the stakes of getting policy and subsequent practices wrong can be very high.

In theory this is all well and good. However, it is also clear that knowing what the 'right' sorts of policy are is notoriously difficult to achieve. Even if a policy appears to be the right one this begs the question 'for how long is this policy assumed to be the right one?'

Furthermore, crafting 'good' policy is an art form just as much as it is a sci-ence. The breadth and depth of knowledge required on a subject area to craft a good policy is something 'spin doctors', 'speech writers', and 'marketing experts' often lack in large measure. The infamous 'axis of evil' comment by President Bush is an especially relevant example of 'policy-on-the-run' driven by short-term considerations that has plagued his administration's term of office and set back international relations for the US in all likelihood for at least a decade.

Moreover, the slip between the 'policy cup' and the 'practice lip' is a constant reality for even 'good' policy. It requires organizational vigilance to keep the gap between policy and practice as small as possible.

It should be obvious by now that KM at a policy level has potential to suffer all these fates and indeed has happened in a number of organizations (Malhotra 2004). Knowledge Management policy in police organizations has no guaran-teed immunity (Home Office 2003).

Thus, there is a real need for police executives to appreciate these policy risk factors (incorrect policy, poor crafting, policy–practice disjunctions) and design them out as far as possible when introducing and/or reworking policies and practices for integrating police KM.

Designing a 'good' policy is never an easy task. What is essential though for designing as relevant a KM policy as possible for the foreseeable future in polic-ing and law enforcement is first and foremost to 'know' the subject area in depth.

The purpose of this book is to provide such 'deep knowledge' of police KM. To that end Figure 10.1 has been designed as a type of 'unifying framework' to guide police and law enforcement officials in their thinking about how to integrate KM meaningfully throughout their organization.

At first glance this 'Fuzzy Pyramid' may appear daunting. Take the time to have a closer look and you will begin to appreciate its significance. The practical usefulness of the pyramid is that it allows you to think about the necessary considerations for designing and implementing an effective, up-to-date KM policy relevant to the specific requirements of your police service's organizational context and global operating environment.

The following subsections will outline and discuss five key considerations that police executives and their staff need to be cognizant of in order to have any chance of successfully designing a relevant, comprehensive, and effective KM policy for policing and law enforcement. These key considerations are embedded in and flow out of the police KM pyramid shown in Figure 10.1.

Knowledge dimensions

The first consideration concerns the dimensions of knowledge as represented along the horizontal (knowledge harvesting) and vertical (knowledge creation) axes of the KM pyramid. This consideration reminds us that KM at a policy level is all about striking the correct balance between the dimensions of 'knowledge harvesting' and 'knowledge creation'.

'Knowledge harvesting' is where existing knowledge captured in an organization's databases, information systems, knowledge repositories, best practices, 'lessons learnt' packages, and so forth is re-used and replicated to achieve pre-specified organizational goals and targets.

According to Malhotra (2004: 3) knowledge harvesting is what passes for much of KM in most organizations. This knowledge harvesting approach to KM

Figure 10.1 Police Knowledge Management as 'fuzzy pyramid' conceptualization

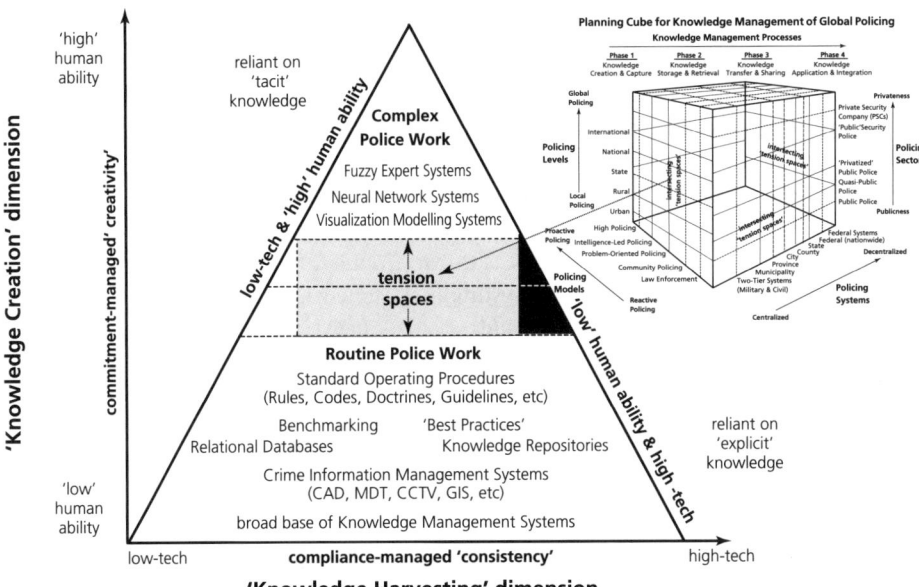

is easy to do for work that is routine and structured. It fits very comfortably with organizations that depend on rules and institutionalized procedures and work in predictable and stable environments.

'Knowledge creation' on the other hand is a much more active and dynamic concept that results from multi-level interactions between data, information, and intelligence combined with rules, procedures, best practices, lessons learnt, and the like by individuals either working in groups or alone that show motivation, commitment, and persistence to think innovatively to come up with new ideas and ways to improve processes and/or solve problems. The critical point about knowledge creation is that its wellspring is in the mind of individuals, not technology. Hence, a knowledge creation approach is most suitable for work that is predominantly non-routine and largely unstructured and where an organization operates in unpredictable and dynamic environments.

The essential difference between these two dimensions is that knowledge harvesting depends on technology for processing routine, structured work in stable environments. Whereas knowledge creation does not depend on technology but rather an individual's innovative thinking, but uses technology to process non-routine, unstructured work in dynamic environments.

This first consideration for designing a good KM policy presents police with 'the overriding challenge for the organizations . . . to effectively address the dialectic of knowledge harvesting and knowledge creation' (Malhotra 2004: 13). This leads into the second policy consideration.

Knowledge Management systems

This second consideration concerns Knowledge Management systems (KMS). As can be seen in Figure 10.1 the horizontal dimension of 'knowledge harvesting' comprises a broad KMS base for undertaking 'routine police work'. Such police KMS cover various types of crime information management systems, relational databases, knowledge repositories, as well as benchmarking, best practices, and an array of standard operating procedures (SOPs) in the form of rules, codes of conduct, doctrines, guidelines, and so forth.

The technological sophistication of such a KMS base varies from 'low-tech' systems to very 'high-tech' systems as shown from left to right along the horizontal axis of this Knowledge Harvesting (KH) dimension. This KH dimension also forms the base of the KM pyramid.

In Figure 10.1 the vertical axis represents the Knowledge Creation (KC) dimension which depends on human ability for its operation. The 'growth' in KC therefore is relative to the amount and quality of human ability that is put into being creative and innovative by individuals within an organization. Hence, as shown the vertical axis, KC, varies from 'low' human ability to 'high' human ability.

Furthermore, the level of human ability put into KC also requires varying degrees of KMS support from an organization in order to realize fully the potential of KC outcomes. Hence, as seen in Figure 10.1, the top half of the KM pyramid is where 'complex police work' occurs. Such complex police work requires a higher level of human ability, often expressed through innovative KC work, to deal effectively with and/or solve problems.

KC work at this higher level of human ability in turn requires more sophisticated technological applications like fuzzy expert systems (Chapter 7—'Cross+Check' Experiential Knowledge Reasoning System), neural network systems (Chapter 8—'Investigative Pathways' Neural Network Mapping System), or visualization modelling systems (Chapter 9—'Interlocking Terrorism Contexts' Knowledge Modelling System), or similar purpose-built KMS for specific police and law enforcement requirements.

'Fuzzy' tension spaces

The third consideration concerns the 'fuzzy' tension spaces that exist at the technological level of KMS for routine and complex police work and at the organizational planning level for KM ranging from local to global policing.

In terms of technological tension spaces, as can be seen in Figure 10.1, these can arise in particular at the intersections between routine and complex police work. This is because new emerging technological innovations and applications are 'disruptive' technologies (Wormeli 2005) when first introduced and may become 'transformative' technologies (Manning 2003) in the longer term. Such technological transformations create organizational tensions especially in terms of budget-draining resources and staffing expertise required to run new applications. The reality of technology-induced tension spaces is very apparent in policing due to a combination of factors concerning the inherent conservatism of the police culture which is generally opposed to any change (Stroshine 2005), varying technological frames (Orlikowski and Gash 1994) of users which can result in technologies being underused with a consequent reduction in organizational effectiveness (Chan *et al.* 2001).

With regard to tension spaces arising from other organizational issues, Figure 10.1 illustrates via the 'planning cube' diagram reproduced on this figure from Chapter 3 how the wide and varied range of intersecting tension spaces arises in policing as a result of incompatibilities, mismatching, and misunderstandings between different policing systems and policing models operating at different levels and across different sectors in the policing and security nexus.

Finally, both types of 'tension space', technological and organizational, are 'fuzzy' as shown on Figure 10.1 by the band of three lines that dissect the middle of the pyramid. The band of lines is meant to indicate the 'fuzziness' of such tension spaces as they will vary greatly as to where a particular set of tensions will draw the line. For example, for some technological tensions the 'space' may be widely or narrowly drawn as to the degree to which routine or complex police work is involved and the resultant technological resources required to support the level and type of police work.

Furthermore, it should be noted that the left side of the 'tension space' band of lines in the middle of the pyramid shows a 'white' triangle while the right side contains a 'black' triangle. These 'black and white' triangles are suggestive of how at the extremities of thinking about 'tension spaces' there is human tendency to see things in 'black and white' terms in order to resolve the tension. People are not comfortable with living with tension for too long. Hence, a quick 'fix' to sort out a problematic issue is a real temptation rather than continuing to grapple with the 'shades of grey' that occupy the middle ground between 'black and white' thinking in order to develop a better-thought-through solution.

This same fuzziness applies to the KM pyramid as a whole, especially, with regard to getting the 'right' balance between the 'knowledge harvesting' and 'knowledge creation' dimensions as this balance will always be a 'matter of degree'. As Zadeh (1996) so succinctly noted fuzzy logic proves 'everything is a matter of degree'. Ironically, 'fuzziness' is 'the constant' in policing and law enforcement environments characterized by knowledge-intensive work (Collier 2006) carried out in rapidly changing landscapes of uncertainty and ambiguity (Snowden 2006) with intersecting tension spaces criss-crossing local and global contexts to forms of 'virtual policing' (Hughes and Love 2004).

Models of police management

The fourth consideration concerns models of police management in relation to the focus of such management. As shown in Figure 10.1 the 'Knowledge Harvesting' dimension is most closely associated with a managerial focus that seeks 'compliance' in order to minimize variance and hence produce a consistent result that is often pre-specified and pre-determined by some type of performance outcome indicator, target, or measurement.

Hence, organizational control is imperative for this type of compliance-based management. Again for routine police work this 'Command and Control' managerial style works up to a certain degree (the 'fuzziness' factor). However, beyond where that 'certain degree' may be drawn a 'command and control' compliance model becomes problematic for a KM policy.

Alternately, as is evident on the vertical axis of the 'Knowledge Creation' dimension of Figure 10.1 the type of managerial focus required to manage the creation of new knowledge is 'Commitment' based. As Malhotra (2004: 11) notes 'a key challenge for managers in the forthcoming turbulent environment will be cultivating commitment of knowledge workers to the organizational vision'.

Creativity and innovative thinking flows from a motivated and committed workforce not one that is told to 'toe the line', 'don't rock the boat', 'keep your head down', and 'just do your job', or in other words be compliant. Viable KMS at the higher end of complex police work can only come about by police managers attending to the sense-making capabilities of their staff or as Butler and Gray (2006) put it adopting 'mindfulness-based approaches' to managing individuals. 'Mindfulness' refers to 'the ability to continuously create and use new categories in perception and interpretation of the world '(Langer 1997: 4).

Butler and Gray (2006: 214) elaborate on such 'mindfulness' approaches as follows:

> Mindfulness-based approaches hold that individuals' and organizations' abili-
> ty to achieve reliable performance in changing environments depends on how
> they think: how they gather information, how they perceive the world around
> them, and whether they are able to change their perspective to reflect the
> situation at hand (Langer, 1989). From this perspective, routines are a double-
> edged sword. They are helpful when they provide options, but detrimental
> when they hinder detection of changes in the task or environment. Whether
> describing individuals or organizations, mindfulness-based approaches posit
> that—more than just consistency of action—properly situated cognition is
> ultimately the basis for reliable performance.

What this consideration of police management models highlights is that police executives need to find the right balance between maintaining a 'com-mand and control' compliance model of management for routine police work while at the same time facilitating the movement towards a more commitment-centred, mindfulness-based management model for some routine police work and for the majority of complex police work. Anything short of this will render even the best-crafted police KM policy ineffectual.

Centrality of tacit knowledge

This fifth and final consideration about designing a good KM policy in police organizations is probably the most difficult challenge to address organizational-ly and managerially. That is, giving the proper credence to the tacit knowledge of individual police officers to be taken seriously in both word and deed by police executives.

The reason this is such a challenge is that there has been a persistent view pro-mulgated in various KM textbooks since the late 1980s that technology will be able to store the 'knowledge' humans have acquired and, to put it bluntly, ren-der the need for reliance on human experience and expertise almost obsolete.

> Information systems will maintain the corporate history, experience and
> expertise that long-term employees now hold. The information systems them-
> selves—not the people—can become the stable structure of the organisation.
> People will be free to come and go, but the value of their experience will be
> incorporated in the systems that help them and their successors run the busi-
> ness. (Applegate *et al.* 1988: 44).

This view is clearly 'out of sync' with much current KM literature but still has some currency in business and technology circles especially those that take a 'knowledge harvesting' approach to KM. A faint echo of this 'technology-reduces-reliance-on-human knowledge' view can still be detected even in some current management texts. In discussing police performance Collier (2006: 115) asserts that 'technology needs to be integrated with working practices to reduce organizational reliance on tacit knowledge'.

While we agree with technological integration into the working practices of police as certainly necessary for a robust KM policy we do not support the view that this needs to be done to 'reduce organizational reliance' on the 'tacit knowledge' of individual police officers. Quite apart from the unlikeliness of this ever being achieved by technology, this view also misses the point that it is precisely the 'tacit knowledge' of creative individuals that is needed to get policing off the fly bottle of outmoded KM thinking. 'Tacit knowledge' is not a commodity that can be downloaded from someone's head and stored in a computer to be considered as the 'holy grail' of KM in a digital chip. Hence, there are at least three significant problems associated with 'stored' tacit knowledge.

The first problem is that knowledge which individuals possess is always 'skewed'. Knowledge is context dependent. That is, knowledge does not exist in a vacuum, it is conditioned and biased by the contexts in which it is collected, discussed, and used. Hence, stored knowledge systems like 'best practices', 'lessons learnt' systems, and so forth are skewed by organizational assumptions that condition individual thinking. Such conditioned thinking can reinforce entrenched folklore and cultural stereotyping that come embedded in 'stored' knowledge.

In this regard, counterintuitively Brown and Brudney (2003: 49) in their study of how police agencies committed to a 'learning-organization' KM paradigm, that presumably values flexibility and adaptability used in their IT systems, found that ironically 'I & T systems may institutionalize old structures and perspectives' rather than advance knowledge.

Moreover, Weick and Sutcliffe (2001) found that organizations operating in dynamic and unpredictable environments like policing and other law enforcement agencies are particularly vulnerable to acquiring IT systems which promote efficiency by routinizing behaviours and hence reduce the involvement of humans in day-to-day activities. Automating IT systems to this degree by reducing human involvement further entrenches and institutionalizes certain thinking patterns desired by the organization, but in the longer term may actually be counterproductive to its survival and certainly the development of new knowledge.

Kogut and Zander (1992) also found that work routines that are embedded in software then restrict and channel user's choices and hence mask variation in data and information that otherwise might have been noticed with less structured software.

Snowden (2006: 277) makes a similar point in regard to police intelligence gathering when he states: 'we also need to understand that the patterns of our own analyst's experience will determine what they pay attention to in large data-sets, so understanding and revealing that bias is critical'.

It can be speculated with some degree of substance that this recognition of the potential for analyst bias—of seeing only what one wants to see—when interpreting data was itself missed by the CIA and other US counter-terrorism agencies in their official assessment and presentation delivered by the then Secretary of State, Colin Powell, to the United Nations of the 'pictures' that 'proved' Saddam had trucks loaded with WMDs ready to unleash death and destruction in the Middle East.

The second problem with 'stored' tacit knowledge is that, once stored, it becomes 'static'. Hence, the richness of its utility is diminished to varying degrees depending on how it is used and for what purpose.

By definition 'tacit knowledge' is an active, dynamic, and richly joined 'composite' construct that depends on human ability operating in concert with various contexts to realize its potential fully as noted previously by several writers (Churchman 1971; Nonaka and Takeuchi 1995; Davenport and Prusak 1998; Ruggles and Holthouse 1999; Sternberg and Horvath 1999; Sternberg, Wagner, and Okagaki 1993; Sternberg 2000; Alavi and Leidner 2002; Muller-Merbach 2004; Leonard and Insch 2005; Malhotra 2004; Butler and Gray 2006; Sastrowarddoyo and Metcalfe 2006).

Given the dynamic and multi-faceted nature of tacit knowledge it may be of little use to 'explicitly store' static representations of individuals' tacit knowledge in databases and knowledge repositories because such a transfer changes the very thing about tacit knowledge—its dynamism—that makes it so valuable. Stored knowledge loses the interactional edge.

Individuals not only can make different 'meanings' out of the same collection of information and data sets, but also at different times and in different contexts. It is this individual variation in interpretations that is so valuable in tacit knowledge. For it introduces variety and differentness to the equation and reduces the risk of the same old thinking being applied again and again to the same old problem with, unsurprisingly, the same old result.

The third problem with 'stored' tacit knowledge is its 'superficiality'. This superficiality is in part a function of the fact that people do not know how much they really know and so can only provide as much as the skill of the interviewer has in eliciting buried or 'deep' tacit knowledge from an individual. However, the larger problem of storing 'superficial' tacit knowledge comes about from the inherent difficulties associated with 'knowledge sharing'.

It is somewhat ironic that in a technological age full of sophisticated technologies for sharing information and knowledge across virtual realities in real time that Malhotra (2006: 10) can so firmly assert that 'it will be almost impossible to ensure that accurate information is available for integration despite presence of enabling technologies that can facilitate such integration'.

The basis of this uninspiring prediction, as Malhotra outlines, lies in the paradoxical roles of collaboration and competition required by organizations of their employees. Malthotra states:

Often, individuals may not willingly share information with their departmental peers, supervisors, or with other departments, because they believe that what they know provides them with an inherent advantage in bargaining and negotiation. Despite availability of most sophisticated 'knowledge sharing' technologies, such human concerns may often result in sharing of partial, inaccurate, or ambiguous information. Even more critical than the absence of information is the propensity of sharing inaccurate or ambiguous information because of competing interests (2006: 10)

As the dictum goes 'Knowledge is Power'. Nowhere is this more evident than when someone is asked to 'share' their knowledge. In a review of the application of 'intelligent' knowledge in British policing, Collier (2006: 114) observes, 'there remain many examples of tacit knowledge being held by police officer(s) not being converted into explicit knowledge that is usable by NIM (National Intelligence Model) processes'.

Given these three problematic areas associated with 'stored' tacit knowledge, that is, its skewed, static, and superficial nature, it should be evident by now that how best to utilize the tacit knowledge of individuals must be of central concern to a KM policy for policing.

In this regard, the fuzzy pyramid in Figure 10.1 provides some guidance as to how to make this immensely important construct called 'tacit knowledge' central to a KM policy for policing and law enforcement. As can be seen the sides of the fuzzy pyramid show 'low-tech' and 'high' human ability going up the left-hand side and 'low' human ability and 'high-tech' going down the right-hand side of the pyramid.

The significance of this depiction is that for the 'Knowledge Creation' dimension to 'grow' in an organization it requires a minimum of some 'low-tech' support and a lot of 'high' human ability in the form of motivation and commitment to kick-start innovative thinking.

The 'high' human ability factor can be either recognized individuals with some talent, experience, or expertise in certain areas, or a composite group of similarly endowed individuals. As is evident on Figure 10.1 at the 'high end' of human ability the reliance on an individual's or group of individuals' tacit knowledge is paramount.

From such a focused concentration of tacit knowledge, then, the basis of KMS in policing and law enforcement can be expected to have some return on this investment in tacit knowledge with the development of innovative technological applications like those noted under the complex police work area of Figure 10.1 and other emerging technologies (Snowden 2006).

Conversely, for the 'Knowledge Harvesting' dimension to 'expand sideways' an organization need only to invest in a range of 'high-tech' applications that require 'little' human ability or involvement of tacit knowledge. To run these high-tech systems only requires training in the procedural documentation (explicit knowledge) relevant to the application.

However 'high-tech' applications become they will never replace the sense-making capacities of human ability. As Snowden (2006: 276) points out in relation to counter-terrorism systems:

> No system will ever of itself predict a terrorist outrage. Focusing on measuring the utility of a system or of a person on their ability to predict the unpredictable is wasteful and dangerous... While we cannot predict outcome, we can know a lot about starting conditions and the nature of attractor and barrier mechanisms (Snowden, 2005) which can influence the evolution of a system for good or evil. There is greater effectiveness in understanding, and therefore influencing, the environment from which events can emerge. In other words, by better managing context we may avoid the need to predict events by making them less likely.

It is the tacit knowledge of people that must be relied upon to make sense of the contexts that lead to events like terrorism, not systems. This does not imply that technological systems are of little use in such circumstances but that it is the combination of their use with human sense-making ability that is the crux of the matter. Hence, various combinations of a 'low–high' tech and 'low–high' human ability mixture range is required based on context-specific considerations.

Moreover, capturing the 'deep' tacit knowledge of individuals is only possible at the time of its occurrence. This is usually when a person is working on solving a problem, either individually or in a group context. It is at this point of occurrence that KMS can make their greatest contribution to capturing tacit knowledge by designing systems that the user 'thinks through' and 'reasons with' to solve a problem. This is precisely why all three applications presented respectively in Chapters 7, 8, and 9 are designed as 'low-tech' systems. They are meant to be 'imprecise' and 'imperfect' systems for it is through the user 'using' the system 'to think with' that it gets 'perfected'; 'perfected' in the sense of the user 'working out' a solution by relying on their tacit knowledge to get the 'system to work' for them.

In this regard Butler and Gray (2006: 221) make the very salient observation based on reported research that 'reliable performance may actually be enhanced by systems that, as a result of inadequacies and errors, encourage individuals to seek out multiple information sources and critically evaluate the data upon which they rely (Hedberg and Jonson 1978)'.

From the above discussion and indeed through the themes in this book it behoves police and law enforcement organizations to fully appreciate and recognize the significance of this final consideration. Making the tacit knowledge of individuals a central focus in any policy on police KM is not an option: it is an imperative to be done—the sooner the better—for both the credibility of policing and the safety of the global community.

The future of police Knowledge Management

The future of police Knowledge Management will depend on several factors coming together at three levels—operationally, managerially, and organizationally. The work in this book offers comprehensive guidance and conceptual clarity for achieving practical applicability and integration at all three levels for police KM.

At the operational level, street/beat/patrol police officers, detectives/ investigators, intelligence officers, crime analysts, and similar operational staff (civilian and uniform) will find much of value to add to their own stock of 'tacit and explicit' police knowledge (Chapter 1, Figure 1.1) and the 'triangles' of police knowledge work (Chapter 7, Figure 7.1) that they operate in and out of in their work contexts.

Particularly, operational staff who invest some time and effort in understanding the applications presented in this book (Chapter 7, 'Cross+Check' Experiential Knowledge Reasoning System; Chapter 8, 'Investigative Pathways' Neural Network Mapping System; Chapter 9, 'Interlocking Terrorism Contexts' Knowledge Modelling System) will find each application addresses very practical issues and concerns which they will face at some time or another or even daily in their various work contexts.

At the managerial level, police supervisors, senior police (inspectors/assistant superintendents/superintendents or similar ranks) and middle-order civilian officials as well as executive police require a holistic planning framework (Chapter 3, Figure 3.5) to manage 'police knowledge work' effectively at three primary levels.

- *The global-contextual level* is proactively to 'plan in' the inevitable 'tension spaces' that arise at the intersections of diverse and different policing sectors, levels, models, and systems.
- *The technological-support level* of KMS using a police-specific 'Technology Matrix' (Chapter 6, Figure 6.1) for mapping out and aligning key policing functions (investigation, analysis, prevention) with key technological functions (communicating, visualizing, reasoning) in order to select the appropriate types of application strategically based on their class, capability, and combination to suit current and future policing needs.
- *The operational-facilitation level* of finding the right balance between maintaining a 'command and control' compliance model of management for routine police work while at the same time facilitating the movement towards a more commitment-centred, mindfulness-based management model for some aspects of routine police work and more importantly for complex police work where the tacit, experiential knowledge of their staff can be more fully valued and utilized.

At the organizational level, it is executive police command (regional commanders, commissioners, or similar ranks) that are required to oversee the present and plan for the future. This oversight and planning responsibility in terms of KM requires the development and implementation of a comprehensive, relevant Police Knowledge Management Policy (PKMP). Such a policy focus will need to ensure a complementary mix of Knowledge Management approaches that are layered throughout a police organization according to their 'knowledge value'. Such knowledge value is realized through economic exchange, use of strategic resources, as well as organizational structures and networks to harvest police knowledge primarily for storage, retrieval, transfer, and sharing such knowledge, and finally to add value through knowledge creation strategies.

The unifying framework of a 'Fuzzy Pyramid' (Chapter 10, Figure 10.1) provides a non-prescriptive conceptual foundation based around five key considerations discussed in detail above. This unifying framework will assist and guide police and law enforcement executive officers and officials in their thinking about how to integrate KM meaningfully throughout their organization locally and globally.

Moreover, any police KM policy, no matter how technologically sophisticated and comprehensively planned, will not work unless proper recognition and acknowledgement is given in word and deed to the community of people who 'are' the organization at one moment in time. The fundamental, significant, and essential character of the contributions that the tacit knowledge and hard-won experience of individual police officers and civilians at all levels of service make within the global policing and law enforcement community can never be underestimated.

Conclusion

In concluding this work a few final observations, remarks and predictions are in order.

Police knowledge work is uniquely distinctive and of fundamental importance to the wellbeing of societies in this global village. However, police knowledge work demands a great deal from its practitioners and managers. It encompasses legal authority to use reasonable force to deal with situations, has wide discretionary and hence 'interpretational' power, it is time- and information intensive in nature, relies strongly on the 'tacit knowledge' of individual officers, and is 'locally' sited in terms of operating practices but, of necessity, must be globally-orientated and focused in perspective. The burden of police work requires not only knowledge but wisdom in how to manage and make best use of such knowledge in policing and law enforcement.

The real key to unlocking the potential of police KM lies in two directions: first, finding better ways to do 'knowledge sharing' and, second, finding better ways to utilize the 'tacit knowledge' of individuals involved in policing and law enforcement. These two issues—sharing knowledge and utilizing tacit knowledge—are not different directions but rather run in parallel and often overlap.

With respect to the first direction for police KM, finding better ways to share knowledge, the problems faced by police forces and other public sector institutions and agencies in the UK clearly establish the case for finding ways to do this better.

Various Audit Commission reports (1996, 2000, 2004, 2005) in the UK as well as the Victoria Climbié Inquiry Report (Laming 2003) into the severe torture, abuse, and death of this eight-year-old girl in 2000, and the damming Bichard Inquiry Report (2004) into intelligence-based record-keeping and vetting practices in Humberside and Cambridgeshire police forces, all highlight the scale of the public sector failures in Britain by government organizations and institutions in not sharing information and knowledge in a timely manner.

Bundred (2006: 129) as Chief Executive of the Audit Commission in London identified 'organisational culture' as the critical element in this consistent pattern of knowledge-sharing failures when he stated 'within organisations or partnerships, culture is the most significant factor in determining the extent of knowledge sharing'. Bichard (2004: 8) goes further in his criticism of the policing system and laid the blame squarely on a key policing body in England and Wales, the Association of Chief Police Officers (ACPO) for being 'unable to foster a culture that properly values the importance of intelligence'.

These examples also provide cause for some sombre reflection on the entrenched nature of the difficulties faced by executives trying to reform an organizational culture. This reality can never be understated nor overlooked.

In relation to the second direction for police KM, finding better ways to capture and utilize the tacit knowledge of individual police officers and teams, the work in this book and particularly the applications presented are illustrative of how tacit knowledge can potentially be utilized at an operational level and in so doing sharing such operational knowledge in a meaningful manner also becomes possible.

To achieve capturing and sharing tacit knowledge the focus will need to be on developing and/or adapting technological innovations, both low-tech and high-tech applications, that can be embedded in the cultural networks of operational policing and law enforcement practices, so that such systems can capture tacit knowledge as it happens in the daily routines of police work. A potential spin-off from focusing on such contextually embedded applications is increasing the possibilities for generating and creating new knowledge from the storehouse of tacit experiential knowledge possessed by individual police officers working with such embedded systems.

Finally, there is no question that police KM will continue to grow in relation to the ever-expanding range of emerging technologies being developed to support knowledge work in a host of industries and businesses. Some of these new technologies will be applicable or can be made adaptable to various areas of police and law enforcement work. But this is primarily a matter of the growth in quantity of IT support available for police KM which looks set to continue in the foreseeable future.

However, in the final analysis the future growth in the 'quality' of police KM rests to a very large extent on the visionary and courageous leadership by police executives in the countries and nations they serve.

Hopefully, this book will find a home on the shelves of people of vision and courage at all levels of policing and law enforcement that want to enhance police knowledge and manage wisely the contexts in which police knowledge evolves, operates, and develops for the good of humankind.

References

Introduction

Keppel, R., and Weis, J. (1993). *Improving the Investigation of Violent Crime: The Homicide Investigation and Tracking System. National Institute of Justice—Research in Brief*. Washington: US Department of Justice.

Personal communication (2001) by SIO responsible for case in Singapore Police Force to Dr Geoff Dean.

Chapter 1

Alavari, M., and Leidner, D. E. (2001). 'Knowledge Management and Knowledge Management Systems: Conceptual Foundations and Research Issues'. *MIS Quarterly*, 25(1): 107–136.

Al-Rasheed, A. (1994). Traditional Arab Management: Evidence from empirical comparative research, conference paper, Arab Management Conference, Bradford: University of Bradford Management Centre.

Anderson, M. L. (2003). 'Embodied cognition: A field guide'. *Artificial Intelligence*, 149(1): 91–130.

Barclay, R., and Murray, P. (2000). 'What is Knowledge Management?'. *Knowledge Praxis*, <http://www.media-access.com/whatis.html>.

Brodeur, J. P., and Dupont, B. (2006). 'Knowledge Workers or "Knowledge" Workers?'. *Policing and Society*, 16(1): 7–26.

Brown, J., and Duguid, P. (2001). 'Knowledge and Organization: A Social-Practice Perspective'. *Organization Science*, 12(2): 198–213.

Chen, H., Schroeder, J., Hauck, R. V., Ridgeway, L., Atabakhsh, H., Gupta, H., Boarman, C., Rasmussen, K., and Clements, A.W. (2002). 'COPLINK Connect: information and knowledge management for law enforcement'. *Decision Support Systems*, 34: 271–285.

Chia, R. (2003). 'From Knowledge-Creation to the Perfection of Action: Tao, Basho and Pure Experience as the Ultimate Ground of Knowing'. *Human Relations*, 56(8): 953–981.

Colaprete, F. (2004). 'Knowledge Management'. *Law & Order*, 52(10): 82–87.

Dean, G. (1995). 'Police Reform: Rethinking Operational Policing'. *American Journal of Criminal Justice*, 23(4): 337–347.

Dreyfus, H. (2002). 'Intelligence without Representation—Merleau Ponty's Critique of Mental Representation'. *Phenomenology and the Cognitive Sciences*, 1(4): 367–383.

Drucker, P. E. (1995). 'The Post Capitalistic Executive', in P. E. Drucker (ed.), *Management in a Time of Great Change*. New York: Penguin.

Eblen, R. A., and Eblen W. (1994). *The Encyclopedia of the Environment*. Boston: Houghton Mifflin Company.

Ekman, G. (1999). *Från text till batong—Om poliser, busar och svennar (From text to bat—about officers)*. Stockholm: Ekonomiska forskningsinstitutet vid Handelshögskolan.

Ericson, R. (1981). *Making Crime: A Study of Detective Work*. Toronto: Butterworths.

——(1990). 'Observations concerning the Work of the Criminal Police', in T. Feltes and E. Rebscher (eds.), *Police and the Community: Contributions concerning the Relationship between Police and the Community and concerning Community Policing*. West Germany: Felix-Verlag.

Foster, J. (2003). 'Police Cultures', in T. Newburn (ed.), *Handbook of Policing*. Devon: Willan Publishing, 196–227.

Glisby, M., and Holden, N. (2003). 'Contextual Constraints in Knowledge Management Theory: The Cultural Embeddedness of Nonaka's Knowledge-creating Company'. *Knowledge and Process Management*, 10(1): 29–36.

Göranzon, B. (1990). *Det pratiktiska intellektet—Datoranvändning och yrkeskunnande (The practical intellect—Computer application and occupational knowledge)*. Stockholm: Carlsson Bokförlag.

Gottschalk, P. (2005). *Strategic Knowledge Management Technology*. Hershey, PA: Idea Group Publishing.

——(2006). *Knowledge Management Systems in Law Enforcement: Technologies and Techniques*. Hershey, PA: Idea Group Publishing.

Gustavsson, B. (2000). *Kunskapsfilosifi. Tre kunskapsformer i historisk belysning (Knowledge Philosophy. Tacit knowledge forms in historical context)*. Stockholm: Wahlström and Widstrand.

Holgersson, S. (2005). *Yrke: POLIS—Yrkeskunnskap, motivasjon, IT-system og andre forutsetninger for politiarbeide (Profession: Police—Occupational knowledge, motivation, IT system and other requirements for police work)*. PhD doctoral dissertation, Institutionen för datavetenskap, Linköping University, Sweden.

Hughes, V., and Jackson, P. (2004). 'The Influence of Technical, Social and Structural Factors on the Effective use of Information in a Policing Environment'. *The Electronic Journal of Knowledge Management*, 2(1): 65–76.

Innes, M. (2003). *Investigating Murder: Detective Work and the Police Response to Criminal Homicide*. Oxford: Clarendon Press.

King, W., Marks, P., and McCoy, S. (2002). 'The Most Important Issues in Knowledge Management'. *Communications of the ACM*, 45(9): 93–97.

Leonard, N., and Insch, G. (2005). 'Tacit Knowledge in Academia: A Proposed Model and Measurement Scale'. *Journal of Psychology*, 139, issue 6: 495–513.

Luen, T. W., and Al-Hawamdeh, S. (2001). 'Knowledge management in the public sector: principles and practices in police work'. *Journal of Information Science*, 27(5): 311–318.

Maquire, M. (2003). 'Criminal Investigation and Crime Control', in T. Newburn (ed.), *Handbook of Policing*. Devon: Willan Publishing, 363–393.

Nelson, R., and Winter, S. (1982). *An economic theory of evolutionary change*. Cambridge, MA: Belknap Press of Harvard University Press.

Newspaper.asia1.com.sg (2004) 'This Matrix has nothing to do with him' at <http://en.wikipedia.org/wiki/Multistate_Anti-Terrorism_Information_Exchange>. Accessed on 16/12/04.

Nonaka, I., and Konno, N. (1998). 'The concept of "Ba": Building a foundation for knowledge creation'. *California Management Review*, 40: 40–54.

Nordenstam, T. (1983). 'Ett pragmatiskt perspektiv på datautveckling (A pragmatic perspective on data evolution)' in B. Göranzon (ed.), *Datautvecklingens filosofi (Philosophy of the computer evolution)*. Stockholm: Carlsson och Jönsson.

Paoline, E. (2003). 'Taking Stock: Towards a richer understanding of police culture'. *Journal of Criminal Justice*, 31(3): 199–214.

Personal communication (2006) with SIO about the murder of a Chinese homosexual in Singapore.

Polanyi, M. (1962). *Personal Knowledge*. Chicago: University of Chicago Press.

—— (1966). *The tacit Dimension*. London: Routledge and Kegan Paul.

—— (1969). *Knowing and Being*. Chicago: University of Chicago Press.

Povey, K. (2002). 'Making Multilateral Agreements Work: The United Kingdom's Commitment to International Cooperation in the Fight Against Transnational Organised Crime', in R. Broadhurst (ed.), *Bridging the Gap: A Global Alliance Perspective on Transnational Organised Crime*. Hong Kong: Hong Kong Police Force, 55–62.

Prusak, L. (2001). 'Where did knowledge management come from?'. *IBM Systems Journal*, 40(4): 1–5.

Reuss-Ianni, E., and Ianni, F. (1983). 'Street cops and management cops: the cultures in policing', in M. Punch (ed.), *Control in the Police Organization*. Cambridge, MA: MIT Press, 251–274.

Schön, D. (1983). *The Reflective Practitioner: How Professionals think in action*. England: Basic Books.

Sheptycki, J. (2002). *In search of Transnational Policing: Towards a sociology of global policing*. Aldershot: Ashgate Publishing.

Spiegler, I. (2000). 'Knowledge Management: A New Idea or a Recycled Concept?'. *Communications of the Association for Information Systems*, 3 (14).

Sternberg, R. L, Forsythe, G. B., Hedlund, J., Horvath, J. A., Wagner, R. K., Williams, W. M., Snook. S., and Grigorenko, E. L. (2000). *Practical Intelligence in Everyday Life*. New York: Cambridge University Press.

Sternberg, R. J., and Horvath, J. A., (1999). *Tacit Knowledge in Professional Practice: Researcher and Practitioner Perspectives*. Mahwah, NJ: Erlbaum.

Sternberg, R. J., Wagner, R. K., and Okagaki, L. (1993). 'Practical intelligence: The nature and role of tacit knowledge in work and at school', in H. Reese, and J. Puckett (eds.), *Advances in Lifespan Development*. Hillsdale, NJ: Erlbaum, 205–227.

Sternberg, R. J., Wagner, R. K., Williams, W. M., and Horvath, J. A. (1995). 'Testing common sense'. *American Psychologist*, 50: 912–927.

Sutcliffe, K., and Weber, K. (2003). 'The high cost of accurate knowledge'. *Harvard Business Review*, May: 75–82.

Tsoukas, H., and Hatch, M. J. (2001). 'Complex Thinking, Complex Practice: The case for a Narrative Approach to Organizational Complexity'. *Human Relations*, 54(8): 979–1013.

249

Tsoukas, H., and Mylonopoulos, N. (2003). 'Part Special Issue Introduction: Modelling Organisational Knowledge'. *Journal of the Operational Research Society*, 54: 911–913.

Tsoukas, H., and Vladimirou, E. (2001). 'What is Organisational Knowledge?'. *Journal of Management Studies*, 38(7): 973–993.

Waddington, P. A. J. (1999). 'Police (canteen) sub-culture: an appreciation'. *British Journal of Criminology*, 39(20): 286–309.

Wagner, R. K., and Sternberg, R. J. (1986). 'Tacit knowledge and intelligence in the everyday world', in R. J. Sternberg, and R. K. Wagner, (eds.), *Practical Intelligence: Nature and Origins of Competence in Everyday World*. New York: Cambridge University Press, 51–83.

Wensley, A. (2001). 'Culture, Knowledge Management and Knowledge Transfer'. *Knowledge and Process Management*, 8(1): 1–2.

Wright, A. (2002). *Policing: An Introduction to Concepts and Practice*. Devon: Willan Publishing.

Wiig, K. (2000). 'Knowledge Management: An Emerging Discipline Rooted in a Long History', in C. Despres and D. Chauvel (eds.), *Knowledge Horizons: The present and the promise of knowledge management*. Boston: Butterworth-Heinemann.

Chapter 2

Alavari, M., and Leidner, D. E. (2001). 'Knowledge Management and Knowledge Management Systems: Conceptual Foundations and Research Issues'. *MIS Quarterly*, 25(1): 107–136.

Barclay, R., and Murray, P. (2000). 'What is Knowledge Management?'. *Knowledge Praxis* at <http://www.media-access.com/whatis.html>.

Bayley, D. H. (1988). 'Community policing: A report from the devil's advocate', in J. R. Greene and S. D. Mastrofski (eds.), *Community policing: Rhetoric or reality* New York: Praeger, 225–238.

Clarke, C. (2006). 'Proactive Policing: Standing on the Shoulders of Community-Based Policing'. *Police Practice and Research: An International Journal*, 7(1): 3–18.

Colvin, C., and Goh, A. (2006). 'Elements Underlying Community Policing: Validation of the Construct'. *Police Practice and Research: An International Journal*, 7(1): 19–34.

'Community Policing: Essential to Homeland Security' (2002) *Sheriff*, 54(5): 36–39.

Cordner, G. (2005). 'Community Policing: Elements and Effects', in R. G. Dunham and G. P. Alpert (eds.), *Critical Issues in Policing: Contemporary Readings (Fifth Edition)*. Prospect Heights, IL: Waveland Press, 401–418.

Earl, M. J. (2000). 'Evolving the E-Business'. *Business Strategy Review*, 11(2): 33–38.

Goldstein, H. (1994). 'Foreword', in D. P. Rosenbaum (ed.), *The challenge of community policing*. Thousand Oaks, CA: Sage, viii–x.

Gottschalk, P. (2005). *Strategic Knowledge Management Technology*. Hershey, PA: Idea Group Publishing.

Hunter, R. D., and Barker, T. (1993). 'BS and buzzwords: The new police operational style'. *American Journal of Police*, 12: 157–168.

King, W., Marks, P., and McCoy, S. (2002). 'The Most Important Issues in Knowledge Management'. *Communications of the ACM*, 45(9): 93–97.

King, W. R., and Teo, T. S. H. (1997). 'Integration Between Business Planning and Information Systems Planning: Validating a Stage Hypothesis'. *Decision Sciences*, 28(2): 279–307.

Klockars, C. (1988). 'The rhetoric of community policing', in J. R. Greene and S. D. Mastrofski (eds.), *Community Policing: Rhetoric or Reality*. New York: Praeger, 239–258.

Maguire, E. and Katz, C. (2002). 'Community policing, loose coupling, and sense-making in American police agencies'. *Justice Quarterly*, 19(3): 565–578.

Manning, P. K. (1989). 'Community policing', in R. G. Dunham and G. P. Alpert (eds.), *Critical issues in policing: Contemporary readings*. Prospect Heights, IL: Waveland, 395–405.

Nolan, R. L. (1979). 'Managing the crises in data processing'. *Harvard Business Review*, March–April: 115–126.

Prusak, L. (2001). 'Where did knowledge management come from?'. *IBM Systems Journal*, 40(4): 1–5.

Skolnick, J. H., and Bayley, D. H. (1988). 'Theme and variation in community policing', in M. Tonry and N. Morris (eds.), *Crime and justice: A review of research*. Chicago: University of Chicago Press, 138.

Spiegler, I. (2000). 'Knowledge Management: A New Idea or a Recycled Concept?', *Communications of the Association for Information Systems*, 3 (14).

Walsh, W., and Vito, G. (2004). 'The Meaning of Compstat: Analysis and Response'. *Journal of Contemporary Criminal Justice*, 20(1): 51–69.

Weatheritt, M. (1988). 'Community policing: Rhetoric or reality?', in J. R. Greene and S. Mastrofski (eds.), *Community policing: Rhetoric or reality?*. New York: Praeger, 153–175.

Wiig, K. (2000). 'Knowledge Management: An Emerging Discipline Rooted in a Long History', in C. Despres and D. Chauvel (eds.), *Knowledge Horizons: The present and the promise of knowledge management*. Boston: Butterworth-Heinemann.

Wycoff, M. A., and Skogan, W. (1994). 'The effect of a community policing management style on officers' attitudes'. *Crime & Delinquency*, 40: 371–383.

Chapter 3

Australian National News Wire, (2006). *Fed: Families try to cope with Bali Nine death penalty news*, 6 Sept.

Avant, D., (2005). *The Market for Force: The Consequences of Privatizing Security*. Cambridge: Cambridge University Press.

Brodeur, J. P., and Dupont, B. (2006). 'Knowledge Workers or "Knowledge" Workers?'. *Policing and Society*, 16(1): 7–26.

Bunyan, T. (2003). 'The birth of the EU's Interior Ministry?'. *Statewatch*, 13(1): 21–23.

Button, M. (2002). *Private Policing*. Devon: Willan Publishing.

Cherney, A., O'Reilly, J., and Grabosky, P. (2006). 'The multilateralization of Policing: The Case of Illicit Synthetic Drug Control'. *Police Practice and Research: An International Journal*, 7(3): 177–194.

Christopher, S. (2004). 'A practitioner's perspective of UK strategic intelligence', in J. Ratcliffe (ed.), *Strategic Thinking in Criminal Intelligence*. Sydney: Federation Press, 3177–3193.

Clarke, C. (2006). 'Proactive Policing: Standing on the Shoulders of Community-Based Policing'. *Police Practice and Research: An International Journal*, 7(1): 3–18.

Cordner, G. (2005). 'Community Policing: Elements and Effects', in R. G. Dunham and G. P. Alpert (eds.), *Critical Issues in Policing: Contemporary Readings (Fifth Edition)*. Prospect Heights, IL: Waveland Press, 401–418.

Deflem, M. (2002). *Policing World Society: Historical Foundations of International Police Cooperation*. Oxford: Clarendon Press.

Dintino, J., and Martens, F. (1983). *Police Intelligence Systems in Crime Control: maintaining a delicate balance in a liberal democracy*. Springfield, IL: C. C. Thomas.

Flood, B. (2004). 'Strategic aspects of the UK National Intelligence Model', in J. Ratcliffe (ed.), *Strategic Thinking in Criminal Intelligence*. Sydney: Federation Press, 37–52.

Gill, P. (2006). 'Not Just Joining the Dots But Crossing the Borders and Bridging the Voids: Constructing Security Networks and 11 September 2001'. *Policing and Society*, 16(1): 27–49.

Goldstein, H. (1994). 'Foreword', in D. P. Rosenbaum (ed.), *The challenge of community policing*. Thousand Oaks, CA: Sage, viii–x.

Holdaway, S. (1983). *Inside the British Police: a force at work*. Oxford: Blackwell.

Home Office (2002). *The National Policing Plan 2003–2006*. London: Home Office.

Illawarra Mercury (2006). *Nightmare in Bali: The Arrests, Trials, and Sentences of the Bali 9*, 13 May.

Johnson, P. (2006). 'Tip-off demands an Aussie role'. *Geelong Advertiser*, 8 Sept: 17.

Johnston, L. (1992). *The Rebirth of Private Policing*. London: Routledge.

—— (2000). *Policing Britain: Risk, Security and Governance*. London: Longman.

Johnston, L., and Shearing, C. (2002). *Governing Security: Explorations in Policing and Justice*.

London: Routledge.

Jones, T. (2003). 'The governance and accountability of policing', in T. Newburn (ed.), *Handbook of Policing*. Devon: Willan Publishing, 603–627.

Karmen, A. (2004). 'Zero tolerance in New York City: hard questions for a get-tough policy', in R. Hopkins Burke (ed.), *Hard Cop, Soft Cop: Dilemmas and debates in contemporary policing*. Devon: Willan Publishing, 23–39.

Kean, T., and Hamilton, L. (2004). *The 9/11 Commission Report*. New York: W. W. Norton.

Killmier, B. (1997). 'Tracking Violent Crime'. *Australian Institute of Criminology Second National Outlook Symposium on* 'Violent Crime, Property Crime and Public Policy'. Canberra: Australian Institute of Criminology.

Kruger, E., and Haggerty, K. (2006). 'Review Essay: Intelligence Exchange in Policing and Security'. *Policing and Society*, 16(1): 86–91.

Lippert, R., and O'Connor, D. (2006). 'Security Intelligence Networks and the Transformation of Contract Private Security'. *Policing and Society*, 16(1): 50–66.

Loader, I. (2000). 'Plural Policing and democratic governance'. *Social and Legal Studies*, 9(3): 323–345.

Maguire, M. (2000). 'Policing by risks and targets: some dimensions and implications of intelligence-led crime control'. *Policing and Society*, 9: 315–336.

Maguire, M., and John, T. (2006). 'Intelligence Led Policing, Managerialism and Community Engagement: Competing Priorities and the Role of the National Intelligence Model in the UK'. *Policing and Society*, 16(1): 67–85.

Mawby, R. (2003). 'Models of Policing', in T. Newburn (ed.), *Handbook of Policing*, Devon: Willan Publishing, 15–40.

Mazerolle, L., and Ransley, J. (2005). *Third Party Policing*. Cambridge: Cambridge University Press.

Michelmore, K. (2005). 'Bali 9 father's fury—"Police told me they would warn my son" '. *The Sydney Daily Telegraph*, 10 Nov: 17.

Noble, R. (2002). 'Interpol's New Approach: A Return to Basics' in R. Broadhurst (ed.), *Bridging the Gap: A Global Alliance Perspective on Transnational Organised Crime*. Hong Kong: Hong Kong Police Force, 37–43.

Quarmby, N. (2004). 'Futures work in strategic criminal intelligence', in J. Ratcliffe (ed.), *Strategic Thinking in Criminal Intelligence*. Sydney: Federation Press, 129–147.

Reiner, R. (2000). *The Politics of the Police*. Oxford: Oxford University Press.

Sarre, R., and Prenzler, T. (2005). *The law of Private Security in Australia*. Pyrmont, N.S.W: Lawbook Co.

Sheptycki, J. (2002). *In search of Transnational Policing: Towards a sociology of global policing*. Aldershot: Ashgate Publishing.

Sheptycki, J., and Ratcliffe, J. (2004). 'Setting the strategic agenda', in J. Ratcliffe (ed.), *Strategic Thinking in Criminal Intelligence*. Sydney: Federation Press, 194–209.

Simmonetti Rosen, M. (2004). 'Terror-oriented policing's big shadow. 2004, a retrospective'. *Law Enforcement News*, December 2004: 1–4.

Tilley, N. (2003). 'Community policing, problem-oriented policing and intelligence-led policing', in T. Newburn (ed.), *Handbook of Policing*. Devon: Willan Publishing, 311–339.

University of Sydney Seminar (2006). *Australians and the death penalty*, 7 June. Available at <http://www.usyd.edu.au/news/84.html?newsstoryid=1090>.

Walker, N. (2003). 'The pattern of transnational policing', in T. Newburn (ed.), *Handbook of Policing*. Devon: Willan Publishing, 111–135.

Walsh, W., and Vito, G. (2004). 'The Meaning of Compstat: Analysis and Response'. *Journal of Contemporary Criminal Justice*, 20(1): 51–69.

Weisburd, D., Mastrofski, S. D., McNally, A. M., Greenspan, R., and Willis, J. J. (2003). 'Reforming to preserve: Compstat and Strategic Problem Solving in American Policing'. *Criminology and Public Policy*, 2(2): 421–456.

Chapter 4

Arnesen, S. A. (2005). *Knowledge Ahead of Time: Utilization of Experience from International Police Deployment—The Norwegian Case*. Working Paper, Norwegian Police University College, Oslo, Norway.

Ashby, D. I., and Longley, P. A. (2005). 'Geocomputation, Geodemographics and Resource Allocation for Local Policing'. *Transactions in GIS*, 9(1): 53–72.

Avery, J. (1981). *Police: force or service?*. Sydney: Butterworths.

Bock, G. W., Zmud, R. W. and Kim, Y. G. (2005). 'Behavioral Intention Formation in Knowledge Sharing: Examining the Roles of Extrinsic Motivators, Social-Psychological Forces, and Organizational Climate'. *MIS Quarterly*, 29(1): 87–111.

Brodeur, J. P. and Dupont, B. (2006). 'Knowledge Workers or "Knowledge" Workers?'. *Policing & Society*, 16(1): 7–26.

Crank, J. P. (2003). 'Institutional theory of police: a review of the state of the art'. *Policing: An International Journal of Police Strategies & Management*, 26(2): 186–207.

Criminal Justice Commission (1995). *Ethical conduct and discipline in the Queensland Police service: the views of recruits, first year constables and experienced officers*. Brisbane: Research and Co-ordination Division, Criminal Justice Commission.

Davenport, T. H. and Prusak, L. (1998). *Working Knowledge*. Boston: Harvard Business School Press.

Dixon, N. M. (2000). *Common Knowledge*. Boston: Harvard Business School Press.

Earl, M. J. (2001). 'Knowledge Management Strategies: Toward a Taxonomy'. *Journal of Management Information Systems*, 18(1): 215–233.

Garud, R., and Kumaraswamy, A. (2005). 'Vicious and Virtuous Circles in the Management of Knowledge: The Case of Infosys Technologies'. *MIS Quarterly*, 29(1): 9–33.

Grover, V., and Davenport, T. H. (2001). 'General Perspectives on Knowledge Management: Fostering a Research Agenda'. *Journal of Management Information Systems*, 18(1): 5–21.

Hansen, M. T., Nohria, N., and Tierney, T. (1999). 'What's your strategy for managing knowledge?'. *Harvard Business Review*, March–April: 106–116.

Hughes, V., and Jackson, P. (2004). 'The Influence of Technical, Social and Structural Factors on the Effective use of Information in a Policing Environment'. *The Electronic Journal of Knowledge Management*, 2(1): 65–76.

McLeod, C. (2003). 'Toward a restorative organization: transforming police bureaucracies'. *Police Practice and Research*, 4(4): 361–377.

Nonaka, I., Toyama, R., and Konno, N. (2000). 'SECI, Ba and Leadership: a Unified Model of Dynamic Knowledge Creation'. *Long Range Planning*, 33(1): 5–34.

Porter, M. E. (1985). *Competitive Strategy*. New York: The Free Press.

Roberg, R., and S. Bonn (2004). 'Higher education and policing: where are we now?'. *Policing: An International Journal of Police Strategies & Management*, 27(4): 469–486.

Smith, N., and Flanagan, C. (2000). *The Effective Detective: Identifying the skills of an effective SIO*. Police Research Series Paper 122, Policing and Reducing Crime Unit, London.

Stabell, C. B., and Fjeldstad, Ø. D. (1998). 'Configuring value for competitive advantage: On chains, shops, and networks'. *Strategic Management Journal*, 19: 413–437.

Woods, J. (2002). *Project Management*. Madison, WI: CWL Publishing.

Chapter 5

Abe, K. (2003). 'Technologies of Surveillance'. *Theory, Culture and Society*, 23(2–3): 265–267.

Adderley, R., and Musgrove, P. (2001). 'Police crime recording and investigation systems'. *Policing*, 24(1): 100–115.

Alavi, M. and Leidner, D. E. (2001). 'Knowledge Management and Knowledge Management Systems: Conceptual Foundations and Research Issues'. *MIS Quarterly*, 25(1): 107–136.

Amarawadi, C. S. (2005). 'Digital repositories for e-government'. *Electronic Government*, 2(2): 2005–218.

Andresen, M. A. (2006). 'Crime measures and the spatial analysis of criminal activity'. *British Journal of Criminology*, 46: 258–285.

Ashby, D. I. and Longley, P. A. (2005). 'Geocomputation, Geodemographics and Resource Allocation for Local Policing'. *Transactions in GIS*, 9(1): 53–72.

Balchen, P. and Børstad, E. (2005). 'Implementing problem-oriented policing'. *International Observer*, edition 40.

Blair, D. C., and Maron, M. E. (1985). 'An Evaluation of Retrieval Effectiveness for a Full-text Document-retrieval System'. *Communications of the ACM*, 28(3): 289–299.

Boba, R. (2001). *Introductory Guide to Crime Analysis and Mapping*. Report to the Office of Community Oriented Policing Services (COPS): US Department of Justice.

Bowen, J. E. (1994). 'An Expert System for Police Investigators of Economic Crimes'. *Expert Systems with Applications*, 7(2): 235–248.

Bowers, K. J., Johnson, S. D., and Pease, K. (2004). 'Prospective Hot-Spotting: The Future of Crime Mapping?'. *British Journal of Criminology*, 44: 641–658.

Brahan, J. W., Lam, K. P., Chan, H., and Leung, W. (1998). 'AICAMS: Artificial Intelligence Crime Analysis and Management System'. *Knowledge-Based Systems*, 11: 355–361.

Carlson, C. (2000). 'Is the FBI tapped into you?'. *Wireless Week*, 16 (19): 3.

Center for Problem-Oriented Policing (2005). *Situational Crime Prevention*, <http://www.popcenter.org/about-situational.htm> (accessed 1 August 2005).

Chainey, S., and Smith, C. (2006). *Review of GIS-based information sharing systems*. Home Office Online Report 02/06, London: Home Office.

Chen, H., Schroeder, J., Hauck, R. V., Ridgeway, L., Atabakhsh, H., Gupta, H., Boarman, C., Rasmussen, K., and Clements, A.W. (2002). 'COPLINK Connect: information and knowledge management for law enforcement'. *Decision Support Systems*, 34: 271–285.

Chen, H., Zheng, D., Atabakhsh, H., Wyzga, W., and Schroeder, J. (2003). 'COPLINK—Managing Law Enforcement Data and Knowledge'. *Communications of the ACM*, 46(1): 28–34.

Clarke, R. V. (2001). 'Effective Crime Prevention: Keeping Pace with New Developments'. *Forum on Crime and Society*, 1(1): 17–33. United Nations Centre for International Crime Prevention.

Coleman, R., and Sim, J. (2000). 'You'll never walk alone: CCTV surveillance, order and neo-liberal rule in Liverpool city centre'. *British Journal of Sociology*, 51: 623–639.

Computer Weekly (2002). Knowledge Management: Surrey Police, 28 Feb.

Cope, N. (2003). 'Crime analysis: principles and practice', in T. Newburn (ed.), *Handbook of Policing*. Devon: Willan Publishing, 340–362.

CPOP (2005) *Center for problem-oriented policing*, <http://www.popcenter.org/default.htm> (accessed 9 December 2005).

'Database Management System' (2004). A Dictionary of Computing: Oxford Reference Online. Oxford University Press, <http://www.oxfordreference.com/views/ENTRY.html?subview=Main&entry=t11.e1188> (accessed, 20 October 2006).

Eppler, M., and Mengis, J. (2004). 'The Concept of Information Overload: A Review of Literature from Organization Science, Accounting, Marketing, MIS, and Related Disciplines'. *The Information Society*, 20: 325–344.

Fazlollahi and Gordon (1993). 'CATCH: Computer Assisted Tracking of Criminal Histories System'. *Interfaces*, 23(2): 51–62.

Garfinkel, S. (2000). *Database Nation: The Death of Privacy in the 21st Century.* Sebastopol, CA: O'Reilly & Associates.

Gips, M. (1999). 'Privacy privation'. *Security Management*, 34(1): 1.

Glomseth, R., and Gottschalk, P. (2005). 'Research propositions for determinants of police investigation performance'. *Electronic Government*, 2(3): 292–304.

Goldstein, H. (2003). 'On further developing problem-oriented policing: the most critical need the major impediments, and a proposal', in J. Knutsson (ed.), *Mainstreaming Problem-Oriented Policing.* Monsey, NY: Criminal Justice Press, 13–47.

Goold, B. (2004). *CCTV and Policing: Public Area Surveillance and Police Practices in Britain.* Oxford: Oxford University Press.

Gottschalk, P. (2006). 'Expert systems at stage IV of the knowledge management technology stage model: The case of police investigations'. *Expert Systems with Applications*, 31: 617–628.

—— (2007). *Knowledge Management Systems in Law Enforcement: Technologies and Techniques.* Hershey, PA: Idea Group Publishing.

Gottschalk, P., and Holgersson, S. (2006). 'Stages of knowledge management technology in the value shop: the case of police investigation performance'. *Expert Systems*, 23(4): 183–193.

Gottschalk, P., and Khandelwal, V. K. (2002). 'Global Comparison of Stages of Growth Based on Critical Success Factors'. *Journal of Global Information Management*, April–June: 40–49.

Gottschalk, P. and Solli-Sæther, H. (2006). 'Maturity model for IT outsourcing relationships'. *Industrial Management and Data Systems*, 106(2): 200–212.

Gottschalk, P. and Tolloczko, P. C. (2006). 'Maturity Model for Mapping Crime in Law Enforcement'. *Electronic Government: An International Journal*, forthcoming.

Haggerty, K. D., and Ericson, R. V. (2001). 'The military technostructures of policing', in P. B. Kraska (ed.), *Militarizing the American Criminal Justice System: The Changing Roles of the Armed Forces and the Police.* Boston: Northeastern University Press.

Haugen, S. (2005). 'E-government, cyber-crime and cyber-terrorism: a population at risk'. *Electronic Government*, 2(4): 403–412.

Hauck, R., and Chen, H. (1999). 'Coplink: A Case of Intelligent Analysis and Knowledge Management'. *20th International Conference of Information Systems*. Atlanta, USA: Association for Information Systems, 15–28.

Home Office (2006). *Review of GIS-based information sharing systems.* Home Office Online Report 02/06.

Hoogeveen and van der Meer (1994). 'Integration of Information Retrieval and Database Management in Support of Multimedia Police Work'. *Journal of Information Science*, 20(2): 79–87.

Hughes, V., and Jackson, P. (2004). 'The Influence of Technical, Social and Structural Factors on the Effective use of Information in a Policing Environment'. *The Electronic Journal of Knowledge Management*, 2(1): 65–76.

Iyer, L. S., Singh, R., Salam, A. F., and D'Aubeterre, F. (2006). 'Knowledge management for Government-to-Government (G2G) process coordination'. *Electronic Government*, 3(1): 18–35.

Julie, R. S. (2000). 'High tech surveillance tools and the fourth amendment: reasonable expectations of privacy in the technological age'. *American Criminal Law Review*, 37, Winter: 127–44.

Kazanjian, R. K. (1988). 'Relation of dominant problems to stages of growth in technology-based new ventures. *Academy of Management Journal*, 31(2): 257–279.

Keppel, R., and Weis, J. (1993). 'Improving the Investigation of Violent Crime: The Homicide Investigation and Tracking System'. *National Institute of Justice—Research in Brief*. Washington: US Department of Justice.

Keppens, J. and Schafer, B. (2006). 'Knowledge based crime scenario modelling'. *Expert Systems with Applications*, 30: 203–222.

'Knowledge-Based System' (2004). *A Dictionary of Computing: Oxford Reference Online*. Oxford University Press, <http://www.oxfordreference.com/views/ENTRY.html?subview=Main&entry=t11.e2814> (accessed 20 October 2006).

'Knowledge Representation' (2004). *A Dictionary of Computing: Oxford Reference Online*. Oxford University Press, <http://www.oxfordreference.com/views/ENTRY.html?subview=Main&entry=t11.e2819> (accessed 20 October 2006).

Lahneman, W. J. (2004). 'Knowledge-Sharing in the Intelligence Community After 9/11'. *International Journal of Intelligence and Counterintelligence*, 17: 614–633.

Lewis (1993). 'Police Information Technology'. *GEC Review*, 9(1): 51–58.

Lingerfelt (1997). 'Technology as a Force Multiplier', in *Proceedings of the Conference on Technology for Community Policing*, National Law Enforcement and Corrections.

'Logic' (2004). *A Dictionary of Computing: Oxford Reference Online*. Oxford University Press, <http://www.oxfordreference.com/views/ENTRY.html?subview=Main&entry=t11.e2814> (accessed 20 October 2006).

Lyon, D. (2001). *Surveillance Society: Monitoring Everyday Life*. Buckingham: Open University Press.

—— (2003). *Surveillance after September 11*. Cambridge: Polity Press.

Lytras, M. D. (2006). 'The Semantic Electronic Government: knowledge management for citizen relationship and new assessment scenarios'. *Electronic Government*, 3(1): 5–17.

Malhotra, Y. (2004). 'Why Knowledge Management Systems Fail? Enablers and Constraints of Knowledge Management in Human Enterprises', in M. E. D. Koenig and T. Kanti Srikantaiah (eds.), *Knowledge Management Lessons Learned: What Works and What Doesn't*. Information Today Inc (American Society for Information Science and Technology Monograph Series): 87–112.

Miller (1996). 'Searchable Databases Help Missouri Solve Crime'. *Government Technology*, 9(8): 18–19.

Newburn, T., and Hayman, S. (2002). *Policing, Surveillance and Social Change: CCTV and Police Monitoring of Suspects*. Cullompton, Devon: Willan Publishing.

NIJ (2005). *Mapping Crime: Understanding Hot Spots*, National Institute of Justice, Office of Justice Programs, 810 Seventh Street NW, Washington, DC 20531, <http://www.ojp.usdoj.gov/nij>.

NIJ (2006). *Mapping and Analysis for Public Safety (MAPS)*, National Institute of Justice, <http://www.ojp.usdoj.gov/nij/maps/>.

Nolan, R. L. (1979). 'Managing the crisis in data processing'. *Harvard Business Review*. March/April: 115–126.

Nunn, S. (2003). 'Seeking tools for the war on terror: A critical assessment of emerging technologies in law enforcement'. *Policing*, 26(3): 454–473.

Paulter, N. G. (2001). 'Guide to the Technologies of Concealed Weapon and Contraband Imaging and Detection'. *NIJ Guide 60200*, Washington, DC, February: National Institute of Justice, Office of Science and Technology.

Personal Communication (2006) Interview with Police Officer on 12 October, *Technology Crime Research Branch*, Singapore Police Force.

Pliant, L. (1996). 'High-technology Solutions'. *The Police Chief*, 5(38): 38–51.

Police Foundation (2002). *Users' Guide of Mapping Software for Police Agencies (fourth edition)* Crime Mapping Laboratory. Report to the Office of Community Oriented Policing Services (COPS): US Department of Justice.

'Production Rule System' (2004). *A Dictionary of Computing: Oxford Reference Online.* Oxford University Press, <http://www.oxfordreference.com/views/ENTRY.html?subview=Main&entry=t11.e4127> (accessed 20 October 2006).

Poston, R. S., and Speier, C. (2005). 'Effective Use of Knowledge Management Systems: A Process Model of Content Ratings and Credibility Indicators'. *MIS Quarterly*, 29(2): 221–244.

Raco, M. (2003). 'Remaking Place and Securitising Space: Urban Regeneration and the Stragtegies, Tactics and Practices of Policing in the UK'. *Urban Studies*, 40(9): 1869–1887.

Ratcliffe, J. H. (2004). 'Crime Mapping and the Training Needs of Law Enforcement'. *European Journal of Criminal Policy and Research*, 10: 65–83.

Rich, T., and Shively, M. (2004). *A Methodology for Evaluating Geographic Profiling Software*. Cambridge, MA: Abt Associates Inc.

Robertson, J. (2004). *Definition of information management terms*. Australia: Step Two Designs.

Rosenberg, A. L. (1998). 'Comment, passive millimeter wave imaging: a new weapon in the fight against crime or a fourth amendment violation?'. *Albany Law Journal of Science and Technology*, 9: 4.

Rowe, J. (2005). 'Process Metaphor and Knowledge Management'. *Kybernetes*, 34(5): 770–784.

Schellenberg, K. (1997). 'Police Information Systems, Information Practices and Individual Privacy'. *Canadian Public Policy—Analyse de Politiques*, 23(1): 23–39.

Schiff, D. (1997). 'Forget X-ray vision specs, try RADAR flashlights'. *Electronic Design*, 45(24): 80.

Sheptycki, J. (2002). *In search of Transnational Policing: Towards a sociology of global policing*. Aldershot: Ashgate Publishing.

Skogan, W. G., and Hartnett, S. M. (2005). 'The Diffusion of Information Technology in Policing'. *Police Practice and Research*, 6(5): 401–417.

Stedje, S. (2004). *The Man in the Street, or the Man in the Suite: An Evaluation of the Effectiveness in the Detection of Money Laundering in Norway*. Master of Arts thesis, Social Sciences and law, UK: University of Manchester.

Stojanovic, L., Stojanovic, N., and Apostolou, D. (2006). 'Change management in e-government: OntoGov case study'. *Electronic Government*, 3(1): 74–92.

Tanriverdi, H. (2005). 'Information Technology Relatedness, Knowledge Management Capability, and Performance of Multibusiness Firms'. *MIS Quarterly*, 29(2): 311–334.

Tilley, N. (2002). *Analysis for Crime Prevention*. Monsey, NY: Criminal Justice Press.

Weisburd, D. and Lum, C. (2005). 'The Diffusion of Computerized Crime Mapping in Policing: Linking Research and Practice'. *Police Practice and Research*, 6(5): 419–434.

Wesley Clark, M. (2006). 'Cell Phone Technology and Physical Surveillance'. *FBI Law Enforcement Bulletin*, 75(5): 25–32.

Witzig, E. (2003). 'The New ViCAP: More User-Friendly and Used by More Agencies'. *FBI Bulletin* (July).

Zukin, S. (1995). *The Cultures of Cities*. Oxford: Blackwell.

Chapter 6

Abt Associates (2005). *Police Department Information Systems Technology Enhancement Project (ISTEP)*. Washington DC: Department of Justice, Office of Community Oriented Policing Services.

Adderley, R., and Musgrove, P. (2001). 'Police crime recording and investigation systems'. *Policing*, 24 (1): 100–115.

Althausen, J., and Mieczkowski, T. (2001). 'The Merging of Criminology and Geography into a Course on Spatial Crime Analysis'. *Journal of Criminal Justice Education*, 12(2): 367–383.

Andresen, M. A. (2006). 'Crime measures and the spatial analysis of criminal activity'. *British Journal of Criminology*, 46: 258–285.

Ashby, D. I., and Longley, P. A. (2005). 'Geocomputation, Geodemographics and Resource Allocation for Local Policing'. *Transactions in GIS*, 9(1): 53–72.

Balchen, P. and Børstad, E. (2005). 'Implementing problem-oriented policing'. *International Observer*, edition 40, <http://www.crime-prevention-intl.org/io_view.php?io_id=128&io_page_id=620> (accessed 10 December 2005).

Borglund, E. (2005). 'Operational use of electronic records in police work'. *Information Research*, 10(4): 1–9.

Bowker, G. (2000). 'Biodiversity datadiversity'. *Social Studies of Science*, 30: 643–683.

Chan, J. B. L. (2003). 'Police and new technologies', in T. Newburn (ed.), *Handbook of Policing*. Devon: Willan Publishing, 655–679.

Chan, J., Brereton, D., Legosz, M., and Doran, S. (2001). *e-Policing: the Impact of Information Technology on Police Practices*. Brisbane: Criminal Justice Commission.

Chu, J. (2001). *Law Enforcement Information Technology: a Managerial, Operational, and Practitioner Guide*. Boca Raton, FLA: CRC Press.

Clarke, R. V. (2001). 'Effective Crime Prevention: Keeping Pace with New Developments'. *Forum on Crime and Society*, 1(1): 17–33. United Nations Centre for International Crime Prevention.

CPOP (2005) *Center for Problem-Oriented Policing*, <http://www.popcenter.org/default.htm> (accessed 9 December 2005).

Coffery, J., Hoffman, R., and Canas, A. (2006). 'Concept Map-based knowledge Modelling: Perspectives from Information and Knowledge Visualization'. *Information Visualization*, 5(3): 192–201.

Cope, N. (2003). 'Crime analysis: principles and practice', in T. Newburn, (ed.), *Handbook of Policing*. Devon: Willan Publishing, 340–362.

DataDetective (2006). *DataDetective Product Outline*, <http://www.sentient.nl/datadetectivetoc.html> (accessed 17 November 2006).

Dean, G. (1995). 'Police Reform: Rethinking Operational Policing'. *American Journal of Criminal Justice*, 23(4): 337–347.

Ekblom, P. (2003). '5Is Framework'. UK: Home Office. Available at <http://www.crimereduction.gov.uk/learningzone/5isguide.htm> (accessed 1 August 2005).

Eppler, M. (2006). 'A comparison between concept maps, mind maps, conceptual diagrams, and visual metaphors as complementary tools for knowledge construction and sharing'. *Information Visualization*, 5(3): 202–210.

Eppler, M., and Burkhard, R. (2005). 'Knowledge Visualization', in D. Schwartz (ed.), *Encyclopedia of Knowledge Management*. New York: Idea Press.

EUROPOL (2006). *Knowledge Management Centre*, <http://www.europol.eu> (accessed 17 November 2006).

Firestone, J. (2005). 'Mining for Information Gold'. *Information Management Journal*, 39(5): 47–51.

Goldstein, H. (2003). 'On further developing problem-oriented policing: the most critical need the major impediments, and a proposal', in J. Knutsson (ed.), *Mainstreaming Problem-Oriented Policing*. Monsey, NY: Criminal Justice Press, 13–47.

Heal, K. (1992). 'Changing perspectives on crime prevention', in D. Evans' N. Fyfe, and D. Herbert (eds.), *Crime, Policing and Place*. London: Routledge.

House, J. (1997). 'Towards a Practical Application of Offender Profiling: the RNC's Criminal Suspect Prioritization System', in J. Jackson and D. Berkerian (eds.), *Offender Profiling: Theory, Research and Practice*. Chichester: John Wiley and Sons, 177–190.

InFlow (2006). Social Network Analysis Software, <http://orgnet.com/> (accessed 20 October 2006).

Krebs, V. (2006). 'Connecting the Dots—Tracking Two Identified Terrorists', <http://www.orgnet.com/prevent.html> (accessed 20 October 2006).

Manning, P. K. (2003). *Policing Contingencies*. Chicago, IL: The University of Chicago Press.

Marks, I. (2006). 'Neural Nets and Scientific Discovery: A Match Made in AI Heaven'. *PCAI* issue 18.3, <http://www.pcai.com/Paid/Issues/PCAI-Online-Issues/18.3_OL/> (accessed 20 October 2006).

Merry, S., and Harsent, L. (2000). 'Intruders, Pilferers, Raiders and Invaders: The Interpersonal Dimension of Burglary', in D. Canter, and L. Alison (eds.), *Profiling Property Crimes*, Aldershot: Ashgate/Dartmouth, 31–56.

NIJ (2006). *Mapping and Analysis for Public Safety (MAPS)*. National Institute of Justice, <http://www.ojp.usdoj.gov/nij/maps/>.

Nogala, D. (1995). 'The future role of technology in policing', in J. P. Brodeur, (ed.), *Comparisons in Policing: An International Perspective*. Aldershot: Avebury.

Novak, J., and Canas, A. (2006). 'The Origins of the Concepts Mapping Tool and the Continuing Evolution of the Tool'. *Information Visualization*, 5(3): 175–184.

Orlikowski, W., and Gash, D. (1994). 'Technological Frames—making sense of information technology in organisations'. *ACM Transactions on Information Systems*, 12(2): 174–207.

Peterson, M., and Ridgeway, R. (1990). 'Analytical Intelligence Training'. *FBI Law Enforcement Bulletin*, 13: 13–17.

Pliant, L. (1996). 'High-technology Solutions'. *The Police Chief*, 5(38): 38–51.

Puonti, A. (2004). 'Tools for Collaboration: Using and Designing Tools in Inter-organizational Economic-Crime Investigation'. *Mind, Culture, and Activity*, 11(2): 133–152.

Ramsland, K. (2001). 'Geographic Profiling: The Predator System'. *The Crime Library*, <http://www.crimelibrary.com/criminal_mind/profiling/geographic/5.html> (accessed 4 June 2001).

Rossmo, K. (1997). 'Geography Profiling', in J. Jackson and D. Berkerian (eds.), *Offender Profiling: Theory, Research and Practice*. Chichester: John Wiley and Sons, 159–176.

Strano, M. (2005). 'A Neural Network Applied to Criminal Psychological Profiling: An Italian Initiative'. *Telematic Journal of Clinical Criminology*, <http://www.criminologia.org>.

Stroshine, M. (2005). 'Information Technology Innovations in Policing', in R. Durham and G. Alpert (eds.), *Critical Issues in Policing: Contemporary Readings* (5th edn.) Illinois: Waveland Press, 172–183.

Tergan, S-O., Keller, T., and Burkhard, R. (2006). 'Integrating knowledge and information: digital concept maps as a bridging technology'. *Information Visualization*, 5: 167–174.

Tilly, N. (ed) (2002). *Analysis for Crime Prevention*. (Crime Prevention Studies, Volume 13). New York: Criminal Justice Press.

Weisburd, D. and Lum, C. (2005). 'The Diffusion of Computerized Crime Mapping in Policing: Linking Research and Practice'. *Police Practice and Research*, 6(5): 419–434.

Welsh, B. (2002). 'Technological innovations for policing: Crime prevention as the bottom line'. *Criminology and Public Policy*, 2(1): 129–132.

Wormeli, P. (2005). *Proactive Knowledge Management in Policing*. Paul Wormeli's Tech-Notes—A commentary on disruptive technologies for public safety and criminal justice information systems, <http://radio.weblogs.com/0126029/stories/2003/06/09/proactiveKnowledgeMangementInPolicing> (accessed 1 August 2005).

Chapter 7

Blum, B. I. (1988). 'A Simple Expert System'. *ACM SIGBIO Newsletter*, 10(1): 22–28

Charniak, E. and Mcdermott, D. (1985). *Introduction to Artificial Intelligence*. Addison-Wesley.

Dale, R. (1987). 'An Introduction To Artificial Intelligence', in M. D. Allan (ed.), *Arms and Artificial Intelligence*. New York: Oxford University Press.

Chen, Z. (1988). 'Building Expert Systems through the Integration of Mental Models', in *Proceedings of the 1st international conference on Industrial and engineering applications of artificial intelligence and expert systems*, Vol 2 IEA/AIE: 754–761.

Cooke, N. M., and. McDonald, J. E (1986). 'A formal methodology for acquiring and representing expert knowledge', in *Proceedings of the IEEE*: 1422–1428.

Cox, E. (1995). *Fuzzy Logic for Business and Industry*. Rockland, MA: Charles River Media.

Dean, G. (2005). 'The "Cross+Check" System: Integrating Profiling Approaches for Police and Security Investigations'. *Journal of Police and Criminal Psychology*, 20(2): 20–43.

——(1995). 'Police Reform: Rethinking Operational Policing'. *American Journal of Criminal Justice*, 23(4): 337–347.

Dean, G. and Schroder, D. (2003). '"Cross+Check" als alternatives model fur die Analyse von Kriminalfaallen'. *Polizel-Heute* (Germany National Police Journal) Marz/April, 32. Jahrgang, 2: 47–49.

Dixon, D. (1999). 'Police investigative procedures', in C. Walker and K. Starmer (eds.), *Miscarriage of Justice: a review of Justice in error*. London: Blackstone.

Durkin, J. (1996). 'Expert Systems—A View of the Field'. *IEEE Expert/Intelligent Systems and Their Applications*, 11(2): 56–63.

Greer, S. (1994). 'Miscarriages of criminal justice reconsidered'. *Modern Law Review*, 57(1): 58–71.

Hall, L., and Kandel, A. (1992). 'The Evolution from Expert Systems to Fuzzy Expert Systems', in A. Kandel (ed.), *Fuzzy Expert Systems*. Boca Raton, FLA: CRC Press.

Hoffman, R. R. (1987). 'The problem of extracting the knowledge of experts from the perspective of experimental psychology'. *AI Magazine*, 8(2): 53–67.

Keppens, J., and Schafer, B. (2006). 'Knowledge based crime scenario modelling'. *Expert Systems with Applications* 30: 203–222.

Klir, G. J., and Folger, T. A. (1988). *Fuzzy Sets, Uncertainty, and Information*. Englewood Cliffs, NJ: Prentice-Hall.

Kosko, B. (1993). *Fuzzy Thinking: The New Science of Fuzzy Logic*. New York: Hyperion.

LeBeuf, M-E. (2001). *Organised Crime and Cybercrime Criminal Investigations and Intelligence on the Cutting Edge*, Technical Report—Information Technology Series. Ottawa: Police Sciences School, Canadian Police College.

Myers, W. (1986). 'Introduction to Expert Systems'. *IEEE Expert*: 100–108.

Rauch-Hindin, W. B. (1986). 'Artificial intelligence in business, science, and industry'. *Fundamentals*, l. Englewood Cliffs, NJ: Prentice-Hall.

Saheb-Tehrani, M. (2005). 'Expert Systems Development: Some Issues of Design Process'. *ACM SIGSOFT Software Engineering Notes*, 30(2): 1–5.

——(1993). 'The Technology of Expert Systems: Some Social Impacts'. *Computers & Society*, 23(1–2): 15–20.

Schank, R. (1982). *Dynamic Memory: A Theory of Reminding and Learning in Computers and People*. Cambridge: Cambridge University Press.

Schneider, M., Kandel, A., Langholz, G., and Chew, G. (1996). *Fuzzy Expert System Tools*. New York: Wiley.

Sedbrook, T. A. (1998). 'A Collaborative Fuzzy Expert System For The Web'. *The DATA BASE for Advances in Information Systems*, 29(3): 19–30.

'System' (2004). *A Dictionary of Computing: Oxford Reference Online*. Oxford University Press, <http://www.oxfordreference.com/views/ENTRY.html?subview=Main&entry=t11.e5243> (accessed 20 October 2006).

Tergan, S-O., Keller, T., and Burkhard, R. (2006). 'Integrating Knowledge and Information: Digital Concept Maps as a Bridging Technology'. *Information Visualization*, 5: 167–174.

Turban, E., and Aronson, J. (1998). *Decision Support Systems and Intelligent Systems*. Englewood Cliffs, NJ: Prentice Hall.

Zadeh, L. A. (1990). 'Fuzzy Logic', in P. Raeth, (ed.), *Expert Systems: A Software Methodology for Modern Applications*. Los Alamitos, CA: IEEE Computer Society Press.

——(1965). 'Fuzzy Sets'. *Information and Control*, 8: 338–353.

Chapter 8

Archbold, C. A. (2005). 'Managing the bottom line: risk management in policing'. *Policing: An International Journal of Police Strategies & Management*, 28(1): 30–48.

Blum, B. I. (1988). 'A Simple Expert System'. *ACM SIGBIO Newsletter*, 10(1): 22–28

Dean, G. (2000). *The Experience of Investigation for Detectives*, unpublished PhD thesis. Brisbane, Australia: Queensland University of Technology.

Dean, G., Fahsing, I. A., and Gottschalk, P. (2007). 'Qualitative and Quantitative Study of Police Investigation Thinking Styles'. *International Journal of Knowledge and Learning*, 3(1): 76–87.

Dean, G., Fahsing, I. A., Gottschalk, P., and Solli-Sæther, H. (2007). 'Investigative Thinking and Creativity: An Empirical Study of Police Detectives in Norway'. *International Journal of Innovation and Learning*. (accepted for publication, forthcoming).

Dean, G., Fahsing, I. A., and Gottschalk, P. (2006). 'Profiling Police Investigative Thinking: A Study of Police Officers in Norway'. *International Journal of the Sociology of Law*, 34(4): 221–228.

Home Office (2005). *Senior Investigating Officer Development Programme*. Police Standards Unit, Home Office of the UK Government, <http://www.policereform.gov.uk> (accessed 11 August 2006).

Kiely, J. A., and Peek, G. S. (2002). 'The Culture of the British Police: Views of Police Officers'. *The Service Industries Journal*, 22(1): 167–183.

Personal communication (2005) by Senior Investigating Officer in Singapore to Dean.

Schwartz, J., Stapp, H., and Beauregard, M. (2005). 'Quantum Physics in Neuroscience and Psychology: A Neurophysical Model of the Mind–Brain Interaction'. Philosophical Transactions of the Royal Society B: Biological Sciences, 360 (1458).

Sternberg, R. (1997). *Thinking Styles*. Cambridge: Cambridge University Press.

Tafti, M. H. A. (1990). 'Neural Networks: A New Dimension in Expert Systems Applications'. *Proceedings of the ACM SIGBDP conference on Trends and directions in expert systems*: 423–433.

Wang, Y.-M. and Elhag, T. (2007). 'A comparison of neural network, evidential reasoning and multiple regression analysis in modelling bridge risks'. *Expert Systems with Applications* 32: 336–348.

Weatherall, D. (1990). 'Neural Networks'. *Management Services* (UK), 34(2): 36–39.

Wilson, A. (1988). 'Cranium Computing: Demystifying Neural Nets'. *ESD: The Electronic Design Magazine*, 16(7): 38–42.

Chapter 9

Abuza, Z. (2005). 'Terrorism, Sectarian Violence and Insurgency in Southeast Asia', <http://www.iseas.edu.sg/rof06/rof06za.pdf> (accessed 22 November 2006).

Ainsworth, P. B. (2001). *Offender Profiling and Crime Analysis*. Devon, UK: Willan Publishing.

Barker, J. (2003). *The No-Nonsense Guide to Terrorism*. Oxford: New Internationalist Publications Ltd.

Batley, B. (2003). *Complexities of Dealing with Radical Islam in Southeast Asia: a case Study of Jemaah Islamiyah*. Canberra: Strategic and Defence Studies Centre, Australian National University.

BBC News (2005). Thailand's restive south at <http://news.bbc.co.uk/2/hi/asia-pacific/3955543.stm>.

Canter, D., and Alison, L. (eds.) (1999). *Profiling in Policy and Practice*. Aldershot: Ashgate/Dartmouth.

Center for Nonproliferation Studies (2002). *Literature Review of Existing Terrorist Behavior Modeling*. Final Report to the Defense Threat Reduction Agency. Monterey Institute of International Studies, CA.

Chance, M. (2005). 'Britain's home-grown terrorists', <http://www.cnn.com/2005/WORLD/europe/07/14/homegrown.terror> (accessed 25 November 2006).

Copson, G. (1995). 'Coals to Newcastle? Part 1: A study of offender profiling'. (Paper 7). London: Police Research Group Special Interest Series, Home Office.

Council of Foreign Relations (2004) at <http://www.terrorismanswers.org/terrorism/introduction.html> (accessed 16 December 2004).

Courier-Mail (2002). 'Enemy Within', 26 October, 31.

Crenshaw, M. (2003). 'The Causes of Terrorism, Past and Present', in C. Kegley (ed.), *The New Global Terrorism*. Englewood Cliffs, NJ: Prentice Hall, 92–105.

Dean, G. (2007). 'Offender Profiling in a Terrorism Context', in R. Kocsis (ed.), *Criminal Profiling: International Theory, Practice & Research*. Totowa, NJ: Humana Press Inc (due for publication early in 2007).

—— (2004). 'Suicide Bombers: Weapons of Mass Terror'. *The Drawing Board: An Australian Review of Public Affairs*, 4(3), <http://www.econ.usyd.edu.au/drawingboard/>.

Douglas, J., Ressier, R. K., Burgess, A. W., and Hartman, C. R. (1986). 'Criminal profiling from crime scene analysis'. *Behavioral Sciences and the Law*, 4: 401–421.

Egger, S. (1999). 'Psychological profiling: Past, present, and future'. *Journal of Contemporary Criminal Justice*, 15(3): 242–261

Encyclopædia Britannica Online (2007). 'Combination lock: system of movements', <http://search.eb.com/eb/art-6407> (accessed 12 February 2007).

Farrington, D., and Lambert, S. (1997). 'Predicting Offender Profiles from Victim and Witness Descriptions', in J. Jackson and D. Bekerian (eds.), *Offender Profiling: Theory, Research and Practice*. Chichester, England: John Wiley and Sons, 133–158.

Ganor, B. (1998). 'Defining Terrorism: Is One Man's Terrorist Another Man's Freedom Fighter?'. The International Policy Institute for Counter-Terrorism, <http://www.ict.org.il/>.

Geberth, V. J. (1981). 'Psychological profiling'. *Law and Order*: 46–52.

—— (1996). *Practical homicide investigation* (3rd edn.). Boca Rotan, FLA: CRC Press.

Griffiths, M., and O'Callagan, T. (2002). *International Relations: The Key Concepts*. London: Routledge.

Groth, N. (1979). *Men who rape: the psychology of the offender*. New York: Plenum Press.

Gunaratna, R. (2003). 'Al Qaeda's Origins, Threat and its Likely Future', in R. Gunaratna (ed.), *Terrorism in the Asia-Pacific: Threat and Response*. Singapore: Times Media Private Limited, 135–160.

Harrower, J. (1998). *Applying Psychology to Crime*. Coventry: Hodder and Stoughton.

Hatyai bombings (2006). <http://www.answers.com/topic/2006-hat-yai-bombing> (accessed 25 November 2006).

Hazelwood, R. R., Ressier, R. K., Depue, R. L., and Douglas, J. E. (1987). 'Criminal personality profiling: An overview', in R. R. Hazelwood and A. W. Burgess (eds.), *Practical aspects of rape investigation: A multidisciplinary approach*. New York: Elsevier, 137–149.

Holmes, R., and Holmes, S. (eds.) (1998). *Contemporary perspectives on serial murder*. Thousand Oaks, CA: Sage.

Horgan, J. (2003). 'The Search for the Terrorist Personality', in A. Silke (ed.), *Terrorists, Victims and Society: Psychological Perspectives on Terrorism and its Consequences*. Chichester: John Wiley and Sons Ltd, 3–28.

——(2003). 'Leaving Terrorism Behind: An Individual Perspective', in A. Silke (ed.), *Terrorists, Victims and Society: Psychological Perspectives on Terrorism and its Consequences*. Chichester: John Wiley & Sons Ltd, 109–130.

InFlow (2006). 'Social Network Analysis Software', <http://orgnet.com/> (accessed 20 October 2006).

Jackson, J., and Bekerian, D. (1997). 'Does Offender Profiling Have a Role to Play?', in J. Jackson and D. Bekerian (eds.), *Offender Profiling: Theory, Research and Practice*. Chichester: John Wiley and Sons, 3–7.

Juergensmeyer, M. (2000). *Terror in the Mind of God: The Global Rise of Religious Violence*. Berkeley, CA: University of California Press.

Kirsch. S. (2001). *Identifying terrorists before they strike by using computerized knowledge assessment (CKA)*, <http://www.skirsch.com/politics/plane/ultimate.htm> (accessed 10 February 2007).

Koepf, C. (2004). 'Terrorism: An Investigator's Handbook'. *FBI Law Enforcement Bulletin*, 73(7): 17.

Krebs, V. (2006). 'Connecting the Dots—Tracking Two Identified Terrorists', <http://www.orgnet.com/prevent.html> (accessed 20 October 2006).

Matassa, M., and Newburn, T. (2003). 'Policing and terrorism', in T. Newburn (ed.), *Handbook of Policing*. Devon: Willan Publishing, 467–500.

Macquarie Dictionary (1982). Australia: The Macquarie Library Pty Ltd.

McCann, J. T. (1992). 'Criminal personality profiling in the investigation of violent crime: Recent advances and future directions'. *Behavioral Sciences and the Law*, 10: 475–481.

Ministry of Home Affairs (2003). 'The Jemaah Islamiyah Arrests and the Threat of Terrorism'. *White Paper*. Singapore: Singapore Government.

Rapoport, D. (2003). 'The Four Waves of Rebel Terror and September 11', in C. Kegley (ed.), *The New Global Terrorism*. Englewood Cliffs, NJ: Prentice-Hall, 36–51.

Reuter, C. (2004). *My Life is a Weapon: A Modern History of Suicide Bombing*. Princeton, NJ: Princeton University Press.

Rossmo, K. (1997). 'Geographic Profiling', in J. Jackson and D. Bekerian (eds.), *Offender Profiling: Theory, Research and Practice*. Chichester: John Wiley and Sons, 159–176.

Rubenstein, R. (2003). 'The Psycho-Political Sources of Terrorism' in C. Kegley (ed.), *The New Global Terrorism*. Englewood Cliffs, NJ: Prentice-Hall, 139–149.

Schbley, A. (2006). 'Towards a Common Profile of Religious Terrorism: Some Psychological Determinants of Christian and Islamic Terrorists'. *Police Practice and Research: An International Journal*, 7(4): 275–292.

Schmidt, A. P., and Jongman, A. I. (1988). *Political Terrorism*. Amsterdam: Transaction Books.

Seger, K. (2003). 'Deterring Terrorists', in A. Silke (ed.), *Terrorists, Victims and Society: Psychological Perspectives on Terrorism and its Consequences*. Chichester: John Wiley and Sons Ltd, 257–269.

Silke, A. (2003). 'Becoming a Terrorist', in A. Silke (ed.), *Terrorists, Victims and Society: Psychological Perspectives on Terrorism and its Consequences*. Chichester: John Wiley and Sons Ltd, 29–54.

—— (2003). 'The Psychology of Suicidal Terrorism', in ibid, 93–108.

Stahelski, A. (2004). 'Terrorists Are Made, Not Born: Creating Terrorists Using Social Psychological Conditioning'. *Journal of Homeland Security*, <http://www.homelandsecurity.org/journal/articles/stahelski.html>.

Strozier, C., and Laughlin, F. (2003). 'Islamic Fundamentalist Ideology, Martyrdom Operations and their Apocalyptic Imagery: "in the Name of Allah, the Compassionate, the Merciful"' at <http://www.jjay.cuny.edu/terrorism/ApocSuicide.pdf.

Townshend, C. (2002). *Terrorism: a Very Short Introduction*. Oxford: Oxford University Press.

Turvey, B. (1999). *Criminal profiling : an introduction to behavioral evidence analysis*. San Diego, CA: Academic Press.

Williams, P. (2002). *Al Qaeda: Brotherhood of Terror*. USA: Alpha Books, Pearson Education Inc.

Wilson, P., Lincoln, R., and Kocsis, R. (1997). 'Validity, utility and ethics of profiling for serial violent and sexual predators'. *Psychiatry, Psychology and Law*, 4: 1–11.

Wise. T. (2005). 'The Tyranny of Common Sense: The Faulty Logic of "Terrorist" Profiling', <http://www.counterpunch.org/wise08022005.html> (accessed 1 November 2006).

Chapter 10

Audit Commission (1996). *Misspent Youth*. London.

Audit Commission (2000). *Calling Time on Crime*. London.

Audit Commission (2004). *Youth Justice*. London.

Audit Commission (2005). *Governance of Partnerships*. London.

Alavi, M., and Leidner, D. (2002). 'Knowledge management systems: issues, challenges and benefits', in S. Barnes (ed.), *Knowledge Management Systems*. London: Thomson Learning, 15–35.

Applegate, L., Cash, J., and Mills, D. Q. (1988). 'Information Technology and Tomorrow's Manager', in W. G. McGowan (ed.), *Revolution in Real Time: Managing Information Technology in the 1990s*. Boston: Harvard Business School Press, 33–48.

Bichard, M. (2004). *The Bichard Inquiry Report*, HC 653. London: The Stationery Office.

Brown, M., and Brudney, J. (2003). 'Learning organizations in the public sector? A study of police agencies employing information and technology to advance knowledge'. *Public Administration Review*, 63(1): 30–43.

Bundred, S. (2006). 'Solutions to Silos: Joining Up Knowledge'. *Public Money & Management*, 26(2): 125–130.

Butler, B., and Gray, P. (2006). 'Reliability, Mindfulness, and Information Systems'. *MIS Quarterly*, 30(2): 211–224.

Chan, J., Brereton, D., Legosz, M., and Doran, S. (2001). *e-Policing: the Impact of Information Technology on Police Practices*. Brisbane: Criminal Justice Commission.

Churchman, C. (1971) *The Design of Inquiring Systems*. New York: Basic Books.

Collier, P. (2006). 'Policing and the Intelligent Application of Knowledge'. *Public Money & Management*, 26(2): 109–116.

Davenport, T. H., and Prusak, L. (1998). *Working Knowledge*. Boston: Harvard Business School Press.

Home Office Science Policy Unit (2003). *Police Science and Technology Strategy*. London: Science Policy Unit.

Hughes, V., and Love, P. (2004). 'Towards cyber-centric management of policing: back to the future with information and communication technology'. *Industrial Management and Data Systems*, 104(7): 604–612.

Huysman, M., and Wulf, V. (2006). 'IT to support knowledge sharing in communities, towards a social capital analysis'. *Journal of Information Technology*, 21: 40–51.

Kogut, B., and Zander, U. (1992). 'Knowledge of the Firm, Combinative Capabilities, and the Replication of Technology'. *Organization Science*, 3(3): 383–397.

Laming, Lord (2003). 'The Victoria Climbié Inquiry: Report of An Inquiry', London: Department of Health and Home Office.

Langer, E. J. (1997). *The Power of Mindful Learning*. Cambridge, MA: Perseus Publishing.

——(1989). *Mindfulness*. Cambridge, MA: Perseus Publishing.

LeBeuf, M-E. (2001). *Organised Crime and Cybercrime Criminal Investigations and Intelligence on the Cutting Edge*. Technical Report—Information Technology Series, Ottawa: Police Sciences School, Canadian Police College

Leonard, N., and Insch, G. (2005). 'Tacit Knowledge in Academia: A Proposed Model and Measurement Scale'. *Journal of Psychology*, 139(6): 495–513.

Malhotra, Y. (2004). 'Why Knowledge Management Systems Fail? Enablers and Constraints of Knowledge Management in Human Enterprises' in M.E.D. Koenig and T. Kanti Srikantaiah (eds.), *Knowledge Management Lessons Learned: What Works and What Doesn't*. Information Today Inc (American Society for Information Science and Technology Monograph Series), 87–112.

Manning, P. K. (2003). *Policing Contingencies*. Chicago, IL: The University of Chicago Press.

Müller-Merbach, H. (2004). 'Socrates' Warning: Knowledge is More than Information'. *Knowledge Management Research & Practice*, 2(1): 61–62.

Nonaka, I., Toyama, R., and Konno, N. (2000). 'SECI, Ba and Leadership: a Unified Model of Dynamic Knowledge Creation'. *Long Range Planning*, 33(1): 5–34.

Nonaka, I., and Takeuchi, H. (1995). *The Knowledge-Creating Company*. New York: Oxford University Press.

Orlikowski, W., and Gash, D. (1994). 'Technological Frames—making sense of information technology in organisations'. *ACM Transactions on Information Systems*, 12(2): 174–207.

Prusak, L. (2001). 'Where did knowledge management come from?'. *IBM Systems Journal*, 40(4): 1–5.

Ruggles, R., and Holthouse, D. (1991). 'Gaining the Knowledge Advantage', in R. Ruggles and D. Holthouse (eds.), *The Knowledge Advantage*. Oxford: Capstone Publishing Ltd, 1–20.

Sastrowarddoyo, S., and Metcalfe, M. (2006). 'Knowledge management as organizing Inquirers'. *Information Knowledge Systems Management*, 5 (2005/2006): 101–116

Snowden, D. (2006). 'Perspectives Around Emergent Connectivity, Sense-Making and Asymmetric Threat Management'. *Public Money & Management*, 26(5): 275–277.

Sternberg, R. J. (2000). 'Images of Mindfulness'. *Journal of Social Issues*, 56(1): 11–26.

Sternberg, R. J., and Horvath, J. A. (1999). *Tacit Knowledge in Professional Practice: Researcher and Practitioner Perspectives*. Mahwah, NJ: Erlbaum.

Sternberg, R. J., Wagner, R. K., and Okagaki, L. (1993). 'Practical intelligence: The nature and role of tacit knowledge in work and at school', in H. Reese and J. Puckett, J. (eds.), *Advances in Lifespan Development*, Hillsdale, NJ: Erlbaum 205–227.

Stroshine, M. (2005). 'Information Technology Innovations in Policing', in R. Durham, and G. Alpert (eds.), *Critical Issues in Policing: Contemporary Readings* (5ᵗʰ edn). Illinois: Waveland Press, 172–183.

Sutcliffe, K., and Weber, K. (2003). 'The high cost of accurate knowledge'. *Harvard Business Review*, May: 75–82.

Weick, K., and Sutcliffe, K. H. (2001). *Managing the Unexpected: Assuring High Performance in an Age of Complexity*. San Francisco: Jossey-Bass.

Wormeli, P. (2005). *Proactive Knowledge Management in Policing*, Paul Wormeli's Tech-Notes—A commentary on disruptive technologies for public safety and criminal justice information systems, <http://radio.weblogs.com/0126029/stories/2003/06/09/proactiveKnowledgeMangementinPolicing> (accessed 1 August, 2005).

Zadeh, L. A. (1965). 'Fuzzy Sets'. *Information and Control*, 8: 338–353.

Index